Lecture Notes in Computer Science 13384

More information about this series at https://link.springer.com/bookseries/558

Paul Groth · Anisa Rula · Jodi Schneider ·
Ilaria Tiddi · Elena Simperl · Panos Alexopoulos ·
Rinke Hoekstra · Mehwish Alam ·
Anastasia Dimou · Minna Tamper (Eds.)

The Semantic Web: ESWC 2022 Satellite Events

Hersonissos, Crete, Greece, May 29 – June 2, 2022
Proceedings

 Springer

Editors
Paul Groth ⒾⒹ
Faculty of Science, Informatics Institute
University of Amsterdam
Amsterdam, Noord-Holland, The Netherlands

Jodi Schneider ⒾⒹ
School of Information Sciences
University of Illinois Urbana-Champaign
Champaign, IL, USA

Elena Simperl ⒾⒹ
Bush House, Strand Campus
King's College London
London, UK

Rinke Hoekstra ⒾⒹ
Elsevier BV
Amsterdam, The Netherlands

Anastasia Dimou ⒾⒹ
Department of Computer Science
KU Leuven
Sint-Katelijne-Waver, Belgium

Anisa Rula ⒾⒹ
Department of Computer Engineering
University of Brescia
Brescia, Italy

Ilaria Tiddi ⒾⒹ
Vrije Universiteit Amsterdam
Amsterdam, The Netherlands

Panos Alexopoulos
Textkernel BV
Amsterdam, The Netherlands

Mehwish Alam ⒾⒹ
FIZ Karlsruhe - Leibniz Institute for
Information Infrastructure
Eggenstein-Leopoldshafen, Germany

Minna Tamper ⒾⒹ
Department of Computer Science
Aalto University
Espoo, Finland

Department of Digital Humanities
University of Helsinki
Helsinki, Finland

ISSN 0302-9743   ISSN 1611-3349 (electronic)
Lecture Notes in Computer Science
ISBN 978-3-031-11608-7   ISBN 978-3-031-11609-4 (eBook)
https://doi.org/10.1007/978-3-031-11609-4

This Springer imprint is published by the registered company Springer Nature Switzerland AG
The registered company address is: Gewerbestrasse 11, 6330 Cham, Switzerland

Preface

This volume contains the satellite proceedings of the 19th edition of the European Semantic Web Conference (ESWC 2022). ESWC is a major venue for discussing the latest in scientific results and innovations related to the Semantic Web, knowledge graphs, and Web data. The satellite events are important aspect of facilitating this discussion.

The satellite events at ESWC 2022 included the poster and demo session, the PhD symposium, the industry track, and project networking, as well as workshops and tutorials. Due to scheduling, the papers from these events are published as post-proceedings.

The poster and demo track received 43 submissions of which 14 posters and 15 demos were accepted. All submissions received three reviews. Posters and demos highlight new research trajectories and ideas within the community and allow for discussions of the latest results. Here, we see topics such as semantics and multi-modality (e.g. video, audio), the importance of Wikidata, methods for dealing with tabular data, and advances in semantic technologies and machine learning.

The PhD symposium is an important venue for doctoral students to present and receive feedback on their research. In total, 13 submissions were received of which 10 papers were accepted. The review process and guidance process was intensive and tailored to helping the students improve their research plans. This included three reviews for each paper as well as peer review by the students themselves. Additionally, all papers were guided by mentors who are senior members of the community. Importantly, senior members of the community attended each presentation to give in-depth feedback. The symposium also featured a keynote by Marieke van Erp. Finally, the students were also given an opportunity to present at the poster and demo session for even more feedback.

The industry track features papers that discuss the adoption and usage of semantic technologies within organizations. Importantly, papers must have a co-author with a non-academic affiliation. We received nine submissions of which six were accepted. All papers received three reviews. The industry track featured papers from a wide variety of organizations including Bosch, Siemens, SNOMED, Wolters Kluwer, and Catalink. Topics included building automation, automotive manufacturing, ontology reshaping, sub-ontology extraction, "semantification" of business, content and data, and data integration.

ESWC 2022 featured a strong collection of ten workshops and two tutorials covering topics ranging from knowledge graph construction and natural language processing to linked data and music and bio-medicine. An addition to this year's program was a main conference presentation of the outcomes of the workshops and tutorials, quickly bringing the learning and observations to the entire community. Later in this volume you will find a more detailed review of the workshops and tutorials.

While not formally part of the proceedings, ESWC has a history of providing network opportunities for projects and particular EU projects. We would like to thank Valentina Presutti and Marieke van Erp for organizing this part of the program for this year.

Lastly, we would like to thank all the contributors to the satellite events: the authors, reviewers, and attendees. These events are crucial for the development of the field and the nurturing of the community.

April 2022

Paul Groth
Jodi Schneider
Anisa Rula
Ilaria Tiddi
Elena Simperl
Rinke Hoekstra
Panos Alexopoulos
Mehwish Alam
Anastasia Dimou
Minna Tamper

Organization

General Chair

Paul Groth — University of Amsterdam, The Netherlands

Workshops and Tutorials Chairs

Mehwish Alam — FIZ Karlsruhe – Leibniz Institute for Information Infrastructure, Germany

Anastasia Dimou — KU Leuven, Belgium

Poster and Demo Chairs

Jodi Schneider — University of Illinois Urbana-Champaign, USA

Anisa Rula — University of Brescia, Italy

Symposium Chairs

Ilaria Tiddi — Vrije Universiteit Amsterdam, The Netherlands

Elena Simperl — King's College London, UK

Industry Track Program Chairs

Rinke Hoekstra — Elsevier, The Netherlands

Panos Alexopoulos — Textkernel, The Netherlands

Sponsoring

Albert Meroño — King's College London, UK

Joe Raad — University of Paris-Saclay, France

Project Networking

Valentina Presutti — University of Bologna, Italy

Marieke van Erp — KNAW Humanities Cluster, The Netherlands

Web and Publicity

Benno Kruit   Vrije Universiteit Amsterdam, The Netherlands

Semantic Technologies

François Scharffe   Columbia University, USA

Proceedings

Minna Tamper   Aalto University and University of Helsinki,
                                           Finland

Program Committee

Ibrahim Abdelaziz	IBM, USA
Maribel Acosta	Ruhr University Bochum, Germany
Alessandro Adamou	The Open University, UK
Nitish Aggarwal	Roku Inc., USA
Céline Alec	Université de Caen Normandie, France
Alsayed Algergawy	University of Jena, Germany
Andreea Iana	University of Mannheim, Germany
Grigoris Antoniou	University of Huddersfield, UK
Ghislain Auguste Atemezing	Mondeca, France
Maurizio Atzori	University of Cagliari, Italy
Sören Auer	TIB Leibniz Information Center Science and Technology and University of Hannover, Germany
Nathalie Aussenac-Gilles	IRIT, CNRS, France
Payam Barnaghi	Imperial College London, UK
Pierpaolo Basile	University of Bari, Italy
Rafael Berlanga	Universitat Jaume I, Spain
Russa Biswas	Karlsruhe Institute of Technology, Germany
Eva Blomqvist	Linköping University, Sweden
Carlos Bobed	everis/NTT Data and University of Zaragoza, Spain
Fernando Bobillo	University of Zaragoza, Spain
Katarina Boland	GESIS - Leibniz Institute for the Social Sciences, Germany
Loris Bozzato	Fondazione Bruno Kessler, Italy
Adrian M. P. Brasoveanu	MODUL Technology GmbH, Austria
Carlos Buil Aranda	Universidad Técnica Federico Santa María, Chile
Davide Buscaldi	LIPN, Université Sorbonne Paris Nord, France

Johann Petrak	University of Sheffield, UK
Guangyuan Piao	National University of Ireland, Maynooth, Ireland
Pierre-Henri Paris	Cnam, France
Lydia Pintscher	Wikimedia Deutschland, Germany
Giuseppe Pirrò	Sapienza University of Rome, Italy
Dimitris Plexousakis	FORTH-ICS, Greece
André Pomp	University of Wuppertal, Germany
María Poveda-Villalón	Universidad Politécnica de Madrid, Spain
Nicoleta Preda	Université Paris-Saclay, Versailles, France
Cédric Pruski	Luxembourg Institute of Science and Technology, Luxembourg
Tara Raafat	University of Surrey, UK
Srinivas Ravishankar	IBM Research, USA
Simon Razniewski	Max Planck Institute for Informatics, Germany
Diego Reforgiato	Università degli studi di Cagliari, Italy
Blake Regalia	University of California, Santa Barbara, USA
Georg Rehm	DFKI, Germany
Achim Rettinger	Trier University, Germany
Artem Revenko	Semantic Web Company GmbH, Austria
Petar Ristoski	IBM Research - Almaden, USA
Giuseppe Rizzo	LINKS Foundation, Italy
Sergio José Rodríguez Méndez	Australian National University, Australia
Roghaiyeh Gachpaz Hamed	Trinity College Dublin, Ireland
Edelweis Rohrer	Universidad de la República, Uruguay
Julian Rojas	Ghent University, Belgium
Maria Del Mar Roldan-Garcia	Universidad de Málaga, Spain
Henry Rosales-Méndez	University of Chile, Chile
Catherine Roussey	INRAE, France
Edna Ruckhaus	Universidad Politécnica de Madrid, Spain
Sebastian Rudolph	TU Dresden, Germany
Harald Sack	FIZ Karlsruhe, Leibniz Institute for Information Infrastructure and KIT Karlsruhe, Germany
Angelo Antonio Salatino	The Open University, UK
Muhammad Saleem	University of Leipzig, Germany
Emanuel Sallinger	TU Wien, Austria
Felix Sasaki	Cornelsen Verlag GmbH and TH Brandenburg, Germany
Ulrike Sattler	University of Manchester, UK
Fatiha Saïs	LISN, Paris-Saclay University, France
Marco Luca Sbodio	IBM Research, Ireland
Stefan Schlobach	Vrije Universiteit Amsterdam, The Netherlands
Daniel Schwabe	PUC-Rio, Brazil

Gezim Sejdiu   University of Bonn, Germany
Juan F. Sequeda   data.world, USA
Barış Sertkaya   Frankfurt University of Applied Sciences,
                               Germany
Dominic Seyler   Baidu Research, USA
Pavel Shvaiko   Informatica Trentina, Italy
Gerardo Simari   Universidad Nacional del Sur and CONICET,
                               Argentina
Evren Sirin   Clark & Parsia, LLC, USA
Hala Skaf-Molli   Nantes University, France
Xingyi Song   University of Sheffield, UK
Adrián Soto   Fintual, Chile
Blerina Spahiu   Università degli Studi di Milano-Bicocca, Italy
Marc Spaniol   Université de Caen Normandie, France
Kavitha Srinivas   IBM, India
Steffen Staab   Universität Stuttgart, Germany, and University of
                               Southampton, UK
Nadine Steinmetz   TU Ilmenau, Germany
Armando Stellato   Tor Vergata University of Rome, Italy
Simon Steyskal   Siemens AG Austria, Austria
Umberto Straccia   ISTI-CNR, Italy
Heiner Stuckenschmidt   University of Mannheim, Germany
Gerd Stumme   University of Kassel, Germany
Vojtěch Svátek   Prague University of Economics and Business,
                               Czech Republic
Ruben Taelman   Ghent University and imec, Belgium
Hideaki Takeda   National Institute of Informatics, Japan
Valentina Tamma   University of Liverpool, UK
Andrea Tettamanzi   University of Nice Sophia Antipolis, France
Andreas Thalhammer   F. Hoffmann-La Roche AG, Switzerland
Tobias Weller   University of Mannheim, Germany
Konstantin Todorov   LIRMM, University of Montpellier, France
Riccardo Tommasini   INSA Lyon, France
Anna Tordai   Elsevier B.V., The Netherlands
Sebastian Tramp   eccenca GmbH, Germany
Cassia Trojahn   IRIT, University of Toulouse-Jean Jaurès, France
Raphaël Troncy   EURECOM, France
Umair ul Hassan   National University of Ireland, Maynooth, Ireland
Jürgen Umbrich   Onlim GmbH, Austria
Ricardo Usbeck   University of Hamburg, Germany
Sahar Vahdati   InfAI, Germany
Ludger Van Elst   DFKI, Germany

Frank Van Harmelen	Vrije Universiteit Amsterdam, The Netherlands
Miel Vander Sande	Meemoo, Belgium
Ruben Verborgh	Ghent University and imec, Belgium
Serena Villata	CNRS, I3S, and 3IA Côte d'Azur Institute, France
Boris Villazón-Terrazas	Majorel, Spain
Fabio Vitali	University of Bologna, Italy
Domagoj Vrgoc	Pontificia Universidad Católica de Chile, Chile
Andreas Wagner	Schaeffler AG, Germany
Kewen Wang	Griffith University, Australia
Ruijie Wang	University of Illinois Urbana-Champaign, USA
Rigo Wenning	W3C, France
Xander Wilcke	Vrije Universiteit Amsterdam, The Netherlands
Cord Wiljes	Nationale Forschungsdateninfrastruktur (NFDI) e.V., Germany
Gregory Todd Williams	Amazon Web Services, USA
Zhe Wu	eBay, USA
Josiane Xavier Parreira	Siemens AG Österreich, Austria
Fouad Zablith	American University of Beirut, Lebanon
Hamada Zahera	Paderborn University, Germany
Ondřej Zamazal	Prague University of Economics and Business, Czech Republic
Songmao Zhang	Chinese Academy of Sciences, China
Ziqi Zhang	University of Sheffield, UK
Rui Zhu	University of California, Santa Barbara, USA
Antoine Zimmermann	École des Mines de Saint-Étienne, France
Matthäus Zloch	GESIS - Leibniz Institute for the Social Sciences, Germany
Amal Zouaq	Ecole Polytechnique de Montréal, Canada
Hanna Ćwiek-Kupczyńska	Institute of Plant Genetics, Polish Academy of Sciences, Poland
Umutcan Şimşek	Semantic Technology Institute Innsbruck, Austria

Additional Reviewers

Ayats, Hugo	Hoppe, Fabian
Braun, Christoph	Hosseini Beghaeiraveri, Seyed Amir
Bruns, Oleksandra	Hosseinzadeh Vahid, Ali
Burgdorf, Andreas	Jain, Nitisha
Eckert, Kai	Kugler, Kai
Ettorre, Antonia	König, Lukas
Flouris, Giorgos	Marcia, Diego
Gesese, Genet Asefa	Marx, Edgard
He, Yuan	Mohtashim, Mirza

Möller, Cedric
Parvin, Parvaneh
Paulus, Alexander
Salman, Muhammad
Santini, Cristian
Schestakov, Stefan
Scrocca, Mario
Sha, Alyssa
Siciliani, Lucia

Sierra-Múnera, Alejandro
Silvestre, Jorge
Simón Ramos, José Manuel
Singh, Gunjan
Tietz, Tabea
Vimercati, Manuel
Werner, Simon
Yan, Xi
Zhuang, Zhiqiang

Sponsors

Platinum Sponsor

VideoLectures.NET is an award-winning free and open access educational video lectures repository. The lectures are given by distinguished scholars and scientists at the most important and prominent events like conferences, summer schools, workshops, and promotional events from many fields of science. The portal is aimed at promoting science, exchanging ideas, and fostering knowledge sharing by providing high-quality didactic contents not only to the scientific community but also to the general public. All lectures, accompanying documents, information, and links are systematically selected and classified through the editorial process taking into account users' comments.

Gold Sponsor

SIEMENS

Siemens AG (Berlin and Munich) is a global technology powerhouse that has stood for engineering excellence, innovation, quality, reliability, and internationality for more than 170 years. The company is active around the globe, focusing on the areas of electrification, automation, and digitalization. One of the largest producers of energy-efficient, resource-saving technologies, Siemens is a leading supplier of efficient power generation and power transmission solutions and a pioneer in infrastructure solutions as well as automation, drive, and software solutions for industry. With its publicly listed subsidiary Siemens Healthineers AG, the company is also a leading provider of medical imaging equipment – such as computed tomography and magnetic resonance imaging systems –

and a leader in laboratory diagnostics as well as clinical IT. In fiscal 2018, which ended on September 30, 2018, Siemens generated revenue of €83.0 billion and net income of €6.1 billion. At the end of September 2018, the company had around 379,000 employees worldwide. Further information is available on www.siemens.com.

Silver Sponsors

Elsevier is a global information analytics business that helps scientists and clinicians to find new answers, reshape human knowledge, and tackle the most urgent human crises. For 140 years, we have partnered with the research world to curate and verify scientific knowledge. Today, we're committed to bringing that rigor to a new generation of platforms. Elsevier provides digital solutions and tools in the areas of strategic research management, R&D performance, clinical decision support, and professional education, including ScienceDirect, Scopus, SciVal, ClinicalKey, and Sherpath. Elsevier publishes over 2,500 digitized journals, including *The Lancet* and *Cell*, 39,000 e-book titles, and many iconic reference works, including *Gray's Anatomy*. Elsevier is part of RELX Group, a global provider of information and analytics for professionals and business customers across industries.

Ontotext is a global leader in enterprise knowledge graph technology and semantic database engines. Ontotext employs big knowledge graphs to enable unified data access and cognitive analytics via text mining and integration of data across multiple sources. Ontotext GraphDBTM engine and Ontotext Platform power business critical systems in the biggest banks, media providers, market intelligence agencies, and car and aerospace manufacturers. Ontotext technology and solutions are spread wide across the value chain of the most knowledge intensive enterprises in the financial services, publishing, health-care, pharma, manufacturing, and public sectors. Leveraging AI and cognitive technologies, Ontotext helps enterprises get competitive advantage, by connecting the dots of their proprietary knowledge and putting in the context of global intelligence.

Springer is part of Springer Nature, a leading global research, educational, and professional publisher, home to an array of respected and trusted brands providing quality content through a range of innovative products and services. Springer Nature is the world's largest academic book publisher, publisher of the world's most influential journals, and a pioneer in the field of open research. The company numbers almost 13,000 staff in over 50 countries and has a turnover of approximately €1.5 billion. Springer Nature was formed in 2015 through the merger of Nature Publishing Group, Palgrave Macmillan, Macmillan Education, and Springer Science+Business Media. Find out more at www.springernature.com.

Bronze Sponsors

IOS Press is an independent, international STM publishing house established in 1987 in Amsterdam. One of our guiding principles is to embrace the benefits a lean organization offers. While our goal is to keep things simple, we strive to meet the highest professional standards. Our business practices are straightforward, transparent, and ethical. IOS Press serves the information needs of scientific and medical communities worldwide. IOS Press now publishes more than 100 international journals and approximately 75 book titles each year on subjects ranging from computer sciences and mathematics to medicine and the natural sciences. Please visit iospress.com to find out more.

metaphacts is a Germany-based company delivering metaphactory – a platform that empowers customers to accelerate their knowledge graph journey and drive knowledge democratization, improve data literacy, and reach smarter business decisions with data. The **metaphacts** team offers unmatched experience and know-how around enterprise knowledge graphs for our clients in areas such as pharma and life sciences, engineering and manufacturing, energy, finance, business, and cultural heritage.

Contents

PhD Symposium

Industry

Summary of Workshops and Tutorials at European Semantic Web Conference 2022

Mehwish Alam[1,2]([✉]) and Anastasia Dimou[3,4,5]([✉])

[1] FIZ Karlsruhe – Leibniz Institute for Information Infrastructure,
Karlsruhe, Germany
mehwish.alam@fiz-karlsruhe.de
[2] Karlsruhe Institute of Technology, Institute AIFB, Karlsruhe, Germany
[3] KULeuven, Department of Computer Science, Sint-Katelijne-Waver, Belgium
anastasia.dimou@kuleuven.be
[4] Flanders Make – DTAI-FET, Leuven, Belgium
[5] Leuven. AI - KU Leuven Institute for AI, 3000 Leuven, Belgium

Abstract. This document summarizes the workshops and tutorials of the 19th European Semantic Web Conference. This edition accepted 10 workshops on different topics revolving around knowledge graphs, such as natural language processing, industrial use of knowledge graphs, biomedical data, etc. Moreover, 2 tutorials were accepted which included knowledge graph construction and music encodings.

Keywords: Semantic technologies · Knowledge graphs · Natural Language Processing · Industrial applications

1 Workshops

This section summarizes and categorizes the 10 workshops accepted to ESWC 2022. 3 workshops were *thematic*: Linked Data in Architecture and Construction Workshop (LDAC), Geospatial Linked Data (GeoLD), and Semantic Web solutions for large-scale biomedical data analytics (SeMWeBMeDA). 3 workshops combined Semantic Web technologies and knowledge graphs with *Natural Language Processing* (NLP): Natural Language Interfaces for the Web of Data (NLI-WOD+QALD), Knowledge Graph Generation from Text (Text2KG) and Deep Learning meets Ontologies and Natural Language Processing (DeepOntoNLP). 2 workshops were focuses on *specific aspects of knowledge graphs*: Modular Knowledge (ModularK) and Knowledge Graph Construction (KGCW). Last, 2 workshops were related to *industry-related topics*: Semantic Digital Twins (SeDIT) and Semantic Industrial Information Modelling (SemIIM). 6 workshops were full-day events and the rest 4 workshops were half-day events. All workshops had high profile keynote speakers from both academia and industry.

© The Author(s), under exclusive license to Springer Nature Switzerland AG 2022
P. Groth et al. (Eds.): ESWC 2022 Satellite Events, LNCS 13384, pp. 1–8, 2022.
https://doi.org/10.1007/978-3-031-11609-4_1

1.1   Workshops on Semantic Technologies

Knowledge Graph Construction (KGCW). More and more knowledge graphs are constructed for private use, e.g., Siri, Alexa, or public use, e.g., DBpedia, Wikidata. While techniques to automate their constructions from existing Web objects exist (e.g., semantic labeling of Web tables), there is still room for improvement. Initially, constructing knowledge graphs from existing datasets was considered an engineering task performed by ad-hoc approaches. However, scientific methods with more declarative-oriented techniques have recently emerged. Several mapping languages for describing rules to construct knowledge graphs and processors to execute those rules emerged. Addressing the challenges related to knowledge graph construction requires both the investigation of theoretical concepts and the development of tools and methods for their evaluation.

This workshop[1] focuses on the automatization of knowledge graph construction methods, analyzing their alignment with previous standard but declarative approaches (i.e., mapping rules). The goal is to provide a venue for scientific discourse, systematic analysis and rigorous evaluation of languages, techniques and tools, as well as practical and applied experiences and lessons-learned for constructing knowledge graphs from academia and industry. The workshop complements and aligns with the activities of the W3C CG on KG construction.

Dr Javier D. Fernández and Dr Selena Baset from Roche were invited to give a talk entitled "From ETL to DIY, or how to democratize the creation of knowledge graphs". The biopharmaceutical industry is embracing knowledge graphs for different purposes, from data integration (e.g. between clinical and biomarker data) for exploration and advanced analytics leading to novel medical insights, to general data representation achieving FAIR data and guiding process automatization. In this scenario of global adoption within complex, multinational companies, scalable techniques are needed to construct, maintain and govern such knowledge graphs, not only by a handful of semantic experts, but also for casual users with domain knowledge. In their presentation, different approaches, challenges, projects, practical tools and solutions used by Roche were shown.

Modular Knowledge (ModularK). The Modular Knowledge workshop[2] offers an interdisciplinary venue for discussing and developing solutions for modularity of knowledge. The workshop combines the efforts of previous experiences (like WoMO, ARCOE-Logic and WOMoCoE workshops) into an interdisciplinary venue for discussing and developing solutions for modularity of knowledge. The aim is to cover and establish connections between various approaches (ranging from rich semantic representations, like Knowledge Graphs and formal ontology, to simpler schemas, like RDF and database schemas) for representing knowledge, its context, its evolution, and for making it accessible to automatic reasoning and knowledge management tasks. The workshop focused on approaches that use of logic-based, subsymbolic, or numerical representations.

---

[1] https://w3id.org/kg-construct/workshop.

[2] https://mk2022.fbk.eu/.

Dr Denny Vrandečić from Wikimedia Foundation was invited to give a talk entitled "Why knowledge must be modular for an Abstract Wikipedia" where he presented the Abstract Wikipedia project, which aims to allow more people to share in a common baseline of knowledge across many languages. In order to do so, the content of a Wikipedia article needs to be represented in a language-independent notation. Such a notation will strongly resemble notations well known in knowledge representation research, and one may argue that Abstract Wikipedia will constitute a knowledge representation project. Denny Vrandečić discussed some implications, raise a lot of open questions, and argue that using a modular approach to knowledge is needed to allow for such a project.

Linked Data in Architecture and Construction Workshop (LDAC). The LDAC workshop[3] series provides a focused overview on technical and applied research on the usage of semantic web, linked data and web of data technologies for architecture and construction (design, engineering, construction, operation, etc.). The workshop aims at gathering researchers, industry stakeholders, and standardization bodies of the broader Linked Building Data (LBD) community. The aim of the workshop is to present current developments, coordinate efforts, gather stakeholders, and elaborate practical insights from industry.

Ian Horrocks was invited to give a talk entitled "Reasoning over Knowledge Graphs: Motivation, Theory and Practice". Knowledge Graphs have rapidly become a mainstream technology that combines features of databases and AI. He briefly introduced knowledge graphs, focusing on the comparison between knowledge graphs and relational databases, and explain why reasoning over knowledge graphs is critical to their effective deployment. He explained the theory behind robust and scalable knowledge graph reasoning, and showed how this has been translated into practice in their RDFox system. Finally, he illustrated the wide applicability of knowledge graphs with some examples of real-world applications.

1.2 Workshops on the Intersection of Knowledge Graphs and Natural Language Processing

Natural Language Interfaces for the Web of Data (NLIWOD+QALD). The NLIWOD workshop[4] focuses on the advancement of Natural Language (NL) Interfaces to the Web of Data. More particularly, it focuses on soliciting discussions on the development of question answering systems, chatbots, and other NL techniques. These dialogue systems and chatbots as increasingly important business intelligence factors. The primary goal of the NLIWOD workshop is to bring together experts on the use of natural-language interfaces (NLI) for answering questions, especially over the Web of Data. The workshop invited Paul Groth from University of Ansterdam to give a keynote on "Understanding Data Search as a Socio-technical Practice/Search Behaviour".

Knowledge Graph Generation from Text (Text2KG). Knowledge Graphs are being recognized as an important and essential resource in many downstream

---

[3] https://linkedbuildingdata.net/ldac2022/.

[4] https://www.nliwod.org/.

tasks such as question answering, recommendation, personal assistants, business analytics, business automation, etc. Even though there are large knowledge graphs built with crowdsourcing such as Wikidata or using semi-structured data such as DBpedia or Yago or from structured data such as relational databases, building knowledge graphs from text corpora still remains an open challenge. This workshop[5] focuses a broad range of topics including the wide range of issues and processes related to knowledge graphs generation from text corpora including, but not limited to entity linking, relation extraction, knowledge representation, and Semantic Web.

Eero Hyvönen from Aalto University and University of Helsinki was invited to give a talk on "Enriching Knowledge Graphs from Texts for Digital Humanities: Biographies, Parliamentary Debates, and Legislation on the Semantic Web". He presented lessons learned in Finland in creating Linked Data services and semantic portals for Digital Humanities, based on a national semantic web infrastructure. Work on creating the Sampo series of systems using textual data is discussed, including the systems "BiographySampo - Finnish Biographies on the Semantic Web", "WarMemoirSampo" on war memoirs of the Second World War", "LawSampo - Finnish Legislation and Case Law on the Semantic Web", and "ParliamentSampo - Parliament of Finland on the Semantic Web".

Deep Learning Meets Ontologies and Natural Language Processing (DeepOntoNLP). In recent years, deep learning has been applied successfully and achieved state-of-the-art performance in a variety of domains, such as image analysis. Despite this success, deep learning models remain hard to analyze data and understand what knowledge is represented in them, and how they generate decisions. Deep Learning (DL) meets Natural Language Processing (NLP) to solve human language problems for further applications, such as information extraction, machine translation, search, and summarization. Previous works have attested the positive impact of domain knowledge on data analysis and vice versa, for example pre-processing data, searching data, redundancy and inconsistency data, knowledge engineering, domain concepts, and relationships extraction, etc. Ontology is a structured knowledge representation that facilitates data access (data sharing and reuse) and assists the DL process as well. DL meets recent ontologies and tries to model data representations with many layers of non-linear transformations. This workshop[6] aims at demonstrating recent and future advances in semantic rich deep learning by using Semantic Web and NLP techniques which can reduce the semantic gap between the data, applications, machine learning process, in order to obtain semantic-aware approaches.

Manolis Koubarakis was invited to give a talk on "Deep learning techniques for Greek legal documents". He discussed the problems of named entity recognition and document classification for legal documents in the Greek language. He presented deep learning models for these problems including various versions of RNNs and the GreekLegalBERT language model. This work was conducted in

---

[5] https://aiisc.ai/text2kg/.
[6] https://sites.google.com/view/deepontonlp2022.

the context of the Greek legal knowledge graph and the platform Nomothesia[7] which makes Greek laws available on the Web as linked open data.

1.3 Industry Oriented Workshops

Semantic Industrial Information Modelling (SemIIM). Information Modelling (IM) has been under the spotlight of both academia and industry for decades. Important aspects of IM include methods and practices of representing concepts, relationships, constraints, rules and operations to specify data semantics for a particular domain. Despite the past success, existing approaches and systems for IM fail to cope with new challenges of overwhelming global industrial digitalization that requires advanced information models and aims at fully computerized, software-driven, automation of production processes and enterprise-wide integration of software components. Such trend and the technological and industrial developments that come with it are an important part of Industry 4.0 and industrial Internet of Things. It requires IM that, for example, allows to capture the functionality of and information flow between different assets in a plant, such as equipment and production processes. Moreover, it requires IM and models that are based on ISA and IEC standards and have a number of desirable properties, e.g., reusable, explainable, scalable, simulatable etc.

This workshop[8] aims at gathering researchers and practitioners who work on addressing these challenges with the help of semantic technologies.

Semantic Digital Twins (SeDIT). The concept of digital twins, as virtual replicas of physical entities, has gained significant traction in recent years in a range of domains such as industry, construction, energy, health or transport. Digital Twins can be used to view the status of the twinned physical object, without the need to interrogate the object itself. The digital twin can be queried by other software without the need to query the device itself thus relieving pressure on devices, which typically have very limited computational capabilities. Digital twins can also be used for monitoring and diagnostics to optimize device performance without impacting on the physical device. It requires unambiguous descriptions of both the entity and its digital counterpart, as well as the ability to integrate data from heterogeneous sources of information (including real-time data) and to interact with the physical world. Given these requirements, semantic technologies can play a significant role in the real-world deployment of digital twin technology. The aims of SeDIT workshop[9] are twofold: to (i) drive the discussion about current trends and future challenges of semantic digital twins; and (ii) support communication and collaboration with the goal of aligning the various efforts and accelerating innovation in the associated fields.

Evgeny Kharlamov from Bosch Center for Artificial Intelligence and University of Oslo was invited to talk about "Semantic Digital Twins: Trends and

---

[7] https://legislation.di.uoa.gr/.

[8] https://sites.google.com/view/semiim-2022/home.

[9] https://sedit.linkeddata.es/.

Shortcomings". He discussed current practices and trends in development and use of semantic digital twins with examples from industry, as well as limitations of existing solutions and requirements for next generation semantic digital twins.

1.4   Domain Specific Workshops

Semantic Web Solutions for Large-Scale Biomedical Data Analytics (SeMWeBMeDA). The life sciences domain has been an early adopter of Linked Data and, a considerable portion of the Linked Open Data cloud is composed of life sciences datasets. The available datasets require integration according to international standards, large-scale distributed infrastructures, specific techniques for data access, and offer data analytics benefits for decision support. Especially in combination with Semantic Web and Linked Data technologies, these promises to enable the processing of large as well as semantically heterogeneous data sources and the capturing of new knowledge. This workshop[10] focused on works related to life sciences and biomedical data processing, as well as the amalgamation with Linked Data and Semantic Web technologies for better data analytics, knowledge discovery and user-targeted applications. This year a special focus is given on the original contributions in regards to the data resources, tools and technologies relevant for research in ongoing Covid19 pandemic.

Catia Pesquita from University of Lisbon was invited to give a talk about Biomedical AI applications increasingly rely on multi-domain and heterogeneous data, especially in areas such as personalised medicine and systems biology. Biomedical Ontologies are a golden opportunity in this area because they add meaning to the underlying data which can be used to support heterogeneous data integration, provide scientific context to the data augmenting AI performance, and afford explanatory mechanisms allowing the contextualization of AI predictions. In particular, ontologies and knowledge graphs support the computation of semantic similarity between objects, providing an understanding of why certain objects are considered similar or different. This is a basic aspect of explainability and is at the core of many machine learning applications. However, when data covers multiple domains, it may be necessary to integrate different ontologies to cover the full semantic landscape of the underlying data. Catia Pesquita presented their recent work on building an integrated knowledge graph that is based on the semantic annotation and interlinking of heterogeneous data into a holistic semantic landscape that supports semantic similarity assessments. She discussed the challenges in building the knowledge graph from public resources, the methodology they used and the road-ahead in biomedical ontology and knowledge graph alignment as AI becomes an integral part of biomedical research.

Geospatial Linked Data (GeoLD). Geospatial data is vital for both traditional applications like navigation, logistics, tourism and emerging areas like autonomous vehicles, smart buildings and GIS on demand. Spatial linked data

---

[10] https://sites.google.com/view/sewebmeda-2021/home.

has recently transitioned from experimental prototypes to national infrastructure. However the next generation of spatial knowledge graphs will integrate multiple spatial datasets with the large number of general datasets that contain some geospatial references (e.g., DBpedia, Wikidata). This integration, either on the public Web or within organizations has immense socio-economic as well as academic benefits. The upsurge in Linked data related presentations in the recent Eurogeographics data quality workshop shows the deep interest in Geospatial Linked Data (GLD) in national mapping agencies. GLD enables a web-based, interoperable geospatial infrastructure. This is especially relevant for delivering the INSPIRE directive in Europe. Moreover, geospatial information systems benefit from Linked Data principles in building the next generation of spatial data applications e.g., federated smart buildings, self-piloted vehicles, delivery drones or automated local authority services. The workshop[11] focused on challenges and solutions for dealing with GLD, especially for building high quality, adaptable, geospatial infrastructures and next-generation spatial applications.

Erwin Folmer gave an invited talk entitle "Lessons Learned from Building the Largest Spatial Knowledge Graph in the Netherlands". Kadaster, the Dutch National Land Registry and Mapping Agency, has been actively publishing their base registries as linked (open) spatial data for several years. To date, a number of these base registers as well as a number of external datasets have been successfully published as linked data and are publicly available. Increasing demand for linked data products and the availability of new linked data technologies have highlighted the need for a new, innovative approach to linked data publication within the organisation in the interest of reducing the time and costs associated with said publication. Both the modelling and publication architecture form part of Kadaster's larger vision for the development of the Kadaster Knowledge Graph through the integration of the various linked datasets. In this presentation Erwin Folmer focused on lessons learned from building (probably) one of the largest spatial knowledge graphs.

2   Tutorials

This section summarizes the two tutorials presented at ESWC 2022.

2.1   Linked Data and Music Encodings

Music encoding, the representation of symbolic music information in a machine-accessible form, is critical to a variety of fields and areas of study, including computational or digital musicology, digital editions, symbolic music information retrieval, and digital libraries. The Linked Data Interest Group of the Music Encoding Initiative (MEI) brings together music encoding specialists with experts in Web science and knowledge organization and regularly organizes training events focusing on applications of Linked Data to music encodings. To this

---

[11] https://i3mainz.github.io/GeoLD2022/.

end, this full-day tutorial[12] details the application of semantic technologies to the domain of music encoding. The tutorial consisted of an overview of music encoding technologies, briefly covering their history and purpose, some terminology, and relevant applications of Linked Data and Semantic Web approaches in this context. Real-life examples and hands-on experience with exercises in interlinking, querying, and annotating various music-related datasets (e.g., RISM, DOREMUS, JazzCats) were introduced.

2.2   Knowledge Graph Construction

Despite the emergence of knowledge graphs, exposed via endpoints or as Linked Data, formats like CSV, JSON or XML are still the most used for exposing data on the web. Some solutions have been proposed to describe and integrate these resources using declarative mapping languages (e.g., RML, R2RML, etc.) and many of those are equipped with associated RDF generators (e.g. RMLMapper, SDM-RDFizer, FunMap, etc.). The use of these technologies enables the construction of knowledge graphs in a declarative way. However, they have a steep learning curve for new users. The aim of this tutorial is, from a practical perspective, to explain in detail the process of constructing knowledge graphs, from writing mappings to their use with suitable tools. From the basic features of mapping languages to the most complex and optimized engines that parse those rules, we take a trip through the most recent history on declarative construction of knowledge graphs from heterogeneous data. More details are available online[13].

---

[12] https://musicenfanthen.gitbook.io/eswc-2022-tutorial.
[13] https://kg-construct.github.io/eswc-dkg-tutorial-2022/.

Posters and Demos

Towards UML-Style Visual Queries
over Wikidata

Kārlis Čerāns(✉)⬤, Jūlija Ovčiņņikova⬤, Mikus Grasmanis⬤, and Lelde Lāce⬤

Institute of Mathematics and Computer Science, University of Latvia, Riga, Latvia
{karlis.cerans,julija.ovcinnikova,mikus.grasmanis,
lelde.lace}@lumii.lv

Abstract. We describe and demonstrate the options for visual UML-style presentation and visual-based creation of SPARQL queries over *Wikidata*, a central Linked Data resource employing a custom data classification encoding. We provide visual presentations of public *Wikidata* example queries, this way adding a visual dimension to their comprehensibility. The process of visual query creation within the tool is supported by auto-completion facilities that consider the context of the already created query part, where possible.

Keywords: SPARQL · Wikidata · Visual queries · Query visualization · ViziQuer

1 Introduction

Visual presentation of information artefacts can help their perception. There is a number of tools available for visual creation of SPARQL queries over RDF data endpoints (cf. e.g., [5,6,8,9]). Visual method has been successfully used for SPARQL query formulation by custom domain experts [8]. *ViziQuer* [5] has shown the possibility to use a UML-style notation to visually create [4] and visualize [3] complex SPARQL queries, involving e.g., basic graph patterns, aggregation and subqueries, complex data expressions and filters.

In this paper we demonstrate for the first time the possibility to ***create visual presentations*** for a large set of generic SPARQL queries (we do this for seven sections of *Wikidata* [10] example query set [11]); we provide a gallery of the visually presented queries in a working visual tool environment (each visual query can be translated back into SPARQL and executed over the *Wikidata* data endpoint[1]).

We also demonstrate an ***auto-completion-supported environment*** for visual query creation over *Wikidata* (involving both schema-level and data-level elements); we believe this to be novel regarding creation of UML-style visual queries over large, heterogeneous and custom-encoded data endpoints, as *Wikidata* is.

We discuss the solutions enabling the *Wikidata* SPARQL query visualization and visual query creation over *Wikidata*.

The supporting material for the paper includes links to the live environment and is available at http://viziquer.lumii.lv/examples/wikidata2022.

---

[1] https://query.wikidata.org/.

P. Groth et al. (Eds.): ESWC 2022 Satellite Events, LNCS 13384, pp. 11–15, 2022.
https://doi.org/10.1007/978-3-031-11609-4_2

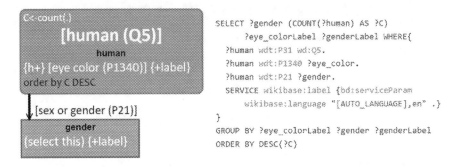

SELECT ?gender (COUNT(?human) AS ?C)
        ?eye_colorLabel ?genderLabel WHERE{
?human wdt:P31 wd:Q5.
?human wdt:P1340 ?eye_color.
?human wdt:P21 ?gender.
SERVICE wikibase:label {bd:serviceParam
        wikibase:language "[AUTO_LANGUAGE],en" .}
}
GROUP BY ?eye_colorLabel ?gender ?genderLabel
ORDER BY DESC(?C)

Fig. 1. Human eye colors by gender

2   Visual Query Notation

A UML-style visual query in *ViziQuer* involves query nodes describing variables or resources; each node can have a possible class name and an attribute specification list. There is a main query node (orange round rectangle) in the query. The edges that connect the nodes usually correspond to links among the node variables or resources (there can be "same-instance" links, labelled by '==', and "empty" links that do not specify a data connection, labelled by '++', as well). Textual condition/filter fields, along with aggregation and query nesting options are available, as well.

We refer the reader to [1] for *ViziQuer* basic constructs and design rationale explanation, [5] for tool description and [4] for its syntax and semantics.

Figure 1 shows a simple query looking for eye color statistics of humans by their gender in both the visual notation and in SPARQL (the prefix definitions are omitted).

For visual queries over *Wikidata* we use a ***presentation by label*** approach for its entities (classes, properties, individuals) to ensure direct readability of the visual query presentation. The entity IRI fragment information is maintained in the entity presentation to ensure that it is unanimous, and to enable easier connecting the visual queries with other approaches for exploring, querying, and analyzing the *Wikidata* data.

The UML-style visual notation allows for a ***single designated classification triple*** to be shown in the prominent UML class position within a query node. Usually, this triple is based on the *rdf:type* property. In *Wikidata*, the most informative classification property is *wdt:P31* ("instance of"), therefore this property is used to link a query node instance corresponding to a query node with the item visualized as UML class name. One also can specify a classification of an instance to be "indirect", thus making the instance-to-class relation to become *wdt:P31/wdt:P279** (*wdt:P279* is a "subclass of" relation).

The visual notation has also custom means (e.g., {+ *label*}) to support the ***label service extension*** in SPARQL queries over *Wikidata* that instructs finding meaningful entity characterization in query results (this option is used widely in the *Wikidata* SPARQL query examples [11]). The languages of the label service, if not being the default set, can be specified on the level of the entire query, or a subquery.

The visual query notation contains full information about a query (in the context of a given data set schema). It is possible to *generate the query SPARQL form*, as well as to *execute the query* from the visual environment. The *reverse translation (visualization)* of SPARQL queries into the visual notation is available, as well (cf. Sect. 3).

3   SPARQL Query Visualization and Visual Query Library

The principal advantages of a *visual UML-style query presentation* of a SPARQL query (presumably used to *accompany*, not to replace the textual query form) lie within

– presenting the *classification and attribute selection triples* in a compact notation (that involves just a class or property name within a query node), and
– splitting the query over *multiple visual elements* to reduce the local complexity of any visually separated query part.

An important feature of visual *Wikidata* SPARQL query presentation comprehension is also inclusion of the *entity labels* within the query presentation.

The automated visualization of SPARQL queries (cf. [3]) can be possible due to the rich visual query constructs supported by the ViziQuer notation (cf. [1]). It has been used to create a visual query library from the *Wikidata* SPARQL query example set (a manual positioning of the query nodes is done after the automated query visualization). The query visualization module has been expanded from [3] to consider the special query encoding and custom query constructs that are typical for the queries over *Wikidata*.

There are currently 105 queries in the library that have been obtained from 120 considered SPARQL queries from the *Wikidata* example query set [11]. A query is said to be visualized successfully if the obtained visual query can be translated back into a query producing the same results (the notion of mathematical equivalence is adopted if both queries time out or produce empty results). The obtained ratio of 87.5% successfully visualized queries is encouraging[2] as the considered queries are meant to make sense to actual SPARQL query writers and illustrate various aspects of the SPARQL query creation.

The visual *Wikidata* query library is available as a project within *ViziQuer* environment, accessible from the paper's support page. The support page also lists the most recent standings regarding the *Wikidata* example query visualization success rates.

4   Visual Query Environment

The visual query environment provides a visual-centered interactive interface for query creation, starting from the query initialization (query seeding) by a class, a property or

---

[2] The current successful visualizations by the example set sections are: Simple queries 20 (of 21), Lexeme queries 17 (17), Wikibase predicates 7 (8), Wikimedia projects 13 (13), Entertainment 17 (20), Computer Science and Technology 9 (11), Biology and Medicine 22 (30). We expect to reach 90% threshold in near future.

an individual, followed by query expansion (query growing) that includes adding information to query nodes (class name, instance URI, attributes and aggregations, filters, ordering and slicing), or adding linked nodes to the query.

The principal element for both query seeding and query growing is auto-completion that is expected to offer to the user meaningful options of choosing the elements relevant for a particular context, including a name text search option.

For seeding a query from a class or property name, as well as for choosing a property in a context of a class name, or a class name in a context of a property, a custom relational database of holding the class and property names, as well as their relations is used (a similar solution over *DBPedia* has been described in [2]); the data has been extracted from the public *Wikidata* SPARQL query endpoint by a similar set of queries. Seeding and growing of queries by individual names is currently done via public *Wikidata* entity search API.

5   Discussion and Conclusions

The demonstrated work shows a possibility to adapt rich UML-style visual query solutions to work with *Wikidata* that is a large and heterogeneous Linked data collection and uses custom data encoding conventions. The implementation of the *ViziQuer* tool has demonstrated the necessary flexibility to incorporate the required custom solutions.

The library of query visualizations demonstrates the richness of extended UML-style visual notation in encoding SPARQL queries of varying complexity. The possibility to obtain a visual presentation of a SPARQL query provides a benefit of an extra structural view over it[3]. The extent of this benefit and the scope of the users and queries over which it is substantial is to be determined within a future work.

The choice of UML-style diagrams for SPARQL query visualizations can be rightfully questioned. The current proposal is an expansion of an existing visual query creation and SPARQL query visualization approach (that has clear benefits in the case of smaller and more class-oriented data endpoints) to handle the queries typical for the *Wikidata* environment. Its shortcomings can be overcome by further improvements or alternative SPARQL query visualization and/or visual query creation approaches that are aimed at serving the SPARQL query comprehensibility and exploit the visual query presentation dimension in query creation.

From the visual query creation perspective an important future work would be to refine the query completion services to allow class-specific instance suggestions (e.g., by integrating a FAAS-style component [7]), property-property connections (like in [2] for *DBPedia*) and property-instance connections (what instances can be subjects and what instances can be objects of triples with a certain property). A general observation, however, is that a context-sensitive auto-completion solution is also going to be demanding in computing resources; therefore, a balance of the auto-completion specificity and available resources is to be sought for.

Acknowledgements. This work has been partially supported by a Latvian Science Council Grant lzp-2021/1-0389 "Visual Queries in Distributed Knowledge Graphs".

---

[3] This would apply to any potential user, encountering a SPARQL query.

References

1. Čerāns, K., et al.: Extended UML class diagram constructs for visual SPARQL queries in ViziQuer/web. In: VOILA@ISWC, vol. 1947, pp. 87–98. CEUR Workshop Proceedings (2017). http://ceur-ws.org/Vol-1947/paper08.pdf
2. Čerāns, K., Lāce, L., Grasmanis, M., Ovčiņņikova, J.: A UML-style visual query environment over DBPedia. In: Garoufallou, E., Ovalle-Perandones, M.A., Vlachidis, A. (eds.) MTSR 2021. Communications in Computer and Information Science, vol. 1537, pp. 16–27. Springer, Cham (2022). https://doi.org/10.1007/978-3-030-98876-0_2
3. Čerāns, K., Ovčiņņikova, J., Lāce, L., Grasmanis, M., Romāne, A.: Visual presentation of SPARQL queries in ViziQuer. In: VOILA@ISWC, vol. 3023, pp. 29–40. CEUR Workshop Proceedings (2021). http://ceur-ws.org/Vol-3023/paper12.pdf
4. Čerāns, K., et al.: ViziQuer: a visual notation for RDF data analysis queries. In: Garoufallou, E., Sartori, F., Siatri, R., Zervas, M. (eds.) MTSR 2018. CCIS, vol. 846, pp. 50–62. Springer, Cham (2019). https://doi.org/10.1007/978-3-030-14401-2_5
5. Čerāns, K., et al.: ViziQuer: a web-based tool for visual diagrammatic queries over RDF data. In: Gangemi, A., et al. (eds.) ESWC 2018. LNCS, vol. 11155, pp. 158–163. Springer, Cham (2018). https://doi.org/10.1007/978-3-319-98192-5_30
6. Haag, F., Lohmann, S., Siek, S., Ertl, T.: QueryVOWL: visual composition of SPARQL queries. In: Gandon, F., Guéret, C., Villata, S., Breslin, J., Faron-Zucker, C., Zimmermann, A. (eds.) ESWC 2015. LNCS, vol. 9341, pp. 62–66. Springer, Cham (2015). https://doi.org/10.1007/978-3-319-25639-9_12
7. de la Parra, G., Hogan, A.: Fast approximate autocompletion for SPARQL query builders. In: VOILA@ISWC, vol. 3023, pp. 41–55. CEUR Workshop Proceedings (2021). http://ceur-ws.org/Vol-3023/paper10.pdf
8. Soylu, A., Giese, M., Jimenez-Ruiz, E., Vega-Gorgojo, G., Horrocks, I.: Experiencing optiquevqs: a multi-paradigm and ontology-based visual query system for end users. Univ. Access Inf. Soc. 15(1), 129–152 (2016)
9. Vargas, H., Buil-Aranda, C., Hogan, A., López, C.: RDF Explorer: a visual SPARQL query builder. In: Ghidini, C., et al. (eds.) ISWC 2019. LNCS, vol. 11778, pp. 647–663. Springer, Cham (2019). https://doi.org/10.1007/978-3-030-30793-6_37
10. Vrandečić, D., Krötzsch, M.: Wikidata: a free collaborative knowledgebase. Commun. ACM 57(10), 78–85 (2014)
11. Web: Wikidata:sparql query service/queries/examples. https://www.wikidata.org/wiki/Wikidata:SPARQL_query_service/queries/examples. Accessed 14 Apr 2022

Using the ODRL Profile for Access Control for Solid Pod Resource Governance

Beatriz Esteves[1(✉)], Víctor Rodríguez-Doncel[1], Harshvardhan J. Pandit[2], Nicolas Mondada[3], and Pat McBennett[3]

[1] Ontology Engineering Group, Universidad Politécnica de Madrid, Madrid, Spain
beatriz.gesteves@upm.es
[2] ADAPT Centre, Trinity College Dublin, Dublin, Ireland
[3] Inrupt, Inc., Boston, USA

Abstract. This demo shows an ODRL editor where RDF policies can be defined and enforced to grant access to personal data stored in Solid Pods. Policies are represented using OAC, the ODRL profile for Access Control, which allows the definition of complex, fine-grained permissive and prohibitive policies that are aligned with GDPR requirements regarding the processing of personal data. In addition, a second demonstrator is presented to simulate an app's request for data and examples of policies and consent record modelling are showcased.

Keywords: ODRL · Policy modelling · Access control · Solid

1 Introduction

Currently, most companies whose business models depend on data, and especially on personal data, for the provision of Web services store the collected data in private data silos, far from the users' control. In this context, a number of emergent solutions to decentralize the Web, and in particular to decentralize the storage of data, such as Solid[1], Hub of All Things[2] and so on, have appeared in recent years. In particular, the Solid specification[3] relies on interoperable data formats and protocols such as the Linked Data Platform[4] or the ACL (Basic Access Control)[5] ontology. However, as we are dealing with personal data, this decentralized storage system falls on the sphere of the General Data Protection Regulation (GDPR)[6] [1] and therefore ACL-based access control policies are not expressive enough for applications to define more complex policies and deal with GDPR requirements regarding the specification of purposes or legal bases

---

[1] https://solidproject.org/.
[2] https://www.hubofallthings.com/.
[3] https://solidproject.org/TR/protocol.
[4] https://www.w3.org/TR/ldp/.
[5] http://www.w3.org/ns/auth/acl#.
[6] https://eur-lex.europa.eu/eli/reg/2016/679/oj.

P. Groth et al. (Eds.): ESWC 2022 Satellite Events, LNCS 13384, pp. 16–20, 2022.
https://doi.org/10.1007/978-3-031-11609-4_3

for the processing of personal data. In addition, by using semantic web vocabularies such as the Open Digital Rights Language (ODRL) [3] and the Data Privacy Vocabulary (DPV) [4], users can easily define more elaborated policy-type preferences when it comes to accessing resources stored in their personal information management system, i.e., to state that only contacts who attended the same university as the user can see their photos.

In this demo[7], we showcase:

– An ODRL editor (SOPE - Solid ODRL access control Policies Editor) which allows for the generation of ODRL policies based on OAC – the ODRL profile for Access Control[8] – to define declarative policies that express permissions and/or prohibitions associated with data stored in a Solid Pod.
– A demonstrator where developers can issue an app request for personal data and receive the respective response based on the architecture and on the access request's authorization algorithm previously described by the authors in [2].

This paper is structured as follows: Sect. 2 presents a description of the demonstration; Sect. 3 details the data modelling used in the work, which relies essentially on OAC, ODRL and DPV; and Sect. 4 concludes the paper and provides future lines of work.

2   Demonstration

The UML sequence diagram in Fig. 1 highlights the components of this demo. The demo set-up consists of two Solid apps that consume and produce Solid Pod resources. SOPE[9] is a Solid ODRL access control Policies Editor for users of Solid apps who wish to define more fine-grained access control policies over their Solid Pod resources. It allows the users to define ODRL policies, based on the OAC profile, to govern the access and storage of Pod resources. To start using SOPE, users need to log into their Solid Pod as the policies will be saved in a private Solid container. Following this step, users only need to choose which type of policy they will be modelling (an ODRL permission or prohibition), select the categories of personal data and purposes to which the policy applies and the access control modes permitted/prohibited by the policy. Finally, the RDF policy will be automatically generated and stored in their Pod under the "/private" container, in a specific sub-container for ODRL policies.

A second app was developed to simulate the process of an app requesting access to certain types of personal data for a specific purpose. It allows Solid app developers to create and launch an access request for specific personal data categories and purposes. This app will match the request's personal data categories, access modes and purposes with the ODRL policies stored in a user's Pod. If a policy exists to authorize the access to such personal data categories then URL paths to Solid Pod resources that contain said personal data categories will be returned.

---

[7] https://protect.oeg.fi.upm.es/eswc-demo/.

[8] https://w3id.org/oac/.

[9] Source code is available on https://github.com/besteves4/solid-sope.

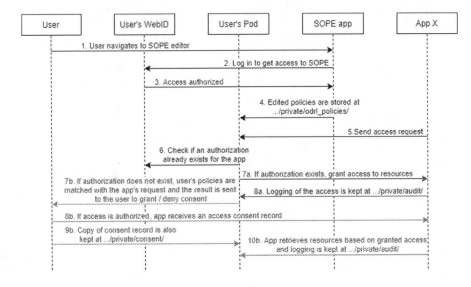

Fig. 1. Sequence diagram of the proposed authorization algorithm demonstration.

3   Data Modelling

In this demo, ODRL[10] is used to define access control policies for the governance of access to resources stored in Solid Pods. In particular, we leverage our previous work, related to the specification of OAC, an ODRL profile to express consent through granular access control policies in Solid [2], and on DPV[11], to invoke specific privacy and data protection terms.

To demonstrate the modelling of policies and consent records, we present two examples in Listings 1.1 and 1.2. In Listing 1.1, a permission over demographic data is set by Anne for the purpose of academic research, which permits read and write access operations over her personal data. In Listing 1.2, a consent record related to an authorized access request, to use and store demographic data for academic research, is specified.

Listing 1.1. Read-Write policy for Demographic data for Academic Research purposes

```
PREFIX rdf: <http://www.w3.org/1999/02/22-rdf-syntax-ns#>
PREFIX odrl: <http://www.w3.org/ns/odrl/2/#>
PREFIX oac: <https://w3id.org/oac/>
PREFIX dpv: <https://w3id.org/dpv#>

:policy-1 a odrl:Policy ;
    odrl:profile oac: ;
    odrl:permission [
        a odrl:Permission ;
        odrl:assigner <https://anne.databox.me/profile/card#me> ;
        odrl:target oac:Demographic ;
        odrl:action oac:Read, oac:Write ;
        odrl:constraint [
            odrl:leftOperand oac:Purpose ;
            odrl:operator odrl:isA ;
            odrl:rightOperand dpv:AcademicResearch ] ] .
```

---

[10] http://www.w3.org/ns/odrl/2/.

[11] https://w3id.org/dpv#.

Listing 1.2. Consent record of an authorized access request

```
PREFIX dpv: <https://w3id.org/dpv#>
PREFIX dct: <http://purl.org/dc/terms/>
PREFIX xsd: <http://www.w3.org/2001/XMLSchema#>
PREFIX dpv-pd: <https://w3id.org/dpv/dpv-pd#>

:consentRecord-1 a dpv:Consent ;
    dct:hasVersion "v1" ;
    dpv:hasIdentifier <https://anne.databox.me/private/consent/record1> ;
    dpv:hasDataSubject <https://anne.databox.me/profile/card#me> ;
    dpv:hasProvisionBy <https://anne.databox.me/profile/card#me> ;
    dpv:hasProvisionTime "2022-03-01T09:27:58"^^xsd:dateTime ;
    dpv:hasPersonalDataHandling [
        a dpv:PersonalDataHandling ;
        dct:language "en" ;
        dpv:hasPolicy :policy-1 ;
        dpv:hasPurpose [
            a dpv:AcademicResearch ;
            dpv:hasLegalBasis dpv:Consent ;
            dpv:hasPersonalData dpv-pd:Demographic ;
            dpv:hasProcessing dpv:Use, dpv:Store ;
            dpv:hasDataController [
                a dpv:DataController ;
                dpv:hasName "Company A" ;
                dpv:hasContact "companyA@example.com"
            ] ;
        ] ;
    ] .
```

4   Conclusions and Future Work

In this demo, we presented a first-of-its-kind web application to generate ODRL policies using the ODRL Profile for Access Control (OAC) and a demonstrator to simulate a Solid app request and the matching authorization mechanism. With SOPE, Solid users have a tool to edit policies in a user-friendly manner, without the need to know about ODRL's inner workings, and with the demonstrator Solid developers can model access requests and obtain the personal data if said request is authorized.

This method is an important advance over the current Solid access control model, enabling richer personal data access policies to be represented and enforced. Moreover, although in the context of this particular work the OAC profile is applied to the governance of access to Solid Pod resources, its use is not limited to the Solid ecosystem, as it does not rely on any Solid-specific terms whatsoever, and it can be applied to other Linked Data platforms in future lines of work.

The system is yet to be complemented by future endeavours: (i) SHACL shapes should be defined to validate the policies, (ii) usability testing must be performed to assess the design choices included in the editor, (iii) other user interfaces beyond this proof of concept should be developed (e.g., UIs to annotate resources with the types of personal data they contain) and (iv) the inferencing power of semantic reasoners should be leveraged in different scenarios where inferred knowledge might simplify validating a policy.

Funding Acknowledgements. This research has been supported by European Union's Horizon 2020 research and innovation programme under the Marie Skłodowska-Curie grant agreement No 813497 (PROTECT). Harshvardhan J. Pandit has received funding from the Irish Research Council Government of Ireland Postdoctoral Fellowship Grant#GOIPD/2020/790. The ADAPT SFI Centre for Digital Media Technology is funded by Science Foundation Ireland through the SFI Research Centres Programme and is co-funded under the European Regional Development Fund (ERDF) through Grant#13/RC/2106_P2.

References

1. REGULATION (EU) 2016/679 of the European parliament and of the council of 27 April 2016 on the protection of natural persons with regard to the processing of personal data and on the free movement of such data, and repealing Directive 95/46/EC (General Data Protection Regulation) (2016)
2. Esteves, B., Pandit, H.J., Rodríguez-Doncel, V.: ODRL profile for expressing consent through granular access control policies in solid. In: 2021 IEEE European Symposium on Security and Privacy Workshops (EuroS&PW), pp. 298–306 (2021). https://doi.org/10.1109/EuroSPW54576.2021.00038, ISSN 2768-0657
3. Iannella, R., Steidl, M., Myles, S., Rodríguez-Doncel, V.: ODRL Vocabulary & Expression 2.2 (2018). https://www.w3.org/TR/odrl-vocab/. Publication Title: W3C Rec
4. Pandit, H..J., et al.: Creating a vocabulary for data privacy. In: Panetto, Hervé, Debruyne, Christophe, Hepp, Martin, Lewis, Dave, Ardagna, Claudio Agostino, Meersman, Robert (eds.) OTM 2019. LNCS, vol. 11877, pp. 714–730. Springer, Cham (2019). https://doi.org/10.1007/978-3-030-33246-4_44

Relation Canonicalization in Open Knowledge Graphs: A Quantitative Analysis

Maria Lomaeva[(✉)] and Nitisha Jain[(✉)]🆔

Hasso Plattner Institute, University of Potsdam, Potsdam, Germany
lomaeva@uni-potsdam.de, nitisha.jain@hpi.de

Abstract. Open Information Extraction (OpenIE) allows the detection of meaningful triples of *(noun phrase, relation phrase, noun phrase)* in unstructured texts in an unsupervised manner. This makes OpenIE highly adaptable for any domain and suitable for creation of an open knowledge graph (KG). The OpenIE methods, however, often result in generation of redundant and ambiguous information. *Canonicalization* is therefore needed to reduce redundancy and improve the quality of the resultant KG. In this work, we create a dataset for a systematic evaluation of relation canonicalization and present a quantitative analysis of existing state-of-the-art methods which has been previously missing.

Keywords: Canonicalization · Information extraction · Knowledge graphs

1 Introduction

Open Information Extraction (OpenIE) techniques are popularly used for the construction of knowledge graphs from raw texts [2]. However, the triples in such open KGs, e.g. Reverb [3], contain noun phrases (NPs) and relation phrases (RPs) that are not canonicalized, for example, *Obama* and *Barack Obama* refer to the same entity and *lives in* and *resident of* have the same intended meaning of the relation. Canonicalization in open KGs is the task of bringing different NPs or RPs having the same meaning to a single normalized form to improve the quality of the KG. Previous works on canonicalization in open KGs have primarily paid attention to noun phrases that represent the entities (subjects and objects) in the triples. The chief reason for this being the lack of a publicly available and large dataset against which the resulting canonicalized relation phrases could be evaluated upon. As such, only a qualitative evaluation or limited manual evaluations of the relation canonicalization has been provided so far. It is, therefore, important to evaluate the performance of existing approaches in a systematic and automated manner, so as to identify their weaknesses and further investigate the ways to improve the techniques. Towards this goal, in this work we present a large dataset comprising canonical relations and their corresponding

P. Groth et al. (Eds.): ESWC 2022 Satellite Events, LNCS 13384, pp. 21–25, 2022.
https://doi.org/10.1007/978-3-031-11609-4_4

relation phrases, which can serve as a gold standard for the evaluation of relation canonicalization methods. We describe the semi-automated process of creation of this dataset and illustrate its utility by performing the quantitative evaluation of existing state-of-the-art canonicalization approaches on it.

Related Work. Canonicalization in open KGs was discussed in detail by Galarraga et al. [4] where they showed that token overlap is an indication of similarity of NPs and RPs. They used Hierarchical Agglomerative Clustering for obtaining canonicalized clusters. Among recent works, CESI [7] used side information (including entity linking, KBP information, morphological normalization etc.) along with word vectors and KG embeddings to perform joint canonicalization of NPs and RPs. Dash et al. [1] proposed a state-of-the-art method called CUVA for canonicalization of entities and relations using variational autoencoders. It improves the canonicalization process on several fronts including entity and relation embeddings, encoding of knowledge graph structure and clustering. However, none of these methods have performed a quantitative evaluation of their performance for relation canonicalization, due to the lack of ground truth annotations for the benchmark datasets. Our work aims to fill precisely this gap.

Putri et al. [6] is one of the few works which focus on canonicalizing relations instead of entities, by aligning the relation phrases (RPs) from an open KG with the ones from Wikidata [8]. The authors show that relation alignment might be a better choice than clustering if most of the relations are likely to have equivalence in a pre-defined knowledge base. Nevertheless, the case when most of the relations of the open KG do not have their analogy in, e.g. Wikidata, is not discussed in the paper.

2   Method

To generate the dataset for relation canonicalization, our approach was to start from an existing ontological KG and derive high-quality relation phrases for its relations that can serve as golden clusters for the evaluation of the canonicalization methods. For this, we chose the NELL KG [5] (iteration 1115) which already has canonical relations. NELL was constructed in an automated way from the ClueWeb09 dataset[1] which also served as the source for other benchmark datasets often used in previous works [1,7] such as *Base, ReVerb45k* and *Ambiguous*. Figure 1 illustrates the overall steps of the dataset generation.

Selection of Representative Relations. Overall, NELL contains 832 unique relations and 2,766,048 triples. We found that not all relations were useful for the task of canonicalization. For example, very specific relations having too few representative triples in the KG would be rarely found in texts, e.g. *inverse_of_agricultural_product_coming_from_vertebrate*. On the other hand, certain relations such as *wikipedia_has_url* with a large number of triples would also

---

[1] http://boston.lti.cs.cmu.edu/Data/clueweb09.

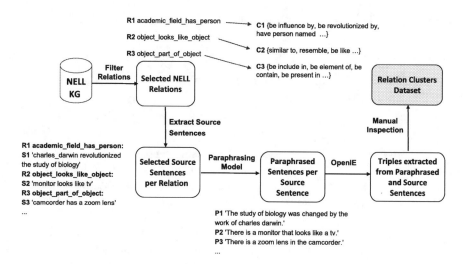

Fig. 1. Steps for creating an annotated dataset of relation clusters for NELL relations.

be undesirable. Therefore, relations with fewer than 20 or more than 300 triples were filtered out, leaving 274 relations.

Extraction of Source Sentences from NELL. The NELL dataset includes the source sentences that the triples in the KG are derived from. This serves as a useful first step for our process - for each of the relations as selected above, we consider the corresponding KG triples that the relation occurs in, and find the source sentences for those triples. Thus, for each relation a set of source sentences is obtained that indicate the relation phrases associated with the canonical relation. Among these, the sentences having no verbs or no explicit entities were filtered out. For uniformity, the maximum number of sentences for each triple was limited to 5, leading to 73,404 sentences overall.

Derivation of Sentence Paraphrases. While the source sentences contained some phrases for the relations, we leveraged a paraphrasing model from HuggingFace [9] to obtain further relation phrases per relation[2]. The number of paraphrases for each sentence was limited to 20; thus each triple had a maximum of 120 paraphrased sentences (max 5 sentences per triple).

Extraction of Relation Phrases. In order to extract the different relation phrases in the set of paraphrased sentences, we used the Stanford OpenIE tool[3] which gave triples of the form ⟨*intuit, was eventually acquired by, mint*⟩. At this stage, the triples having no subjects or objects were filtered out and we obtained a set of relation phrases for each relation. The triples which mentioned original noun phrases in an inverse form (e.g. *yellow, is the colour of, sun* instead of *sun, has colour, yellow*) were marked as inverse and added to the set of extracted relation phrases.

---

[2] https://huggingface.co/tuner007/pegasus_paraphrase.
[3] https://stanfordnlp.github.io/CoreNLP/openie.html.

Table 1. Results for relation canonicalization for CUVA and CESI

	Base		Ambiguous		ReVerb45k	
	Macro	*Micro*	*Macro*	*Micro*	*Macro*	*Micro*
CESI	**0.6301**	**0.5169**	**0.6284**	**0.5149**	0.6284	**0.5149**
CUVA	0.5	0.104	0.4043	0.2113	**0.6301**	0.4717

Manual Inspection. The process of paraphrasing sentences automatically contributed to a wide range of possible interesting relation phrases for each relation, in many cases even better than what could have been obtained manually. However, to ensure the quality of the resulting dataset, we performed a manual cleanup to remove the noisy paraphrases. The noise for the relation varied between 10% to 50% and the took from 5 to 20 min depending on the relation. At this step, further nearly duplicate relations were discovered with identical RPs, e.g., *color_of_object* and *color_associated_with_visualizable_attribute*, such relations were merged.

The final dataset[4] consists of 162 canonical relations (and their inverse relations) along with their corresponding RPs, with the mean number of non-normalised RPs being 29. A few representative examples from the dataset are : **organization_acronym_has_name:** {stand for, abbreviate for, be short for} *inverse:* {full name for, be briefly know as}; **person_has_religion:** { worship, follow, believe} *inverse:* {be religion of}.

3   Evaluation and Conclusion

Quality of the Dataset. We performed manual evaluation of the generated dataset by randomly selecting 50 relations and asking two annotators to mark the corresponding RPs as correct or incorrect (1 or 0). This manual check took a couple of person hours and reported a Fleiss' Kappa agreement score of 0.80. A third annotator then independently resolved the conflicts to create the final dataset. The disagreements were mainly attributed to ambiguous or polysemous RPs that would fit well for multiple relations, as each annotator might differently imagine the necessary granularity of the dataset. The average accuracy of the RPs in the dataset after this process was 0.95.

Evaluation of Existing Methods. With our dataset serving as the ground-truth, we evaluated the relation clusters obtained from CESI and CUVA for the *Base, Ambiguous* and *ReVerb45k* datasets, with the macro and micro precision metrics [4]. The results of this evaluation, as presented in Table 1, provided some interesting insights. The scores for CESI are generally higher except for *ReVerb45k*. The reason could be that the main model used in CUVA (variational autoencoders) requires more data to learn appropriate word representations. As soon as it is provided a larger corpus, it slightly outperforms CESI. In case of

---

[4] https://github.com/veerlosar/rp_canonicalisation.

Base, CUVA came up with about 10 relation clusters - one out of which contained over 90% of relation phrases. Such clustering results significantly affected the macro and micro precision for both *Base* and *Ambiguous* datasets.

Conclusion. In this work, we have presented a dataset for relation canonicalization that can be used for a quantitative evaluation of existing as well as future techniques. We hope this paves the way for further improvements in this direction. As future work, we continue to refine the proposed dataset further. In particular, we would like to avoid any bias in the dataset which could be introduced due to use of specific open-source tools such as HuggingFace and Stanford OpenIE (currently the dataset might favour the relation phrases extracted via these tools as compared to others). We plan to alleviate this issue while expanding the current dataset to include more relations and applying the pipeline to different knowledge bases. Additionally, we plan to perform a more thorough analysis for relation canonicalization and propose ways to mitigate the shortcomings of existing solutions.

References

1. Dash, S., Rossiello, G., Mihindukulasooriya, N., Bagchi, S., Gliozzo, A.: Open knowledge graphs canonicalization using variational autoencoders. In: Proceedings of the 2021 Conference on Empirical Methods in Natural Language Processing, pp. 10379–10394, November 2021
2. Dessì, D., Osborne, F., Recupero, D.R., Buscaldi, D., Motta, E.: Generating knowledge graphs by employing natural language processing and machine learning techniques within the scholarly domain. Futur. Gener. Comput. Syst. **116**, 253–264 (2021)
3. Fader, A., Soderland, S., Etzioni, O.: Identifying relations for open information extraction. In: Proceedings of the 2011 Conference on Empirical Methods in Natural Language Processing, pp. 1535–1545, July 2011
4. Galárraga, L., Heitz, G., Murphy, K., Suchanek, F.M.: Canonicalizing open knowledge bases. In: Proceedings of the 23rd ACM International Conference on Information and Knowledge Management, pp. 1679–1688 (2014)
5. Mitchell, T., et al.: Never-ending learning. In: Proceedings of the Twenty-Ninth AAAI Conference on Artificial Intelligence (AAAI-15) (2015)
6. Putri, R.A., Hong, G., Myaeng, S.H.: Aligning open ie relations and kb relations using a siamese network based on word embedding. In: Proceedings of the 13th International Conference on Computational Semantics - Long Papers, pp. 142–153. Association for Computational Linguistics, Gothenburg, Sweden, May 2019
7. Vashishth, S., Jain, P., Talukdar, P.: CESI: canonicalizing open knowledge bases using embeddings and side information. In: Proceedings of the 2018 World Wide Web Conference, pp. 1317–1327 (2018)
8. Vrandečić, D., Krötzsch, M.: Wikidata: a free collaborative knowledgebase. Commun. ACM **57**(10), 78–85 (2014)
9. Wolf, T., et al.: Transformers: state-of-the-art natural language processing. In: Proceedings of the 2020 Conference on Empirical Methods in Natural Language Processing: System Demonstrations, pp. 38–45, October 2020

Harmonizing and Using Numismatic Linked Data in Digital Humanities Research and Application Development: Case DigiNUMA

Heikki Rantala[1]([✉]) [iD], Eljas Oksanen[2,3] [iD], and Eero Hyvönen[1,3] [iD]

[1] Semantic Computing Research Group (SeCo), Aalto University, Espoo, Finland
{heikki.rantala,eero.hyvonen}@aalto.fi
[2] Department of Cultures, University of Helsinki, Helsinki, Finland
[3] Helsinki Centre for Digital Humanities (HELDIG), University of Helsinki,
Helsinki, Finland
eljas.oksanen@helsinki.fi
https://seco.cs.aalto.fi, https://heldig.fi

Abstract. This paper outlines the ongoing work of the DigiNUMA project for creating solutions in data harmonisation, analysis, and dissemination of pan-European archaeological and numismatic Cultural Heritage, using linked data and semantic web technologies. The project focuses on Viking Age (800–1150 AD) Finnish and English numismatic data as a case study. A broader context is gained by research into harmonizing collection data of the National Museum of Finland, the British Museum, and the Fitzwilliam Museum in Cambridge for compatibility with the international Nomisma.org ontology, and by creating tools that can be used to work with other Nomisma.org datasets.

1 Introduction and Related Work

During the recent years the number of archaeological finds made by the public across Europe, mainly through hobby metal-detecting, has grown considerably. Coins form a special case of finds worth concentrating on for several reasons. Coin finds are relatively easy to recognise when found in the ground with a detector and are usually the most numerous object type reported by the public [5]. Coin types can be identified more precisely than other common finds, producing higher quality record data and making them specially suitable for Digital Humanities (DH) analysis; for example, dates and places of minting can often be determined with reference to existing numismatic scholarship. Historical coins also moved internationally, making harmonizing and comparing international data especially relevant.

DigiNUMA – Digital Solutions for European Numismatic Heritage[1] [6] is an ongoing research project that responds to a set of new needs in Cultural Heritage

---

[1] Project homepage: https://seco.cs.aalto.fi/projects/diginuma.

P. Groth et al. (Eds.): ESWC 2022 Satellite Events, LNCS 13384, pp. 26–30, 2022.
https://doi.org/10.1007/978-3-031-11609-4_5

(CH) data management, research, and dissemination using Linked Open Data (LOD). The project collaborates with two international LOD data projects in archaeological CH: ARIADNEplus[2] [8] and Nomisma.org[3] [2]. ARIADNEplus is a pan-European research infrastructure and aggregation project for all archaeological data, while Nomisma.org concerns numismatic data.

The project contributes to the state-of-the-art by developing new tools and approaches for DH analyses on numismatic collection data mainly based on the ontology framework of Nomisma.org. Another contribution of the DigiNUMA project is to create a generic semantic portal model, application, and LOD service for archaeological coin finds based on the "Sampo-model" [3] and Sampo-UI framework [4], a new part of the "Sampo" series of portals[4].

2   Data and Ontologies

As a case study the project concentrates on Viking Age (800–1150 AD) coins, selected owing to high degree of geographic circulation (therefore diversity in different national collections) of coins from this period in north-western and northern Europe and beyond from western Asia. DigiNUMA will mainly draw upon the existing numismatic data maintained by the Finnish National Museum Coin Cabinet and the Finnish Heritage Agency. In order to provide an international comparison, and to identify possible biases inherent in national numismatic datasets, DigiNUMA will also investigate English early medieval coin data from the British Museum, and data from the Corpus of Early Medieval Coins at the Fitzwilliam Museum in Cambridge, UK.

Digitisation of archaeological CH has advanced in many European countries in the recent years. Issues related to data harmonisation of archaeological data (alignment of dataset structures and object classifications) remain, however, a significant challenge for collating, studying and disseminating CH data at a transnational scale, as existing collections management practices and typologies typically descend from a broad variety of long-standing national or institutional practices and traditions. In this context numismatic data makes an excellent case study in LOD data harmonisation owing to a strong existing foundation of internationally shared typological practices. Nomisma.org was started by the American Numismatic Society in 2010, to facilitate the presentation of numismatic concepts using LOD [2,9]. More than 30 different institutions have provided datasets[5] for the project.

Nomisma.org includes ontologies for many different aspects of numismatic data such as mints and rulers, and even deities depicted on the coins. Currently Nomisma.org mostly includes data related to classical era owing to the breadth of international scholarship on Greek and Roman numismatics, but expanding the ontologies to cover medieval era is planned. DigiNUMA project will aim to

---

[2] https://ariadne-infrastructure.eu.

[3] http://Nomisma.org.

[4] Sampo portals: https://seco.cs.aalto.fi/applications/sampo.

[5] See: http://Nomisma.org/datasets.

be a part of this process, and share the ontologies created with Nomisma.org. The ontology work done within the DigiNUMA project will be limited mainly to concepts relevant to the available Finnish data.

3   Using the LOD Service and Applications

As far as is possible, the research data will also be opened as a data service, but some elements of the data may not be possible to make public due to rights issues. Harmonized data together with ontologies, published as a LOD service on the Linked Data Finland platform,[6] is used in three ways: 1) the data can be filtered, uploaded and reused in external DH tools and applications. 2) The SPARQL endpoint can be used for data analyses using tools such as the YAS-GUI editor[7] and Jupyter Notebooks. 3) A new semantic portal "CoinSampo" is being developed on top of the SPARQL endpoint that can be used without programming skills. It demonstrates how the LOD service can be used effectively in application development. All data and software developed in DigiNUMA will be published openly using the CC BY 4.0 license, whenever this is allowed by the original data providers' copyright.

The CoinSampo web application is currently in early development, and is based on the Sampo-UI framework[8]. While the application is mainly developed for the Finnish data, using an international Nomisma.org ontology makes it possible to easily use the application to work with other data as well.

To test the early prototype of CoinSampo application, and it's applicability to international data, we have used the Seleucid Coins Online[9] dataset created by the American Numismatic Society. This dataset, like many others, can be downloaded from the Nomisma.org website and depicts coin types of the ancient Seleucid Empire (312 BC to 63 BC). As an example of the application prototype, Fig. 1 shows the relative numbers of coin denominations associated with the mint of Susa as a pie chart.[10] It is easy to see that most coin are of denomination "Tetradrachm". This can be very quickly compared to numbers from other mints.

Importantly, *DigiNUMA* seeks to develop applications for types of data analysis and visualisation that have been previously largely inaccessible without training in programs such as R or Python. Three examples are given. First, medieval numismatic data is typically "fuzzy data" in terms of its dating, with coins being dated within a range of possible dates of manufacture. In this context it is difficult to construct precise chronological charts displaying variation in coin observations across time using common statistical tables. Aoristic analysis is a temporal analysis technique for creating an aggregate picture of a set of temporally imprecise data [7]. The planned application assigns the fractional

---

[6] https://ldf.fi.

[7] http://yasgui.triply.cc/.

[8] https://github.com/SemanticComputing/sampo-ui.

[9] http://numismatics.org/sco.

[10] The application uses the ApexCharts library https://apexcharts.com to create chart visualizations.

probability of each observation in a dataset falling into a given temporal bin, adding them together and depicting the results as a bar chart that shows probabilistic patterns of increase and decrease in observations across time. Second, the application will also include various maps useful for analysis. Coin findspot data yields critical information on historical economic patters, yet, where findspots are numerous or clustered, simple point-based are inefficient for their close study. A kernel density estimation based "heat map" yields more useful map views [1]. Third, historic coin circulation can be visualised with radial diagrams that connect mint locations and coin findspots. On technical level, we use existing open source libraries[11] and the existing faceted search framework and modules of Sampo-UI to implement various kinds of visualizations. A researcher or hobbyist can use CoinSampo's faceted search functionality to create these kind of visualizations quickly and without technical know-how.

In an example use case a user interested in eleventh-century English coin economy could produce a chronological overview of all coins issued at a particular mint town, identify main periods of high output, and follow up by comparing spatial distributions to study changes in coin circulation patterns across time - possibly producing new information on growth and development of medieval regional economies. Should harmonised data be possible to add from different countries, such analysis could be extended to cover aspects of international trade.

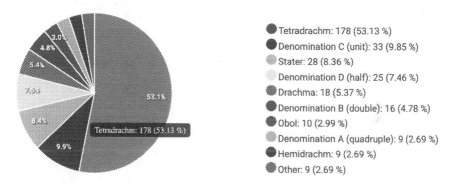

Fig. 1. An example of a visualization created with CoinSampo application showing coin denominations of Seluidic coins from the mint of Susa.

4   Discussion

In our experience, the current data in Nomisma.org datasets can sometimes have errors and inconsistencies, perhaps due to different data providers applying the model in slightly differing ways. The ontology infrastructure is moreover currently limited for the post-classical era. However, the fundamental fact that a series of international datasets, arriving from institutions with divergent collections managements histories and policies, have nevertheless been described using

---

[11] For example ApexCharts: https://apexcharts.com.

a similar ontological framework makes it possible to reuse applications created in the DigiNUMA project for analysis and dissemination of this diverse body of numismatic data, with only slight alterations. The shared ontology infrastructure also makes creating new data easier. This demonstrates the significant potential of LOD and data harmonisation approaches in bringing together and creating added value from international and traditionally heterogeneous CH material.

A significant quantity of archaeological CH data in many European countries is today generated by the public. This is but one aspect that plays into the need to increase the accessibility of CH data, including its interoperability in scientific analysis internationally but also in lowering the threshold for anyone to discover, learn and create new knowledge, as a critical issue in European heritage management. To this end, *DigiNUMA* will lay the groundwork for future collaboration, secure international and interdisciplinary networks between Finnish and European partners, and develop solutions to current challenges.

Acknowledgements. The project has been funded by the Jenny and Antti Wihuri Foundation. CSC – IT Center for Science has provided computational resources.

References

1. Bevan, A.: Spatial methods for analysing large-scale artefact inventories. Antiquity **86**, 492–506 (2012). https://doi.org/10.1017/S0003598X0006289X
2. Gruber, E., Meadows, A.: Numismatics and linked open data. ISAW Papers 20.6 (2021). http://hdl.handle.net/2333.1/q83bkdqf
3. Hyvönen, E.: Digital humanities on the semantic web: sampo model and portal series. Semant. Web - Interoperabil. Usabil. Appl. (2022, submitted)
4. Ikkala, E., Hyvönen, E., Rantala, H., Koho, M.: Sampo-UI: a full stack Javascript framework for developing semantic portal user interfaces. Semant. Web - Interoperabil. Usabil. Appl. **13**(1), 69–84 (2022). https://doi.org/10.3233/SW-210428
5. Leahy, K., Lewis, M.: Finds Identified: Portable Antiquities Scheme. Greenlight Publishing, Witham (2018)
6. Oksanen, E., et al.: Digital humanities solutions for pan-European numismatic and archaeological heritage based on linked open data (2022, submitted)
7. Orton, D., Morris, J., Pipe, A.: Catch per unit research effort: sampling intensity, chronological uncertainty, and the onset of marine fish consumption in historic London. Open Quater. **3**, 1–20 (2017). https://doi.org/10.5334/oq.29
8. Richards, J., Niccolucci, F. (eds.): The Ariadne Impact. Archaeolingua, Budapest (2019). https://doi.org/10.5281/zenodo.3476712
9. Wigg-Wolf, D., Duyrat, F.: La révolution des linked open data en numismatique: les exemples de nomisma.org et online Greek coinage. Archéol. Numér. **17**(1), 1–12 (2017). https://doi.org/10.21494/ISTE.OP.2017.0171 https://doi.org/10.21494/ISTE.OP.2017.0171

Extending AgreementMakerLight
to Perform Holistic Ontology Matching

Marta Contreiras Silva[✉], Daniel Faria, and Catia Pesquita

LASIGE, Faculdade de Ciências da Universidade de Lisboa, Lisbon, Portugal
mcdsilva@fc.ul.pt

Abstract. Creating rich knowledge graphs that allow the representation of data encompassing multiple domains requires the integration of different ontologies. However, the challenge of matching multiple ontologies is not properly addressed by the current pairwise strategy espoused by state-of-the-art ontology alignment systems.

We have extended the ontology alignment system AgreementMakerLight (AML) to address this particular challenge through a scalable cluster-based incremental matching strategy. We make use of AML's fast and precise matching algorithms to determine the semantic affinity between the ontologies and cluster them, then apply AML's full ontology matching pipeline incrementally, within each cluster, by matching and then merging ontologies pairwise. The strategy was applied to the integration of 28 biomedical ontologies and achieved a runtime reduction of almost 50%.

This poster expands on the extensions applied to the AML system as the technical contribution that accompanies our In-Use Technology accepted submission "Matching Multiple Ontologies to Build a Knowledge Graph for Personalized Medicine".

Keywords: Ontology matching · Holistic ontology matching · Biomedical ontologies

1 Introduction

Sophisticated Semantic Web applications often depend on a comprehensive and holistic view of their domain. In many domains, there are several ontologies available that provide different scopes or perspectives, and which could be aligned and integrated into a full-fledged semantic network, circumventing the burden of developing a new encompassing ontology. However, this requires a paradigm shift in Ontology Matching from the current pairwise approach of state-of-the-art systems to holistic ontology matching [6].

A naive application of the traditional pairwise alignment strategy would be to align all possible pairs of ontologies and then merge them all to obtain a single alignment. This would require a quadratic number of ontology matching steps, which is not very scalable. As such, the challenge of holistic ontology

© The Author(s), under exclusive license to Springer Nature Switzerland AG 2022
P. Groth et al. (Eds.): ESWC 2022 Satellite Events, LNCS 13384, pp. 31–35, 2022.
https://doi.org/10.1007/978-3-031-11609-4_6

matching [7,9] has been addressed in one of two ways: either by partitioning the search space and then running the pairwise alignments within [4] or matching incrementally in a predefined order [5,10]. However, these works do not tackle the alignment of ontologies whose domains although related are not exactly the same.

To address the challenge of holistic ontology matching to build a multi-domain graph we have developed a strategy[1] that considers both partitioning and incremental alignment strategies, taking also into account how to support user input. Our strategy aims to strike a balance between quality, coverage and scalability of the alignment process.

2 Holistic OM Strategy

The starting point of our approach is the AML system [3], which has been one of the top performing systems in the Ontology Alignment Evaluation Initiative (OAEI) over the last nine years [1,8]. However, AML, like other state-of-the-art OM systems is prepared solely to produce alignments between two ontologies, and lacks the functionality of integrating two ontologies through their alignment, which is critical to enable a pairwise matching strategy to be applied incrementally to holistic matching. Our holistic matching strategy, Clustering Incremental Alignment (CIA) (Fig. 1), is geared to tackle multi-domain matching problems where the overlap between some ontologies might be small or even

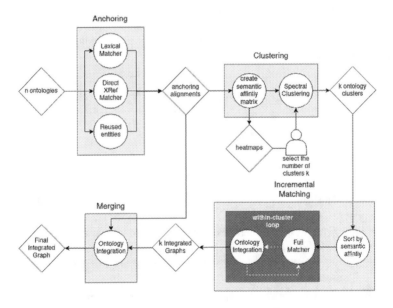

Fig. 1. Overview of the Clustering Incremental Alignment (CIA) strategy.

---

[1] https://github.com/liseda-lab/holistic-matching-aml.

non-existent. For those ontologies, sophisticated matching algorithms would not only be a likely waste of computation time, but could potentially result in lower quality alignments by finding more false positives. However, for highly overlapping ontologies, we do want to use sophisticated matching algorithms, as they are expected to increase the quality of the alignment. Thus, our CIA strategy starts with an anchoring step that aims at defining the level of semantic affinity between all of the ontologies, using fast matching techniques with a high degree of confidence. From these anchoring alignments that are produced, a semantic affinity matrix is created that serves as input for both Spectral Clustering and the development of a heatmap that allows the visualization of more closely related sets of ontologies. This aids the user in defining the number of clusters to select in the Spectral Clustering process. The ontologies are then separated into clusters and further sorted in descending order of semantic affinity. The full AML matching pipeline is then run within each cluster in an incremental fashion, where the first pair of ontologies is matched, then the ontologies are merged through their alignment, then the resulting merged ontology is matched with the third ontology, and so on and so forth. This process results in one integrated graph per cluster, which will be merged together using the initial anchoring alignments to produce a final integrated graph.

3   Application to the Biomedical Domain

The KATY project[2] aims to develop an AI-empowered personalized medicine system to use in clinical decision support that is based on a Knowledge Graph to support Explainable AI.

To develop this KG we need to integrate 28 biomedical ontologies which are, most often than not, incredibly complex and large. This means that in addition to the challenges in Holistic OM, we are also tacling the challenges in aligning biomedical ontologies [2]. We applied the CIA strategy over this set of 28 ontologies and compared it to the standard AML pairwise strategy, where all possible pairs are matched and then all resulting alignments merged, henceforth referred to as Global Pairwise Alignment (GPA) [11]. Table 1 summarizes the runtimes, number of mappings, and number of tasks from both strategies.

The GPA strategy runs in almost 32 h, while CIA only requires roughly 16 h, which corresponds to a decrease in runtime of almost half. Although CIA requires longer loading times (since ontologies are loaded for Anchoring and for Incremental Matching), it spends only 15% of the time in Matching tasks that is required for GPA. The integrated graph produced by CIA is 25% smaller than the one produced by GPA, which can be explained by the lack of semantically redundant mappings that are produced when using basic pairwise matching.

---

[2] http://katy-project.eu/.

Table 1. Alignment results

	Runtime (hh:mm)			Alignment	
Strategy	Load	Match	Total	Mappings	Tasks
GPA	11:47	19:51	31:37	554, 547	378
CIA	12:52	03:04	15:56	417, 131	378* + 24

GPA: global pairwise alignment. CIA: within cluster incremental alignment.
* from the Anchoring step

4   Conclusions

The CIA strategy decreased the overall runtime required in matching these 28 biomedical ontologies when compared to the state-of-the-art, which makes progress in addressing the issue of scalability. Moreover, the combination of approaches in CIA is expected to ensure high precision across less closely related domains (different clusters) by employing high precision lexical matching, while improving recall for closely related ontologies (same cluster) by employing more computationally expensive algorithms. This expectation is supported by the evaluation of the matching algorithms of AML in the OAEI campaign where the full AML strategy achieves median performances of 90.6% in precision and 76.31% in recall in the anatomy and large biomed tracks, whereas the lexical matching achieves 98.9% precision and 40.6% recall [1,2].

The next step in this work is to perform a expert-based validation study over a set of selected mappings to ensure that the produced alignment is correct and coherent. The use of this type of validation is vital since the available reference alignments are incapable of supporting our alignments tasks.

Acknowledgments. This work was supported by FCT through the LASIGE Research Unit (UIDB/00408/2020 and UIDP/00408/2020). It was also partially supported by the KATY project funded the European Union's Horizon 2020 research and innovation program (GA 101017453).

References

1. Faria, D., Lima, B., Silva, M.C., Couto, F.M., Pesquita, C.: AML and AMLC results for OAEI 2021, p. 6
2. Faria, D., Pesquita, C., Mott, I., Martins, C., Couto, F.M., Cruz, I.F.: Tackling the challenges of matching biomedical ontologies. J. Biomed. Semant. **9**(1), 1–19 (2018)
3. Faria, D., Pesquita, C., Santos, E., Palmonari, M., Cruz, I.F., Couto, F.M.: The agreementmakerlight ontology matching system. In: Meersman, R. (ed.) OTM 2013. LNCS, vol. 8185, pp. 527–541. Springer, Heidelberg (2013). https://doi.org/10.1007/978-3-642-41030-7_38
4. Gruetze, T., Böhm, C., Naumann, F.: Holistic and scalable ontology alignment for linked open data. LDOW **937**, 1–10 (2012)

5. Hertling, S., Paulheim, H.: Order matters: matching multiple knowledge graphs. arXiv preprint arXiv:2111.02239 (2021)
6. Megdiche, I., Teste, O., Trojahn, C.: An extensible linear approach for holistic ontology matching. In: Groth, P. (ed.) ISWC 2016. LNCS, vol. 9981, pp. 393–410. Springer, Cham (2016). https://doi.org/10.1007/978-3-319-46523-4_24
7. Otero-Cerdeira, L., Rodríguez-Martínez, F.J., Gómez-Rodríguez, A.: Ontology matching: a literature review. Expert Syst. Appl. **42**(2), 949–971 (2015)
8. Pour, M.A.N., et al.: Results of the ontology alignment evaluation initiative (2021)
9. Rahm, E.: Towards large-scale schema and ontology matching. In: Schema matching and mapping, pp. 3–27. Springer (2011). https://doi.org/10.1007/978-3-642-16518-4_1
10. Saleem, K., Bellahsene, Z., Hunt, E.: Porsche: performance oriented schema mediation. Inf. Syst. **33**(7–8), 637–657 (2008)
11. Silva, M.C., Faria, D., Pesquita, C.: Matching multiple ontologies to build a knowledge graph for personalized medicine. In: International Semantic Web Conference (2022). https://doi.org/10.1007/978-3-031-06981-9_27

It's All in the Name: Entity Typing Using Multilingual Language Models

Russa Biswas[1,2(✉)], Yiyi Chen[1,2], Heiko Paulheim[3], Harald Sack[1,2], and Mehwish Alam[1,2]

[1] FIZ Karlsruhe – Leibniz Institute for Information Infrastructure, Karlsruhe, Germany
{russa.biswas,yiyi.chen,harald.sack,mehwish.alam}@fiz-karlsruhe.de
[2] Karlsruhe Institute of Technology, Institute AIFB, Karlsruhe, Germany
[3] University of Mannheim, Mannheim, Germany
heiko@informatik.uni-mannheim.de

Abstract. The entity type information in Knowledge Graphs (KGs) of different languages plays an important role in a wide range of Natural Language Processing applications. However, the entity types in KGs are often incomplete. Multilingual entity typing is a non-trivial task if enough information is not available for the entities in a KG. In this work, multilingual neural language models are exploited to predict the type of an entity from only the name of the entity. The model has been successfully evaluated on multilingual datasets extracted from different language chapters in DBpedia namely German, French, Spanish, and Dutch.

Keywords: Entity type prediction · Knowledge graph completion · Multilingual language models · Classification

1 Introduction

Entity typing is the task of assigning entities in a Knowledge Graph (KG) with similar characteristic features to the same semantic type. The type information of entities plays a fundamental role in KG completion. In KGs such as DBpedia, YAGO, Wikidata, etc., the entity types are extracted automatically from structured data such as Wikipedia Infoboxes, generated using heuristics, or are human-curated. Therefore, the entity type information in KGs is often incomplete. Recent research focuses on automated entity type prediction models exploiting the triples in a KG using heuristics (Paulheim and Bizer 2013) and neural network-based models (Biswas et al. 2020; Jin et al. 2019; Biswas et al. 2021b). The multi-level representations of entities are learned in MuLR (Yaghoobzadeh and Schütze 2017) by using character embeddings, word embeddings, and entity embeddings using the Structured SKIP-gram (SSKIP) model followed by a multi-label classification approach to predict the entity types. The pre-trained RDF2Vec entity embeddings in (Sofronova et al., 2020) coupled with a supervised approach using a neural network based classifier and

P. Groth et al. (Eds.): ESWC 2022 Satellite Events, LNCS 13384, pp. 36–41, 2022.
https://doi.org/10.1007/978-3-031-11609-4_7

a vector similarity based unsupervised approach are used to predict the types of the entities in DBpedia.

Nevertheless, it is still a challenging problem to predict the type information for non-popular entities or new entities that are added to the KG, i.e., entities with less or no triples associated with them. The meaningfulness of the entity names in the Semantic Web has been studied in (de Rooij et al., 2016). To this end, entity names have been leveraged to predict the types of the entities using Neural Language Models (NLMs) in (Biswas et al., 2021a) for the English DBpedia chapter. However, to be able to predict the types of the entities just by their names, one has to understand multiple languages. Therefore, this originates the necessity of an automated multilingual entity type prediction framework for different chapters in DBpedia. For example, *Is it possible to predict the types of the entities dbr: Lachse, dbr: Saumon, dbr: Salmo, and dbr: Zalm from their names?* These are the names of *Salmon fish* in German, French, Spanish, and Dutch respectively. Therefore, this paper focuses on predicting the types of entities just by their names for different language chapters of DBpedia, namely German (DE), French (FR), Spanish (ES), and Dutch (NL).

This paper focuses on tackling two main challenges: (*i*) predict the types of the entities for which significantly less or no triples are available in the KGs, and (*ii*) predict the types of the entities in different languages. This lack of available information is compensated by exploiting the Multilingual Neural Language Models (Multilingual-NLMs), namely Wikipedia2Vec, and m-BERT. They are trained on a huge amount of textual data in multiple languages, and they provide implicit contextual information about the entities in their corresponding language-agnostic vector representations. The main contributions are:

– A multi-class classification framework is proposed to predict the missing entity types in multilingual DBpedia chapters exploiting the NLMs.
– A benchmark dataset for multilingual entity typing consisting of entities from German (DE), French (FR), Spanish (ES), and Dutch (NL) DBpedia chapters are published for re-usability purposes for future research.

2 Entity Typing Using Language Models

This section discusses the Multilingual-NLMs and the classification model used for entity typing only from the names of the entities.

m-BERT. **B**idirectional **E**ncoder **R**epresentations from **T**ransformers (Devlin et al., 2019) is a contextual embedding approach in which pretraining on bidirectional representations from the unlabeled text by using the left and the right context in all the layers is performed. Multilingual-BERT (m-BERT) supports 104 languages trained on text from the Wikipedia content with a shared vocabulary across all the languages. However, the size of Wikipedia varies greatly for different languages. The low-resource languages are underrepresented in the neural network model compared to the popular languages. The training on the low-resource languages of Wikipedia for a large number of epochs results in overfitting of the model. To combat the content imbalance of Wikipedia, less popular languages are over-sampled, whereas the popular languages are under-sampled. An exponential smoothing weighting of the data during the pre-training data creation is used. For tokenization, a 110k shared WordPiece vocabulary is used. The word counts are weighted following the same method for the pre-training data creation. Therefore, the low-resource languages are up-weighted by some factors. Given an entity name $E_i = (w_1, w_2, ..., w_n)$, the input sequence to the m-BERT model is given by $([CLS], w_1, w_2, ..., w_n, [SEP])$, where E_i is the ith entity and $w_1, w_2, .., w_n$ are the n words in the entity name. $[CLS]$ and $[SEP]$ are special tokens that mark the beginning and the end of the input sequence.

Wikipedia2vec. (Yamada et al., 2020) The model jointly learns word and entity embeddings from Wikipedia, where similar words and entities are close to one another in the vector space. It uses three submodels to learn the representation: Wikipedia Link Graph Model, Word-based skip-gram model, and Anchor context model. The skip-gram model forms the basis of these three submodels with a training objective to find embeddings useful for predicting context words or entities given a target word or entity. A Wikipedia Link Graph is generated in which the nodes are the entities in Wikipedia, and the edges are the links between them. There exists an edge between two nodes if the Wikipedia page of one entity has a link to that of the Wikipedia page of the other entity or if both the pages are linked to each other. Entity embeddings are learned from this Wikipedia Link Graph by predicting the neighboring entities following the skip-gram model. The second submodel is the Word-based skip-gram model, which learns word embeddings by predicting neighboring words given each word in a text contained on a Wikipedia page. Lastly, the Anchor context model learns the embeddings by predicting the neighboring words for each entity. This submodel focuses on putting similar words and the entities closer to each other in the vector space which helps in a deeper understanding of the interactions between the embeddings of the entities and the words in Wikipedia. In this work, pre-trained Wikipedia2vec models[1] for each of the languages, i.e., DE, FR, ES, and NL are used.

Embeddings of the Entity Names. In this work, the m-BERT base model has been used, in which each position outputs a vector of dimension equal to that of its hidden layer and its corresponding dimension is 768 for the base model. Each entity name is considered as a sentence for the input to m-BERT. The average of the last four hidden layers is taken to represent the entities. For Wikipedia2vec, the average of all word vectors in each entity name is taken as the vector representation of the entity.

Classification. Entity typing is considered a classification task with the types of entities as classes. A two-layered Fully Connected Neural Network (FCNN) model consisting of two dense layers with ReLU as an activation function has been used on the top of the entity vectors. This work considers non-overlapping classes. Therefore it is a multi-class classification problem. A softmax function used in the last layer calculates the probabilities of the entities in different classes.

---

[1] https://wikipedia2vec.github.io/wikipedia2vec/pretrained/.

Table 1. Dataset statistics

DBpedia chapters	Train	Test	Valid	Total entities	#coarse-grained class	#fine-grained class
German	38500	23100	15400	77000	38	77
French	57999	34799	23199	115997	51	116
Spanish	42000	25200	16800	84000	45	84
Dutch	44000	26400	17600	88000	42	88

Table 2. Entity typing results on DE, FR, ES, and NL DBpedia chapters

DBpedia chapters	#classes	m-BERT			Wikipedia2vec			m-BERT + Wikipedia2vec		
		Accuracy	Ma-F1	Mi-F1	Accuracy	Ma-F1	Mi-F1	Accuracy	Ma-F1	Mi-F1
German	38	0.818	0.760	0.818	0.870	0.817	0.870	**0.918**	**0.884**	**0.918**
	77	0.674	0.676	0.674	0.763	0.762	0.763	0.831	0.829	0.831
French	51	0.794	0.689	0.794	0.833	0.718	0.833	**0.867**	**0.780**	**0.867**
	116	0.544	0.542	0.544	0.611	0.612	0.611	0.678	0.680	0.678
Spanish	45	0.782	0.694	0.782	0.843	0.764	0.843	**0.894**	**0.846**	**0.894**
	84	0.629	0.627	0.629	0.681	0.682	0.681	0.788	0.788	0.788
Dutch	42	0.885	0.825	0.885	0.812	0.735	0.812	**0.908**	**0.859**	**0.908**
	88	0.664	0.665	0.664	0.753	0.757	0.753	0.825	0.825	0.825

Table 3. Comparison of our approach with SDType common entities

DBpedia chapters	#Common test entities	SDType accuracy	Wikipedia2vec	m-BERT
German	1103	43%	66.2%	61.4%
French	9223	75.4%	79.1%	75.3%
Spanish	3486	84.57%	85.3%	84%
Dutch	7977	73.09%	77.34%	73.13%

3   Evaluation

Datasets. The work focuses on predicting the types of the entities in different DBpedia chapters, namely, DE, FR, ES, and NL. The entities are extracted from the language versions of DBpedia-version 2016–10[2]. The most popular classes from each DBpedia chapter are chosen with 1000 entities per class. The coarse-grained classes are the parent classes of the fine-grained classes in the hierarchy tree. In this dataset, no entity belongs to two different classes in different hierarchy branches. Further details about the dataset are provided in Table 1 and are made available via Github[3].

---

[2] http://downloads.dbpedia.org/wiki-archive/downloads-2016-10.html.
[3] https://github.com/russabiswas/MultilingualET_with_EntityNames.

Results. It is observed from the results as depicted in Table 2 that the static NLM Wikipedia2Vec trained on different languages of Wikipedia performs better than the m-BERT model for all the DBpedia chapters. BERT is a contextual embedding model that generates better latent representations where the context is available in the input sequence. The entity names are considered input sentences to the m-BERT model that do not provide any contextual information. On the other hand, the Wikipedia2Vec models trained on different Wikipedia languages perform better as they provide the fixed dense representation of the words or entities in the pre-trained models. It is noticeable that the concatenated vectors from m-BERT and Wikipedia2vec yield the best result as both the features are combined. Furthermore, Table 2 shows that the model performs better for coarse-grained classes compared to the fine-grained because it is often not possible to identify if a certain entity is of the type *Scientist* or an *Actor* from its name. However, it is possible to identify if the entity is of type *Person*. Also, the proposed model is compared with SDType in Table 3. For this, the publicly available results of the SDType method[4] are used. However, only a small fraction of the entities are common between the available results and DBpedia test datasets. The accuracy provided in Table 3 is calculated based on the number of common entities, and the proposed model with Wikipedia2Vec outperforms the SDType model.

4   Conclusion and Outlook

This paper analyzes multilingual NLMs for entity typing in a KG using entity names. In the future, fine-grained type prediction using other textual entity descriptions from the KG using the multilingual NLMs will be explored.

References

Biswas, R., Sofronova, R., Alam, M., Sack, H.: Entity type prediction in knowledge graphs using embeddings. DL4KG @ ESWC2020 (2020)

Biswas, R., Sofronova, R., Alam, M., Heist, N., Paulheim, H., Sack, H.: Do judge an entity by its name! entity typing using language models. In: Verborgh, R. (ed.) ESWC 2021. LNCS, vol. 12739, pp. 65–70. Springer, Cham (2021). https://doi.org/10.1007/978-3-030-80418-3_12

Biswas, R., Sofronova, R, Sack, H., Alam, M.: Cat2Type: wikipedia category embeddings for entity typing in knowledge graphs. In: K-CAP (2021b)

Devlin, J., Chang, M., Lee, K., Toutanova, K.: BERT: pre-training of deep bidirectional transformers for language understanding. In: NAACL-HLT (2019)

Jin, H., Hou, L., Li, J., Dong, T.: Fine-grained entity typing via hierarchical multi graph convolutional networks. In: EMNLP-IJCNLP (2019)

Paulheim, H., Bizer, C.: Type inference on noisy RDF data. In: Alani, H. (ed.) ISWC 2013. LNCS, vol. 8218, pp. 510–525. Springer, Heidelberg (2013). https://doi.org/10.1007/978-3-642-41335-3_32

---

[4] https://bit.ly/3eggWP0.

de Rooij, S., Beek, W., Bloem, P., van Harmelen, F., Schlobach, S.: Are names meaningful? quantifying social meaning on the semantic web. In: Groth, P. (ed.) ISWC 2016. LNCS, vol. 9981, pp. 184–199. Springer, Cham (2016). https://doi.org/10.1007/978-3-319-46523-4_12

Sofronova, R., Biswas, R., Alam, M., Sack, H.: Entity typing based on RDF2Vec using supervised and unsupervised methods. In: Harth, A., et al. (eds.) ESWC 2020. LNCS, vol. 12124, pp. 203–207. Springer, Cham (2020). https://doi.org/10.1007/978-3-030-62327-2_35

Yaghoobzadeh, Y., Schütze, H.: Multi-level representations for fine-grained typing of knowledge base entities. In: EACL (2017)

Yamada, I.: Wikipedia2Vec: an efficient toolkit for learning and visualizing the embeddings of words and entities from wikipedia. In: EMNLP (2020)

The Supervised Semantic Similarity Toolkit

Rita T. Sousa$^{(\boxtimes)}$, Sara Silva, and Catia Pesquita

LASIGE, Faculdade de Ciências da Universidade de Lisboa, Lisbon, Portugal
{risousa,sgsilva,clpesquita}@ciencias.ulisboa.pt

Abstract. Knowledge graph-based semantic similarity measures have been used in several applications. Although knowledge graphs typically describe entities according to different semantic aspects modeled in ontologies, state-of-the-art semantic similarity measures are general-purpose since they consider the whole graph or depend on expert knowledge for fine-tuning.

We present a novel toolkit that can tailor aspect-oriented semantic similarity measures to fit a particular view on similarity. It starts by identifying the semantic aspects, then computes similarities for each semantic aspect, and finally uses a supervised machine learning method to learn a supervised semantic similarity according to the similarity proxy. The toolkit combines six taxonomic semantic similarity and four embedding similarity measures and provides baseline evaluation approaches.

This extended abstract is related to the paper "Towards Supervised Biomedical Semantic Similarity" accepted to the SeWeBMeDA 2022 but focuses on our work's technical contribution whereas the workshop submission focuses on the use case for biomedical informatics.

Keywords: Ontology · Knowledge graph · Graph embedding · Semantic similarity · Machine learning

1   Introduction

Semantic similarity between entities in knowledge graphs (KGs) is essential for several tasks, especially in data mining and machine learning. State-of-the-art semantic similarity measures (SSMs), both taxonomic and graph embedding-based measures, are general-purpose and either consider the graph as a whole or depend on domain expert knowledge. However, KGs provide multiple semantic aspects (SAs) (Definition 1) or perspectives over an entity and, depending on our viewpoint of the domain, different SAs should be considered in similarity computation. In previous work, we developed a methodology to predict protein interactions that uses genetic programming, a machine learning (ML) method, to evolve combinations of aspect-oriented semantic similarities [8]. The positive results inspired us to hypothesize that, not only in the biomedical domain, if data regarding a similarity proxy (Definition 2) is available, we can learn a supervised semantic similarity tailored to capture a specific similarity view that combines different SAs.

© The Author(s), under exclusive license to Springer Nature Switzerland AG 2022
P. Groth et al. (Eds.): ESWC 2022 Satellite Events, LNCS 13384, pp. 42–46, 2022.
https://doi.org/10.1007/978-3-031-11609-4_8

Definition 1. *A **semantic aspect** represents a perspective of the representation of KG entities. It can correspond to portions of the graph (e.g., describing a protein only through the biological process subgraph of the Gene Ontology) or a given set of property types (e.g., describing a person only through properties having geographical locations as a range).*

Definition 2. *A **similarity proxy** is an estimation of the similarity between two entities that relies on objective representations of entities and calculate similarity using mathematical expressions or other algorithms.*

We have developed a toolkit[1] that learns a supervised semantic similarity between entities represented in KGs tailored towards a specific similarity proxy. This tailoring is achieved by using supervised ML methods where the input values are the similarities for different SAs, and the expected outputs are the proxy similarity values. Currently, our toolkit supports 10 SSMs (4 based on KG embeddings and 6 based on taxonomic similarity) coupled with 8 ML methods (classical ML approaches and neural network-based approaches). Since our toolkit is especially suited to KGs with several SAs, such as biomedical KGs, we applied it in a collection of benchmark datasets for KG-based similarity in the biomedical domain [2]. It is, however, domain-independent and readily applicable to other applications, such as recommender systems where the similarity computation between users is essential.

2   The Toolkit

Our toolkit, shown in Fig. 1, needs a KG and a list of instance pairs with proxy similarity values and is able to: (1) identify the SAs that describe the KG entities (2) compute KG-based similarities according to different SAs and using different SSMs; (3) train supervised ML algorithms to learn a supervised semantic similarity according to the similarity proxy for which we want to tailor the similarity; (4) evaluate the supervised semantic similarity against a set of baselines. This framework is independent of the SAs, the specific implementation of KG-based similarity and the ML algorithm employed in supervised learning.

Semantic Aspects Selection. In this work, we consider KGs where real-word entities are annotated with classes from ontologies. Ontologies structure their classes and the relationships between them as a directed acyclic graph. A semantic annotation is about assigning real-world entities to ontology classes describing them. Therefore, our toolkit takes as input an ontology file and an instance annotation file to generate the KG, where the nodes represent ontology classes and real-world entities, and edges are employed in representing ontology classes' relations and semantic annotations.

As default, our toolkit uses subgraphs rooted in the classes at a distance of one from the KG root class or the subgraphs when the KGs have multiple roots as SAs. However, SAs can also be manually defined by selecting the root classes that anchor the aspects.

---

[1] https://github.com/liseda-lab/Supervised-SS.

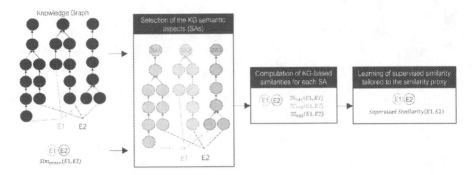

Fig. 1. Overview of the proposed framework. Considering a KG with its three SAs, each instance of the dataset representing a pair between an entity E1 and an entity E2 is characterized by three SS values corresponding to the semantic similarity between them for the three SAs, and a proxy similarity value. The models returned in the second step are then the combinations of the similarity scores of the three SAs.

Similarity Computation for Each Semantic Aspect. For the computation of KG-based similarities for each SA, our toolkit employs 10 KG-based SSMs.

Taxonomic Semantic Similarity. The taxonomic semantic similarity can be calculated using six state-of-the-art measures, from combining two information content (IC) approaches (IC_{Seco}, IC_{Resnik}) with one of three set similarity measures (ResnikBMA, ResnikMax, SimGIC). IC is a measure of how specific and informative a concept is, giving SSMs the ability to weigh the similarity of two concepts according to their specificity. IC_{Resnik} [5] is an extrinsic IC based on the number of occurrences of a concept in a corpus of texts. IC_{Seco} [7] is a structure-based approach based on structural information extracted from the ontology, namely the number of direct and indirect descendants.

Two types of approaches can be employed to calculate semantic similarity for two entities, each annotated with a set of concepts: pairwise approaches, where pairwise comparisons between all concepts annotating each entity are considered, or groupwise approaches. Resnik [5] is a pairwise class-based measure in which the similarity between two classes corresponds to the IC of their most informative common ancestor. Pairwise scores are then summarised using an aggregation strategy. For *ResnikBMA*, only the best-matching pair for each term is considered. For *ResnikMax*, the maximum of the pairwise similarities is used instead. *SimGIC* [4] is a groupwise approach based on a Jaccard index in which each term is weighted by its IC.

Graph Embedding Similarity. Four different representative graph embedding approaches can be employed to generate graph embeddings. *TransE* [1] is a translational distance approach, where each fact represents the distance between the two entities after a translation carried out by the relations. *distMult* [9] is a semantic matching approach that exploits similarity-based scoring functions by matching latent semantics of entities and relations embodied in their vector space representations. *RDF2Vec* [6] is a path-based approach that performs random walks over the RDF graph to train a neural language model. *OWL2Vec** [3] is also a path-based approach but focuses on OWL ontologies instead of typical KGs to preserve the semantics of the graph structure, the lexical information and the logical constructors.

After generating the entities' embeddings for each SA, the cosine similarity between the vectors representing each entity in the pair corresponds to the graph embeddings similarity.

Supervised Similarity Learning Tailored to Similarity Proxy. To train a supervised semantic similarity according to the similarity proxy for which we want to tailor the similarity, eight representative ML algorithms for regression can be employed. *Linear Regression* and *Bayesian Ridge* assume there is a linear relationship between the independent and dependent variables. *K-Nearest Neighbor* explores the feature space and reaches a prediction for each sample based on the expected outputs of its neighbors. *Genetic Programming* is an evolutionary algorithm that tries to optimize a combination of variable and operators. *Decision Tree* predicts the value of a target variable by learning simple decision rules inferred from the data features. *Multi-layer Perception* is a class of feedforward artificial neural networks that learn non-linear functions through backpropagation of errors. *Random Forest* and *Extreme Gradient Boosting* (also known as XGBoost) are ensemble methods that combine the decisions from multiple decision trees to improve the overall performance.

These algorithms receive as input the semantic similarity values for the different SAs and the proxy similarity values as expected outputs. The output is an aggregated similarity score.

Supervised Similarity Evaluation. The focus of the evaluation is to assess the ability of ML methods to learn combinations of SAs that improve the calculation of similarity. For each combination of an SSM with an ML algorithm, the Pearson's correlation coefficient is computed between the similarity proxies (expected values) and the obtained supervised similarity (predicted values). As baselines, our toolkit also computes the Pearson's correlation coefficient with the whole KG similarity, the single SA similarities and two well-known strategies for combining the single aspect scores (average and maximum).

3   Use Case for the Biomedical Domain

Our toolkit was successfully applied in a set of protein and gene benchmark datasets [2], and two KGs including data from two biomedical ontologies, Gene Ontology and Human Phenotype Ontology. These biomedical datasets rely on three proxies of similarity calculated based on mathematical expressions or other algorithms: protein function family similarity, protein sequence similarity and phenotype-based gene similarity. The results demonstrated our toolkit's ability to significantly produce semantic similarity models that fit different biological perspectives.

4   Conclusion

Our approach is independent of the SSM and the chosen ML method. Until now, we have used SSMs that take into consideration semantic and structural information. The inclusion of embedding methods that also consider lexical information should be incorporated into our toolkit in the future. In addition, although we only applied supervised ML algorithms to tailor semantic similarity to different biomedical similarity proxies, the proposed approach is versatile. As future work, we can evaluate our toolkit in other domain gold standards, such as the Lee50[2] where the similarity between news articles pairs has been been rated multiple times by humans and so it can be considered a similarity proxy.

Acknowledgements. This work was funded by FCT through LASIGE Research Unit (UIDB/00408/2020, UIDP/00408/2020); projects GADgET (DSAIPA/DS/0022/2018) and BINDER (PTDC/CCI-INF/29168/2017); PhD grant SFRH/BD/145377/2019. It was also partially supported by the KATY project funded by European Union's Horizon 2020 research and innovation programme (GA 101017453).

References

1. Bordes, A., Usunier, N., Garcia-Durán, A., Weston, J., Yakhnenko, O.: Translating embeddings for modeling multi-relational data. In: Proceedings of the 26th International Conference on NIPS (2013)
2. Cardoso, C., Sousa, R.T., Köhler, S., Pesquita, C.: A collection of benchmark data sets for knowledge graph-based similarity in the biomedical domain. Database **2020**, baaa078 (2020)
3. Chen, J., Hu, P., Jimenez-Ruiz, E., Holter, O.M., Antonyrajah, D., Horrocks, I.: OWL2Vec*: embedding of owl ontologies. Mach. Learn. **11**, 1–33 (2021)
4. Pesquita, C., Faria, D., Bastos, H., Falcao, A., Couto, F.: Evaluating GO-based semantic similarity measures. In: Proceedings of the 10th Annual Bio-Ontologies (2007)
5. Resnik, P.: Using information content to evaluate semantic similarity in a taxonomy. In: Proceedings of the 14th International Joint Conference on AI (1995)
6. Ristoski, P., Paulheim, H.: RDF2Vec: RDF graph embeddings for data mining. In: Groth, P., et al. (eds.) ISWC 2016. LNCS, vol. 9981, pp. 498–514. Springer, Cham (2016). https://doi.org/10.1007/978-3-319-46523-4_30
7. Seco, N., Veale, T., Hayes, J.: An intrinsic information content metric for semantic similarity in WordNet. In: Proceedings of the 16th European Conference on AI (2004)
8. Sousa, R.T., Silva, S., Pesquita, C.: Evolving knowledge graph similarity for supervised learning in complex biomedical domains. BMC Bioinform. **21**, 1–19 (2020)
9. Yang, B., tau Yih, W., He, X., Gao, J., Deng, L.: Embedding entities and relations for learning and inference in knowledge bases (2015)

---

[2] https://webfiles.uci.edu/mdlee/LeePincombeWelsh.zip.

Tab2Onto: Unsupervised Semantification with Knowledge Graph Embeddings

Hamada M. Zahera[1(✉)], Stefan Heindorf[1], Stefan Balke[3], Jonas Haupt[2], Martin Voigt[2], Carolin Walter[4], Fabian Witter[3], and Axel-Cyrille Ngonga Ngomo[1]

[1] DICE Group, Paderborn University, Paderborn, Germany
{hamada.zahera,heindorf,axel.ngonga}@upb.de
[2] elevait GmbH & Co. KG, Dresden, Germany
{jonas.haupt,martin.voigt}@elevait.de
[3] pmOne AG, Paderborn, Germany
{stefan.balke,fabian.witter}@pmone.com
[4] USU Software AG, Karlsruhe, Germany
carolin.walter@usu.com

Abstract. A large amount of data is generated every day by different systems and applications. In many cases, this data comes in a tabular format that lacks semantic representation and poses new challenges in data modelling. For semantic applications, it then becomes necessary to lift the data to a richer representation, such as a knowledge graph that adheres to a semantic ontology. We propose Tab2Onto, an unsupervised approach for learning ontologies from tabular data using knowledge graph embeddings, clustering, and a human in the loop. We conduct a set of experiments to investigate our approach on a benchmarking dataset from a medical domain and learn the ontology of diseases. Our code and datasets are provided at https://tab2onto.dice-research.org/.

Keywords: Ontology learning · Tabular data · Knowledge graph embeddings · Human-in-the-loop

1 Introduction

Data-driven companies collect large amounts of data from various sources to improve their business analytic and decision-making processes. In most cases, this data comes in a tabular format (e.g., as CSV files). The lack of semantic information in tabular data leads to machines often being unable to assign unique semantics to their content.

Semantification [2] is the process of converting data into a representation with unique semantics, e.g., an RDF knowledge graph, that tackles the aforementioned drawback of tabular data. It also simplifies data integration [5] and explainable machine learning [3]. However, current semantification frameworks rely on numerous hand-crafted scripts, which require expensive maintenance

P. Groth et al. (Eds.): ESWC 2022 Satellite Events, LNCS 13384, pp. 47–51, 2022.
https://doi.org/10.1007/978-3-031-11609-4_9

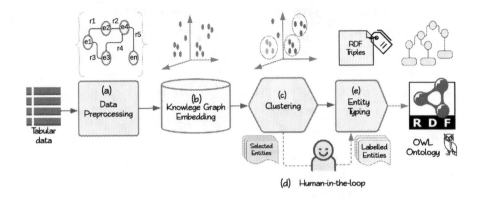

Fig. 1. Tab2Onto pipeline for semantification.

by IT service providers. We propose the Tab2Onto approach, an unsupervised semantification process which exploits knowledge graph (KG) embeddings. Our approach works as follows (see Fig. 1): (i) construct a KG from tabular data, (ii) employ KG embeddings to represent entities and relations, (iii) apply hierarchical, unsupervised clustering, (iv) have a human in the loop to assign labels for the computed clusters, and (v) generate an ontology.

2   Related Work

Recently, many approaches have been proposed to construct ontologies from *textual* data. We refer to the survey paper [8] for more details about ontology learning from text. Few studies on constructing ontologies from *tabular* data (e.g., CSV, spreadsheets) have been carried out in recent research. For example, the authors of [2] propose a *user-driven* approach that requires considerable manual work. The approach in [4] only populates an existing ontology from tabular data. Furthermore, the work presented in [6] demonstrates the significance of transforming tabular data into RDF to capture semantic information. The authors propose an ontology-driven approach for generating RDF from multiple CSV files. However, they assume that each CSV file contains entities from the same domain, which is not the case for most real-world data. To deal with entities from different domains, we use entity clustering to group similar entities together. To the best of our knowledge, this is the first attempt that combines KG embeddings, clustering, and a human in the loop for ontology learning.

3   Approach

Our approach takes a single[1] CSV file as input and generates an OWL ontology as output. Figure 1 shows the pipeline of the Tab2Onto approach, including five

---
[1] In case of multiple CSV files, they are joined into a single file.

Table 1. Clustering for type prediction on FB15k-237. Best results in bold.

Algorithm	TRANSE		DISTMULT		ROTATE		QMULT	
	Acc.	F_1	Acc.	F_1	Acc.	F_1	Acc.	F_1
K-Means	0.784	0.751	0.771	0.741	0.282	0.200	**0.785**	**0.803**
Agglomerative	0.779	0.746	0.781	0.749	0.284	0.201	0.744	0.775
HDBSCAN	0.678	0.624	0.475	0.362	0.276	0.119	0.276	0.119

steps. In the *data preprocessing* step (Fig. 1a), we convert the input data to an RDF graph using the Vectograph library[2] that transforms each cell entry $e_{i,j}$ in row i and column j to a $<subject\text{-}predicate\text{-}object>$ triple, i.e., $(e_i, e_j, e_{i,j})$ where e_i denotes the name of row i and e_j the name of column j. Further, we represent entities and relations in the RDF graph using KG embeddings (Fig. 1b). Each entity and relation is represented as a d-dimensional vector ($\mathbb{R}^d$) in the embedding space, where similar entities are close to each other. In the clustering step (Fig. 1c), we use the K-Means algorithm to identify clusters of entities. Each cluster contains a set of entities with similar properties and common relations. In the next step (Fig. 1d), our goal is to assign labels (i.e., classes or types) to the clustered entities. For this purpose, we employ a *human in the loop* to assign one label to each cluster. We ask said human to specify labels for a few entities from each cluster. For each cluster, we sample some entities close to its centroid and present a set of RDF triples about these entities via a web interface. The user can then manually assign a label to each entity. After that, we *propagate* the majority label to all entities within the same cluster (Fig. 1e). Finally, we construct an OWL ontology based on the labelled clusters using the OWLready2 library.[3] The learned ontology contains a taxonomy of OWL classes and entities (i.e., OWL individuals) with type information.

4 Experiments

We aim to answer the following questions: **(Q1)** *Which KG embeddings yield the best clusters of entities in the embedding space?* **(Q2)** *Which clustering approach yields the best clusters of entities?* **(Q3)** *How well does our pipeline work for the semantification of tabular data?*

Evaluation Setup: For research questions **Q1** and **Q2**, we use the popular KG benchmark *FB15k-237* with types such as `movie`, `person`, etc. The dataset includes a subset of the Freebase Knowledge Graph with $14{,}951$ entities and 237 relations. For **Q3**, we use the *Lymphography*[4] dataset, which contains tabular data about 148 instances of lymphography diagnoses with 18 attributes. As metrics, we use *accuracy* and *macro*-F_1 to evaluate the predicted types of entities

---

[2] https://github.com/dice-group/Vectograph.
[3] https://github.com/pwin/owlready2.
[4] https://archive.ics.uci.edu/ml/datasets/Lymphography.

Table 2. Tab2Onto semantification of *Lymphography* with QMULT embeddings and K-Means clustering.

Approach	Acc.	F_1
Tab2Onto (*unsupervised*)	**0.666**	**0.728**
Random (*unsupervised*)	0.533	0.485
Logistic regression (*supervised*)	0.833	0.818

compared to the ground-truth types in the *FB15k-237* dataset. Furthermore, we use Evolearner [3] from the Ontolearn library to evaluate the generated ontology.

4.1 Embedding-Based Clustering for Type Prediction

To answer **Q1**, we experimented with the KG embeddings TRANSE, DISTMULT, ROTATE, and QMULT [1]. Table 1 shows the evaluation results in terms of *accuracy* (**Acc.**) and *macro-*F_1 (**F_1**) measure. Our results demonstrate that QMULT embeddings achieve superior performance over other embedding models, with an F_1-score of 0.803 compared to 0.751 by TRANSE (K-Means clustering).

To answer **Q2**, we evaluated the performance of different clustering methods: K-Means, agglomerative clustering, and HDBSCAN. Table 1 reports our evaluation results for each method with the KG embedding models used in **Q1**. We observe that K-Means achieves the best performance in clustering entities. In particular, K-Means outperforms agglomerative clustering by absolute +0.028 in terms of F_1-score (for QMULT embeddings). Based on these findings, we employ the best combination of KG embeddings (QMULT) and clustering algorithm (K-Means) in the full pipeline of our approach in the next section.

4.2 Semantification of Tabular Data

To answer **Q3**, we investigated the application of our pipeline in the medical domain. We used the benchmarking dataset *Lymphography*, which provides lymphograms and their attributes as tabular data (e.g., *lymphatics, lymNodesEnlar, defectInNode, extravasates*). Our goal is to infer types of lymphatic diseases (*Normal, Fibrosis, Metastases, Malign-Lymph*) and represent them as OWL classes in the generated ontology. Starting from tabular data, we apply the full pipeline of Tab2Onto as follows: we transform the tabular data of Lymphography into an RDF graph in step (a); then we learn QMULT embeddings in step (b); we cluster entities using the K-Means approach in step (c); we employ a human in the loop to assign labels (*Normal, Fibrosis, Metastases or Malign-Lymph*) to a set of sampled entities from each cluster in step (d). Finally, the output of Tab2Onto is an ontology that contains a taxonomy of OWL classes based on the cluster labels, in step (e).

To evaluate the predicted lymphatic types, we compared our *unsupervised* approach to *random-labelling* with probabilities reflecting the class distribution. Further, we used *supervised* logistic regression as an upper-bound baseline for type prediction. Table 2 shows that Tab2Onto outperforms *random-labelling* with a large margin, up to +0.13 accuracy and +0.24 *macro*-F_1 scores; we are reasonably close to the *supervised* logistic regression approach. In addition, we evaluated the application of the generated ontology in a concept learning task. Using the positive and negative examples of the Lymphography dataset in SML-Bench [7], the state-of-the-art concept learner EvoLearner [3] learns a concept with an F_1-score of 0.82 on the automatically generated ontology compared to 0.84 for a concept learned on SML-Bench's manually created ontology.

5 Conclusion

We present Tab2Onto, an unsupervised semantification approach for learning an ontology from tabular data without requiring any labelled training data. Our approach clusters entities using their KG embeddings to derive their types. By employing embedding-based clustering and a human in the loop, our approach can efficiently convert tabular data into a machine-readable format that can be linked to knowledge graphs. In future work, we will explore density-based clustering with further hyperparameter tuning. We will also conduct more experiments with semi-supervised approaches to learn ontology with few labelled data.

Acknowledgements. This work has been supported by the German Federal Ministry of Education and Research (BMBF) within the project DAIKIRI under grant number 01IS19085B and the German Federal Ministry for Economic Affairs and Climate Action (BMWK) within the project RAKI under grant number 01MD19012B.

References

1. Demir, C., Moussallem, D., Heindorf, S., Ngomo, A.C.N.: Convolutional hypercomplex embeddings for link prediction. In: Asian Conference on Machine Learning, pp. 656–671. PMLR (2021)
2. Ermilov, I., Auer, S., Stadler, C.: User-driven semantic mapping of tabular data. In: I-SEMANTICS, pp. 105–112. ACM (2013)
3. Heindorf, S., et al.: EvoLearner: learning description logics with evolutionary algorithms. In: WWW (2022)
4. Nederstigt, L.J., Aanen, S.S., Vandic, D., Frasincar, F.: FLOPPIES: a framework for large-scale ontology population of product information from tabular data in e-commerce stores. Decis. Support Syst. **59**, 296–311 (2014)
5. Ngonga Ngomo, A.C., et al.: LIMES: a framework for link discovery on the semantic web. KI-Künstliche Intell. **35**(3), 413–423 (2021)
6. Sharma, K., Marjit, U., Biswas, U.: Automatically converting tabular data to RDF: an ontological approach. Int. J. Web Semant. Technol. **6**(3) (2015)
7. Westphal, P., Bühmann, L., Bin, S., Jabeen, H., Lehmann, J.: SML-bench - a benchmarking framework for structured machine learning. Semantic Web **10**(2), 231–245 (2019)
8. Wong, W., Liu, W., Bennamoun, M.: Ontology learning from text: a look back and into the future. ACM Comput. Surv. **44**(4), 20:1–20:36 (2012)

DataSpecer: A Model-Driven Approach to Managing Data Specifications

Štěpán Stenchlák[✉][ID], Martin Nečaský[ID], Petr Škoda[ID], and Jakub Klímek[ID]

Faculty of Mathematics and Physics, Department of Software Engineering,
Charles University, Malostranské nám. 25, 118 00 Prague 1, Czechia
s.stenchlak@gmail.com

Abstract. In this paper, we demonstrate DataSpecer, a tool for effortless management of data specifications based on a domain ontology. Using DataSpecer, the users can generate technical artifacts such as data schemas, e.g., in JSON Schema or XML Schema, and human-readable documentation for a specific dataset based on the provided ontology while maintaining the semantic mapping from the generated artifacts to the ontology. This significantly eases the task of developing data specifications and keeping the corresponding technical artifacts consistent in the process. The tool is based on a previously studied model-driven development (MDD) approach [5] that divides data modeling into layers. This approach was already partially implemented in the tools XCase [2] and eXolutio [3], however, only for XML Schemas and only based on a manually created model, not on an existing domain ontology. Our current tool provides support for the implementation of artifact generators for any target format, including human-readable documentation, and supports domain ontologies as the starting point of the MDD. The tool is already in use in Czechia with the Semantic Government Vocabulary (SGOV) [4] serving as the domain ontology.

Keywords: Data schema · Data modeling · Ontology · Automation

1 Introduction

To support the exchange of structured data among different parties, a common data specification must be agreed upon. To create the specification, the parties must agree on the domain semantics of the data to be exchanged. The result of the agreement is typically recorded in the form of a domain ontology and its documentation. Then, a data schema based on a chosen data format, such as CSV, XML, JSON or RDF, is created. The schema defines a specific data structure to be used to express the exchanged data. It typically comprises several data fields, i.e. CSV columns, XML elements, JSON keys, or RDF class and predicate IRIs. The data specification itself then contains human-readable documentation and a set of technical artifacts such as the data schema, data examples, etc.

This work was partially supported by the Charles University grant SVV 260588.

P. Groth et al. (Eds.): ESWC 2022 Satellite Events, LNCS 13384, pp. 52–56, 2022.
https://doi.org/10.1007/978-3-031-11609-4_10

Developing the technical artifacts can be a complex and error-prone task. This is further complicated as different versions of the artifacts must be maintained. Moreover, in complex data exchange environments, there are data providers and consumers with different needs and technical backgrounds. Agreeing on a single data format may be unnecessarily difficult, and the result is typically not comfortable for everyone. Therefore, it would be useful if multiple formats could be defined while the semantic consistency of their defining technical artifacts would be preserved. However, the more technical artifacts there are to be maintained, the bigger is the challenge to keep all of them consistent.

Consider as an example the exchange of open data about tourist destinations. The data can be published both by a small village trying to attract tourists to visit using only basic information about interesting places and by a large tourist agency managing detailed information about destinations in a whole country. On the other hand, there are also consumers with different needs. Advanced consumers require the RDF representation respecting the domain ontology. Application programmers expect data available in JSON or XML formats depending on their favorite data processing libraries. Data scientists or journalists use tools that usually support only tabular data expressed in CSV or JSON.

In this demonstration, we present DataSpecer, a tool that automates the design and maintenance of such a complex set of semantically related technical artifacts from a given domain ontology. We demonstrate how the tool can be used to define a specification of data formats for exchanging open data about tourist destinations. As the domain ontology, we use an existing ontology defined and used by the Ministry of the Interior of the Czech Republic (MinIntCZ) called Semantic Government Vocabulary (SGOV) [4]. We show how two data structures for publishing open data about tourist destinations can be created from the domain ontology in DataSpecer using a graphical user interface. We also show how data schemas and human-readable documentation defining different data formats for these two data structures can be generated automatically by technical artifact generators. The purpose of this demo is to demonstrate the overall approach to generating technical artifacts. Specific technical artifact generators are our work-in-progress. Currently, DataSpecer supports generators of XML and JSON schemas and their human-readable documentation.

2   DataSpecer

DataSpecer[1] follows the model-driven development (MDD) approach. It considers models at three levels of MDD. The computation independent model (CIM) represents the domain semantics which is defined by a given domain ontology. The platform independent model (PIM) is a computational model which describes technical but platform independent details for expressing domain data. For example, it adds data types and technical labels to concepts from CIM. The platform specific model (PSM) specifies the details of how the data is expressed in various data formats and structures.

---

[1] https://dataspecer.com/.

At the CIM level, DataSpecer reads a given domain ontology on the input and extracts classes and properties. An ontology can be expressed in various ontology specification languages. The typical languages are RDF Schema or OWL. However, there are more options, such as SHACL or the Unified Foundational Ontology (UFO) [1]. There are also proprietary approaches used by Schema.org or Wikidata to express ontologies. DataSpecer is not restricted to a specific ontology language. For a given language, it needs a specific adapter. We currently support only ontologies based on UFO-A, a subset of UFO incorporating only endurants - objects and their ontology, applied by MinIntCZ in SGOV [4] to design various government ontologies.

PIM is represented as a subset of CIM. It describes the semantics of a given data specification comprising one or more data structures. PSM is then represented by individual data structures designed in DataSpecer. To design a data specification comprising a set of data structures, a designer follows this typical workflow, which is also demonstrated in a video[2]:

1. Data Specification. First, the designer initializes the data specification, which is a set of data structures to express the same data using different structures. In our demonstration, we aim at a sample data specification for publishing open data about tourist destinations.

Fig. 1. A data structure for Tourist destinations represented in DataSpecer and its JSON schema. Attributes are blue; edges are red. (Color figure online)

2. Data Structures. The designer then creates one or more data structures in the data specification. A data structure is a rooted oriented tree that is agnostic to a specific serialization in a chosen syntax (see Fig. 1). Its nodes represent classes from the domain ontology (CIM). Its edges represent properties from the ontology connecting the classes. The nodes specify individual data fields for representing data semantically described by the ontology. The edges represent how the data fields are nested in the data structure.

In our demonstration, the designer creates two data structures. The first one aims at publishing generic information about tourist destinations, such as their

---

[2] https://youtu.be/lZoM794_uFk.

titles and contact points. The other defines how information about the accessibility of tourist destinations shall be published. For a new empty data structure, the designer selects its root by selecting a class from the CIM, i.e., the class *Tourist destination*. For a non-empty data structure, the designer can choose an existing node mapped to an ontology class and define its content by choosing one or more properties related to the class from the ontology. The designer can also refine the resulting data structure by adding technical details such as technical labels to be used in the schemas, data types, etc. In the demonstration, we show how the designer selects *Tourist destination* as a root for both data structures and how different content for them can be derived from the CIM.

DataSpecer represents the data structure created by the designer as a PSM mapped to the PIM of the data specification. The tool maintains the PIM as a subset of the CIM automatically as the designer creates new nodes and edges in the PSM. We demonstrate these mappings from the data structures to the CIM by showing how chosen nodes and edges are mapped to the domain ontology.

3. Data Schemas and Their Previews. For each data structure, the designer can choose a data format in which the data structure shall be represented. DataSpecer currently supports XML and JSON. The data structure, together with the chosen generic format, defines a specific data format. In the demonstration, we will show how the designer can choose the data formats and how the corresponding data schemas can be generated not only when a data structure is finished but also during its creation as a live preview.

4. Technical Artifacts Generation. Finally, the designer requests DataSpecer to generate technical artifacts for the specified data formats. DataSpecer executes the selected technical artifacts generators and bundles the result as a single archive which can be downloaded by the designer. Currently, DataSpecer contains generators for XML Schema, JSON Schema[3], and a human-readable documentation in Bikeshed[4]. In the demonstration, we will show how the designer can download the technical artifacts for both resulting specific data formats.

3   Current Usage and Future Work

DataSpecer has been applied by the MinIntCZ to design recommended JSON data structures for publishing open data. This included data specifications for tourist destinations, bulletin boards of local governments, etc. Another application in the context of MinIntCZ was to design XML data structures for sharing data among government information systems. We demonstrated the usage of DataSpecer on a set of information systems in the field of road traffic and personal transport. While the first application produces only JSON structures and the second only XML structures, both rely on SGOV as the common ontology.

---

[3] https://json-schema.org/.

[4] https://tabatkins.github.io/bikeshed/.

DataSpecer is still under development. We are working on adding support for domain ontologies expressed in RDF Schema and OWL as well as for proprietary ontologies such as Schema.org and Wikidata as CIM. We are also working on adding support for the CSV format and support for more detailed configuration for data schema generators regarding preferred constructs in the individual schema languages. Our vision is that data specification authors use existing public ontologies, possibly combined with their own ontologies, to design their data specifications in a systematic, MDD based way.

We are also working on the interoperability of the generated data specifications. In the same way, we generate data schemas, we are working on deriving transformations among the individual data structures. For each data structure, there will be a lifting transformation transforming the data expressed using this structure to the RDF representation corresponding to the domain ontology. Moreover, there will be a lowering transformation transforming the data from the RDF representation back to the defined structure. Therefore, data represented using one data structure can be transformed to a representation using another data structure via the RDF representation using the generated transformations.

Another crucial objective is supporting modifications and change propagation, both on the ontology and schema levels. Changes introduced in the ontology will be used to derive new schemas automatically, thus creating data transformations between the old and new schemas.

Last but not least, DataSpecer currently supports only manual data structure design, where the designer needs to go through the individual properties of a chosen class from the domain ontology and manually select which will be represented in the data structure. We plan to extend DataSpecer with support for a semi-automated process of data structure definition.

References

1. Guizzardi, G., Benevides, A.B., Fonseca, C.M., Porello, D., Almeida, J.P.A., Sales, T.P.: UFO: unified foundational ontology. Appl. Ontol. **Pre-press**(Pre-press), 1–44 (2021). https://content.iospress.com/articles/applied-ontology/ao210256
2. Klímek, J., Kopenec, L., Loupal, P., Malý, J.: XCase - a tool for conceptual XML data modeling. In: Grundspenkis, J., Kirikova, M., Manolopoulos, Y., Novickis, L. (eds.) ADBIS 2009. LNCS, vol. 5968, pp. 96–103. Springer, Heidelberg (2010). https://doi.org/10.1007/978-3-642-12082-4_13
3. Klímek, J., Malý, J., Nečaský, M., Holubová, I.: eXolutio: methodology for design and evolution of XML schemas using conceptual modeling. Informatica **26**(3), 453–472 (2015). https://content.iospress.com/articles/informatica/inf1065
4. Křemen, P., Nečaský, M.: Improving discoverability of open government data with rich metadata descriptions using semantic government vocabulary. J. Web Semant. **55**, 1–20 (2019). https://doi.org/10.1016/j.websem.2018.12.009
5. Nečaský, M., Mlýnková, I., Klímek, J., Malý, J.: When conceptual model meets grammar: a dual approach to XML data modeling. Data Knowl. Eng. **72**, 1–30 (2012). https://doi.org/10.1016/j.datak.2011.09.002

Towards Query Processing over Heterogeneous Federations of RDF Data Sources

Sijin Cheng[✉] and Olaf Hartig

Linköping University, Linköping, Sweden
{sijin.cheng,olaf.hartig}@liu.se

Abstract. A federation of RDF data sources offers enormous potential when answers or insights of queries are unavailable via a single data source. As various interfaces for accessing RDF data are proposed, one challenge for querying such a federation is that the federation members are heterogeneous in terms of the type of data access interfaces. There does not exist any research on systematic approaches to tackle this challenge. To provide a formal foundation for future approaches that aim to address this challenge, we have introduced a language, called *FedQPL*, that can be used for representing query execution plans in this setting. With a poster in the conference we generally want to outline the vision for the next generation of query engines for such federations and, in this context, we want to raise awareness in the Semantic Web community for our language. In this extended abstract, we first discuss challenges in query processing over such heterogeneous federations; thereafter, we briefly introduce our proposed language, which we have extended with a few new features that we did not have in the version published originally.

Keywords: Heterogeneous federations · Query plan language

1 Motivation and Challenges

Efficiently processing queries over federation members that provide the same type of interface (i.e., SPARQL endpoint) has been explored extensively [2]. However, as different types of interfaces are proposed to publish RDF data sources, such as Triple Pattern Fragment (TPF) interface [16], Bindings-Restricted TPF (brTPF) interface [8], Star Pattern Fragments (SPF) [3], SaGe interface [11], smart-KG interface [5], and WiseKG [4], providers of RDF data sources may choose to publish their RDF data via a different type of interface depending on the properties of these interfaces [9, 12]. As a result, federations of RDF data sources may become heterogeneous in terms of access interfaces. Due to this heterogeneity, query processing over such federations faces extra challenges, involving the key sub-tasks of federated query processing, such as source selection, query decomposition, planning and optimization, and query execution.

Example 1. *As a motivating example, consider a federation F_{ex} with two members: Federation member fm_1 provides a SPARQL endpoint interface for the RDF*

P. Groth et al. (Eds.): ESWC 2022 Satellite Events, LNCS 13384, pp. 57–62, 2022.
https://doi.org/10.1007/978-3-031-11609-4_11

graph $G_1 = \{(a, foaf{:}knows, c), (c, foaf{:}knows, d)\}$, whereas fm_2 provides a TPF interface for the RDF graph $G_2 = \{(c, foaf{:}name, "Alice"), (c, foaf{:}age, 21)\}$.

Example 2. *Consider a basic graph pattern (BGP) $B_{ex} = \{tp_1, tp_2, tp_3\}$ with the three triple patterns $tp_1 = (?x, foaf{:}knows, ?y)$, $tp_2 = (?y, foaf{:}name, ?z)$ and $tp_3 = (?y, foaf{:}age, ?g)$. When evaluating B_{ex} over the example federation F_{ex}, we expect to obtain one solution mapping: $\mu_1 = \{?x \rightarrow a, ?y \rightarrow c, ?z \rightarrow$ "Alice", $?g \rightarrow 21\}$.*

In order to devise an efficient solution for answering the BGP B_{ex}, the properties and constraints of each member's interface must be considered. In terms of source selection, existing engines [1, 6, 13, 14] generally rely on a set of SPARQL ASK queries or on metadata about federation members to determine which federation member(s) can evaluate each triple pattern. Due to the fact that the TPF interface, however, cannot answer such SPARQL ASK queries, it is necessary to consider the type of interface during source selection in heterogeneous federations. In addition, we are unable to apply an existing query decomposition approach easily since not all forms of subqueries can be answered directly by every interface. For instance, FedX [14] would group the triple patterns tp_2 and tp_3 into a subquery as they can be evaluated exclusively at federation member fm_2. While such an exclusive group is beneficial for, e.g., a SPARQL endpoint, the TPF interface provided by fm_2 cannot answer such a group pattern directly. Furthermore, some works leverage information and metadata about the federation member for query planning and optimization, such as estimating join cardinality or pruning data sources that do not contribute to the final results. This process should consider the properties of each interface as different interfaces provide different types of metadata and support exploring of different information.

When it comes to physical plans, different interfaces may require the engine to leverage specific physical operators. For instance, possible algorithms for the implementation of a *join* operator are a standard (local) nested-loops join, or RDF-specific variations of the semijoin and the bind join [2]. The latter algorithms rely on a data access interface in which the given input solution mappings can be captured as part of the requests. If the interface is more expressive (e.g., a SPARQL endpoint), concrete examples of such algorithms can be found in the SPARQL endpoint federation engines [6, 14]. However, for less expressive interfaces (such as the TPF interface), the algorithm can be implemented using a variation of an index nested-loops join in which a separate request is created for each input solution mapping [16].

Therefore, for the next generation of federation engines, it is not sufficient to merely combine and integrate existing solutions as the features and constraints of each interface must be thoroughly considered in the context of heterogeneous federations. Some work has been done on dealing with query processing for heterogeneous interfaces. Comunica [15] is a modular engine that can be used to run queries on heterogeneous data sources, however it simply handles query execution at the triple pattern level, without considering features and optimization options for heterogeneous federations. We believe that any principled approach to querying heterogeneous federations of such RDF data sources must be based on a solid formal foundation. In recent work, Heling and Acosta [10] introduce interface-aware approaches for query decomposition and query planning. Similar to our work, they also formalize the concept of federations. We argue that the formal foundation should provide not only a formal data model capturing the federation concepts, including the corresponding query semantics, but also formal concepts that precisely define the artifacts produced by the various steps of query processing, including source selection, query decomposition, planning and optimization, and query execution.

2 FedQPL: A Language for Query Plans over Federations

We have defined *FedQPL* [7], a language for formally specifying logical query plans. This language can be applied to more precisely define query planning and optimization approaches, as well as to represent the logical plans in a query engine. The key innovations of this language over the standard SPARQL algebra are that it contains operators to make explicit which federation member is accessed in each part of a query plan and to distinguish different ways of accessing a federation member. FedQPL features operators that explicitly capture the intention to execute a certain subquery at a specific federation member, as well as explicitly distinguish whether such access is meant to be based solely on the given subquery or also on intermediate results obtained for other subqueries. While approaches that focus on homogeneous federations can also benefit from these features, we argue that such features are essential for any principled approach to query planning in heterogeneous federations where the properties and the limitations of different data access interfaces must be considered.

To give an intuition of what FedQPL provides, we briefly go through the syntax of FedQPL expressions in this poster paper. Note that we have extended FedQPL with four additional operators that we did not have in the original paper. With this extension, FedQPL can now capture plans for the complete version 1.0 fragment of SPARQL. In our original paper, we also provide an extensive set of equivalences for FedQPL expressions that can be used as query rewriting rules for query optimization.

Definition 1. *A **FedQPL expression** φ can be constructed from the following grammar, in which req, tpAdd, bgpAdd, join, union, mj, mu, (,), filter, leftJoin, tpOptAdd, and bgpOptAdd are terminal symbols.[1] ρ is an expression in the request language L_{req} of some interface [7], fm is a federation member, tp is a triple pattern, B is a BGP, F is a SPARQL filter expression, and Φ is a nonempty set of FedQPL expressions.*

$$\varphi ::= req_{fm}^{\rho} \mid tpAdd_{fm}^{tp}(\varphi) \mid tpOptAdd_{fm}^{tp}(\varphi) \mid bgpAdd_{fm}^{B}(\varphi) \mid bgpOptAdd_{fm}^{B}(\varphi) \mid$$
$$join(\varphi,\varphi) \mid leftjoin(\varphi,\varphi) \mid union(\varphi,\varphi) \mid mj\,\Phi \mid mu\,\Phi \mid filter^{F}(\varphi)$$

---

[1] The operators captured by the last four symbols are the ones that we have added.

While these operators are generally independent of the type of interface provided by the corresponding federation member fm, some operators can be used only for federation members with an interface that has specific properties.

The first operator, req, captures the intention to retrieve the result of a certain (sub)query ρ from a given federation member. For instance, the aim to retrieve solution mappings for tp_1 (of B_{ex} in Example 2) from the member fm_1 (of F_{ex} in Example 1) can be represented as $req_{fm_1}^{tp_1}$. The forms of the (sub)queries ρ that can be used for this operator depend on the interface provided by the federation member, which our formalization abstracts by the notion of request languages [7]. For instance, with req we can represent a request with a whole BGP, but only for interfaces that support BGP requests.

The unary operator $tpAdd$ captures the intention to access a federation member to obtain solution mappings for a single triple pattern that must be compatible with solution mappings obtained from the plan represented by the given subexpression. For instance, in our running example we observe that only one of the solution mappings for tp_1 from fm_1 can be joined with solution mappings for tp_2 from fm_2. To produce the join between the two sets of solution mappings we may use the output of $req_{fm_1}^{tp_1}$ as input to retrieve only the compatible solution mappings for tp_2 from fm_2, which can be represented as the following FedQPL expression: $tpAdd_{fm_2}^{tp_2}\left(req_{fm_1}^{tp_1}\right)$. The operator $bgpAdd$ is a BGP-based variation of $tpAdd$. In contrast to these operators, $join$ is a binary operator that joins two inputs, capturing the intention to get the input sets of solution mappings independently, and then join them in the query federation engine.

The operator $leftjoin$ is binary operator that captures the intention to extend information using an optional part. If the optional part (right input) has no matching solution mappings, no bindings are created but it does not eliminate the solutions. Consider query pattern P_{opt} as a variation of the example BGP B_{ex} where $\{tp_2, tp_3\}$ are optional. Federation member fm_1 contributes two solution mappings for tp_1. Although $?y \rightarrow d$ is not compatible with solution mappings in the optional part, querying the federation F_{ex} (cf. Example 1) results in two solution mappings for P_{opt} as the non-optional information is returned anyway. Similar to the difference between $join$ and $tpAdd$ (respectively $bgpAdd$), $tpOptAdd$ and $bgpOptAdd$ are unary variations of $leftjoin$ that access a federation member to obtain bindings for a given triple pattern, respectively a BGP, to optionally extend the solution mappings of a given intermediate query result.

The operator $filter$ captures the intention to impose a constraint on the solution mappings obtained from the plan represented by the given subexpression. Continuing with the example BGP B_{ex}, if adding a filter condition ($?g < 20$) on the solutions, the query engine will return no solution mapping.

As for the remaining operators, $union$ lifts the standard SPARQL algebra operator union into the FedQPL language, whereas mj and mu are multiway variations of $join$ and $union$ to capture the intention to apply a multiway algorithm that can combine an arbitrary number of inputs.

3   Future Work

So far we have focused on providing the formal foundations of query processing approaches over heterogeneous federations. We believe that establishing these foundations is a necessary prerequisite for a systematic study of the next generation of federation engines. Consequently, we first plan to investigate what adaptations are needed in source selection approaches and query decomposition in the scenario of heterogeneous interfaces. Secondly, we plan to design effective and efficient query planning and optimization approaches for queries over heterogeneous federations. We will implement these approaches in a new federation engine for federated query processing over heterogeneous interfaces.

References

1. Abdelaziz, I., Mansour, E., Ouzzani, M., Aboulnaga, A., Kalnis, P.: Lusail: a system for querying linked data at scale. Proc. VLDB Endow. **11**, 485–498 (2017)
2. Acosta, M., Hartig, O., Sequeda, J.F.: Federated RDF query processing. In: Encyclopedia of Big Data Technologies (2019)
3. Aebeloe, C., Keles, I., Montoya, G., Hose, K.: Star pattern fragments: accessing knowledge graphs through star patterns. arXiv preprint arXiv:2002.09172 (2020)
4. Azzam, A., Aebeloe, C., Montoya, G., Keles, I., Polleres, A., Hose, K.: WiseKG: balanced access to web knowledge graphs. In: Proceedings of the Web Conference (2021)
5. Azzam, A., Fernández, J.D., Acosta, M., Beno, M., Polleres, A.: SMART-KG: hybrid shipping for SPARQL querying on the web. In: Proceedings of the Web Conference (WWW) (2020)
6. Charalambidis, A., Troumpoukis, A., Konstantopoulos, S.: SemaGrow: optimizing federated SPARQL queries. In: Proceedings of the 11th International Conference on Semantic Systems (SEMANTICS) (2015)
7. Cheng, S., Hartig, O.: FedQPL: a language for logical query plans over heterogeneous federations of RDF data sources. In: Proceedings of the 22nd International Conference on Information Integration and Web-based Applications & Services (2020)
8. Hartig, O., Buil-Aranda, C.: Bindings-restricted triple pattern fragments. In: Debruyne, C., et al. (eds.) OTM 2016. LNCS, vol. 10033, pp. 762–779. Springer, Cham (2016). https://doi.org/10.1007/978-3-319-48472-3_48
9. Hartig, O., Letter, I., Pérez, J.: A formal framework for comparing linked data fragments. In: d'Amato, C., et al. (eds.) ISWC 2017. LNCS, vol. 10587, pp. 364–382. Springer, Cham (2017). https://doi.org/10.1007/978-3-319-68288-4_22
10. Heling, L., Acosta, M.: Federated SPARQL query processing over heterogeneous linked data fragments. In: Proceedings of the Web Conference (WWW) (2022)
11. Minier, T., Skaf-Molli, H., Molli, P.: SaGe: web preemption for public SPARQL query services. In: Proceedings of the Web Conference (WWW) (2019)
12. Montoya, G., Aebeloe, C., Hose, K.: Towards efficient query processing over heterogeneous RDF interfaces. In: 2nd Workshop on Decentralizing the Semantic Web (DeSemWeb) (2018)
13. Saleem, M., Ngonga Ngomo, A.-C.: HiBISCuS: hypergraph-based source selection for SPARQL endpoint federation. In: Presutti, V., d'Amato, C., Gandon, F., d'Aquin, M., Staab, S., Tordai, A. (eds.) ESWC 2014. LNCS, vol. 8465, pp. 176–191. Springer, Cham (2014). https://doi.org/10.1007/978-3-319-07443-6_13

14. Schwarte, A., Haase, P., Hose, K., Schenkel, R., Schmidt, M.: FedX: optimization techniques for federated query processing on linked data. In: Aroyo, L., et al. (eds.) ISWC 2011. LNCS, vol. 7031, pp. 601–616. Springer, Heidelberg (2011). https://doi.org/10.1007/978-3-642-25073-6_38
15. Taelman, R., Van Herwegen, J., Vander Sande, M., Verborgh, R.: Comunica: a modular SPARQL query engine for the web. In: Vrandečić, D., et al. (eds.) ISWC 2018. LNCS, vol. 11137, pp. 239–255. Springer, Cham (2018). https://doi.org/10.1007/978-3-030-00668-6_15
16. Verborgh, R., et al.: Triple pattern fragments: a low-cost knowledge graph interface for the web. J. Web Semant. **37**, 184–206 (2016)

SAND: A Tool for Creating Semantic Descriptions of Tabular Sources

Binh Vu[✉] and Craig A. Knoblock

USC Information Sciences Institute, Marina del Rey, CA 90292, USA
{binhvu,knoblock}@isi.edu

Abstract. Building semantic descriptions of tables is a vital step in data integration. However, this task is expensive and time-consuming as users often need to examine the table data, its metadata, and ontologies to find the most appropriate description. In this paper, we present SAND, a tool for creating semantic descriptions semi-automatically. SAND makes it easy to integrate with semantic modeling systems to predict or suggest semantic descriptions to the users, as well as to use different knowledge graphs (KGs). Besides its modeling capabilities, SAND is equipped with browsing/querying tools to enable users to explore data in the table and discover how it is often modeled in KGs.

Keywords: Semantic descriptions · Semantic models · Knowledge graph · Semantic web · Linked data · Ontology

1 Introduction

There is a large number of tables available on the Web and Open Data Portals. However, these tables come with various formats and vocabularies describing their content, thus making it difficult to use them. To address this problem, a semantic description of a table is created that encodes column types, relationships between columns, and additional context values needed to interpret the table. Given the semantic description, the table can be automatically converted to linked data or RDF triples providing the ability to quickly combine multiple tables for downstream tasks/applications to consume data using the same representation. Nevertheless, creating semantic descriptions is time-consuming. They are difficult to write manually, and during the creation process, the developers often need to switch back and forth between the ontology and the data to find the appropriate terms. Therefore, a user interface (UI) to assist and guide the developers in creating the descriptions is needed.

There are several UIs developed for creating semantic descriptions. Notable examples include Karma [2] and MantisTable [1]. Karma is a data integration tool that can ingest data from various types of sources (e.g., spreadsheets, databases, etc.), map them to an ontology that users choose, and export the normalized data to RDF or store it in a database. MantisTable can import tables

© The Author(s), under exclusive license to Springer Nature Switzerland AG 2022
P. Groth et al. (Eds.): ESWC 2022 Satellite Events, LNCS 13384, pp. 63–67, 2022.
https://doi.org/10.1007/978-3-031-11609-4_12

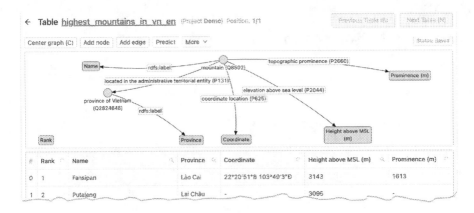

Fig. 1. The semantic description of the table about mountains shown as a graph on top of the table. Green nodes are ontology classes, yellow nodes are columns. Edges depicts the types (e.g., `rdfs:label`) and relationships of columns (e.g., `located in administrative teritorial entity (P131)`). (Color figure online)

from files and create semantic descriptions to map them to KGs such as Wikidata. In both cases, these systems are strongly integrated with their semantic modeling algorithms for suggesting candidate descriptions and hence difficult to extend with state-of-the-art algorithms. In addition, when mapping tables to KGs, we often need to explore the data through filtering and browsing entities to find rows that do not match the semantic descriptions, yet such features are lacking in the aforementioned systems.

In this paper, we introduce SAND a novel system that addresses the above limitations. The contributions of SAND are: (1) a UI for creating semantic descriptions with a full pipeline from raw table data to RDF/JSON-LD output; (2) browsing/querying features for exploring the data and how it is modeled in KGs; and (3) an open design enabling easy integration with semantic modeling algorithms for semi-automatically creating semantic descriptions while supporting different knowledge graphs (e.g., Wikidata, DBPedia). SAND is available as an open source tool under the MIT License[1].

2   Creating Semantic Descriptions in SAND

In this section, we will show how a user can build the semantic description of a table of mountains using the Wikidata ontology and then export the data as RDF. First, we discuss the overall process as if the user performs all steps manually. Then, we demonstrate how the user can do it semi-automatically.[2]

Manual Process. The process begins by uploading tables to SAND. SAND supports reading tables from various formats such as `.json`, `.csv`, `.xlsx`, and

---

[1] https://github.com/usc-isi-i2/sand.
[2] Demo: https://github.com/usc-isi-i2/sand/wiki/Demo.

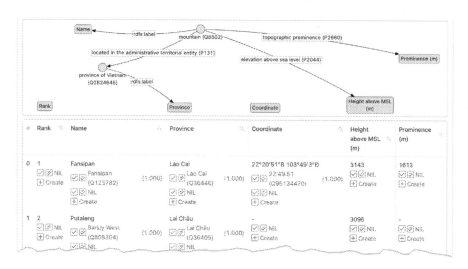

Fig. 2. The auto-generated semantic description and linked entities of the table. If a cell is linked to an entity, it is shown as a hyperlink and its candidate entities are displayed below it. The user can update the linked entity of a cell by clicking on a single-check or a double-check button. Differing from the single-check button, the double-check button will apply the operation to all cells (same column) that have the same value as the current cell.

allows the user to refine the parsing options for different formats. The next step is to create the semantic description of the uploaded table. In particular, the user assigns semantic types to columns containing entities (called entity columns) and relationships (ontology predicates) between the entity columns and the remaining columns. Figure 1 shows the final outcome of this step. For example, the 2nd column *Name* is assigned to type `mountain (Q8502)` (via the link `mountain... → rdfs:label`) and the 3rd column *Province* is assigned to type `province of Vietnam (Q2824648)`. The description also tells us that these mountains are located in the provinces by the relationship `located in ... (P131)` between the two nodes: `mountain...` and `province....` The third step is to link cells with existing entities in KGs (e.g., Wikidata). This step is optional, but we recommend doing it in SAND as during exporting, any cell in the entity columns that does not link to any entity is treated as a new entity. In this table, many entities are already in Wikidata so by doing entity linking, we can avoid creating duplicated data. Finally, once the user is satisfied with the semantic description, they can export and download the RDF of the table. Note that in the RDF data, raw values of the coordinates and heights are converted to the correct types thanks to the value constraints provided by the semantic description. Exporting the data via the UI may not be ideal if the user has a huge table or many tables of the same schema. Therefore, SAND also allows exporting an internal D-REPR specification of the table, which is used to transform the table to RDF by the D-REPR engine [5] programmatically.

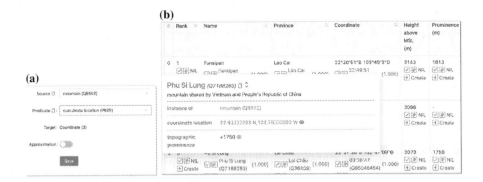

Fig. 3. (a) Add/Update relationship dialog box (b) Entity browsing

Semi-automatic Process. As the whole process is quite lengthy, hence at the beginning, the user can tell SAND to generate the semantic description and link entities for them by clicking the predict button. Under the hood, SAND will invoke semantic modeling and entity linking algorithms that are integrated to SAND via its plugin systems. Currently, SAND provides plugins for MTab [3] and GRAMS [4]. Figure 2 shows the result after prediction. Notice that it cannot predict the correct relationship of the 3rd column and some of the linked entities are incorrect. The user can fix the missing relationship by clicking on the yellow node representing the 3rd column, and selecting the source node and the relationship as shown in Fig. 3a. Another way to add the missing relationship is to click on the add edge button. To fix the incorrectly linked entities, the user can deselect them or right-click on the column and choose a filter to deselect cells containing entities that do not belong to the current semantic type (mountain) all at once.

Exploring the Data. Assuming that the last column in the table is ambiguous and the user is unsure if the predicted relationship topographic prominence (P2660) is correct, they can choose to filter rows that have entities having the property P2660 and use SAND's entity browsing capability to check if any values of the properties are different from the values in the table (Fig. 3b).

3   System Design and Configurations

To integrate with KGs, we define common schemas for entities, ontology classes, and ontology predicates. Then, we create their data access objects (DAOs), each of which has two functions: (1) querying an object by its ID or URI; and (2) searching the objects by their label. The DAOs also convert objects from their original schema in the KG to the common schema in SAND. This approach makes it easy to set up SAND since DAOs can be implemented using KG's public APIs. In other words, we do not require to build a local database containing KG's entities and ontology.

To integrate with a semantic modeling algorithm, we declare an abstract class that predicts the semantic description of a given table and links table cells to entities in KGs.

The DAOs and semantic modeling algorithms are specified in SAND's configuration file by their paths (e.g., `plugins.wikidata.get_entity_dao`) and imported dynamically when the server starts.

4   Discussions and Future Work

With SAND, users can quickly model and convert their tables to RDF or JSON-LD for integrating with their dataset or knowledge graph. SAND reduces the amount of work that the users need to do via its semi-automatic semantic modeling, entity linking, and data cleaning features. For the researchers or developers, customizing SAND's components is straightforward via its plugin system. They can implement and test their semantic modeling algorithm on SAND or adapt SAND to their use cases without having to develop a new UI from scratch.

For future work, we plan to add more data source types such as databases and APIs. We also plan to support writing custom data cleaning scripts and incorporating data cleaning algorithms into the system.

References

1. Cremaschi, M., Rula, A., Siano, A., De Paoli, F.: MantisTable: a tool for creating semantic annotations on tabular data. In: Hitzler, P., et al. (eds.) ESWC 2019. LNCS, vol. 11762, pp. 18–23. Springer, Cham (2019). https://doi.org/10.1007/978-3-030-32327-1_4
2. Gupta, S., Szekely, P., Knoblock, C.A., Goel, A., Taheriyan, M., Muslea, M.: Karma: a system for mapping structured sources into the semantic web. In: Simperl, E., et al. (eds.) ESWC 2012. LNCS, vol. 7540, pp. 430–434. Springer, Heidelberg (2015). https://doi.org/10.1007/978-3-662-46641-4_40
3. Nguyen, P., Yamada, I., Kertkeidkachorn, N., Ichise, R., Takeda, H.: Demonstration of MTab: tabular data annotation with knowledge graphs (2021)
4. Vu, B., Knoblock, C.A., Szekely, P., Pham, M., Pujara, J.: A graph-based approach for inferring semantic descriptions of Wikipedia tables. In: Hotho, A., et al. (eds.) ISWC 2021. LNCS, vol. 12922, pp. 304–320. Springer, Cham (2021). https://doi.org/10.1007/978-3-030-88361-4_18
5. Vu, B., Pujara, J., Knoblock, C.A.: D-REPR: a language for describing and mapping diversely-structured data sources to RDF. In: Proceedings of the 10th International Conference on Knowledge Capture, pp. 189–196 (2019)

BLAST: Block Applications for Things

Michael Freund[1]([☒])[ID], Thomas Wehr[1][ID], and Andreas Harth[1,2][ID]

[1] Fraunhofer Institute for Integrated Circuits IIS, Nürnberg, Germany
{michael.freund,thomas.wehr,andreas.harth}@iis.fraunhofer.de
[2] Friedrich-Alexander-Universität Erlangen-Nürnberg, Nürnberg, Germany

Abstract. We introduce a block-based visual programming language called BLAST for programs involving connected devices with a Web of Things abstraction. We developed an editor and an execution environment for BLAST programs that runs in a web browser. We demonstrate that BLAST can be used to create programs that interact with a variety of devices. In particular we show the use of connected devices in a geofencing scenario.

Keywords: Block-based programming · Web of Things · Graphical programming

1 Introduction

Connected devices form the basis for a wide variety of applications in industry settings, such as condition monitoring, energy consumption analysis, simulation and optimisation [3]. The Web of Things (WoT)[1] aims at providing a set of standardised technologies to help simplify creating applications involving connected devices. At the same time, casual users should be able to quickly program applications involving connected devices. The programming languages currently in use for accessing devices are primarily text-based and are difficult to access for casual users. One possible approach to improve accessibility and ease the creation of computer programs is the visual programming paradigm.

Visual programming does not require the user to enter any text; instead, programs are based on graphical elements like blocks, graphs, tables or diagrams. Programs are created by arranging predefined blocks with images or text via a drag-and-drop interface. Blocks can be geometrically aligned with other compatible blocks, like in a jigsaw puzzle, to form complex programs. Since blocks can only be arranged in the correct way, no syntax errors can occur [5,6,10].

The block-based approach can be used not only for learning programming concepts, but also for more complex problems. Block languages have been successfully used in constructing SPARQL queries [2] or programming industrial robots [9,11], both areas which normally require advanced programming skills.

---

[1] https://www.w3.org/WoT/.

© The Author(s), under exclusive license to Springer Nature Switzerland AG 2022
P. Groth et al. (Eds.): ESWC 2022 Satellite Events, LNCS 13384, pp. 68–72, 2022.
https://doi.org/10.1007/978-3-031-11609-4_13

We present BLAST, a visual programming environment that works with devices following the Web of Things interface. BLAST programs can be created in a web browser, based on Google's Blockly[2], a JavaScript library for creating block-based languages and editors. BLAST programs can be translated into JavaScript and executed in the web browser. BLAST implements the Web of Things abstraction to devices with Bluetooth Low Energy (BLE) and USB Human Interface Devices (HID) interface via APIs of modern web browsers.

The currently best known tool for programming IoT devices using visual programming is Node-RED[3]. Node-RED's programming paradigm is based on dataflows; in contrast, BLAST focuses on control flow constructs. The use cases in industrial settings we envision for BLAST involve mostly control flow, and in such scenarios a dataflow abstraction can lead to programs that are difficult to understand and maintain.

Another system similar to BLAST is Punya [8], an Android app development system based on the MIT App Inventor[4]. Like BLAST, Punya offers a block-based programming environment for writing programs that can include SPARQL queries and access online services. Punya focuses on creating applications for Android devices that can access the mobile phone's internal hardware. Punya also acts as a client to publish and access data on servers supporting the Constrained Application Protocol (CoAP). BLAST programs, on the other hand, run in modern web browsers and support devices based on a WoT abstraction.

In the following we first introduce the BLAST language using a geofencing scenario, next describe the browser-based editor and execution environment for BLAST programs, followed by a short usability evaluation, and then conclude.

2   BLAST Language

When choosing the vocabulary for our block-based language BLAST, we decided on a mixture of natural language and computer language [7]. In BLAST, the blocks are arranged into readable sentences, as in a natural language, but the blocks also contain a few technical programming terms, such as "repeat while true" instead of "forever".

The BLAST language includes standard elements from other programming languages such as loops, functions, and variables. In addition, the BLAST language provides blocks related to interacting with WoT devices. These WoT-related blocks can be grouped under the three interaction affordances Properties (that can be read and written), Actions (that can be invoked), and Events (that can be observed). Further, the BLAST language includes blocks to send HTTP requests with arbitrary headers, request method and request body. The BLAST language also includes blocks to load RDF graphs from a URI and execute SPARQL queries, which allows for the interaction with Read-Write Linked Data APIs or other REST APIs. Finally, if the available blocks are not sufficient

---

[2] https://developers.google.com/blockly/.

[3] https://nodered.org/.

[4] https://appinventor.mit.edu/.

to implement a desired functionality, there is a block in which native JavaScript code can be entered, and thus almost everything that is possible in JavaScript is also possible in BLAST.

Fig. 1. Example BLAST program that implements a geofencing scenario: when the beacon gets close, the light is turned off; when the beacon leaves the close range, a sound is played and the light is turned red. (Color figure online)

For an example of a BLAST program see Fig. 1. The program involves a LED light with a BLE interface and a small battery-powered BLE beacon. The BLE controller (the "BLE central") is implicitly used when reading the signal-strength property. The functionality of these devices ("Things") can be accessed via reading and writing properties. The LED light, for example, has a property "colour" that can be written. To enable an event abstraction, the program includes a block that defines a state with a condition on the signal strength of the BLE beacon. On entering or exiting the defined state, the event blocks, which itself can contain arbitrary blocks, are triggered.

3   BLAST Editor and Execution Environment

We have implemented an editor and an execution environment for BLAST programs that run in modern web browsers.

The editor uses the Blockly library and provides custom control and command blocks that make up the BLAST language. The custom blocks and the BLAST environment follow almost all of the design principles introduced by Fraser [4], such as a clear border style or the avoidance of transitive connections. Not implemented, however, are the varying color choices for different loop types.

Based on the user's arrangement of the blocks, the editor generates JavaScript code that can then be executed in the browser. The system builds on the Web Bluetooth API[5] and the WebHID API[6] to interact with devices. BLAST uses the

---

[5] https://webbluetoothcg.github.io/web-bluetooth/.

[6] https://wicg.github.io/webhid/.

Web of Things abstraction as interface; we have implemented the WoT interface for eight devices that use the BLE GAP and GATT profiles as well as the USB and Bluetooth HID interface. The WoT interface contains the metadata and interaction affordances as well as the JavaScript code needed for communication. In addition, the system includes access to the camera and sound output via browser APIs using the WoT interface. Further, the system includes access to the Web Speech API[7]. The functionality to issue HTTP requests is based on the Fetch API[8], Social Linked Data (Solid) authentication is based on the Inrupt client libraries[9], and SPARQL query support is based on μRDF.js[10]. Next to the presented small scenario around geofences, we have developed BLAST programs to accomplish five use cases with varying complexity. These use cases include switching on a light, temperature monitoring, and movement detection. Each use case introduces a different challenge that requires the use of programming patterns in combination with the built-in blocks for properties, actions, events, requests, and queries.

4   Usability Evaluation

For evaluating the usability of BLAST, we employ the System Usability Scale (SUS) questionnaire. According to Assila et al. [1], SUS provides reliable results for different sample sizes and converges quickly to the correct conclusion.

We conducted an evaluation with nine participants. None of the participants had background knowledge regarding the Web of Things, RDF, or SPARQL. Participants were asked to solve four tasks using BLAST, these included a simple "Hello World!" program, periodic polling of RSSI data by using a loop, reading data from a connected IoT device, and as a final task, reading data and processing it using logical operators. After the completion of these tasks, the participants filled out the SUS questionnaire. The achieved SUS score across all questionnaires is 81.4 out of 100 points, which corresponds to good usability.

It must be noted that the survey was conducted with an older version of BLAST. This is due to the fact that BLAST is under constant development. Since the user interface has undergone only minor changes since the evaluation, the results are still relevant.

5   Conclusion

We have introduced BLAST, a block-based language that simplifies the interaction with IoT devices, digital twins or other web resources without the need for a deeper understanding of different programming languages or network protocols. We are currently working on an execution environment that runs on Node.js as a way to execute BLAST programs independently of browsers, which impose restrictions on accessing devices to provide security and privacy protection.

---

[7] https://wicg.github.io/speech-api/.

[8] https://fetch.spec.whatwg.org/.

[9] https://docs.inrupt.com/developer-tools/javascript/client-libraries/.

[10] https://github.com/vcharpenay/uRDF.js/.

References

1. Assila, A., Ezzedine, H., et al.: Standardized usability questionnaires: features and quality focus. Electron. J. Comput. Sci. Inf. Technol. **6**(1) (2016)
2. Bottoni, P., Ceriani, M.: Using blocks to get more blocks: exploring linked data through integration of queries and result sets in block programming. In: IEEE Blocks and Beyond Workshop, pp. 99–101 (2015)
3. Cimino, C., Negri, E., Fumagalli, L.: Review of digital twin applications in manufacturing. Comput. Ind. **113**, 103130 (2019)
4. Fraser, N.: Ten things we've learned from blockly. In: 2015 IEEE Blocks and Beyond Workshop (Blocks and Beyond), pp. 49–50 (2015). https://doi.org/10.1109/BLOCKS.2015.7369000
5. Kelleher, C., Pausch, R.: Lowering the barriers to programming: a taxonomy of programming environments and languages for novice programmers. ACM Comput. Surv. **37**(2), 83–137 (2005)
6. Maloney, J., Resnick, M., Rusk, N., Silverman, B., Eastmond, E.: The scratch programming language and environment. ACM Trans. Comput. Educ. (TOCE) **10**(4), 1–15 (2010)
7. Pasternak, E., Fenichel, R., Marshall, A.N.: Tips for creating a block language with blockly. In: IEEE Blocks and Beyond Workshop, pp. 21–24 (2017)
8. Patton, E.W., Van Woensel, W., Seneviratne, O., Loseto, G., Scioscia, F., Kagal, L.: The Punya platform: building mobile research apps with linked data and semantic features. In: Hotho, A., et al. (eds.) ISWC 2021. LNCS, vol. 12922, pp. 563–579. Springer, Cham (2021). https://doi.org/10.1007/978-3-030-88361-4_33
9. Tomlein, M., Grønbæk, K.: A visual programming approach based on domain ontologies for configuring industrial IoT installations. In: Proceedings of the Seventh International Conference on the Internet of Things, pp. 1–9 (2017)
10. Weintrop, D.: Block-based programming in computer science education. Commun. ACM **62**(8), 22–25 (2019)
11. Weintrop, D., Shepherd, D.C., Francis, P., Franklin, D.: Blockly goes to work: block-based programming for industrial robots. In: IEEE Blocks and Beyond Workshop, pp. 29–36 (2017)

Leibniz Data Manager – A Research Data Management System

Anna Beer[1], Mauricio Brunet[1], Vibhav Srivastava[1],
and Maria-Esther Vidal[1,2]([✉])

[1] TIB - Leibniz Information Centre for Science and Technology, Hannover, Germany
{Anna.Beer,Mauricio.Brunet,Vibhav.Srivastava,Maria.Vidal}@tib.eu
[2] Leibniz University Hannover, Hannover, Germany

Abstract. FAIR principles aim to enhance machine-actionability of research data management, and enable data consumers and providers to scale up to incoming data avalanches. This demo paper describes Leibniz Data Manager (LDM), a research data management repository that resorts to Semantic Web technologies to empower FAIR principles. During the demonstration, the attendees will create various digital objects, and observe the crucial role of metadata in efficient and effective management and analysis of research data management. LDM is publicly available: https://service.tib.eu/ldmservice/.

Keywords: Research data management · RDF · FAIR principles

1 Introduction

FAIR data principles emphasize the crucial role of machine-processable metadata to find, access, interoperate, and reuse data with minimal human intervention [3]. Leibniz Data Manager is built on Semantic Web technologies to support researchers in documenting, analyzing, and sharing research datasets. LDM solves interoperability across repositories and integrates datasets published in other repositories. To present dataset metadata, it relies on existing vocabularies, e.g., DCAT[1] and DataCite[2]. Also, data services implemented as Jupyter notebooks[3] enable the execution of live code over LDM repositories. The definition of various access privileges facilitates the access and management of the LDM datasets and data services. Lastly, a wide variety of available data visualizations enables the preview of the main characteristics of a dataset without downloading it. This demo demonstrates the LDM features in the whole lifecycle of research data management [2]. First, attendees will collect and describe a dataset, and generate a Digital Object Identifier (DOI)[4] that will persistently and globally

---

[1] https://www.w3.org/TR/vocab-dcat-2/.
[2] https://schema.datacite.org/.
[3] https://jupyter.org/.
[4] https://www.doi.org/.

identify their datasets. Next, they will explore metadata, describing the defined datasets, in various RDF serializations. Previews of the uploaded data will be visualized using a myriad of plots. Jupyter notebooks will be included as data services to demonstrate on-the-flight analyses. Lastly, datasets from other data repositories or data providers will be integrated; the attendees will be able to set up different synchronization schedules to keep datasets up to date.

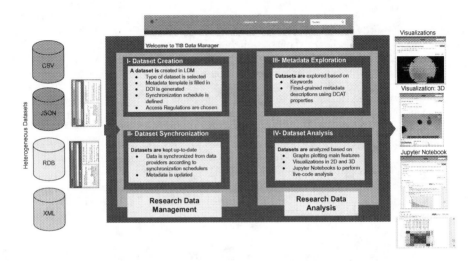

Fig. 1. The Leibniz Data Manager main components.

2 The Leibniz Data Manager Architecture

Leibniz Data Manager aims at supporting the lifecycle of research data management: a) Planning research; b) Collecting data; c) Processing and Analyzing data; d) Publishing and Sharing; e) Preserving data, and f) Re-using data. Figure 1 depicts the main components for research data management and analysis. Data is collected from datasets in heterogeneous formats; also, data catalogs can be integrated from existing repositories (e.g., the data repository of the Leibniz University Hannover[5]). Metadata describing a dataset is collected from the data provider; and existing vocabularies, e.g., DCAT and DataCite are utilized to describe the metadata following the Linked Data[6] and FAIR principles. The newly created dataset is uniquely and persistently identified by generating a DOI. Moreover, the user can define a scheduler for synchronizing the dataset with the other dataset providers [1]. Lastly, the user can describe the dataset access regulations. Once a dataset is part of the LDM catalog, data and metadata are created and synchronized according to the schedule defined during the data

---

[5] https://data.uni-hannover.de/.

[6] https://www.w3.org/wiki/LinkedData.

creation step. At the analysis level, LDM enables users to explore the datasets based on keyword queries or searches defined on DCAT properties (e.g., object types, formats, licenses). Metadata is presented in various RDF serializations and described using DCAT or DataCite. Datasets can be explored using multiple plots or visualized in 2D or 3D. Lastly, data services allow for the analysis of datasets via the use of interactive programming via Jupyter notebooks. LDM is implemented as an open source and extends the open data repository system CKAN[7] along with extra features developed on top of CKAN extensions, e.g., ckanext-dcat[8]. LDM is available as a Docker container to facilitate installing LDM distributions[9]. LDM is a publicly available resource maintained by the TIB – Leibniz Information Center for Science and Technology in Hannover[10]. TIB is one of the largest libraries for Science and Technology in the world[11], and actively promotes open access to digital research artifacts, e.g., research data, scientific literature, non-textual material, and software. Similar to other TIB services, LDM is regularly maintained and supported.

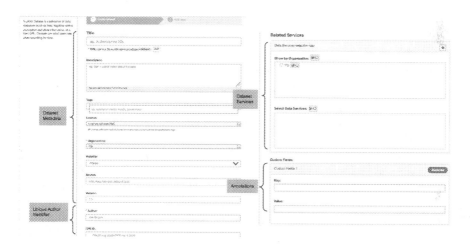

Fig. 2. Dataset creation step. Metadata is collected to describe datasets, licenses, authors, data services, and semantic annotations.

3   Demonstration of Use Cases

The demonstration aims at illustrating the LDM main functionalities and the support provided in each of the steps of the research data management lifecycle. During the demonstration, the attendees will be able to interact with LDM, and experiment the tasks of dataset creation and management, and dataset analysis.

---

[7] https://ckan.org/.

[8] https://github.com/ckan/ckanext-dcat.

[9] https://github.com/SDM-TIB/LDM_Docker/.

[10] https://www.tib.eu/en/research-development/scientific-data-management/.

[11] https://www.tib.eu/en/tib/profile/.

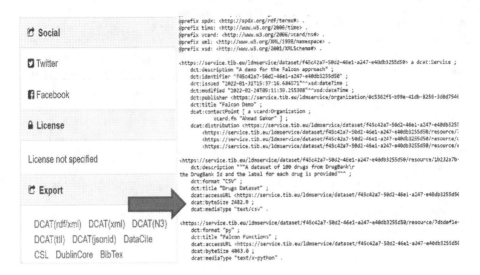

Fig. 3. Semantically describing datasets.

3.1 Dataset Creation and Management

Attendees will go through dataset creation and specify metadata that characterizes the defined dataset; it includes title, description, tags, and license. Additionally, the dataset authors can be uniquely identified using their ORCID[12] identifiers. Similarly, attendees will define data services for the datasets, and use controlled vocabularies, to express the meaning of the published data. Figure 2 illustrates the part of the interface used to collect this metadata and create a dataset. Attendees will create two types of datasets, i.e., local and imported from other repositories. Different schedulers for data synchronization will be defined. They will explore metadata in various vocabularies, e.g., DataCite, DCAT, or DublinCore, to analyze machine-readable descriptions of the defined datasets (Fig. 3). Furthermore, attendees will be able to explore and search the datasets based on metadata represented using these vocabularies. Different schedulers for data synchronization will allow for LDM adaptability and synchronization.

3.2 Dataset Analysis

Three types of datasets are available: (i) Local datasets, including data resources presented in various formats (e.g., CSV, JSON, text, or MP4). (ii) Imported datasets collected from existing data repositories on the Web. (iii) Data services running on top of datasets and providing data processing results in the form of non-alterable Python code. The attendees will publish these three different types of data resources (Fig. 4) and analyze main properties using live code implemented as Jupyter notebook services[13].

---

[12] https://orcid.org/.

[13] https://service.tib.eu/ldmservice/service/.

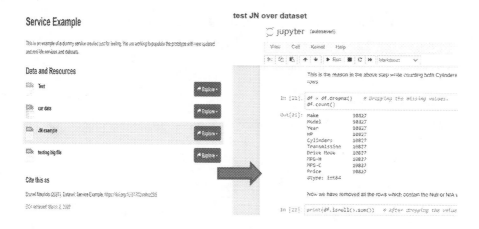

Fig. 4. Jupyter notebook integrated over dataset for live code analysis.

4 Conclusions

We demonstrate a data management system for supporting the lifecycle of research data management, i.e., data creation, documentation, analysis, preservation, and sharing. Datasets from other repositories can be imported and maintained up to date. The LDM demo puts in perspective the crucial role of Semantic Web technologies, and W3C recommended vocabularies, in the generation of machine-readable metadata respecting Linked Data and FAIR principles.

Acknowledgements. The project is funded by Deutsche Forschungsgemeinschaft (DFG, German Research Foundation) in the LIS Funding Programme *e-Research Technologies* (grant no. 438302423).

References

1. Chamanara, J., Kraft, A., Auer, S., Koepler, O.: Towards semantic integration of federated research data. Datenbank-Spektrum **19**(2), 87–94 (2019). https://doi.org/10.1007/s13222-019-00315-w
2. Mosconi, G., et al.: Three gaps in opening science. Comput. Support. Coop. Work **28**(3–4), 749–789 (2019). https://doi.org/10.1007/s10606-019-09354-z
3. Wilkinson, M., et al.: The fair guiding principles for scientific data management and stewardship. Sci. Data **3**(1), 1–9 (2016). https://doi.org/10.1038/sdata.2016.18

Towards Knowledge Graph-Agnostic SPARQL Query Validation for Improving Question Answering

Aleksandr Perevalov[1,2($\boxtimes$)] ⓘ, Aleksandr Gashkov[3] ⓘ, Maria Eltsova[3] ⓘ,
and Andreas Both[2,4] ⓘ

[1] Anhalt University of Applied Sciences, Köthen, Germany
aleksandr.perevalov@hs-anhalt.de
[2] Leipzig University of Applied Sciences, Leipzig, Germany
[3] Perm National Research Polytechnic University, Perm, Russia
[4] DATEV eG, Nuremberg, Germany

Abstract. A Knowledge Graph Question Answering (KGQA) system needs to generate a SPARQL query over a knowledge graph (KG) that is reflecting a user's information need expressed by the given natural-language question. Yet, many of these generated queries might be completely mismatching. To deal with this problem, we developed a KG-agnostic approach that is intended to increase the KGQA quality while validating SPARQL query candidates and finally removing the incorrect ones. In this demonstration, we provide the research community a Web user interface and a RESTful API to experiment with the processing of our approach and experience the possible impact of such an approach.

Keywords: Question answering · Knowledge graphs · Query validation · Query ranking · API · Demonstrator

1 Introduction

The Web was established to manifest a major information source for many people worldwide. While aiming at better knowledge modeling and representation, the Semantic Web initiative was proposed and is permanently growing. The objective of this initiative is to make Web data machine-readable and machine-understandable by describing concepts, entities, and relations between them [1]. Today, the Semantic Web may be considered as a giant Knowledge Graph (KG). In this regard, Knowledge Graph Question Answering (KGQA) systems are actively developing already for more than a decade [4,5].

KGQA systems typically transform a natural-language question to produce a set (or ranked list) of SPARQL[1] *Query Candidates* (QC), i.e., a common interface is present for input information (question text) and output information (SPARQL query), where the first QC should be usable to retrieve the

---

[1] https://www.w3.org/TR/rdf-sparql-query/.

© The Author(s), under exclusive license to Springer Nature Switzerland AG 2022
P. Groth et al. (Eds.): ESWC 2022 Satellite Events, LNCS 13384, pp. 78–82, 2022.
https://doi.org/10.1007/978-3-031-11609-4_15

correct answer from the considered KG. There are different structures in the KGs (e.g., different basic graph modeling patterns[2]). However, the *label attribute* (e.g., rdfs:label[3]) is one of the few common properties used very often in KGs. Therefore, such commonly used attribute like rdfs:label enables us to transform the queries in a way that they can be "understood" without depending on structures of particular KGs. In our previous research, we introduced a KG-agnostic approach for validating SPARQL query candidates with the intention to decide whether one could be used to retrieve the correct answer to the given question or not [8].

The approach allows filtering out the incorrect SPARQL queries from the query candidates list by training a binary classifier on positive and negative examples (considering questions and queries) to distinguish between correct and incorrect queries, respectively. Hence, the possible impact of the eliminating the incorrect query candidates is as follows: (1) improving the QA quality by moving the correct QCs to the top of the list and by reducing the cardinality of the QCs list, consequently (2) improving the efficiency of a KGQA system if it executes top-N candidates from the list, and (3) decreasing the probability of misinformation by removing all the QCs given an unanswerable question.

In our recent research papers [7,8], we have demonstrated the applicability of the approach on different KGQA benchmarks' datasets. Specifically, we observed that the query validation approach helps to relatively increase QA quality by up to 382% given Precision@1 (=NDCG@1) score.

In this demo[4], we are providing an interactive Web user interface (Web UI) and a corresponding RESTful API for interacting with the SPARQL query validation model. The Web UI also enables its users to send the feedback given a particular prediction to contribute for further evaluation and optimization of the approach. The API provides the research community with the opportunity to integrate the corresponding approach into their QA systems and to test it interactively.

This paper is structured as follows: Sect. 2 briefly describes the suggested approach. In Sect. 3 the demo application is presented. We draw conclusions in the Sect. 4.

2   Query Candidate Validation

Our approach is based on the assumption that a SPARQL query expressing a user's information need can be transformed to a natural-language text (i.e., verbalized) that should be similar to the original question. Therefore, we assume that it is possible to establish such a decision algorithm that can determine whether a SPARQL query is correctly representing a question (i.e., to validate a SPARQL query with respect to the original question).

---

[2] https://www.w3.org/TR/rdf-sparql-query/#BasicGraphPatterns.

[3] https://www.w3.org/2000/01/rdf-schema#label.

[4] The demo application and the video of presentation are available at http://demos. swe.htwk-leipzig.de/sparql_query_validation_demo.

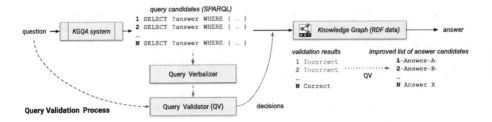

Fig. 1. General overview of the query validation process. The core component is the *Query Validator* intended to filter incorrect query candidates.

The general overview of the query validation approach is given in Fig. 1.

The core component of the entire process is the *Query Validator (QV)* module. This module receives question text and verbalizes SPARQL query as an input. The query is verbalized by replacing URIs with its rdfs:label value and leaving all the variable names while removing the rest of the query [8]. The QV module makes binary decisions on whether a *Query Candidate* (QC) is correct or not, given a textual question (in our research paper QAnswer [3] is used for computing the QCs). Therefore, for each QC a decision is done, the set of these decisions form the list of *validation results*. If a decision was negative, then a QC is eliminated, otherwise it stays in the list of query candidates. Hence, a new (probably improved) list of validated query candidates is created. Thereafter, (depending on the used KGQA system) all validated queries might be executed on a KG to get the actual answer. Finally, the obtained answers are used for answering the question. The more detailed description of the QV approach is available in our corresponding research paper [8].

3   Demo Application

The demo application consists of two parts: Web interface and RESTful API. The interface allows a user to "play" with the QV approach in interactive mode (see Fig. 2). One should fill the "Question text" and "SPARQL query" fields. Alternatively, one of the examples on the right side of the screen can be selected to make the system infer the validation decision in the "Results" area. The examples are taken from the well-known QA benchmark dataset LC-QuAD [6]. Each result contains the entered question, the query and its verbalization, the confidence score, the validation decision, and also will show two feedback buttons. The RESTful API is used by the Web UI and can also be called independently. Therefore, we require the same input parameters for the GET request (question and query). The response returns validationResult and confidence. We intend to use the users' feedback collected in our future work to improve our approach. We encourage researchers and developers to integrate the QV approach in their systems and applications using the provided API or even establish reusable QA components (e.g., using a QA framework like [2]).

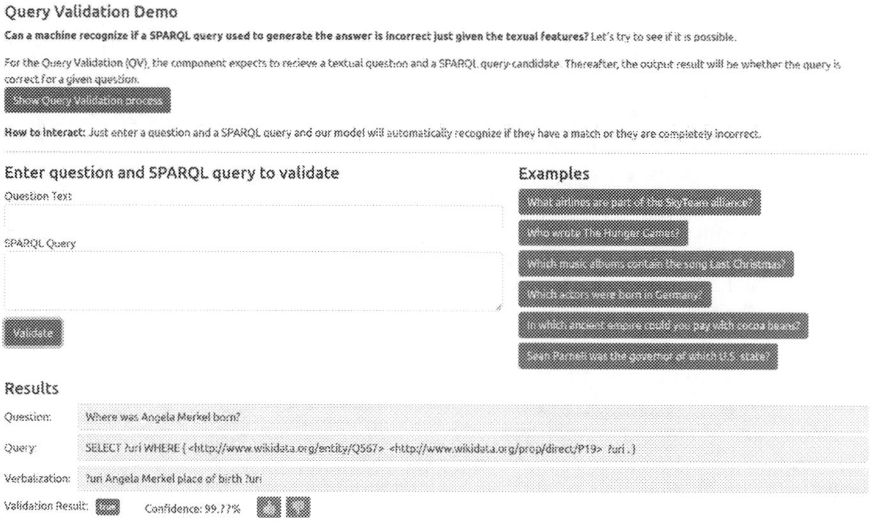

Query Validation Demo

Can a machine recognize if a SPARQL query used to generate the answer is incorrect just given the texual features? Let's try to see if it is possible.

For the Query Validation (QV), the component expects to recieve a textual question and a SPARQL query-candidate. Thereafter, the output result will be whether the query is correct for a given question.

Show Query Validation process

How to interact: Just enter a question and a SPARQL query and our model will automatically recognize if they have a match or they are completely incorrect.

Enter question and SPARQL query to validate

Question Text

SPARQL Query

Validate

Examples

What airlines are part of the SkyTeam alliance?

Who wrote The Hunger Games?

Which music albums contain the song Last Christmas?

Which actors were born in Germany?

In which ancient empire could you pay with cocoa beans?

Sean Parnell was the governor of which U.S. state?

Results

Question: Where was Angela Merkel born?

Query: SELECT ?uri WHERE { <http://www.wikidata.org/entity/Q567> <http://www.wikidata.org/prop/direct/P19> ?uri .}

Verbalization: ?uri Angela Merkel place of birth ?uri

Validation Result: ▓▓▓ Confidence: 99.77% ▨ ▨

Fig. 2. Screenshot of the demo interface

4 Conclusion

Providing high quality for Question Answering is crucial to enable information access for any user (without the need to learn a technical query language like SPARQL). Here, we provide access to an KG-agnostic approach for analyzing SPARQL queries and deciding whether these queries are correct w.r.t. the given question or not. Hence, our demonstrator enables users to experience possible straightforward verbalizations of generated SPARQL queries, which hopefully will also inspire additional integrations and novel approach with the intention to increase the quality of QA methods. Additionally, our implemented API can be used to test the functionality with an own dataset and to easily integrate our approach into existing QA systems. In the future, we will integrate different verbalizations into our approach to enable users to experience the impact of different verbalization methods.

References

1. Berners-Lee, T., Hendler, J., Lassila, O.: The semantic web. Sci. Am. **284**(5), 34–43 (2001). http://www.jstor.org/stable/26059207
2. Both, A., Diefenbach, D., Singh, K., Shekarpour, S., Cherix, D., Lange, C.: Qanary – a methodology for vocabulary-driven open question answering systems. In: Sack, H., Blomqvist, E., d'Aquin, M., Ghidini, C., Ponzetto, S.P., Lange, C. (eds.) ESWC 2016. LNCS, vol. 9678, pp. 625–641. Springer, Cham (2016). https://doi.org/10.1007/978-3-319-34129-3_38
3. Diefenbach, D., Both, A., Singh, K., Maret, P.: Towards a question answering system over the semantic web. Semant. Web **11**, 421–439 (2020). https://doi.org/10.3233/SW-190343

4. Diefenbach, D., Lopez, V., Singh, K., Maret, P.: Core techniques of question answering systems over knowledge bases: a survey. Knowl. Inf. Syst. **55**(3), 529–569 (2017). https://doi.org/10.1007/s10115-017-1100-y
5. Dimitrakis, E., Sgontzos, K., Tzitzikas, Y.: A survey on question answering systems over linked data and documents. J. Intell. Inf. Syst. **55**(2), 233–259 (2019). https://doi.org/10.1007/s10844-019-00584-7
6. Dubey, M., Banerjee, D., Abdelkawi, A., Lehmann, J.: LC-QuAD 2.0: a large dataset for complex question answering over Wikidata and DBpedia. In: Ghidini, C., et al. (eds.) ISWC 2019. LNCS, vol. 11779, pp. 69–78. Springer, Cham (2019). https://doi.org/10.1007/978-3-030-30796-7_5
7. Gashkov, A., Perevalov, A., Eltsova, M., Both, A.: Improving the question answering quality using answer candidate filtering based on natural-language features. In: 16th International Conference on Intelligent Systems and Knowledge Engineering (ISKE 2021) (2021)
8. Gashkov, A., Perevalov, A., Eltsova, M., Both, A.: Improving question answering quality through language feature-based SPARQL query candidate validation. In: Groth, P., et al. (eds.) ESWC 2022, pp. 217–235. Springer, Cham (2022). https://doi.org/10.1007/978-3-031-06981-9_13

Towards Generalized Welding Ontology in Line with ISO and Knowledge Graph Construction

Muhammad Yahya[1,2(✉)], Baifan Zhou[3], Zhuoxun Zheng[4,5],
Dongzhuoran Zhou[3,4], John G. Breslin[1,2], Muhammad Intizar Ali[6],
and Evgeny Kharlamov[3,4]

[1] Confirm Smart Manufacturing, National University of Ireland, Galway, Ireland
[2] Insight Centre for Data Analytics, National University of Ireland, Galway, Ireland
m.yahya1@nuigalway.ie
[3] SIRIUS Centre, University of Oslo, Oslo, Norway
[4] Bosch Center for Artificial Intelligence, Renningen, Germany
[5] Department of Computer Science, Oslo Metropolitan University, Oslo, Norway
[6] School of Electronic Engineering, Dublin City University, Dublin, Ireland

Motivation. Industry 4.0 [1,2] comes with unprecedented amounts of heterogeneous industrial data [3–5]. This opens new horizons for AI technology in making manufacturing smarter, more optimal [6,7] and eventually circular and sustainable. A prominent AI approach that has recently attracted a considerable attention in industry is semantic technologies that allow to uniformly integrate manufacturing data via declarative ontologies, transform it into Knowledge Graphs (KG) and then layer Machine Learning [8] and Reasoning over the resulting KGs [9,10].

An important challenge with the use of semantic technologies in plants and with scaling them from single production lines to the entire factory and beyond to clusters of factories [11] is the development of high quality standardised ontologies that will be accepted by multiple stakeholders ranging from engineers to managers [12–14]. In particular, it is common to develop ontologies that follow expert heuristics and opinions rather than commonly accepted practices and standards.

In order to address this challenge we advocate to ontologies that on the one hand are in line with international industrial standards provided by, e.g., International Organization for Standardization (ISO) or International Society of Automation (ISA) and on the other hand that are tailored towards KGs that allow for a wide range of AI methods over them including Machine Learning via vector space embedding [15].

In particular in our work we focus on ontologies for a particular type of manufacturing – welding – that is crucial in the automotive industry and for Bosch [16], one of the top global suppliers of automated welding solutions for car bodies. Welding is a sophisticated manufacturing technology in which (typically) metal parts are joined together using an energy source to produce a connection between the parts [17,18]. Besides car building welding is heavily

P. Groth et al. (Eds.): ESWC 2022 Satellite Events, LNCS 13384, pp. 83–88, 2022.
https://doi.org/10.1007/978-3-031-11609-4_16

used in shipbuilding, railways, and aerospace. Welding is well established and regulated by ISO and ISA.

Despite to the high number of welding standards, the topic of shared, generalized, and reusable formal welding ontological models is insufficiently discussed in the literature. Most of previous ontologies were rather tailored to one or some welding domains [19], or some specific applications such as solving the interoperability conflict in welding standards [20] or enhancing the machine learning pipeline [21,22]. In addition, instead of commonly agreed best practice, heuristic knowledge is often followed for ontology engineering and KG construction.

In this poster we give a preliminary report of our ongoing work on welding ontologies with standardised and generic vocabularies. In particular we discuss In particular we aim at a generic *welding core ontology (WCO)* that is in line with ISO standards and existing ontologies, aiming at a common ground for ontology engineering and KG construction for welding. In the following we describe our approach by first giving requirements, then by describing our modelling process, and finally by describing our core ontology and KG.

Requirements to the Welding Ontology. The following requirements help us to ensure that our ontology can be effectively used in the welding domain.

R1. *Capture Domain Knowledge:* The developed ontology needs to capture domain knowledge properly. In particular, this includes to reflect the information provided by the domain documents, domain experts, and to obtain knowledge in which the conflicts are sorted out, terminologies are unified and concepts are disambiguated. This requirement is evaluated with the competency questions.

R2. *Quality Ontology:* A quality ontological model should have good performance in terms of established metrics: e.g., clarity, completeness, and conciseness. This requirement is evaluated with the Ontology Pitfall Scanner (OOPS!).

R3. *Adherence to Industry Standards and Existing Ontologies:* The concepts and relations in the ontology must be possibly in line with ISO welding standards and the existing generic and core vocabularies. For example, ISO 4063, ISA 95, Reference Generalized Ontological Mode (RGOM)[1], DOLCE[2], Time ontology[3], etc. This requirements is evaluated in generalizability and reusablity section.

Welding Ontology Development Process. To develop the welding ontology, We adopt the ontology development process depicted in Fig. 1.

– *Step 1: Domain Analysis and Knowledge Gathering.* During the initial phase of the ontology development process, a series of workshops with Bosch experts

---

[1] http://industryportal.enit.fr/ontologies/RGOM.

[2] http://www.loa.istc.cnr.it/dolce/overview.html.

[3] https://www.w3.org/TR/owl-time/.

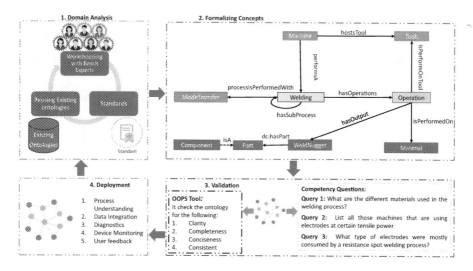

Fig. 1. The workflow for ontology modelling and knowledge construction

were held in order to comprehend the domain Knowledge. Furthermore, welding standards such as ISO 4063 in line with those for production line integration i.e. ISA 95 were identified for gathering extensive knowledge. A comparison study is then conducted with ISO 4063, ISA-95, RGOM, and existing vocabularies are analyzed and compared.

- *Step 2: Formalizing Concepts.* The second step involves the codification of knowledge collected to a formalized structure i.e. classes and the relationship between it, and it's axioms. The classes and relations are semantically modelled in the prospect of welding and manufacturing resources, depicted in Fig. 1.2.
- *Step 3: Validation.* The validation step mainly consists of ontology evaluation with respect to the defined requirements, explained in detail in Sect. 3.
- *Step 4: Deployment.* The WCO is deployed in various activities, e.g., process understanding, data integration [23]. User feedbacks are collected constantly and lead to further domain analysis. The workflow is naturally iterative.

Welding Core Ontology. Our preliminary version of the WCO covers four areas of the welding industry: *Physical Entity, Product, Process, Business.* The initial version of WCO incorporate the domain knowledge from Bosch welding experts, ISO 4063, ISA95, RGOM and other existing ontologies. It consists of 216 classes, 71 object properties, and 32 data properties.

Enterprise Cross-Domain Knowledge Graph. The idea of cross-domain KGs is to construct KGs following the WCO as the upper-level schema, which we create beforehand for a wide range of welding processes. The hierarchy of cross-domain KGs are in this: *Individuals → Welding Domain Ontologies → WCO*, in which the *individuals* follow the class definitions in the *welding domain ontologies*, which are all sub-classes of the WCO. Bosch has data from many welding processes, locations, customers and we are working towards enterprise cross-domain KGs [24,25] to have a seamless collaboration between the manufacturing experts, resources, equipment, etc.

Evaluation. We plan to conduct an evaluation of our ontology in multiple ways. First, we plan to study *Competence Questions* with Bosch experts to analyse the coverage of the domain knowledge (R1) from three aspects in the manufacturing:

– data inspection, e.g., *What are the different materials used in the welding?*
– information summary, e.g., *List the number of welding programs used by the machines?*
– diagnostics, e.g., *Which machine generates the most abnormal welding operations?*

Next, we plan to conduct the *Ontology Pitfall Scanner (OOPS!) evaluation* of the ontology quality (R2) with the metrics such as clarity, completeness, and conciseness. Next we plan to analyse *generalizability and reusablity* of WCO, where the later is achieved by reusing the terminology from ISO standards and existing vocabularies (R3), e.g., 'machine' and 'tool' are from the RGOM, 'sensors' concept from SOSA ontology, 'isPartOf' from Dublin core ontology. The competency questions, OOPS! and generalizability and reusablity metrics were used to assess the R1, R2 and R3, respectively.

Acknowledgements. This work was partially supported by SFI (Grant 16/RC/ 3918), and the H2020 projects Dome 4.0 (Grant Agreement No. 953163), Onto-Commons (Grant Agreement No. 958371), and DataCloud (Grant Agreement No. 101016835) and the SIRIUS Centre, Norwegian Research Council project number 237898. For the purpose of Open Access, the author has applied a CC BY public copyright licence to any Author Accepted Manuscript version arising from this submission.

References

1. Yahya, M., Breslin, J.G., Ali, M.I.: Semantic web and knowledge graphs for industry 4.0. Appl. Sci. **11**(11), 5110 (2021)
2. Sudharsan, B., et al.: Tinyml benchmark: executing fully connected neural networks on commodity microcontrollers. In: 2021 IEEE 7th World Forum on Internet of Things (WF-IoT), pp. 883–884. IEEE (2021)
3. Zhou, B., Chioua, M., Bauer, M., Schlake, J.-C., Thornhill, N.F.: Improving root cause analysis by detecting and removing transient changes in oscillatory time series with application to a 1, 3-butadiene process. Ind. Eng. Chem. Res. **58**, 11234–11250 (2019)
4. Zhou, B., Chioua, M., Schlake, J.-C.: Practical methods for detecting and removing transient changes in univariate oscillatory time series. IFAC-PapersOnLine **50**(1), 7987–7992 (2017)

5. Chand, S., Davis, J.: What is smart manufacturing. Time Mag. Wrapper **7**, 28–33 (2010)
6. Mikhaylov, D., Zhou, B., Kiedrowski, T., Mikut, R., Lasagni, A.-F.: High accuracy beam splitting using slm combined with ML algorithms. Opt. Lasers Eng. **121**, 227–235 (2019)
7. Mikhaylov, D., Zhou, B., Kiedrowski, T., Mikut, R., Lasagni, A.F.: Machine learning aided phase retrieval algorithm for beam splitting with an LCoS-SLM. In: Laser Resonators, Microresonators, and Beam Control XXI, vol. 10904, International Society for Optics and Photonics, p. 109041M (2019)
8. Zhou, B., Pychynski, T., Reischl, M., Kharlamov, E., Mikut, R.: Machine learning with domain knowledge for predictive quality monitoring in resistance spot welding. J. Intell. Manuf. **33**, 1–25 (2022). https://doi.org/10.1007/s10845-021-01892-y
9. Zhou, D., et al.: Enhancing knowledge graph generation with ontology reshaping - Bosch case, in: ESWC (Demos/Industry). Springer (2022)
10. Mailis, T., Kotidis, Y., Christoforidis, S., Kharlamov, E., Ioannidis, Y.E.: View selection over knowledge graphs in triple stores. Proc. VLDB Endow. **14**(13), 3281–3294 (2021)
11. Zhou, B., Zhou, D., Chen, J., Svetashova, Y., Cheng, G., Kharlamov, E.: Scaling usability of ML analytics with knowledge graphs: exemplified with a bosch welding case. In: IJCKG, pp. 54–63. ACM (2021)
12. Svetashova, Y., et al.: Ontology-enhanced machine learning: a bosch use case of welding quality monitoring. In: Pan, J.Z. (ed.) ISWC 2020. LNCS, vol. 12507, pp. 531–550. Springer, Cham (2020). https://doi.org/10.1007/978-3-030-62466-8_33
13. Zhou, B., Svetashova, Y., Pychynski, T., Kharlamov, E.: Semantic ML For manufacturing monitoring at Bosch. In: ISWC (Demos/Industry), vol. 2721, p. 398 (2020)
14. Svetashova, Y., Zhou, B., Schmid, S., Pychynski, T., Kharlamov, E.: SemML: Reusable ML for condition monitoring in discrete manufacturing. In: ISWC (Demos/Industry), vol. 2721, pp. 213–218 (2020)
15. Ho, V.T., Stepanova, D., Gad-Elrab, M.H., Kharlamov, E., Weikum, G.: Learning rules from incomplete KGs using embeddings. In: ISWC Posters & Demos, vol. 2180, CEUR-WS.org (2018)
16. Zhou, B.: Machine learning methods for product quality monitoring in electric resistance welding, Ph.D. thesis, Karlsruhe Institute of Technology, Germany (2021)
17. Zhou, B., Pychynski, T., Reischl, M., Mikut, R.: Comparison of machine learning approaches for time-series-based quality monitoring of resistance spot welding (RSW). Arch. Data Sci. Series A (Online First) **5**(1), 13 (2018)
18. Zhou, B., Svetashova, Y., Byeon, S., Pychynski, T., Mikut, R., Kharlamov, E.: Predicting quality of automated welding with machine learning and semantics: a Bosch case study. In: CIKM. ACM, pp. 2933–2940 (2020)
19. Chang, X., Rai, R., Terpenny, J.: Design for manufacturing (DFM) ontology: implementation of a mechanical assembly through welding process. In: IIE Annual Conference. Proceedings, p. 1690 (2007)
20. Saha, S., Usman, Z., Li, W., Jones, S., Shah, N.: Core domain ontology for joining processes to consolidate welding standards. Robot. Comput.-Integr. Manuf. **59**, 417–430 (2019)
21. Zhou, B., Svetashova, Y., Pychynski, T., Baimuratov, I., Soylu, A., Kharlamov, E.: SemFE: facilitating ML pipeline development with semantics. In: CIKM. ACM, pp. 3489–3492 (2020)
22. Zhou, B., et al.: SemML: Facilitating development of ML models for condition monitoring with semantics. J. Web Semant. **71**, 100664 (2021)

23. Zhou, B., et al.: The data value quest: a holistic semantic approach at Bosch. In: ESWC (Demos/Industry). Springer (2022)
24. Zhou, D., Zhou, B., Chen, J., Cheng, G., Kostylev, E., Kharlamov, E.: Towards ontology reshaping for KG generation with user-in-the-loop: applied to Bosch welding. In: IJCKG. ACM, pp. 145–150 (2021)
25. Zheng, Z., et al.: Query-based industrial analytics over knowledge graphs with ontology reshaping. In: ESWC (Posters & Demos). Springer (2022)

O'FAIRe: Ontology FAIRness Evaluator in the AgroPortal Semantic Resource Repository

Emna Amdouni[1] , Syphax Bouazzouni[1] , and Clement Jonquet[1,2(✉)]

[1] LIRMM, University of Montpellier and CNRS, Montpellier, France
{emna.amdouni,syphax.bouazzouni,jonquet}@lirmm.fr
[2] MISTEA, University of Montpellier, INRAE and Institut Agro, Montpellier, France

Abstract. O'FAIRe, the *Ontology FAIRness Evaluator,* is a methodology to automatically assess to which level a semantic resource or ontology respects the FAIR Principles. This paper describes the online tool implementing O'FAIRe within the AgroPortal ontology repository, through 61 questions/tests, among 80% are based on the ontology metadata description. For a specific ontology or a group of semantic resources, O'FAIRe web service outputs both global and detailed scores (normalized) against the 15 FAIR Principles. O'FAIRe results are visualized and explained with new specific user-friendly interfaces (such as the FAIRness wheel) in order to help AgroPortal users improve the FAIRness of their resources. O'FAIRe is currently implemented in three different public ontology repositories as they offer the required metadata descriptions. In the future, we will deploy the service in other OntoPortal repositories.

Keywords: FAIR Principles · FAIRness assessment · Ontologies and semantic resources · Ontology metadata · Ontology repository

1 Context and Motivations

In 2014, the FAIR Principles established fundamental guidelines to make scientific data interoperable, persistent, and reusable for humans and machines [1]. Since then, several assessment methodologies and tools have been proposed to manually or automatically evaluate to what extent data or different research objects adhere to the FAIR Principles. For instances, FAIRdat, FAIR metrics [3], FAIRshake [2], F-UJI [3], or FAIR-checker [4]. Only one specific tool for ontologies called FOOPS! was released end of 2021 [5]. Early 2018, we argued that rich metadata descriptions and ontology repositories offer a means to facilitate the implementation of "FAIR ontologies" [6]. Later, we demonstrated the impact of harmonized and standardized metadata descriptions on the ontology identification and selection process [7]. More recently, other community efforts have also expressed the need for recommendations and guidelines on how to provide FAIR semantic resources or "artefacts" including the FAIRsFAIR H2020 project [8], or expert group guidelines [9, 10]. However, these works focus on recommendations and guidelines but do not specify a methodology for assessing the FAIRness of semantic resources (vocabularies, terminologies, thesaurus, etc.) and automating this task. FOOPS! is a good starting

P. Groth et al. (Eds.): ESWC 2022 Satellite Events, LNCS 13384, pp. 89–94, 2022.
https://doi.org/10.1007/978-3-031-11609-4_17

point for automatic FAIRness assessment, still, it has several limits: it does not cover all the sub-principles, and does not consider and test all the related aspects of a sub-principle (e.g., "I1/I2" are evaluated with straightforward tests), and does not provide actionable guidelines to address the detected issues. It does not work with a group of ontologies. One strong difference is that FOOPS! does not rely on any ontology repository nor a standard way to describe ontologies/metadata, which is somehow both an advantage and a limitation.

From our point-of-view, clear metadata descriptions and open semantic repositories are two key elements of making semantic resources FAIR. In a previous paper, we introduced an *integrated quantitative FAIRness assessment grid* for ontologies and semantic resources [11] which dispatches 478 credits to each FAIR principle, depending on its importance when assessing the FAIRness of semantic resources. The proposed grid is based on the *Metadata for Ontology Description and Publication Ontology* [11], previous work harmonizing several metadata vocabularies into one model that has been implemented within AgroPortal [7]. With O'FAIRe, extensively presented in [REF], we go a step further and define a clear generic and customizable methodology, based on 61 questions to automatically assess the FAIRness level of ontologies, guide semantic stakeholders to make their semantic resources FAIR, and select relevant FAIR semantic resources for use. This methodology considers FAIRness assessment of ontologies should as much as possible be based on the evaluation of their metadata properties, which ones shall be ideally indexed, shared, and standardized by reference ontology repositories or libraries. As illustrated hereafter, we have implemented O'FAIRe as a web service working with any OntoPortal installation (https://ontoportal.org) [12] respecting MOD 1.4 properties and implemented specific visualizations illustrated here in the AgroPortal ontology repository [13].

2 O'FAIRe: Design, Implementation and Demonstration

O'FAIRe is based on 61questions that describe the unambiguous tests to determine to which level a semantic resource respects a particular aspect of FAIR. The distribution of the 61 questions is as follows: Findable (13), Accessible (13), Interoperable (15), Reusable (20). Each question disposes of certain number of credits (as defined by the grid [11]) to assign to an ontology depending on how it passes the test. When assigned to an ontology, credits become points that are added and normalized into scores. The higher the number of points, the better the test is passed. For instance, for the principle R1.1 ("Ontologies and ontology metadata are released with a clear and accessible usage license."), O'FAIRe relies on 3 questions:

Q1. Is the ontology license clearly specified, with an URI that is resolvable and supports content negotiation? 15 pts (assessed with the property `dct:license`*).*
Q2. Are the ontology access rights specified and permissions documented? 7 pts (assessed with the property `dct:accessRights`*).*
Q3. Are the ontology usage guidelines and copyright holder documented? 15 pts (assessed with the properties `cc:morePermissions`, `cc:useGuidelines` *and* `dct:rightsHolder`*).*

We implemented O'FAIRe into a web service which executes tests automatically evaluating how a semantic resource stored within AgroPortal responds to the 61 questions. The tool provides a score for each sub-principles as well as a global normalized [0–100] FAIR score. Formally speaking, we use AgroPortal's metadata record to evaluate the level of FAIRness of the corresponding semantic resource. Consequently, we do not evaluate the level of FAIRness of an ontology but the level of FAIRness of the ontology stored within AgroPortal. This distinction is important as several FAIR sub-principles are linked to the repository in which the ontology is hosted.

The questions and the web service have been implemented in a Java Servlet application, which consumes as entry the JSON ontology metadata descriptions returned by AgroPortal's web service API. The code is open-source, fully documented and available for reuse/customization on GitHub: https://github.com/agroportal/fairness. Over O'FAIREe questions: 45 are dependent of the ontology and 16 are determined simply by the fact that the ontology is stored in AgroPortal; which means the repository automatically gives 93 points to an ontology (19% of the total points). Currently, the prototype implements 50/61 questions (82%). The rest of the questions are not yet implemented because we do not have: (i) either a metadata property to store the information necessary to assess the question or (ii) implemented a mechanism to analyze the ontology content. This means that the maximum score an ontology can currently obtain in AgroPortal is 387/478 (normalized score of 81/100).

O'FAIRe prototype (v2) was released in AgroPortal v2.2 release (on 2/2/22) (http://agroportal.lirmm.fr); as well as in the SIFR BioPortal (http://bioportal.lirmm.fr), a repository of French biomedical terminology and the IndustryPortal (http://industryportal.eni t.fr) developed in the context of the H2020 OntoCommons project. The three are open ontology-repositories based on the OntoPortal technology and implementing MOD 1.4. O'FAIRe web service in AgroPortal is accessible at following base URL: http://services. agroportal.lirmm.fr/ofaire. It takes as input parameter an *ontology acronym* or a list of ontology acronyms. It returns a *JSON output* which contains the FAIR scores obtained for each question aggregated by sub-principle, principle and then in total (`score`). The total score is maximized by 478 and normalized for convenience and comparison (`normalizedScore`). Every test result is justified by a short sentence (`explanation`) and when relevant the list of MOD1.4 metadata properties used (`properties`), so users may be aware of how this score was obtained.

Equipped with O'FAIRe, we have revisited or developed new user interfaces within AgroPortal to display FAIR scores. For instance, it is now possible to order all the semantic resources by FAIR score on the "Browse" page, which lists all the semantic resources in AgroPortal. Figure 1 shows an overview of the results returned for an individual evaluation of the Basic Formal Ontology (BFO) in AgroPortal: the *FAIRness wheel* shows the obtained scores over the 15 FAIR sub-principles; the *bar chart* details for each FAIR principle: the total score obtained (i.e., green part) as well as non-obtained points (yellow part) and credits that cannot yet be assigned (gray part) per limits of current implementation. Other interfaces (e.g., the *Summary page*) provides details about an ontology score, metadata properties used and explanations.

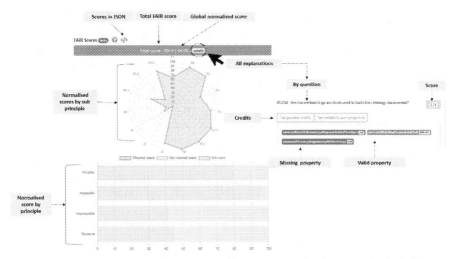

Fig. 1. Overview of O'FAIRe evaluation of BFO in AgroPortal. The normalized global FAIR score is 64 (equivalent to 306 points).

When a list of ontologies is passed as entry, the `combined` parameter computes metrics for the group of ontologies requested (average, min, max and median and returns the average scores). Figure 2. shows an illustration in AgroPortal for a group of ontologies.

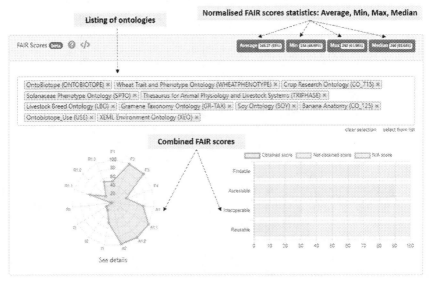

Fig. 2. O'FAIRe combined FAIRness evaluation of 11 ontologies in the OBO group in AgroPortal: average = 55, min = 48, max = 61, and median = 55.

3   Conclusion

O'FAIRe offers both a methodology and a tool (illustrated here in AgroPortal) to enable automatic FAIRness assessment of ontologies. It differs from existing initiatives, as it is specialized for ontologies or semantic resources and it is based on metadata description harmonized in an ontology repository. O'FAIRe main goal is to offer a metric to measure the level of FAIRness and thus guide semantic stakeholders to make their semantic resources more FAIR, and select relevant FAIR semantic resources for their use. The grid on which O'FAIRe is conceived as well as its methodology (e.g., list of questions) can be customized, extended, or improved by other semantic experts in further studies. Currently, O'FAIRe can be used in the AgroPortal an ontology repository dedicated to agronomy, the SIFR BioPortal and IndustryPortal. Collaborations within the OntoPortal Alliance will enable us to extend and maybe customize O'FAIRe for other repositories such as the BioPortal, EcoPortal or MatPortal.

Since its release, O'FAIRe was received with good interest from AgroPortal users and we have already seen some semantic resources metadata modified to 'get a better score'. In a near future, we will conduct a user survey to evaluate and improve the tool and the underlying methodology. We acknowledge that the set of questions and credit assignments are discussable and will work to reach the largest consensus in subsequent versions of O'FAIRe.

Acknowledgement. *Data to Knowledge in Agronomy and Biodiversity* project (D2KAB – www. d2kab.org – ANR-18-CE23–0017) and the project ANR *French participation in GO FAIR Food Systems Implementation Network* (FooSIN – https://foosin.fr – ANR19-DATA-0019).

References

1. Wilkinson, M.D., et al.: The FAIR guiding principles for scientific data management and stewardship. Sci. Data **3**, 1–9 (2016). https://doi.org/10.1038/sdata.2016.18
2. Clarke, D.J.B., et al.: FAIRshake: Toolkit to Evaluate the FAIRness of research digital resources. Cell Syst. **9**(5), 417–421 (2019)
3. Devaraju, A., Huber, R.: An automated solution for measuring the progress toward FAIR research data. Patterns **2**(11), 100370 (2021). https://doi.org/10.1016/j.patter.2021.100370
4. Rosnet, T., Lefort, V., Devignes, M.-D., Gaignard, A.: FAIR-checker, a web tool to support the findability and reusability of digital life science resources, July 2021
5. Garijo, D., Corcho, O., Poveda-Villalón, M.: FOOPS!: an ontology pitfall scanner for the FAIR principles. In: 20th International Semantic Web Conference, ISWC 2021: Posters, Demos, and Industry Tracks, CEUR Workshop Proceedings, 2980, October 2021
6. Jonquet, C.: FAIR data requires FAIR ontologies, how do we do? F1000Res, vol. 7, March 2018. https://doi.org/10.7490/F1000research.1115343.1
7. Jonquet, C., Toulet, A., Dutta, B., Emonet, V.: Harnessing the power of unified metadata in an ontology repository: the case of AgroPortal. J. Data Semant. **7**(4), 191–221 (2018). https://doi.org/10.1007/s13740-018-0091-5
8. Franc, Y.L., Coen, G., Essen, J.P., Bonino, L., Lehväslaiho, H., Staiger, C.: D2.2 fair semantics: first recommendations, March 2020. https://doi.org/10.5281/zenodo.3707985

9. Garijo, D., Poveda-Villalón, M.: Best practices for implementing FAIR vocabularies and ontologies on the web. In: Applications and Practices in Ontology Design, Extraction, and Reasoning. IOS Press (2020). https://doi.org/10.3233/SSW200034

10. Malone, J., Stevens, R., Jupp, S., Hancocks, T., Parkinson, H., Brooksbank, C.: Ten simple rules for selecting a bio-ontology. PLoS Comput. Biol. **12**(2), 6 (2016)

11. Dutta, B., Toulet, A., Emonet, V., Jonquet, C.: New generation metadata vocabulary for ontology description and publication. In: Garoufallou, E., Virkus, S., Siatri, R., Koutsomiha, D. (eds.) MTSR 2017. CCIS, vol. 755, pp. 173–185. Springer, Cham (2017). https://doi.org/10.1007/978-3-319-70863-8_17

12. Graybeal, J., Jonquet, C., Fiore, N., Musen, M.A.: Adoption of BioPortal's ontology registry software: the emerging ontoportal community (2019)

13. Jonquet, C., et al.: AgroPortal: a vocabulary and ontology repository for agronomy. Comput. Electron. Agric. **144**, 126–143 (2018). https://doi.org/10.1016/j.compag.2017.10.012

domOS Common Ontology: Web of Things Discovery in Smart Buildings

Amir Laadhar[✉], Christian Thomsen, and Torben Bach Pedersen

Aalborg University, Aalborg, Denmark
{amirl,chr,tbp}@cs.aau.dk

Abstract. According to the 2021 energy efficiency report of the European Union (EU), 75% of the existing buildings in the EU have been assessed as energy-inefficient. Internet of Things (IoT) services are developed to increase energy efficiency in buildings. The W3C recommends the use of the W3C Web of Things (WoT) standard to enable IoT interoperability on the Web. However, the ability to discover IoT devices available in the WoT remains a challenge due to the lack of ontologies integrating WoT Thing Descriptions in smart buildings. We present in this paper the domOS Common Ontology (dCO) to achieve the W3C WoT discovery in smart residential buildings in 5 demonstration sites of the H2020 EU domOS project. This ontology integrates the WoT Thing Description with IoT concepts, i.e. IoT devices and building topology, in order to leverage the W3C WoT Discovery. We made the WoT Discovery implementation available for the community.

Keywords: Semantic interoperability · Internet of Things · Web of Things · Web of Things discovery

1 Introduction

The WoT Thing Description [9] is a key specification for the W3C Web of Things [6]. A Thing Description describes the metadata and interfaces of Things to participate in the WoT. However, in order to use a Thing, its Thing Description first has to be stored and obtained. A WoT Thing Description Directory (WoT TDD) [1] allows the registration, management, and search of a database of Thing Descriptions and allows authenticated and authorized entities to find WoT Thing Descriptions satisfying a set of criteria, such as being in a certain location, or having certain semantics, or containing certain interactions. This can be achieved using the W3C WoT discovery embedded in the Thing Description Directory. IoT consumers should be able to send semantic queries to the WoT discovery. For instance, an IoT service provider would like to know the set of devices related to smart space heating in a given apartment or room of a building. Semantic interoperability eases the scalable development of energy efficiency IoT applications and services. The WoT discovery requires a common ontology to semantically annotate Thing Descriptions in order to allow their

P. Groth et al. (Eds.): ESWC 2022 Satellite Events, LNCS 13384, pp. 95–100, 2022.
https://doi.org/10.1007/978-3-031-11609-4_18

semantic querying from the WoT Thing Description Directory. However, there is a lack of ontologies integrating the WoT into smart buildings. To achieve WoT discovery, the domOS Common ontology integrates the WoT ecosystem in smart buildings. The contributions of this paper are: (i) The domOS Common Ontology (dCO) ontology, as a common information model to allow semantic discovery in the WoT. (ii) An open-source implementation of the WoT semantic discovery capability to allow a context-based search of the IoT devices and their metadata in the WoT.

2   Example Use Case

In this section, we present a use case related to semantic discovery. We consider a space heating service, which aims to reduce the energy required for a residential house located in the demonstrator site of Sion, Switzerland. The house contains a heat pump appliance, which heats a water tank. An electricity meter measures the consumed energy by the heat pump. The water from the tank is pumped to the heating pipes of the house floor to ensure space heating. A temperature sensor measures the ambient temperature of a given room. A thermostat enables and disables heating for each room. The space heating service algorithm computes the optimal temperature needed in each room based on the input measurements from the ambient sensors. The heating service achieves energy efficiency when automatically turning off the heater. This house also contains other services which require other devices such as sensors and actuators. One of the main challenges of IoT ecosystems in smart buildings is to enable IoT consumers to search for the right IoT devices without having any prior knowledge about them. Therefore, IoT consumers need a semantic discovery capability in the Web of Things. We present the following user stories are example of the semantic discovery capability for the space heating service use case: The IoT service provider wants to know the list of sensors and heating controllers related to the space heating service in a given apartment; The IoT service provider wants to know the temperature sensors measuring a temperature above 26 °C in the rooms heated by the space heating. These user stories, would not be possible to answer their related semantic queries if the relevant metadata of IoT devices are not stored in a semantic knowledge base to allow their discovery. Therefore, in this work, we propose the domOS Common Ontology to semantically annotate Thing Descriptions and store them in a semantic knowledge base to ensure the WoT Discovery in the context of WoT ecosystems.

3   Ontology Design and Competency Questions

Conforming to the NeOn ontology engineering methodology [10], we identified a set of competency questions (CQs) as part of our ontology requirement specification document (ORSD). The ORSD was made in collaboration with our partners from 5 demonstration sites of the H2020 EU domOS project (https:// www.domos-project.eu/). The purpose of the dCO is to integrate the WoT Thing

Descriptions with smart buildings. We have identified the following use cases of dCO: (i) Semantic annotation of Thing Descriptions, which are JSON-LD files that describe the metadata of a WoT Thing. (ii) WoT Semantic discovery in smart buildings. Both the CQs and the ORSD can be found in our GitHub repository (https://github.com/AmirLaa/TDD). We integrate an ontology FAIRification activity into the NeOn methodology following the best practices for implementing FAIR principles in ontologies introduced by Garijo et al. [3]. Based on the CQs, the ontology should both support the WoT and the IoT domain in order to allow the WoT discovery of IoT devices and their metadata in smart buildings. Therefore, dCO integrates the SAREF [4] core ontology with SAREF4ENER, the Thing Description ontology, IoT devices, Units of Measurements Ontology and Building Topology Ontology (BOT) [8].

4   Ontology Construction and Evaluation

Figure 1 shows the main classes and properties of dCO, which is based on a modular design to enhance the maintainability of the ontology and facilitate its integration in other projects.

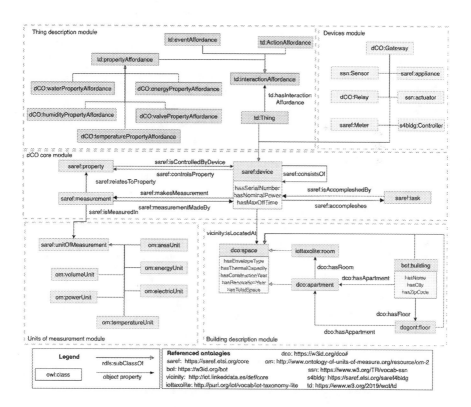

Fig. 1. dCO design overview

We depict the graphical representations of the modules in the dCO documentation (https://w3id.org/dco/). dCO should be used for the semantic annotation of the JSON-LD Thing Descriptions (cf. dCO documentation). A Thing Description can be annotated using a device term (e.g., `dco:temperatureSensor`), its location (e.g., `dco:Apartment01`), its interaction affordances (e.g., `dco:temperaturePropertyAffordance`), and the units of measurements (e.g., `dco:celsius`).

The dCO core module reuses the SAREF core ontology [4] and allows the integration of the other modules to ensure WoT discovery queries in smart buildings. This module is integrated with the Thing description module and the device module using a subsumption relationship. The core module is integrated with the building description module, the units of measurement module, respectively, using the property `vicinity:isLocatedAt` and `saref:isMeasuredIn`.

The devices module represents the set of devices in an IoT ecosystem. Devices are structured in categories, that reflect different types of devices (e.g., `ssn:sensor`, `saref:meter`).

The units of measurements module represents all the units of measurements of the IoT devices. This module reuses the Units of Measurement Ontology. A `saref:measurement` is a measurement using a unit of measurement.

The thing description module integrates the W3C WoT Things Descriptions ontology [2] with the core module. A `td:Thing` subsumes a `ssn:device`. A `td:Thing` inherits properties of a `saref:device`. A `td:Thing` can be related to one or more `ssn:tasks` and associated to one or more `td:actionAffordances`, `td:eventAffordances`, and `td:propertyAffordances`.

The building description module contains the representation of building-related metadata and building topology. We reuse concepts from the W3C Building Topology Ontology (BOT) [8]. We define four types of spaces: `bot:building`, `dogont:floor`, `dco:apartment`, and `iottaxolite:room`.

Ontology Evaluation: To ensure that the concepts correctly implement the ontology requirements and CQs, we created several SPARQL queries to answer the CQs. We have also evaluated dCO using Description Logic (DL) reasoners for satisfiability, incoherence, and inconsistency. We have validated dCO using the OOPS! (OntOlogy Pitfall Scanner!) [7] tool. This tool detects the most common pitfalls appearing when developing ontologies. We assessed and validated the FAIRness of dCO using a tool called FOOPS! [5], which assesses the compliance of ontologies against 24 different checks distributed across the FAIR principles.

5   WoT Thing Description Directory Implementation

To enable the WoT Discovery, Thing Descriptions should be stored in a Thing Description Directory. This directory allows CRUD operations of Thing Descriptions, their syntactic validation, and WoT discovery using an API interface. We implemented a WoT Discovery service and made it available using a Swagger API (https://herald.aau.dk/docs/). We made the implementation of the Thing Description Directory and the WoT Discovery available for the WoT community on GitHub (https://github.com/AmirLaa/TDD). Things Descriptions are synchronously stored, updated, and deleted from a document database and a triple store. The document database (MongoDB) allows the CRUD operation of the JSON-LD Thing Descriptions. The RDF triple store (Apache Jena Fuseki) stores the RDF transformation of the JSON-LD Things Description in order to allow WoT semantic discovery via a SPARQL endpoint. An example of an RDF Thing Description is available in the dCO ontology documentation. Things Descriptions have to be semantically annotated to allow their WoT Discovery via the Thing Description Directory. To validate our implementation of the WoT discovery capability, we converted the user stories of the space heating use case and CQs into SPARQL queries. We used the WoT discovery API interface to query the semantic knowledge. We have also concluded that the queries return the expected results. Moreover, we have implemented the Thing and Building Description Directory in 5 demonstrator sites across Europe of the domOS project. We have tested and validated the implementation in an agile development process in collaboration with our stakeholders.

In future work, we will consider making a building description JSON-LD file for the WoT, which will contain all metadata of a building itself, building topology, and IoT services metadata. The building description should be integrated into the semantic discovery of the Thing Description Directory in order to allow more advanced SPARQL queries in the WoT.

Acknowledgements. Research funded by the European Union through the Horizon 2020 domOS project (grant agreement 894240).

References

1. Cimmino, A., McCool, F.T.M., Toumura, K.: Web of things (wot) discover. W3C Working Draft Recommendation (2021)
2. Charpenay, V., Käbisch, S.: On modeling the physical world as a collection of things: the w3c thing description ontology. In: Harth, A. (ed.) ESWC 2020. LNCS, vol. 12123, pp. 599–615. Springer, Cham (2020). https://doi.org/10.1007/978-3-030-49461-2_35
3. Cota, G., et al.: Best practices for implementing fair vocabularies and ontologies on the web. In: Applications and Practices in Ontology Design, Extraction, and Reasoning
4. Daniele, L., den Hartog, F., Roes, J.: Created in close interaction with the industry: the smart appliances reference (SAREF) ontology. In: Cuel, R., Young, R. (eds.) FOMI 2015. LNBIP, vol. 225, pp. 100–112. Springer, Cham (2015). https://doi.org/10.1007/978-3-319-21545-7_9
5. Garijo, D., Corcho, O., Poveda-Villalón, M.: Foops!: an ontology pitfall scanner for the fair principles. In: Proceedings of the ISWC (2021)
6. Kovatsch, M., Matsukura, R., Lagally, M., Kawaguchi, T., Toumura, K., Kajimoto, K.: Web of things (wot) architecture. W3C Recommendation (2020)
7. Poveda-Villalón, M., Suárez-Figueroa, M.C., Gómez-Pérez, A.: Did you validate your ontology? OOPS! In: Simperl, E. (ed.) ESWC 2012. LNCS, vol. 7540, pp. 402–407. Springer, Heidelberg (2015). https://doi.org/10.1007/978-3-662-46641-4_35

8. Rasmussen, M.H., Lefrançois, M., Schneider, G.F., Pauwels, P.: Bot: the building topology ontology of the w3c linked building data group. Semantic Web (2021)
9. Käbisch, S., Kamiya, T., McCool, M., Charpenay, V., Kovatsch, M.: Web of things (wot) thing description. W3C Recommendation (2020)
10. Suárez-Figueroa, M.C., Gómez-Pérez, A., Fernández-López, M.: The NeOn methodology for ontology engineering. In: Suárez-Figueroa, M.C., Gómez-Pérez, A., Motta, E., Gangemi, A. (eds.) Ontology Engineering in a Networked World, pp. 9–34. Springer, Heidelberg (2012). https://doi.org/10.1007/978-3-642-24794-1_2

WeKG-MF: A Knowledge Graph of Observational Weather Data

Nadia Yacoubi Ayadi$^{(\boxtimes)}$ ⓘ, Catherine Faronⓘ, Franck Michelⓘ,
Fabien Gandonⓘ, and Olivier Corbyⓘ

University Côte d'Azur, Inria, CNRS, I3S (UMR 7271), Sophia-Antipolis, France
{nadia.yacoubi-ayadi,fabien.gandon,olivier.corby}@inria.fr,
{faron,fmichel}@i3s.unice.fr

Abstract. In this paper, we present the WeKG-MF Knowledge Graph
constructed from open weather observations published by Météo-France
institution. WeKG-MF relies on a semantic model that formalizes knowledge about meteorological observational data. The model is generic
enough to be adopted and extended by meteorological data providers
to publish and integrate their sources while complying with Linked Data
principles. WeKG-MF offers access to a large number of meteorological
variables described through spatial and temporal dimensions and thus
has the potential to serve several scientific case studies from different
domains including agriculture, agronomy, environment, climate change
and natural disasters.

Keywords: Knowledge graph · Semantic modelling · Observational
data · Linked data · Meteorology

1 Introduction

Meteorological data are crucial for many application domains. They typically
include measurements of several weather parameters such as wind direction and
speed, air pressure, rainfall, humidity and temperature. However, these data are
most commonly collected and stored separately in different files using a tabular
data format that lacks explicit semantics, which impedes their integration and
sharing to serve researchers from different domains such as agriculture, climate
change studies or natural disaster monitoring. A typical approach in integrating
and publishing such data is to formalize a knowledge graph relying on linked
data and semantic Web standard models and practices. To deal with the complexity of the knowledge domain to be modelled, we adopted the SAMOD agile
methodology [6]. The SAMOD process is initiated by a motivating scenario that
leads to a set of competency questions that, in turn, provide requirements on
the knowledge graph model. As output, we designed a semantic model in which
meteorological variables are semantically defined and described at a fine grained
level, including aspects of time, location, units of measurement, etc. The WeKG-
MF knowledge graph, constructed from open weather observations published by

Météo-France, is compliant with the proposed semantic model. The first release of the WeKG-MF includes weather observations from January 2019 till December 2021. The paper is structured as follows. Section 2 presents an overview of WeKG semantic model and highlights its design principles. Section 3 presents the RDF-based knowledge graph WeKG-MF constructed from weather data archives of Météo-France and illustrates how it serves use cases identified in the context of the D2KAB French research project[1].

2   Semantic Model for Weather Data

In order to propose a self-contained model for representing and publishing meteorological data, we extend the SOSA/SSN [3,4] ontologies with three new classes. First, `weo:MeterologicalObservation` is the core class of our model; it supports the description of a single, atomic observation that is related to a particular feature of interest, instance of the `weo:MeteorologicalFeature` class, and an observable property, instance of class `weo:WeatherProperty`. These three classes specialize classes from the SOSA/SSN ontologies [3,4] as reflected by their formal definitions. These definitions express that only one weather property and one meteorological feature is used for a given meteorological observation:

$$
\begin{aligned}
weo: MeteorologicalFeature \quad \equiv \quad & sosa: FeatureOfInterest \ \cap \\
& \forall ssn: hasProperty.weo: WeatherProperty \ \cap \\
& \geq 1ssn: hasProperty.weo: WeatherProperty
\end{aligned}
$$

$$
\begin{aligned}
weo: WeatherProperty \quad \equiv \quad & sosa: ObservableProperty \ \cap \\
& \forall ssn: isPropertyOf.weo: MeteorologicalFeature \ \cap \\
& \geq 1ssn: isPropertyOf.weo: MeteorologicalFeature
\end{aligned}
$$

$$
\begin{aligned}
weo: MeteorologicalObservation \ \equiv \quad & sosa: Observation \ \cap \\
& \forall sosa: observedProperty.weo: WeatherProperty \ \cap \\
& = 1sosa: observedProperty \ \cap \\
& \forall sosa: hasFeatureOfInterest.weo: MeteorologicalFeature \ \cap \\
& = 1sosa: hasFeatureOfInterest
\end{aligned}
$$

We reused the Value Sets[2] (VP) ontology design pattern and, because we can enumerate the values, this led us to define a SKOS vocabulary whose concepts are instances of `weo:WeatherProperty` or `weo:MeteorologicalFeature` and represent the possible values of observable properties and features of interest. Inline with Linked Data best practices, we aligned the weather properties of our SKOS vocabulary with terms from the NERC Climate and Forecast Standard Names

---

[1] http://www.d2kab.org.
[2] https://www.w3.org/TR/swbp-specified-values/.

vocabulary[3]. To avoid redundancies of measurements units among observations, we define for each SKOS weather property an applicable unit re-using QUDT Unit vocabulary[4]. Thus, observation results are modelled as literals and an observation is linked to its result by RDF property `sosa:hasSimpleResult`. Finally, since observable properties of our vocabulary are also defined as instances of the `qudt:QuantityKind` class, we aligned them with terms from the QUDT Quantity Kind vocabulary. Figure 1 presents an RDF graph of a meteorological observation relative to the wind feature of interest and reporting the average wind speed observable property.

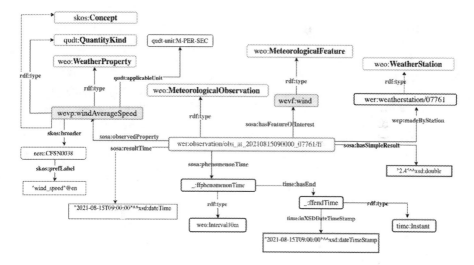

Fig. 1. Example of a meteorological observation reporting the wind speed average property

Our semantic model deals with both temporal and spatial dimensions of meteorological observations. Along temporal dimension, the model captures the instant or interval at/during which the weather parameter is measured. Since duration of time intervals are described in the official documentation of the World Meteorological Organization (WMO)[5], we defined different time interval classes, based on the `time:Interval` class [2], by expressing OWL restrictions on their duration that may be declared in seconds, minutes or hours. The interest of doing this is that these time intervals are declared once in our semantic model and are reused for all observations, and thus avoid substantial redundancy. In Fig. 1, the `wevp:windAverageSpeed` weather property is measured during a period of 10 min. This is denoted by `sosa:phenomenonTime` property whose value is an instance of `weo:Interval10m` class, while the end time of the interval is an instance of class `time:Instant`.

---

[3] http://vocab.nerc.ac.uk/collection/P07/.
[4] http://qudt.org/vocab/quantitykind/.
[5] https://public.wmo.int/en/.

Meteorological observations are provided by weather stations which spatial information, such as longitude, latitude and altitude. We introduce the `weo:WeatherStation` class as a subclass of the `geosparql:Feature` class and `sosa:Platform`. According to GeoSPARQL vocabulary [1], each instance of `weo:WeatherStation` has a geometry with specific coordinates which enables us to query weather observations based on spatial information. The OWL version of our semantic model as well as the related SKOS vocabularies are available in our Github repository[6]. The prefixes of ontologies and vocabularies reused or introduced in this paper are listed in the repository's README[7].

3 WeKG-MF: Weather Knowledge Graph - Météo-France

We constructed the *WeKG-MF* knowledge graph according to the model presented in Sect. 2 from open weather observations published by Météo-France[8]. We first downloaded from Météo-France's portal the list of SYNOP weather stations in GeoJSON format, as well as the monthly observation reports generated by these stations as CSV files. Then, we implemented a reproducible pipeline to generate WeKG-MF in compliance with the proposed semantic model where the mapping is performed by the Morph-xR2RML tool [5]. The first version of WeKG-MF covers the period from January 2019 to the end of December 2021. Key statistics of the dataset are presented in Table 1.

Table 1. Key statistics of the WeKG-MF dataset

Category	
Downloadable RDF dump	https://doi.org/10.5281/zenodo.5925413
Total Nr. of triples	62.306.102
Nr. of Observations	8.335.258
Nr. of weather stations	62
Nr. of weather properties	22
Nr. of meteorological features	6
Nr. of Observations per weather property	≈416.762
Nr. of links to Wikidata	92

To illustrate how observations in the WeKG-MF can be queried and aggregated, we first developed a set of SPARQL queries available on the Github repository of the project[9]. Beyond this, we initially started this work to address

---

[6] https://github.com/Wimmics/d2kab/tree/main/meteo/ontology.

[7] https://github.com/Wimmics/d2kab/tree/main/meteo.

[8] https://www.meteofrance.com/.

[9] https://github.com/Wimmics/d2kab/tree/main/meteo/sparql-examples.

the needs of the D2KAB French project whose primary objective is to create a framework to turn agronomy and biodiversity data into semantically described, interoperable, actionable, and open knowledge. A preliminary needs analysis pointed to competency questions that potential users may want to get answers. We only present some of them due to space constraints. Experts in agronomy investigate the correlations between the development rate of plants and weather parameters. They are especially interested in comparing aggregated values of a weather parameter for the same period of time in the same geographic location across years, e.g. the Growing Daily Degrees (GDD) calculated from the daily average air temperature minus a certain threshold called base temperature.

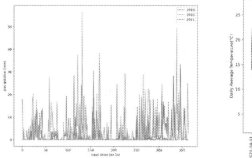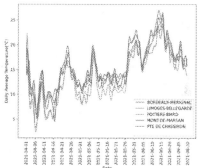

Fig. 2. Examples of visualisation of daily precipitations and average temperature

We developed, together with the set of SPARQL queries, a Jupyter Notebook that demonstrate how the results of queries can be used to generate visualizations from the WeKG-MF knowledge graph. As an example, Fig. 2 presents two plots. The first one shows daily cumulative precipitations measured at the '*Bordeaux-Merignac*' station and the second one shows the evolution of daily average temperature collected from weather stations located in the French region of '*Nouvelle Aquitaine*'. Each plot shows a comparison of aggregated values calculated based on two weather parameters (precipitation and air temperatures) available in the WeKG-MF knowledge graph. Several use cases in agronomy can benefit from pre-calculated spatio-temporal slices of observations. For this, our model supports the definition of SPARQL CONSTRUCT queries with respect to a specific structure. Taking again the example of the GDD, we have defined SPARQL queries to construct a set of slices of daily min., max. and avg. temperatures for each weather station and for each year.

4   Conclusion and Future Work

In this paper, we presented WeKG-MF, a knowledge graph of weather observational data generated from Météo-France's open data archives. It is based on a reusable, formal model exploiting and extending a network of well-known ontologies. In terms of sustainability, we released a fully automatic pipeline that enables anyone to generate and update the WeKG-MF graph over time with new data downloaded from Météo-France. In the short term, we will investigate identified use cases in the agronomy and agriculture domains in which our meteorological knowledge graph will be integrated with other knowledge sources in order to meet D2KAB project partners requirements.

References

1. Battle, R., Kolas, D.: Enabling the geospatial semantic web with parliament and GeoSPARQL. Semant. Web **3**(4), 355–370 (2012)
2. Cox, S., Little, C.: Time ontology in OWL (2020). https://www.w3.org/TR/owl-time/
3. Haller, A., et al.: The modular SSN ontology: a joint W3C and OGC standard specifying the semantics of sensors, observations, sampling, and actuation. Semant. Web **10**(1), 9–32 (2019)
4. Janowicz, K., Haller, A., Cox, S.J.D., Phuoc, D.L., Lefrançois, M.: SOSA: a lightweight ontology for sensors, observations, samples, and actuators. J. Web Semant. **56**, 1–10 (2019)
5. Michel, F., Djimenou, L., Faron-Zucker, C., Montagnat, J.: Translation of relational and non-relational databases into RDF with xR2RML. In: Proceedings of the WEBIST 2015 Conference, Lisbon, Portugal, pp. 443–454. SciTePress (2015)
6. Peroni, S.: SAMOD: an agile methodology for the development of ontologies. In: Dragoni, M., Poveda-Villalón, M., Jimenez-Ruiz, E. (eds.) OWL: Experiences and Directions - Reasoner Evaluation, pp. 55–69. Springer, Heidelberg (2016)

DAGOBAH UI: A New Hope
for Semantic Table Interpretation

Christophe Sarthou-Camy[1], Guillaume Jourdain[1], Yoan Chabot[1(✉)],
Pierre Monnin[1], Frédéric Deuzé[1], Viet-Phi Huynh[1], Jixiong Liu[1,2],
Thomas Labbé[1], and Raphael Troncy[2]

[1] Orange, Belfort, France
yoan.chabot@orange.com
[2] EURECOM, Sophia-Antipolis, Biot, France

Abstract. The past few years have seen a growing research interest in
Semantic Table Interpretation (STI), i.e. the task of annotating tables
with elements defined in knowledge graphs (KGs). These semantic annotations make use of entities and standardized types and relations and can,
in turn, support several downstream use cases for tabular data such as
dataset profiling and indexing, recommender systems, or dataset search.
In this paper, we introduce DAGOBAH UI, a user-friendly Web interface that enables to visualize, validate, and manipulate results of STI
methods such as the DAGOBAH API. Through an interactive demonstration on real world datasets, we illustrate how such a UI can ease the
adoption and mass usage of STI techniques by end-users. A video of the
demonstration is available at https://tinyurl.com/dagobah-ui-demo. An
access to the DAGOBAH API can also be requested at https://developer.
orange.com/apis/table-annotation (for logged in users).

Keywords: Semantic table interpretation · Table enrichment ·
Knowledge graph · DAGOBAH

1 Introduction

Large parts of available data either on the Web or in internal repositories
of companies are encoded in tabular formats (e.g. Excel or CSV files) or as
web tables [1]. Hence, there is a strong interest in understanding the semantics of such tables to pave the way for semantic-based services such as dataset
search/recommendation, or enrichment of heterogeneous tabular datasets [2].
This process is known as Semantic Table Interpretation (STI) and has seen
a growing research interest over the past few years, for example, through the
SemTab challenge [6]. The 2021 edition of the SemTab challenge has featured a
"Usability" track to foster research in user-friendly interfaces that will ease mass
adoption of STI techniques. In this line of research, we propose DAGOBAH UI, a
Web user interface that makes use of the RESTful API exposing the DAGOBAH
SL system [5] – the best performing system at the SemTab 2021 Challenge – and
the Wikidata KG [9].

© The Author(s), under exclusive license to Springer Nature Switzerland AG 2022
P. Groth et al. (Eds.): ESWC 2022 Satellite Events, LNCS 13384, pp. 107–111, 2022.
https://doi.org/10.1007/978-3-031-11609-4_20

2   Related Work

The closest tools to DAGOBAH UI are MantisTable [3] and the MTab interface [8]. MantisTable is a Web application that enables to import and manage tables as well as trigger specific annotation methods of the STI process. MTab is a Web interface that allows to upload a table and display the resulting semantic annotations provided by the MTab tool. An entity search functionality from a text input by the user is also provided. DAGOBAH UI offers additional functionalities such as the enrichment of tables with information from the knowledge graph, and conversely the enrichment of the knowledge graph with information from the tables. OpenRefine[1] is a powerful Web-based tool for cleaning, transforming, and extending tabular data with external data. The reconciliation functionalities are closed to the Cell-Entity Annotation task of the STI process and benefit now from a standardized protocol.[2] However, while a end-user has to manually instruct OpenRefine how to annotate specific columns via ad-hoc rules, the STI process is fully automatic in DAGOBAH UI.

3   System Description

DAGOBAH UI is a user-friendly Web interface that allows the manipulation, interpretation, and enrichment of relational tabular data. From a technical point of view, DAGOBAH is made of a NodeJS API using the Open API standard[3] and a frontend developed with VueJS and Boosted[4].

Tabular data files can be loaded in DAGOBAH UI from the local file system similarly to what OpenRefine and MantisTable [3] offer. In addition, DAGOBAH UI provides pre-loaded tabular data from the most commonly used benchmarks such as the SemTab datasets [6] and T2Dv2 [7].

3.1   Table Interpretation

DAGOBAH UI makes use of the RESTful API exposing DAGOBAH-SL [5], a system providing functionalities for table pre-processing and Semantic Table Interpretation. DAGOBAH-SL annotates tabular data with elements of KGs such as Wikidata or DBpedia. This system leverages *(i)* an Elasticsearch-based lookup service, and *(ii)* a disambiguation algorithm that relies on syntactic distances and comparisons between the context of an entity in the table and in the knowledge graph. This system was empirically evaluated during the three editions of the SemTab challenge [6] and has shown competitive performance with a 1st prize in the Accuracy track of the 2021 edition.

The preprocessing toolbox of DAGOBAH UI allows to clean a table (encoding problems, cell misalignment, etc.) as well as to extract information about the

---

[1] https://openrefine.org/.
[2] https://reconciliation-api.github.io/specs/latest/.
[3] https://www.openapis.org/.
[4] https://boosted.orange.com/.

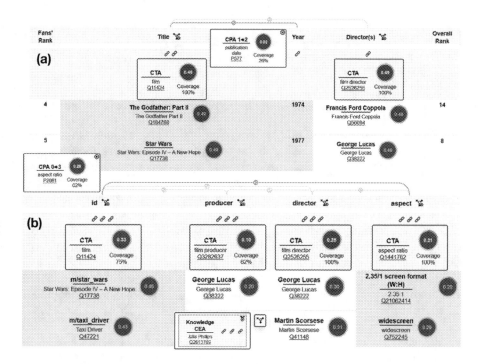

Fig. 1. DAGOBAH UI depicting the semantic annotations on the SemTab and Movie tables with the associated confidence scores.

table topology (orientation, header, etc.) which are crucial for the annotation process.

The user can then launch the semantic annotation process. The results of this process on Table *77694908_0_6083291340991074532.csv* (from SemTab 2019 dataset [4]) are presented in Fig. 1.a. Three tasks are carried out. Cell-Entity Annotation (CEA) aims at associating each cell of the table with an entity of the KG. In DAGOBAH UI, the CEA results are presented together with the original mentions. For example, "Star Wars" has been annotated with the Wikidata entity Q177738 (Star Wars: Episode IV - A New Hope). Column-Type Annotation (CTA) aims to map each column with an entity type. In the user interface, these annotations are presented in the upper part of the table (in the headers). In the example, the system has annotated the "Title" column with the entity Q11424 (film). Columns-Property Annotation (CPA) seeks to associate pairs of table columns with a property of the KG. The relationships found are symbolised by links at the top of the table. When the user clicks on a link, the associated Wikidata property is displayed. In the example, the relationship P577 (publication date) has been identified between the columns "Title" and "Year". Figure 1.b shows the annotation results for another Web table about movies generated partly from Wikidata. This example illustrates the power of the semantic elevation enabled by the annotation process. Indeed, the system found that "Star Wars" in the SemTab table and "m/star_wars" in the Movie table actually denote the same entity: Q177738 (Star Wars: Episode IV - A New Hope). This data reconciliation capability is particularly interesting for use cases involving heterogeneous datasets.

3.2 Table Enrichment with KGs

The life cycle of tabular data and the coverage of background knowledge represented in open or enterprise KGs can vary. This situation generates differences between tables published by organisations and open or enterprise KGs that are continuously curated: information is missing, dimensions are eluded since they are deemed useless by the data producer, etc. However, in many use cases (e.g. dataset search, profiling and recommendation), the completeness and richness of the data have positive effects and are desirable qualities. Once annotated, tables can be enriched with additional elements from the supporting KG. For example, missing values can be filled and new columns can be appended using the KG background knowledge. The enriched table can then be exported by the user for subsequent analysis. Figure 2 shows DAGOBAH UI modal window for selecting new columns to add to the Movie table. SPARQL queries are used to identify the most representative properties (e.g. cast member, cost, award received, etc.) of the entities in the column for which the user has requested suggestions (button next to the header). In the example, after selecting the P1476 (title) property, the user interface allows to preview the added values before confirming the operation.

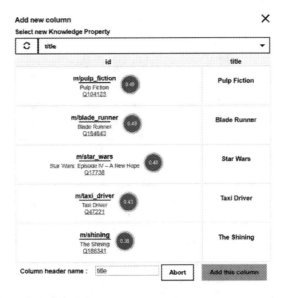

Fig. 2. Modal window for choosing new columns to add to the movie table.

4   Demonstration

The demonstration at the conference will showcase the annotation and enrichment features of DAGOBAH UI. This will be done on different scenarios and datasets from various sectors such as creative industries, news and sports, and the pharmaceutical domain. Attendees will be able to discover how DAGOBAH UI can automatically interpret a table via CEA, CTA and CPA tasks. Table enrichment features will also be presented to show how the tool can generate richer and more complete tables. We provide a demonstration video on YouTube at https://tinyurl.com/dagobah-ui-demo.

Our future work includes the development of new features around KG enrichment from tables. As discussed in this paper, tables can benefit from KGs through cell completion and table expansion with new columns. Conversely, tables are also a great source of dormant knowledge that can be leveraged to enrich open or enterprise KGs. To this aim, DAGOBAH UI will enable to export the annotations as RDF triples to refine KGs. Future work also includes the evaluation of DAGOBAH UI usability with real users. To this aim, the availability of DAGOBAH UI within the company will allow to collect interesting feedbacks to progress on the adoption of STI tools.

References

1. Chabot, Y., et al.: A framework for automatically interpreting tabular data at orange. In: ISWC Posters, Demos and Industry Tracks. CEUR Workshop Proceedings, vol. 2980 (2021)
2. Chapman, A., et al.: Dataset search: a survey. VLDB J. **29**(1), 251–272 (2019). https://doi.org/10.1007/s00778-019-00564-x
3. Cremaschi, M., Rula, A., Siano, A., De Paoli, F.: MantisTable: a tool for creating semantic annotations on tabular data. In: European Semantic Web Conference (ESWC), pp. 18–23 (2019)
4. Hassanzadeh, O., Efthymiou, V., Chen, J., Jiménez-Ruiz, E., Srinivas, K.: SemTab 2019: semantic web challenge on tabular data to knowledge graph matching data sets. Zenodo (2019). https://doi.org/10.5281/zenodo.3518539
5. Huynh, V.P., et al.: DAGOBAH: table and graph contexts for efficient semantic annotation of tabular data. In: SemTab 2021: Semantic Web Challenge on Tabular Data to Knowledge Graph Matching (2021)
6. Jiménez-Ruiz, E., Hassanzadeh, O., Efthymiou, V., Chen, J., Srinivas, K., Cutrona, V.: Results of semtab 2020. In: SemTab 2020: Semantic Web Challenge on Tabular Data to Knowledge Graph Matching, vol. 2775, pp. 1–8 (2020)
7. Lehmberg, O., Ritze, D., Meusel, R., Bizer, C.: A large public corpus of web tables containing time and context metadata. In: 25th International Conference Companion on World Wide Web (WWW Companion), pp. 75–76 (2016)
8. Nguyen, P., Yamada, I., Kertkeidkachorn, N., Ichise, R., Takeda, H.: SemTab 2021: tabular data annotation with MTab tool. In: SemTab 2021: Semantic Web Challenge on Tabular Data to Knowledge Graph Matching (2021)
9. Vrandecic, D., Krötzsch, M.: Wikidata: a free collaborative knowledgebase. Commun. ACM **57**(10), 78–85 (2014)

KartoGraphI: Drawing a Map of Linked Data

Pierre Maillot[(✉)][ID], Olivier Corby[ID], Catherine Faron[ID], Fabien Gandon[ID], and Franck Michel[ID]

University Cote d'Azur, Inria, CNRS, I3S, Nice, France
{Pierre.Maillot,Olivier.Corby,Catherine.Faron,Fabien.Gandon,
Franck.Michel}@inria.fr

Abstract. A large number of semantic Web knowledge bases have been developed and published on the Web. To help the user identify the knowledge bases relevant for a given problem, and estimate their usability, we propose a declarative indexing framework and an associated visualization Web application, KartoGraphI. It provides an overview of important characteristics for more than 400 knowledge bases including, for instance, dataset location, SPARQL compatibility level, shared vocabularies, etc.

1   Introduction

In recent years, a large number of semantic Web knowledge bases (KB) have been developed and published on the Web. The reuse and joint exploitation of multiple KBs requires them to comply with a number of good practices. To help the user identify a set of relevant and usable KB that answers her need, we propose the *KartoGraphI* Web application[1] that provides visualizations of certain characteristics of KBs. It relies on a (meta)dataset describing KBs available on the Web, automatically generated by the *IndeGx* framework by querying KBs with SPARQL.

This paper presents a demonstration of KartoGraphI together with an illustration of the main features of IndeGx. It is organized as follows: Sect. 2 presents the IndeGx framework and generated dataset. Section 3 presents the KartoGraphI Web application. Section 4 presents the proposed demonstration and concludes.

2   IndeGx: Description of Semantic Web KB

IndeGx is a framework designed to index public KBs that are available online through a SPARQL endpoint. The indexing process uses SPARQL queries to either extract the available metadata from a KB or to generate as much metadata as the endpoint allows it. The RDF data generated by IndeGx is expressed using a combination of well-established description vocabularies such

---

[1] KartoGraphI: http://prod-dekalog.inria.fr/.

P. Groth et al. (Eds.): ESWC 2022 Satellite Events, LNCS 13384, pp. 112–117, 2022.
https://doi.org/10.1007/978-3-031-11609-4_21

as SPARQL Service Description, VoID and DCAT. The generated metadata not only describes KBs but also conveys an estimation of certain quality criteria. These metadata can be used either by humans e.g. to select suitable sources, or agents to automate processes such as query optimization or rewriting.

IndeGx processes publicly available KBs whose endpoints are listed on the LOD Cloud, Wikidata, SPARQLES [3], Yummy Data [4] and Linked Wiki. At the time of writing, IndeGx has processed and indexed 553 KBs. The generation of a KB description depends on the capabilities of its endpoint. In particular, complex queries, such as those using counting and string-based operators on large quantities of triples or disjunctions, may fail due to the limits in time and resources of the endpoint.

IndeGx can be extended with new KB description features as long as they can be extracted with SPARQL queries. Those new features will be used in future indexations. The operations made by IndeGx to extract metadata are described in RDF in a GitHub repository using the EARL and the Manifest vocabularies. This structure makes it possible to add operations used in other similar approaches. IndeGx already uses the operations described in the approaches SPORTAL [2] and SPARQLES.

Asserted Dataset Descriptions. Provenance information concerns, among others, a dataset's authors, contributors, editors, license, source datasets, generation method, date of creation and modification. Those provenance metadata are important for transparency of and trust in the KB. They are generally asserted by the KB creators as part of a VoID description, but are difficult to discover when they are not given. IndeGx extracts the available provenance information of a KB by looking in its dataset for metadata descriptions made using VoID, DCAT or SPARQL-SD vocabularies. We separate the most basic provenance metadata into 4 categories: the authorship, the licensing, the time, and the source. The results show that less than 1% of KBs with a public SPARQL endpoint contain such metadata.

Endpoint Capabilities. The content of a KB is only as reachable as its endpoint is available. Approaches such as SPARQLES [3] estimate the performance of SPARQL endpoints using SPARQL queries. IndeGx reuses SPARQLES queries and extends them to survey the implementation of the features of the SPARQL language by endpoints.

Data Quality Measures. Several criteria have been identified as indicators of the quality of a KBs, such as those listed in [1,4]. IndeGx evaluates KBs according to several of those quality criteria using SPARQL queries.

Traceability of the Indexing Process. IndeGx generates traceability metadata for every operation done on every dataset. The metadata contain information such as the start and end time of each operation, the query submitted and the error returned if it so happens. The generated traces support the study of the average performance of endpoints and of the responses of each endpoint to determine some of their characteristics.

3   KartoGraphI: Drawing a Map from Semantic Web KBs

KartoGraphI is a Web application visualizing the data generated by IndeGx. It draws various visualizations and statistics grouped along several view points described below.

Used/Shared Vocabularies. The (re)use of well-known vocabularies in a dataset facilitates its re-usability by others and is one of the core principles of Linked Data. IndeGx extracts the list of vocabularies from the namespaces of classes and properties a dataset uses.

KartoGraphI first generates a visualization of the endpoints linked to all the vocabularies, including the vocabularies used by no other KB (Fig. 1). Secondly, a refined version of this visualization focuses on well-known vocabularies by showing only a subset of 3487 namespaces extracted from Linked Open Vocabularies (LOV) and prefix.cc. A major advantage of this refined visualization is to filter out any unknown vocabulary that may result of a typographical error or the non-respect of naming conventions. However, it can also filter out new or very specialized vocabularies that are not listed on those sites.

KartoGraphI also offers a third visualization that connects the endpoints to the keywords associated to their well known vocabularies. This association of endpoints and keywords can be used to identify the domains a KB pertains to.

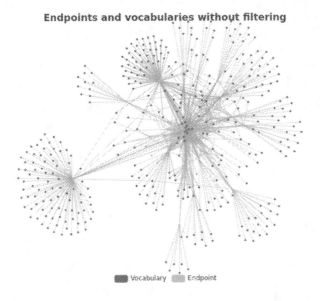

Fig. 1. Graph of the endpoints listed on LOD Cloud website and their vocabularies. The vocabularies are extracted by IndeGx from the namespaces of classes and properties of the datasets.

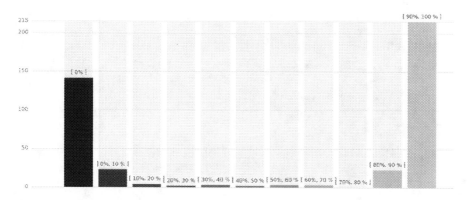

Fig. 2. Bar chart of the distribution of the endpoints according to their coverage of SPARQL features.

Dataset Population. VoID allows to give statistics about the triples and instances present in a dataset. Such metadata give an idea of the scale of a dataset and the most advanced statistics can be used to optimize queries. After trying to retrieve such information from the metadata given in a KB, IndeGx uses SPARQL queries to update the retrieved metadata and as much as possible extract all the possible statistics that can be expressed with VoID. They include statistics such as the number of triples using a certain property with an instance of a certain class as an object. Such statistics are extracted using CPU- and/or memory-intensive queries that only endpoints backed by large hardware resources can answer.

Endpoint Capabilities. The results displayed by KartoGraphI (Fig. 2), show that two-thirds of the endpoints tested by IndeGx support at least 80% of all tested SPARQL features. The endpoints from the remaining third either returned errors or did not answer any SPARQL query.

Data Quality Measures. The quality of the data of a KB can be measured according to different criteria. Among them, one of the structural quality measures depends on the respect of community best practices such as avoiding the usage of blank nodes and RDF data structures such as lists, sequences, and bags. It is to be noted that vocabularies such as OWL and SHACL use blank nodes and data structures to define vocabularies. Due to that, this measure may not be adapted as it is for datasets such as ontology repositories. This kind of criteria appears to be well complied with among the KBs processed. The proportion of resources that are not blank nodes in a dataset is close to 100%. The proportion of triples that are not part of the definition of RDF data structures is 76.2%. Other quality measures include the interlinking of a KB with others, through the use of shared vocabularies. They also include the readability of the KB by humans, based on the presence of labels and short readable URIs. The interlinking of KBs is generally good among the KBs processed, with on average 75% of the vocabularies used in a KB being listed on vocabulary portals. On the other

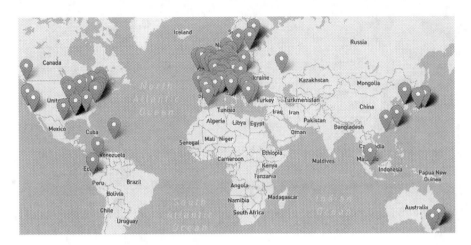

Fig. 3. Geolocation of the endpoints in KartoGraphI: green items represent an endpoints' IP locations; orange items represent endpoints that gave a timezone not matching this location. (Color figure online)

side, the readability of KBs is not good in general according to our measures: an average 42% of the resources have no label, and an average 49% of them do not have short URIs.

Geolocation. The geolocation of endpoints is often overlooked as metadata of a KB. Using only SPARQL queries, IndeGx could only get endpoint timezones as an indicator of their location. To work around this lack, KartoGraphI uses external APIs to determine the location of endpoints from their URL. The resulting map, shown in Fig. 3, illustrates that, although the Linked Data is an international effort, it is over-represented in Europe whereas there is an "empty diagonal" from South-West to North-East, containing no publicly available KBs. It is however possible that KBs hosted by countries in this zone be listed in resources currently not considered by IndeGx.

4   Proposed Demonstration

The demo will be as follow: Attendees will be guided through the different visualizations of the KartoGraphI Web application. A commentary of the notable features observed in the KBs descriptions created by IndeGx from publicly accessible endpoints will be given, as shown in the video available at http://prod-dekalog.inria.fr/SubmissionESWC2022.

KartoGraphI and IndeGx offer a systematic evaluation of sets of publicly available endpoints based on SPARQL. They show that among the KBs with an endpoint listed as publicly available, one third of them are not reachable. The remaining two thirds are usable thanks to their reuse of common vocabularies. By contrast, the readability of their content is not high on average, very few contain self-descriptions. Their resources are in majority not labeled to describe their content to humans.

In future works, KartoGraphI and IndeGx will extract and present new features present in KBs such as the language tag present. In the future, KartoGraphI will also offer a query editor using IndeGx metadata to guide federated query writing using IndeGx metadata.

Acknowledgments. This work is supported by the ANR DeKaloG project, ANR-19-CE23-0014, and the ANR D2KAB project, ANR-18-CE23-0017.

References

1. Debattista, J., Lange, C., Auer, S., Cortis, D.: Evaluating the quality of the LOD cloud: an empirical investigation. Semant. Web **9**(6), 859–901 (2018)
2. Hasnain, A., Mehmood, Q., Zainab, S.S.E., Hogan, A.: SPORTAL: profiling the content of public SPARQL endpoints. Int. J. Semant. Web Inf. Syst. (IJSWIS) 134–163 (2016). https://doi.org/10.4018/IJSWIS.2016070105
3. Vandenbussche, P.Y., Umbrich, J., Matteis, L., Hogan, A., Buil-Aranda, C.: SPARQLES: monitoring public SPARQL endpoints. Semant. Web **8**(6), 1049–1065 (2017). https://doi.org/10.3233/SW-170254
4. Yamamoto, Y., Yamaguchi, A., Splendiani, A.: YummyData: providing high-quality open life science data. Database J. Biol. Databases Curation **2018** (2018)

WikidataComplete – An Easy-to-Use Method for Rapid Validation of Text-Extracted New Facts Applied to the Wikidata Knowledge Graph

Kunpeng Guo[1,2]([⊠]) [ID], Dhairya Khanna[3] [ID], Dennis Diefenbach[1,2] [ID],
Aleksandr Perevalov[4,5] [ID], and Andreas Both[5,6] [ID]

[1] The QA Company, Saint-Etienne, France
`kunpeng.guo@univ-st-etienne.fr`
[2] Laboratoire Hubert Curien, UMR CNRS 5516, Lyon, France
[3] Maharaja Agrasen Institute of Technology, New Delhi, India
[4] Anhalt University of Applied Sciences, Köthen, Germany
[5] Leipzig University of Applied Sciences, Leipzig, Germany
[6] DATEV eG, Nuremberg, Germany

Abstract. Wikidata is one of the most used knowledge graphs (KG) and it plays a vital role in the Semantic Web community. Many industries have integrated Wikidata into solutions dedicated to intelligent assistance, information retrieval, or knowledge integration. As one of the biggest KGs, Wikidata receives millions of edits every year. However, it is still far from complete. Generally, a natural workflow to ingest a new fact into Wikidata starts by searching the relative information in a free-text document collection (e.g., Wikipedia articles). This information is used to create a new fact (or update a fact) on Wikidata. The entire process is labor-intensive. In this paper, we present WikidataComplete, a plugin that facilitates Wikidata editors to contribute to the completion of the Wikidata KG. For the implementation of WikidataComplete, we integrated the latest question-answering (QA) technologies in order to extract the new facts. We embed our fact-ingestion workflow directly on the Wikidata entity page to make the insertion of facts smooth and efficient. Ultimately, WikidataComplete can be a handy tool for Wikidata contributors, and it has the potential to complete millions of missing facts in the Wikidata KG.

Keywords: WikidataComplete · Wikidata · Knowledge graph completion · Question answering

1 Introduction

WikidataComplete tackles the task of *Knowledge Graph Completion* (KGC) which aims at adding missing relation for existing entities in a KG [5]. The

P. Groth et al. (Eds.): ESWC 2022 Satellite Events, LNCS 13384, pp. 118–122, 2022.
https://doi.org/10.1007/978-3-031-11609-4_22

task is particularly an important issue for community-based KGs such as Wikidata[1]. Despite the Wikidata KG receiving millions of edits each year[2] it is far from complete. For instance, for the newspaper entities, Wikidata only lists the property *place of publication*[3] for 40% of them. There are two main paradigms to solve the task of KGC: (1) link prediction-based, which predicts missing relation based on the current graph structure [2]; (2) machine reading-comprehension technique that can leverage missing relations from free texts [3].

In this work, we present *WikidataComplete*, a Wikidata plugin that facilitates the process of fulfilling the missing facts in the Wikidata KG. The plugin follows the second paradigm to perform the KGC task. It includes a fact-verification step to have a human in the loop to guarantee the inserted fact is valid. Besides, the new ingested fact is accompanied automatically by evidence from where it was extracted, which is increasing the providence data quality too. Therefore, the new facts inserted by WikidataComplete into Wikidata KG will be both accurate and self-explanatory.

2 Demo

Finding and ingesting a new fact into Wikidata is a relatively labor-intensive process. For example, let us consider "Canaan", a "Japanese anime television series" (Wikidata URI: https://www.wikidata.org/wiki/Q10319021). By exploring the entity on Wikidata, it is not immediately clear if it is complete or not. Only after a more careful analysis (e.g., using the Recoin Plugin[4] [1]) one can detect that the property "director" (P57) is missing. A Wikidata editor who wants to improve the KG needs to find a source that contains this missing fact. One natural choice is to go to the Wikipedia and to check if the missing information is available in the text of an article. By reading the corresponding Wikipedia article, one will identify the following paragraph "The series was animated by the animation studio P.A. Works, *directed by Masahiro Andō*, who previously directed ....". In the next step, the editor can start completing the missing fact. Identifying the property (director) is not problematic. since this was its original intention. On the other hand, identifying the object entity by its label can be difficult if it is ambiguous. This is the case for the label *Masahiro Andō* which could correspond to the following URIs Q9128134 (anime director), Q11451348 (Japanese animator) or Q1982546 (Japanese association football player). After having correctly disambiguated the object entity, the editor can finally insert the identified statement and improve the completeness of the Wikidata Knowledge Graph.

WikidataComplete automatically addresses this workflow. While exploring Wikidata entities, editors will be directly be pointed to incomplete ones and new facts are ready to be reviewed. For the example, WikidataComplete directly

---

[1] https://www.wikidata.org/.

[2] https://www.wikidata.org/wiki/Wikidata:Statistics.

[3] https://www.wikidata.org/wiki/Property:P291.

[4] https://www.wikidata.org/wiki/Wikidata:Recoin.

Fig. 1. Screenshot of WikidataComplete showing a new fact for "Canaan"

proposes the fact depicted in Fig. 1. One can see that it has identified that the entity is incomplete concerning to a certain relation. Thereafter, it identifies a text segment in Wikipedia containing the relevant information (see "evidence" statement), provides a disambiguated entity, and asks the editor only for publishing or rejection. To allow the editor to judge the fact, a source and evidence are provided. The source redirects the user to the Wikipedia page containing the answer in highlighted text. In case of approval, both are inserted into the graph. This enables other editors to better trace back where the knowledge is coming from.

The code with instructions to activate the plugin can be found on GitHub.

3   Process

The workflow of WikidataComplete contains three main modules: *(1)* Incomplete Triplet Curation, *(2)* Dedicated Relation Extraction, *(3)* Target Entity Linking.

Incomplete Triplet Curation: A triple in a KG is composed of three main elements: Subject Entity, Property, and Object Entity. A triple is incomplete if for one subject entity (e.g., "Canaan (Japanese anime television series)"), the property "director" is missing from the Wikidata KG. WikidataComplete collects the missing triples via the process consisting of 3 steps:

- *Fix a class*: The plugin first fixes a class (i.e., *"anime television series"*) and collect the subject entities that match to it.
- *Find Most Frequent Properties*: The plugin analyzes the subject entities that belong to the *fixed* class to get the most frequent properties that exist among all of them. The plugin tries to complete the entities of this class with respect to these properties.
- *Resource Availability Verification*: The plugin fixes the class and the property and conducts a collection of missing triplets *(Subject - Property - ?)*. Before moving forward to *(2) relation extraction*, the triplets are filtered out if the subject does not have a corresponding Wikipedia page.

Dedicated Relation Extraction: This module first receives a collection of missing triplets. The problem of finding the missing object entity is solved with the task of question answering (QA) over free-text. The QA task takes a question and a paragraph and tries to identify in the paragraph the corresponding answer. The plugin downloads the Wikipedia article of the subject entity and treats it as our target passage. Then it constructs the questions by putting together the subject entity label and property entity label (e.g., *"Canaan director?"*). The QA model will indicate a set of candidates in the form of text spans for the object entity.

Object Entity Linking: The output of the *(2) Relation Extraction* module is a list of candidates for the object entity in the textual span format. For the fact ingestion, we need to link the spans to their corresponding entity in the Wikidata KG. This is achieved by a pre-trained KG linker model [4]. This module can help to filter out unreasonable answer choices made by the *(2) Relation Extraction* module.

Finally, the new triples together with snippets (pieces of evidence) from where they were extracted are obtained. This is presented in the UI of WikidataComplete as in Fig. 1 for user approval or rejection.

4   Conclusion

In this paper, we introduced WikidataComplete, a Wikibase plugin that integrates Question-Answering technologies and human-in-loop verification strategy to help complete the Wikidata Knowledge Graph. The proposed workflow has the potential to add millions of missing facts in the Wikidata KG by extracting them from textual resources and reducing the required time investments for the Wikidata editors. We plan in the future to generalize our approach to other sources than Wikipedia, to increase its precision, and to apply it to other domains.

This work was partially funded by the Google Summer of Code program 2021.

References

1. Balaraman, V., Razniewski, S., Nutt, W.: Recoin: relative completeness in Wikidata. In: Companion Proceedings of the The Web Conference 2018, pp. 1787–1792 (2018)
2. Chen, Z., Wang, Y., Zhao, B., Cheng, J., Zhao, X., Duan, Z.: Knowledge graph completion: a review. IEEE Access **8**, 192435–192456 (2020)
3. Han, X., Liu, Z., Sun, M.: Joint representation learning of text and knowledge for knowledge graph completion. arXiv preprint arXiv:1611.04125 (2016)
4. Kratzwald, B., Kunpeng, G., Feuerriegel, S., Diefenbach, D.: IntKB: a verifiable interactive framework for knowledge base completion. In: Proceedings of the 28th International Conference on Computational Linguistics, pp. 5591–5603. International Committee on Computational Linguistics, Barcelona, Spain (Online), December 2020
5. Lin, Y., Liu, Z., Sun, M., Liu, Y., Zhu, X.: Learning entity and relation embeddings for knowledge graph completion. In: Twenty-ninth AAAI conference on artificial intelligence (2015)

Query-Based Industrial Analytics over Knowledge Graphs with Ontology Reshaping

Zhuoxun Zheng[1,2(✉)], Baifan Zhou[3], Dongzhuoran Zhou[1,3], Gong Cheng[4], Ernesto Jiménez-Ruiz[3,5], Ahmet Soylu[2], and Evgeny Kharlamov[1,3]

[1] Bosch Center for Artificial Intelligence, Renningen, Germany
zhengzx712@gmail.com
[2] Department of Computer Science, Oslo Metropolitan University, Oslo, Norway
[3] SIRIUS Centre, University of Oslo, Oslo, Norway
[4] State Key Laboratory for Novel Software Technology, Nanjing University,
Nanjing, China
[5] Department of Computer Science, City, University of London, London, UK

Abstract. Industrial analytics that includes among others equipment diagnosis and anomaly detection heavily relies on integration of heterogeneous production data. Knowledge Graphs (KGs) as the data format and ontologies as the unified data schemata are a prominent solution that offers high quality data integration and a convenient and standardised way to exchange data and to layer analytical applications over it. However, poor design of ontologies of high degree of mismatch between them and industrial data naturally lead to KGs of low quality that impede the adoption and scalability of industrial analytics. Indeed, such KGs substantially increase the training time of writing queries for users, consume high volume of storage for redundant information, and are hard to maintain and update. To address this problem we propose an ontology reshaping approach to transform ontologies into KG schemata that better reflect the underlying data and thus help to construct better KGs. In this poster we present a preliminary discussion of our on-going research, evaluate our approach with a rich set of SPARQL queries on real-world industry data at Bosch and discuss our findings.

1 Introduction

Industrial analytics includes among others equipment diagnosis and anomaly detection [1]. It helps to reduce the downtime of manufacturing equipment, resource consumption, error rates, etc. and aims at enhancing the overall production value-chain which is one of the key goals of Industry 4.0 [2,3]. Industrial analytics heavily relies on integration of heterogeneous production data. Knowledge Graphs (KGs) as the data format for integration and ontologies as the unified data schemata are a prominent solution that offers not only a high quality data integration [4] but also a convenient and standardised way to exchange data and to layer analytical applications over it [5,6].

However, poor design of ontologies or high degree of mismatch between them and industrial data, e.g., when the ontology is designed to reflect the general domain of

P. Groth et al. (Eds.): ESWC 2022 Satellite Events, LNCS 13384, pp. 123–128, 2022.
https://doi.org/10.1007/978-3-031-11609-4_23

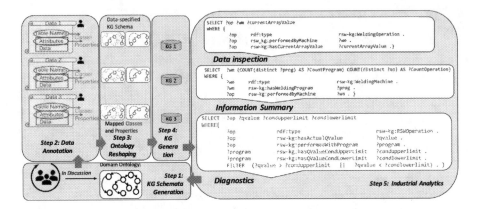

Fig. 1. Our workflow of enhancing industrial analytics with ontology reshaping ($\mathcal{OR}$)

knowledge or exported, rather than data particularities [7] naturally lead to KGs of low quality that impede the adoption and scalability of industrial analytics. Indeed, such KGs often have deep structure or have many blank nodes thus they are sparse and consume a high volume of storage for redundant information, and are hard to maintain and update. Moreover, accessing such data requires long and cumbersome SPARQL queries that are counterintuitive and this substantially increases the training time of users such as engineers [8] in writing such queries.

In order to address this problem, we propose an ontology reshaping approach to transform ontologies into KG schemata that better reflect the given underlying industrial data and thus help to construct better KGs. In this poster, we present a preliminary discussion of our on-going research, evaluate our approach with a rich set of SPARQL queries on real-world industry data at Bosch and discuss the our findings.

2   Our Approach

We now describe our approach of enhancing KG generation with $\mathcal{OR}$ that consists of five steps and summarised in Fig. 1.

KG Schemata Generation (Step 1, left-bottom part of Fig. 1). In this step, we adopt the approach of generating KG schemata by extending domain ontologies from upper level ontologies [9,10]. The users, i.e. domain experts, participate heavily in ontology extension. They have intensive discussions and create good quality ontologies that reflect the general domain knowledge.

Data Annotation (Step 2, Fig. 1). In this step experts annotate heterogeneous industrial raw data with diverse formats and structures collected from production with unified terms in the domain ontology created in Step 1. Here we consider the raw data in the format of relational tables. The table names are mapped to classes in the ontology and attribute names to properties. In some complex cases, attribute names with endings like "ID" or "NAME" are elevated to classes according to users' inputs.

Ontology Reshaping (Step 3, Fig. 1). In this step our ontology reshaping algorithm $\mathcal{OR}$ takes a knowledge-oriented domain ontology, a raw dataset, a mapping between them, and some optional user heuristics as the input and outputs a data-oriented ontology, which serves as the KG schemata. The resulting ontology is a (compact) version of the original one and essentially consists of (1) all corresponding information (table names and attributes) from the raw data and (2) other essential connecting elements, which are partially from the original ontology and partially from users, to attain some optimality defined by user heuristics, efficiency, simplicity, etc. We adopt our $\mathcal{OR}$ algorithm [11]. In the nutshell $\mathcal{OR}$ firstly selects a subset of nodes and edges in the domain ontology [12], creating its sub-graph, which is a sparse sub-graph that consists of many disconnected small graph fragments; secondly, it extends the sub-graph to a KG schema with the help of two sources of information: (a) retaining other nodes and edges of the domain ontology to preserve part of its knowledge, (b) some optional information given by users (welding experts) that help to connect the fragments in the sub-graph.

KG Generation (Step 4, Fig. 1). In this step the KG schemata are populated in the ETL fashion with the actual data based on the annotated table names and attributes in the relational table to generate the KGs. The generated KGs are data-oriented and (often) more compact.

Industrial Analytics (Step 5, Fig. 1). In this step, we layer industrial analytics upon the generated KG. In this paper, we consider three types of SPARQL queries written by engineers or generated by users' keywords inputs. The queries account for retrieving or summarising specific information of interest from huge datasets that come from running production lines, and to perform basic diagnostics over them. The details follow in the next section. During the application, the user feedback is constantly collected and the workflow can go back to Step 1 and the whole process restarts. For example, after the application stage, users may realise they can scale the system to more tasks and thus go back to extend the domain ontology for more tasks.

Related Work. The most related work to ours are the one on ontology modularisation [13], summarisation [14,15], and summarisation forgetting. They focus on selecting subsets of ontologies, but they do not address the data particularity issue. We thus propose to rely on ontology reshaping ($\mathcal{OR}$), which transforms domain ontologies to its often compacter versions that reflect more data specificities. The resulting KGs will contain no blank-nodes and become less deep, and thus the queries will become less deep and more user-friendly.

3   Evaluation with Industrial Dataset

We now present evaluation of our approach with a real industrial dataset.

Data Description. The dataset D is collected from a German factory, in which reside production lines that consist of 27 welding machines of an impactful automated welding process widely applied in automotive industry: the resistance spot welding [16,17]. D contains a high number of welding operation records and a series of welding sensor measurements. These data account for 1000 welding operations, estimated to be related

Table 1. Our approach enhanced by ontology reshaping (Onto-Reshape) outperforms the baseline significantly in terms of query simplicity, avg.: average, max: maximum

Subset		Set 1	Set 2	Set 3	Set 4	Set 5	Set 6
Raw data	#Attributes	20	40	60	80	100	120
Baseline	Avg. query depth	4.2	4.4	4.3	4.3	4.2	4.3
	Max. query depth	5.0	5.0	5.0	5.0	5.0	5.0
Onto reshape	Avg. query depth	2.3	2.5	2.6	2.7	3.0	3.1
	Max. query depth	3.0	4.0	3.0	4.0	3.0	4.0

to 100 cars. In this work, we select a section of D for discussion, which contains 4.315 million records and 176 attributes. The knowledge-oriented domain ontology O is generated by welding experts and contains 206 classes, 203 object properties, and 191 datatype properties. The mapping maps all 176 attributes in D to classes in O.

Query Description. We consider SPARQL queries of three types as follows: *Type I: Data inspection*, where the experts need to inspect these data for generating a first handful of insights. The desired answer to such query is a listing of some attributes. An example see Step 5 in Fig. 1, which will return all arrays of currents with the corresponding operation-names and machine-IDs. *Type II: Information summary*, where the welding experts need to gain overview information of arbitrarily selected datasets, e.g. how many different programs does every welding machine perform (Step 5 in Fig. 1)? *Type III: Diagnostics*, where the welding experts need to perform various diagnostic tasks, such as detecting abnormal machines, operations, etc. Moreover, the users would also like to find the surroundings of the abnormalities, to figure out what happened near the abnormalities, so that they can better understand for root-causes. One example for this kind of queries would be: Where are the abnormal welding operations whose quality indicators exceed the conditional tolerance limit? (Step 5 in Fig. 1).

Experiment Design. To test our approach, we randomly sub-sample D to 6 sub-datasets (Set 1–6 in Table 1). Each set contains a subset of the attributes of D, reflecting different data complexity. The numbers of attributes in the subsets increase by twenty each time, from 20 to 120. We repeat the sub-sampling for each subset 10 times to decrease the randomness. We compare our approach with a *baseline* of KG generation without ontology reshaping, which is a naive approach to use the domain ontology directly as the KG schema. This work considers 729 queries and 324, 189, 216 queries for query Type I, II, III, respectively. The evaluation metrics are set as the average and maximal query depth, which characterises the number of edges to connect two nodes in the query graph via the shortest path (the query is essentially also a graph with variable nodes).

Results and Discussion. The results (Table 1) show that for retrieving the same answers, the queries are significantly simplified with our approach: the query depths are reduced by about 2 for both its average and maximum. This indicates the generated KG becomes more practical, because shorter queries are needed to get the same information. In addition, we also observe that the KGs after Onto-Reshape become more efficient and simpler: their generation becomes 7 to 8 times faster, the number of entities are reduced to 1/2 to 1/6 of the baseline, storage space to 2/3, and the number of blank nodes to zero.

4   Conclusion and Outlook

In this paper, we present our ongoing research of knowledge graph-based industrial query analytics at Bosch. We have preliminary results that show the benefit of our approach for industrial analytics. Our work falls into the big picture of KG-based industrial applications [18]. As future work we will investigate transforming queries across different KG schemata, and study more query properties.

Acknowledgements. The work was partially supported by the H2020 projects Dome 4.0 (Grant Agreement No. 953163), OntoCommons (Grant Agreement No. 958371), and DataCloud (Grant Agreement No. 101016835) and the SIRIUS Centre, Norwegian Research Council project number 237898.

References

1. ur Rehman, M.H., et al.: The role of big data analytics in industrial internet of things. Future Gener. Comput. Syst. **99**, 247–259 (2019)
2. Kagermann, H.: Change through digitization—value creation in the age of industry 4.0. In: Albach, H., Meffert, H., Pinkwart, A., Reichwald, R. (eds.) Management of Permanent Change, pp. 23–45. Springer, Wiesbaden (2015). https://doi.org/10.1007/978-3-658-05014-6_2
3. Zhou, B., Pychynski, T., Reischl, M., Mikut, R.: Comparison of machine learning approaches for time-series-based quality monitoring of resistance spot welding (RSW). Arch. Data Sci. Ser. A (First) **5**(1), 13 (2018)
4. Horrocks, I., Giese, M., Kharlamov, E., Waaler, A.: Using semantic technology to tame the data variety challenge. IEEE Internet Comput. **20**(6), 62–66 (2016)
5. Zhou, D., et al.: Enhancing knowledge graph generation with ontology reshaping - Bosch case. In: Groth, P., et al. (eds.) ESWC (Demos/Industry) 2022. LNCS, vol. 13384, pp. 299–302. Springer, Cham (2022)
6. Zou, X., A survey on application of knowledge graph. In: Journal of Physics: Conference Series, vol. 1487, p. 012016. IOP Publishing (2020)
7. Yahya, M., Towards generalized welding ontology in line with ISO and knowledge graph construction. In: Groth, P., et al. (eds.) ESWC (Posters & Demos) 2022. LNCS, vol. 13384, pp. 83–88. Springer, Cham (2022)
8. Soylu, A., et al.: OptiqueVQS: a visual query system over ontologies for industry. Seman. Web **9**(5), 627–660 (2018)
9. Zhou, B., et al.: SemML: facilitating development of ML models for condition monitoring with semantics. J. Web Seman. **71**, 100664 (2021)
10. Svetashova, Y., et al.: Ontology-enhanced machine learning: a BOSCH use case of welding quality monitoring. In: Pan, J.Z., et al. (eds.) ISWC 2020. LNCS, vol. 12507, pp. 531–550. Springer, Cham (2020). https://doi.org/10.1007/978-3-030-62466-8_33
11. Zhou, D., Zhou, B., Chen, J., Cheng, G., Kostylev, E.V., Kharlamov, E.: Towards ontology reshaping for KG generation with user-in-the-loop: applied to BOSCH welding. In: IJCKG (2021)

12. Svetashova, Y., Zhou, B., Schmid, S., Pychynski, T., Kharlamov, E.: SemML: reusable ML for condition monitoring in discrete manufacturing. In: ISWC (Demos/Industry), vol. 2721, pp. 213–218 (2020)
13. Doran, P., Ontology reuse via ontology modularisation. In: KnowledgeWeb PhD Symposium, vol. 2006. Citeseer (2006)
14. Zhang, X., Cheng, G., Qu, Y.: Ontology summarization based on RDF sentence graph. In: WWW 2007, pp. 707–716 (2007)
15. Pouriyeh, S., et al.: Ontology summarization: graph-based methods and beyond. Int. J. Semant. Comput. **13**(2), 259–283 (2019)
16. Zhou, B., Pychynski, T., Reischl, M., Kharlamov, E., Mikut, R.: Machine learning with domain knowledge for predictive quality monitoring in resistance spot welding. J. Intell. Manuf. **33**(4), 1139–1163 (2022). https://doi.org/10.1007/s10845-021-01892-y
17. Zhou, B., Zhou, D., Chen, J., Svetashova, Y., Cheng, G., Kharlamov, E.: Scaling usability of ML analytics with knowledge graphs: exemplified with a Bosch welding case. In: IJCKG, pp. 54–63. ACM (2021)
18. Zhou, B., et al.: The data value quest: a holistic semantic approach at Bosch. In: Groth, P., et al. (eds.) ESWC (Demos/Industry) 2022. LNCS, vol. 13384, pp. 287–290. Springer, Cham (2022)

Semantic Video Entity Linking

Tim Grams, Honglin Li, Bo Tong, Ali Shaban, and Tobias Weller[✉]

Data and Web Science Group, University of Mannheim, Mannheim, Germany
{tim.grams,honglin.li,bo.tong,ali.shaban,tobias.weller}@uni-mannheim.de

Abstract. Knowledge graphs are an established technology in the field of information retrieval and question answering. However, the focus is mostly on searching web pages and related documents and less on video formats, resulting in the fact that queries on videos for refining the search are often neglected. In this demo, we show a framework for recognizing faces in YouTube videos and linking them to the matching entities in DBpedia using the thumbnails available in DBpedia. By linking the videos from YouTube with the information from DBpedia, more complex search queries can be made possible. We will present both the frontend of the application, including the search, adding more YouTube videos and formulating complex queries, as well as the architecture and the libraries used in the application.

Keywords: Knowledge graph · Face recognition · Video annotation

1 Introduction

Knowledge graphs (KGs) allow to model information in a semi-structured way and are used especially in information retrieval and question answering. For years, knowledge graphs have been used to improve search queries in search engines, but mostly for web pages and related documents. Using knowledge graphs to optimize search queries about video files is rarely used. In video search engines, searches are commonly based on the title and description, available tags for the video, and meta information such as the video format type and the length of the clip. The content itself and valuable information from a knowledge graph are not taken into account to improve the search results. Yet this information is of considerable use and can significantly improve the search, as demonstrated in the past with text search engines. For example, a search query *Give me scenes showing female actors born before 1970 in California* could not be answered by current video search engines. In order to answer such a query, the content of the video has to be analyzed if this information is not available in the title and description and information stored in a knowledge graph such as DBpedia and Wikidata can be considered. As a further challenge, the title and description of the video does not have to match the actual content of the video, making the analysis of the content of the video essential. For answering search queries such as the one posed above, we propose to link the entities occurring in the

P. Groth et al. (Eds.): ESWC 2022 Satellite Events, LNCS 13384, pp. 129–132, 2022.
https://doi.org/10.1007/978-3-031-11609-4_24

video to the corresponding entities of a knowledge graph. Within this work, we have linked videos from the online video platform YouTube based on the people present in them to the matching entities of the DBpedia knowledge graph. We used state-of-the-art edge face-recognition techniques to link the faces recognized in the videos to the thumbnails provided by DBpedia. We used additional images obtained from search requests to increase the performance of the correct matching. The information about the entities presented in the video with the associated link to the matching entity in a knowledge graph is stored in an RDF graph, using existing standards such as Foaf [2] and Dublin Core [3], and is freely available. Using the information linked in this RDF graph, we can answer queries such as the one posed above, as well as more complex queries as the following within this demo:

– Give me scenes showing the founder of Apple
– Give me scenes showing the winner of the 2017 Grand Prix in Hungary
– Give me scenes showing female actors born before 1970 in California
– Give me videos in which the German chancellor of 2019 speaks together with Emmanuel Macron for at least 20 s

The remainder of the paper is structured as follows: In Sect. 2 we introduce the approach and analyze the performance of matching recognized persons in videos to entities of the knowledge graph. In Sect. 3 we describe what exactly is shown during the demo and specify the added value for the community. In Sect. 4 we summarize the demo and present an outlook for future work.

2   Multi-modal Entity Linking

First, thumbnails of entities of type person were extracted from DBpedia. Furthermore, to improve the performance of the recognition of persons in videos, additional images of the corresponding entities were automatically crawled using a Google search. In order to avoid noise and distortion, a maximum of three additional images were extracted from the Google search. The videos are broken down into frames. For a faster processing, a batch of frames at a time is considered. Multitask cascaded convolutional networks were used to extract five landmark key points for each face from the video frames. For improved matching of the DBpedia thumbnails with the later recognized faces from the videos it is important that the input to the face recognition model is always similar in terms of colors and pose. Since the DeepFace library [6] only performs rotations and no affine transformations, we implemented an own alignment function. Using Arcface [4] we created a 512 dimensional vector representing the face of a person. Afterwards, a k-nearest neighbor algorithm was trained with all of the thumbnails representations to find predictions for unknown faces. Experiments have shown that using an approximation of the classification algorithm provides a better balance between runtime and accuracy. Therefore we used the Non-Metric Space Library [1]. The achieved accuracy on the training benchmark of the Arcface representations of the thumbnails from DBpedia and three additional extracted images from Google with the videos from YouTube was 0.85. We used the l2 metric to measure the distance between the representations of the thumbnails and the representations of the detected faces from the videos. If the distance was less than 1.25, the video was linked to the entity.

We store the information about the linked videos in a Virtuoso knowledge graph. The basic structure builds on previous work on semantic description of videos [7]. Foaf [2], Dublin Core [3] and MPEG-7 [5] are used for annotation. Figure 1 shows the structure for storing the annotations using one video as an example. The upper half of the structure shows the video itself. It has a title and an identifier which points to the link on YouTube. A video can have multiple scenes with each having a start- and endtime and depicting entities.

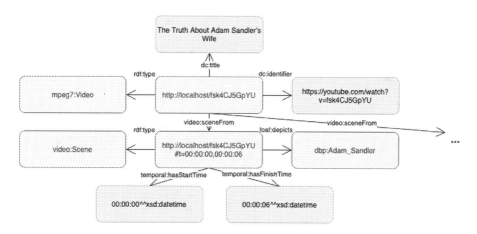

Fig. 1. Example of annotation and linking the recognized entity to DBpedia.

3   Demonstration

Within this demo we will show the application, which is available online[1], including its functionalities and architecture. Interested persons can use a text-based search function to enter names of persons and search for their associated videos, which are publicly available on YouTube. We will suggest examples of persons such as Barack Obama in the demonstration to assist the user in carrying out the demonstration of the application. A complete list of linked entities are available online[2]. The embedded videos from YouTube are annotated with the start and end time in which the entity occurs in the video and the entity linked to DBpedia. In addition to a text-based search, we will also demonstrate a complex search using a SPARQL query. Complex queries can be made and answered using the available information in DBpedia. For example, this can be used to

---

[1] http://westpoort.informatik.uni-mannheim.de/search.
[2] https://bit.ly/3Kfb2fp.

retrieve all videos featuring a Canadian actor who lives in Los Angeles. This search query shows the power and the possibilities which are made possible by this application. Along with search, we show how users can index new YouTube videos for our system, thus making them accessible for search. Furthermore, we show how the knowledge graph with the linked entities to the videos can be exported completely or filtered based on a search query using a Virtuoso Knowledge Graph[3]. The code of the demo is available online[4] so that the demo can be run on a local machine.

4   Conclusion and Future Work

In this demo, we show how faces in YouTube videos can be automatically linked to the matching entities from DBpedia to enable complex queries about videos. The information about the recognized entities in the videos is stored in a Virtuoso Knowledge Graph, whose endpoint is publicly available, so that the information can be queried and exported at any time. The source code of the demo is publicly available so that the entire process, including face recognition and link storage, can also be performed locally.

As future work, we aim to use this framework to create a large dataset of YouTube videos linked to DBpedia entities and make the produced data publicity available on the web. Besides, the change in accuracy between images of a person at a different age offers another research opportunity. Therefore, we would like to further refine face recognition by performing age-invariant face recognition to smooth out any outdated thumbnail images of entities in DBpedia.

References

1. Boytsov, L., Naidan, B.: Engineering efficient and effective non-metric space library. In: Brisaboa, N., Pedreira, O., Zezula, P. (eds.) SISAP 2013. LNCS, vol. 8199, pp. 280–293. Springer, Heidelberg (2013). https://doi.org/10.1007/978-3-642-41062-8_28
2. Brickley, D., Miller, L.: FOAF Vocabulary Specification. Namespace Document 2 Sept 2004, FOAF Project (2004). http://xmlns.com/foaf/0.1/
3. DCMI Usage Board: DCMI metadata terms. DCMI recommendation, Dublin Core Metadata Initiative, December 2006. published online on 18th December 2006. http://dublincore.org/documents/2006/12/18/dcmi-terms/
4. Deng, J., Guo, J., Xue, N., Zafeiriou, S.: ArcFace: additive angular margin loss for deep face recognition. In: Proceedings of the IEEE Conference on Computer Vision and Pattern Recognition, pp. 4690–4699 (2019)
5. Martinez, J.: Mpeg-7 overview (version 10), October 2005. http://www.chiariglione.org/mpeg/standards/mpeg-7/mpeg-7.htm
6. Serengil, S.I., Ozpinar, A.: Hyperextended lightface: a facial attribute analysis framework. In: 2021 International Conference on Engineering and Emerging Technologies (ICEET), pp. 1–4. IEEE (2021)
7. Sikos, L.F.: VidOnt: a core reference ontology for reasoning over video scenes. J. Inf. Telecommun. 2(2), 192–204 (2018)

---

[3] http://westpoort.informatik.uni-mannheim.de/sparql.

[4] https://github.com/face-hunters/face-hunter.

Walk This Way!

Entity Walks and Property Walks for RDF2vec

Jan Portisch[1,2]([envelope]) [iD] and Heiko Paulheim[2] [iD]

[1] SAP SE, Walldorf, Germany
[2] Data and Web Science Group, University of Mannheim, Mannheim, Germany
{jan,heiko}@informatik.uni-mannheim.de

Abstract. RDF2vec is a knowledge graph embedding mechanism which first extracts sequences from knowledge graphs by performing random walks, then feeds those into the word embedding algorithm word2vec for computing vector representations for entities. In this poster, we introduce two new flavors of walk extraction coined *e-walks* and *p-walks*, which put an emphasis on the structure or the neighborhood of an entity respectively, and thereby allow for creating embeddings which focus on similarity or relatedness. By combining the walk strategies with order-aware and classic RDF2vec, as well as CBOW and skip-gram word2vec embeddings, we conduct a preliminary evaluation with a total of 12 RDF2vec variants.

Keywords: RDF2vec · Embedding · Similarity · Relatedness

1 Introduction

RDF2vec [7] is an approach for embedding entities of a knowledge graph in a continuous vector space. It extracts sequences of entities from knowledge graphs, which are then fed into a word2vec encoder [2]. Such embeddings have been shown to be useful in downstream tasks which require numeric representations of entities and rely on a distance metric between entities that captures entity similarity and/or relatedness [4].

Different variants for walk extraction in RDF2vec have been proposed in the past, including the inclusion of weights in the random component [1] and the use of other walk strategies such as community hops and walklets [8]. Moreover, it has been shown recently that using an order-aware variant instead of classic word2vec improves the resulting embeddings [6].

RDF2vec mixes the notion of similarity and relatedness. This can be seen, for example, in Table 1: The closest concepts in the vector space for *Mannheim* are comprised of the city timeline, a person, the local ice hockey team, and close cities. All of these are *related* to the city in a sense that they have a semantic relation to Mannheim (Peter Kurz, for instance, is Lord mayor of Mannheim). However, these concepts are not *similar* to the city since a person and a city do not have much in common.

P. Groth et al. (Eds.): ESWC 2022 Satellite Events, LNCS 13384, pp. 133–137, 2022.
https://doi.org/10.1007/978-3-031-11609-4_25

Table 1. 5 nearest neighbors to *Mannheim* in RDF2vec (classic), p-RDF2vec, and e-RDF2vec trained on DBpedia (SG)

#	RDF2vec	p-RDF2vec	e-RDF2vec
1	Ludwigshafen	Arnsberg	Ludwigshafen
2	Peter Kurz	Frankfurt	Timeline of Mannheim
3	Timeline of Mannheim	Tehran	Peter Kurz
4	Karlsruhe	Bochum	Adler Mannheim
5	Adler Mannheim	Bremen	Peter Kurze

In this paper, we present two new variants of RDF2vec: *p-RDF2vec* emphasizes structural properties of entities, i.e. their attributes, and consequently has a higher exposure towards similarity. *e-RDF2vec* emphasizes the neighboring entities, i.e. the context of entities, and consequently has a higher exposure towards relatedness.

2   New Walk Flavors

In the following, we define a knowledge graph $\mathcal{G}$ as a labeled directed graph $\mathcal{G} = (\mathcal{V}, \mathcal{E})$, where $\mathcal{E} \subseteq \mathcal{V} \times \mathcal{R} \times \mathcal{V}$ for a set of relations $\mathcal{R}$. Vertices are subsequently also referred to as *entities* and edges as *predicates*.

Classic RDF2vec creates sequences of random walks. A random walk of length n (for an even number n) for w_0 has the form

$$w = (w_{-\frac{n}{2}}, w_{-\frac{n}{2}+1}, ..., w_0, ..., w_{\frac{n}{2}-1}, w_{\frac{n}{2}}) \tag{1}$$

where $w_i \in \mathcal{V}$ if i is even, and $w_i \in \mathcal{R}$ if i is odd. For better readability, we stylize $w_i \in \mathcal{V}$ as e_i and $w_i \in \mathcal{R}$ as p_i:

$$w = (e_{-\frac{n}{2}}, p_{-\frac{n}{2}+1}, ..., e_0, ..., p_{\frac{n}{2}-1}, e_{\frac{n}{2}}) \tag{2}$$

In the case of loops, it is possible that a walk contains an entity or edge more than once.

From the definition of random walks, we derive two other types of random walks (see Fig. 1): A *p-walk* w_p is a subsequence of a walk w which consists of only the focus entity e_0 and the predicates in the walk, i.e.,

$$w_p = (p_{-\frac{n}{2}+1}, p_{-\frac{n}{2}+3}, ..., e_0, ..., p_{\frac{n}{2}-3}, p_{\frac{n}{2}-1}) \tag{3}$$

In contrast, an *e-walk* consists only of the entities in the walk, i.e.,

$$w_e = (e_{-\frac{n}{2}}, e_{-\frac{n}{2}+2}, ..., e_0, ..., e_{\frac{n}{2}-2}, e_{\frac{n}{2}}) \tag{4}$$

In other words: p-walks capture the *structure* around an entity, while e-walks capture the *context*. Thus, we hypothesize that embeddings computed from p-walks capture (structural) *similarity*, while those computed from e-walks capture contextual similarity, which can also be understood as *relatedness*.

Fig. 1. Illustration of the different walk types

3 Evaluation

We evaluate embeddings obtained using three different walk extraction strategies, i.e., classic walks, p-walks and e-walks, and training with classic word2vec as well as order-aware word2vec, using both the CBOW and skip-gram variants. This, in total, yields 12 different configurations for RDF2vec.[1] All embedding models are publicly available to download via KGvec2go [5][2].

For evaluation, we use the framework proposed in [3], which consists of different tasks (classification, regression, clustering, analogy reasoning, entity relatedness, document similarity). We use a recent DBpedia release[3]. The results are depicted in Table 2. We can make a few interesting observations:

1. In 12/20 cases, the best results are achieved with classic walks. p-walks yield the best results in 3/20 cases, e-walks do so in 5/20 cases.
2. For entity relatedness, e-walks yield the best results, showing that those walks actually capture relatedness best.
3. For document similarity, p-walks outperform the other approaches. One explanation could be that structural similarity of entities (e.g., politicians vs. athletes) is more important for that task.
4. Semantic analogies are known to require both, relatedness and similarity.[4] Therefore, one may expect both p-walks and e-walks to perform poorly which is indeed verified by our experiments.
5. As observed in [6], the ordered variants almost always outperform the non-ordered ones, for all kinds of walks, except for the semantic analogy problems.

---

[1] We generated 500 walks per node with a depth of 4, i.e., we perform 4 node hops. All embeddings are trained with a dimensionality of 200. The experiments were performed with jRDF2vec (https://github.com/dwslab/jRDF2Vec), which implements all the different variants used in this paper.

[2] http://kgvec2go.org/download.html.

[3] https://www.dbpedia.org/blog/snapshot-2021-09-release/.

[4] For solving an analogy task like *Paris is to France like Berlin is to X*, X must be similar to *France*, as well as related to *Berlin*.

Table 2. Result of the 12 RDF2vec variants on 20 tasks. The best score for each task is printed in bold. The suffix $_{oa}$ marks the ordered variant of RDF2vec.

Task	Metric	Dataset	Classic RDF2vec				e-RDF2vec				p-RDF2vec			
			sg	sg$_{oa}$	cbow	cbow$_{oa}$	sg	sg$_{oa}$	cbow	cbow$_{oa}$	sg	sg$_{oa}$	cbow	cbow$_{oa}$
Classification	ACC	AAUP	0.706	0.713	0.643	0.690	0.696	**0.717**	0.703	0.690	0.564	0.623	0.551	0.612
		Cities	**0.818**	0.803	0.725	0.723	0.770	0.743	0.750	0.702	0.606	0.677	0.501	0.707
		Forbes	**0.623**	0.605	0.575	0.600	0.608	0.605	0.612	0.600	0.581	0.610	0.560	0.578
		Metacritic Albums	0.586	0.585	0.536	0.532	0.596	0.583	0.564	0.584	0.634	0.632	0.569	**0.667**
		Metacritic Movies	0.726	0.716	0.549	0.626	0.724	**0.732**	0.686	0.676	0.610	0.660	0.535	0.663
Clustering	ACC	Cities and Countries (2k)	0.789	0.900	0.520	**0.917**	0.726	0.726	0.668	0.660	0.605	0.520	0.637	0.733
		Cities and Countries	0.587	0.760	0.783	0.720	0.749	0.766	**0.820**	0.745	0.687	0.782	0.787	0.728
		Cities, Albums Movies, AAUP, Forbes	0.829	**0.854**	0.547	0.652	0.759	0.828	0.557	0.719	0.598	0.798	0.663	0.748
		Teams	0.909	0.931	0.940	0.925	0.889	0.926	0.916	0.931	**0.941**	0.938	0.940	0.580
Regression	RMSE	AAUP	65.985	63.814	77.250	66.473	67.337	65.429	70.482	69.292	80.318	72.610	96.248	77.895
		Cities	15.375	**12.782**	18.963	19.287	17.017	16.913	17.290	20.798	20.322	17.214	24.743	20.334
		Forbes	36.545	**36.050**	39.204	37.067	38.589	38.558	39.867	36.313	37.146	36.374	37.947	38.952
		Metacritic Albums	15.288	15.903	15.812	15.705	15.573	15.785	15.574	**14.640**	15.178	14.869	15.000	16.679
		Metacritic Movies	**20.215**	20.420	24.238	23.362	20.436	20.258	23.348	22.518	23.235	22.402	23.979	22.071
Semantic Analogies	ACC	capital country entities	**0.957**	0.864	0.810	0.789	0.794	0.747	0.660	0.397	0.008	0.091	0.000	0.036
		all capital country entities	**0.905**	0.857	0.594	0.758	0.657	0.591	0.359	0.592	0.014	0.073	0.002	0.052
		currency entities	**0.574**	0.535	0.338	0.447	0.309	0.193	0.198	0.297	0.006	0.076	0.002	0.085
		city state entities	**0.609**	0.578	0.507	0.442	0.459	0.484	0.250	0.361	0.009	0.048	0.000	0.036
Entity Relatedness	Kendall Tau		0.747	0.716	0.611	0.547	**0.832**	0.800	0.726	0.779	0.432	0.768	0.568	0.737
Document Similarity	Harmonic Mean		0.237	0.230	0.283	0.209	0.275	0.250	0.170	0.111	0.193	**0.382**	0.296	0.256

This effect is even slightly stronger for p-walks and e-walks than for classic RDF2vec.

6. Generally, skip-gram (and its ordered variant) are more likely to yield better results than CBOW.

Table 1 shows the five closest concepts for classic RDF2vec and the extensions presented in this paper. It can be seen that classic and e-RDF2vec have an exposure towards relatedness while p-RDF2vec results in similar entities (i.e., only cities) being retrieved.

4   Conclusion and Future Work

In this work, we have shown that p-walks and e-walks are interesting alternatives, which, in particular in combination with the order-aware variant of RDF2vec, can outperform classic RDF2vec embeddings. Moreover, we have seen that using p-walks and e-walks can help create embeddings whose distance function reflects similarity and relatedness respectively.

At the same time, the evaluation is still not very conclusive. Therefore, we aim at compiling collections of synthetic test cases which will allow us to make clear statements about which techniques are promising for which kind of problem.

Another interesting avenue for future research is the combination of different embeddings. In cases where aspects of two or three different embedding techniques are relevant, those can be combined and fed into a downstream classification system.

References

1. Cochez, M., Ristoski, P., Ponzetto, S.P., Paulheim, H.: Biased graph walks for RDF graph embeddings. In: WIMS, pp. 1–12 (2017)
2. Mikolov, T., Sutskever, I., Chen, K., Corrado, G.S., Dean, J.: Distributed representations of words and phrases and their compositionality. NIPS **26** (2013)
3. Pellegrino, M.A., Altabba, A., Garofalo, M., Ristoski, P., Cochez, M.: GEval: a modular and extensible evaluation framework for graph embedding techniques. In: Harth, A., et al. (eds.) ESWC 2020. LNCS, vol. 12123, pp. 565–582. Springer, Cham (2020). https://doi.org/10.1007/978-3-030-49461-2_33
4. Portisch, J., Heist, N., Paulheim, H.: Knowledge graph embedding for data mining vs. knowledge graph embedding for link prediction–two sides of the same coin? Semantic Web (to appear) (2022)
5. Portisch, J., Hladik, M., Paulheim, H.: KGvec2go–knowledge graph embeddings as a service. In: LREC 2020, pp. 5641–5647. ELRA (2020)
6. Portisch, J., Paulheim, H.: Putting RDF2Vec in order. In: ISWC 2021 Posters and Demos (2021)
7. Ristoski, P., Paulheim, H.: RDF2Vec: RDF graph embeddings for data mining. In: Groth, P., et al. (eds.) ISWC 2016. LNCS, vol. 9981, pp. 498–514. Springer, Cham (2016). https://doi.org/10.1007/978-3-319-46523-4_30
8. Vandewiele, G., et al.: Walk extraction strategies for node embeddings with RDF2Vec in knowledge graphs. In: Workshop on Machine Learning and Knowledge Graphs (2021)

Self-verifying Web Resource Representations Using Solid, RDF-Star and Signed URIs

Christoph H.-J. Braun$^{(\boxtimes)}$ (ID) and Tobias Käfer (ID)

Institute AIFB, Karlsruhe Institute of Technology (KIT), Karlsruhe, Germany
{braun,tobias.kaefer}@kit.edu

Abstract. Our demo showcases a Solid-based Web where the integrity of a Web resource's representation is directly verifiable using its content and its identifier: A Web resource is available at some URI described in RDF. Each such representation includes a Linked Data Signature, which we model using RDF-star. In addition, each Web resource's URI includes the signature's value as a suffix, which we call *Signed URI*. In a Web of such resource representations, modifications to a resource are detectable unless all resources that transitively reference the original are updated as well. We present a Solid-based Web application where such a Web of resources with self-verifying representations can be created and verified.

1 Introduction

Anybody can publish anything on the Web; and later modify or delete it. No commonly accepted mechanism ensures that the published data is not altered after it was first made accessible on the Web. In addition, declaring authorship of information on the Web is not required by design.

However, with the recent trend of Self-Sovereign Identity [1] and the growing Solid ecosystem [9], users claim more control over their digital life. The ability to express verifiable information on the Web in a self-sovereign manner is becoming evermore important. While some may sense a possible blockchain use-case, as previously presented in [2], we argue: The Web is all we need.

Our demo is built with the following components: We rely on the Solid Protocol [3]. Web resource representations in RDF are stored in the user's personal online data storage (Pod). These representations are signed by the user using a Linked Data Signature, which models all information necessary for verification. To this end, we propose to use RDF-star [5] for modeling Linked Data Signatures. Inspired by Trusty URIs [8], we use a suffix in the Web resource's URI, where we include the signature value, instead of the content hash as with Trusty URIs. We call such a URI a *Signed URI*. When accessing a Signed URI, a user can expect a specific content with matching signature value to be served. In other

---

Website http://people.aifb.kit.edu/co1683/2022/eswc/.
Code https://github.com/uvdsl/solid-web-ldsig.

© The Author(s), under exclusive license to Springer Nature Switzerland AG 2022
P. Groth et al. (Eds.): ESWC 2022 Satellite Events, LNCS 13384, pp. 138–142, 2022.
https://doi.org/10.1007/978-3-031-11609-4_26

words, Signed URIs allow users to reference a resource together with its state. This way, a graph of signed resource representations is created. A change in resource state thus becomes detectable, unless all resource representations that transitively reference the changed resource, are updated as well. In this demo, we showcase:

- Creation and Verification of Linked Data Signatures using a Solid App.
- Modeling of Linked Data Signatures using RDF-star.
- Signed URIs, which allow to reference a resource in a specific state.

This paper is structured as follows: First, we give a short overview on related work. Next, we provide a very basic walkthrough of our demo. Then, we touch on modeling Linked Data Signatures. Hereafter, we ponder the implications of Signed URIs. Finally, we conclude.

2 Related Work

We briefly survey related work in the realm of Linked Data integrity and Solid. An early description about the Solid project is provided in [9].

The integrity of Linked Data is typically verified by calculating and comparing cryptographic hashes of the underlying RDF graphs. We use the algorithm of Hogan [6] for graph canonicalisation as it handles blank nodes most gracefully.

The W3C recently released the Verifiable Credential (VC) data model [10] as a recommendation for sharing verifiable claims. We do not use the VC data model as we concentrate more on the signature itself than on the claim. Mentioned by the VC recommendation as a valid signature scheme, the draft specification of Linked Data Proofs has been renamed Data Integrity[1], now noting the usage of Linked Data only as an optional feature. Also in recent discussion, a proposal for standardization of Linked Data Signatures[2] has sparked fierce discourse within the community, albeit recognizing the need for standradized RDF canonicalization and hashing.

Trusty URIs [8] aim to make digital resources verifiable, immutable and permanent by extending the usual URI scheme with a cryptographic hash of the resource as a URI suffix. Our approach builds on and extends the conceptional idea of Trusty URIs with digital signatures to *Signed URIs*.

Nanopublications [7] aim at publishing data on the Web using Trusty URIs such that links among nanopublications contribute to data integrity. With only hash values ensuring integrity of data, authorship of publications is not preserved. The centralised yet distributed nanopublication-server-network ensures publications' discoverability, permanence and immutability.

Web Publishing using Named Graphs has first been proposed by Carroll et al. [4]. The approach relies on ontology-defined terms to indicate if a graph is to be interpreted as assertive or non-assertive by an information consumer. We use RDF-star [5] instead of Named Graphs, thereby allowing the information creator to normatively define which triples are (non-)assertive.

---

[1] https://w3c-ccg.github.io/data-integrity-spec/.

[2] https://lists.w3.org/Archives/Public/semantic-web/2021Oct/0020.html.

3   Basic Demo Walkthrough

Adhering to the Solid Protocol, users are identified by a WebID and store their data on a personal online data storage (Pod) under access control. A user logs in to our demo app with their WebID. The user then creates an RDF graph and signs it with a Linked Data Signature: First, the created RDF graph is canonicalised using the algorithm of Hogan [6]. Next, SHA-256 is applied as message digest and the Elliptic Curve Digital Signature Algorithm (ECDSA) with curve P-256 creates the signature value. The app takes care of creating, storing and handling the user's cryptographic keys in the user's Solid Pod under access control. The signature value is appended to the URI to create a *Signed URI*. The user stores the signed resource representation on her Pod at that URI.

Upon dereferencing a URI, the app validates the resource in three steps: First, the app checks if all triples quoted by the Linked Data Signature are in fact asserted. Second, the app checks if the signature value is verifiable using the quoted triples and the specified algorithms. Here, the signature suffix is removed prior to resolving relative URIs. Third, the app checks if the signature value matches with the signature suffix from the URI.

The user can not only verify the content from its Linked Data Signature but also expect it specifically to be served from its Signed URI. Moreover, the user is able to reference a resource in a specific state from another resource representation, thereby creating a Web of self-verifying resource representations.

4   Modeling Linked Data Signatures Using RDF-Star

Linked Data Signatures (LDS) are a way of modelling a cryptographic signature of an RDF graph or dataset. LDS are listed as one possible signature scheme in the Verifiable Credentials (VC) data model [10]. However, the VC data model is heavily influenced by the JSON syntax. Examining the data model from a pure RDF perspective, we took issue (1) in the use of RDF datasets, which have underspecified semantics [11], and (2) in the assertion of claimed statements, which are a result of the use of Named Graphs [4]. To avoid these issues, we model LDS using RDF-star. For an example of our data model, we recommend the inclined reader to take a look at our website which is linked on the first page. RDF-star allows for quoting triples, i.e. referencing without asserting. We argue that the LDS only provides meta-information on the signed triples and does not necessarily have to assert those triples. This may be useful, for instance, when the truth-value of the signed triples can change over time: a digital student id card becomes invalid once the student graduates. The signature, however, is always valid as it makes no statement about the truth-value of the signed triples.

5   Pondering the Implications of Signed URIs

Inspired by Trusty URIs [7,8], a *Signed URI* is a URI that includes the hexadecimal value of the content's signature as a suffix, delimited by two underscores,

e. g. http://ex.org/test_0x12. Specifically, the suffix ends the hierarchical part of a URI that does not have a query part. In a Web of resource representations with Linked Data Signatures available at Signed URIs, links among representations contribute the integrity of the resources' representations. When a resource's state changes, the signature value changes, the existing Signed URI mismatches, and the modification becomes detectable. For an undetectable modification, a new Signed URI is to be used and all resources that transitively reference the changed resource have to be updated with respective new Sigend URIs. Since on the Web, resources are typically under control of many different users, all those users have to agree on such updates. Otherwise, *some* evidence will remain.

6   Conclusion

In this demo, we showcased a Web of self-verifying resource representations using Linked Data Signatures and Signed URIs. In a Web of such resource representation, modifications to a resource's state become detectable unless all other resource representations that transitively reference the modified state are also changed. We envision a Web where such resources are under decentralised control of many different users, thereby providing a basis for trust in tamper-evident information.

Acknowledgements. This work is partially supported by the German federal ministry of education and research (BMBF) in MANDAT (FKZ 16DTM107B).

References

1. Allen, C.: The path to self-sovereign identity. http://www.lifewithalacrity.com/2016/04/the-path-to-self-sovereereign-identity.html (2016)
2. Braun, C., Käfer, T.: Verifying the integrity of hyperlinked information using linked data and smart contracts. In: Acosta, M., Cudré-Mauroux, P., Maleshkova, M., Pellegrini, T., Sack, H., Sure-Vetter, Y. (eds.) SEMANTiCS 2019. LNCS, vol. 11702, pp. 376–390. Springer, Cham (2019). https://doi.org/10.1007/978-3-030-33220-4_28
3. Capadisli, S., Berners-Lee, T., Verborgh, R., Kjernsmo, K.: Solid Protocol. Version 0.9.0. W3C Solid Community Group (2021). https://solidproject.org/TR/protocol
4. Carroll, J.J., Bizer, C., Hayes, P.J., Stickler, P.: Named graphs. J. Web Semant. **3**(4), 247–267 (2005)
5. Hartig, O., Champin, P.-A., Kellogg, G., Seaborne, A.: RDF-star and SPARQL-star. W3C Draft Community Group Report. https://w3c.github.io/rdf-star/cg-spec/editors_draft.html (2022)
6. Hogan, A.: Canonical forms for isomorphic and equivalent RDF graphs: algorithms for leaning and labelling blank nodes. ACM Trans. Web **11**(4), 1–62 (2017)
7. Kuhn, T., et al.: Decentralized provenance-aware publishing with nanopublications. PeerJ Comput. Sci. **2**, e78 (2016)
8. Kuhn, T., Dumontier, M.: Trusty URIs: verifiable, immutable, and permanent digital artifacts for linked data. In: Presutti, V., d'Amato, C., Gandon, F., d'Aquin, M., Staab, S., Tordai, A. (eds.) ESWC 2014. LNCS, vol. 8465, pp. 395–410. Springer, Cham (2014). https://doi.org/10.1007/978-3-319-07443-6_27

9. Mansour, E., et al.: A demonstration of the solid platform for social web applications. In: Proceesings of Posters & Demos at the 25th International Conference on World Wide Web (WWW) (2016)

10. Sporny, M., Noble, G., Longley, D., Burnett, D.C., Zundel, B., Den Hartog, K.: Verifiable Credentials DataModel. W3C Recommendation. https://www.w3.org/TR/vc-data-model/ (2021)

11. Zimmermann, A.: RDF 1.1: On Semantics of RDF Datasets. W3C Working Group Note. https://www.w3.org/TR/rdf11-datasets/ (2014)

From OWL to Graphol: Importing Ontologies into Eddy the Editor

Maria Rosaria Fraraccio[1], Manuel Namici[1], and Valerio Santarelli[2(✉)]

[1] Sapienza Università di Roma, Rome, Italy
{fraraccio,namici}@diag.uniroma1.it
[2] OBDA Systems, Rome, Italy
santarelli@obdasystems.com

Abstract. In this demo we showcase the most recent enhancement to EDDY, the visual editor for ontologies in the graphical language GRAPHOL, which is the capability of fully importing ontologies expressed in the W3C standard OWL 2 language. We will illustrate and motivate the innovative choices we have adopted for achieving this goal, which are geared towards a more incremental approach to the importing process, designed to mitigate the commonly recurring challenges of providing a visually and conceptually rational layout of the ontology in graphical form.

1 Introduction

EDDY [7] is an open-source editor specifically designed for creating ontologies in GRAPHOL [6], which is a completely visual ontology language that is equivalent to OWL 2 [1], meaning that any OWL 2 ontology can be specified in GRAPHOL, and viceversa. The main characteristics of GRAPHOL are that ontologies are represented as diagrams, rather than written as sets of formulas, as commonly happens in popular ontology design and engineering environments, and that the basic visual elements of the language are rooted in the Entity-Relationship model, in such a way as to make a GRAPHOL ontology assume the form of a graph, built through nodes and edges. This makes GRAPHOL, and consequently EDDY, ideally suited for users such as engineers or analysts who are more familiar with diagramatic languages for conceptual modeling rather than with typical ontology formalisms, as is often required in non-academic and industrial contexts. While EDDY has provided since its earliest releases a wide variety of intuitive functionalities for drawing GRAPHOL diagrams, for guaranteeing their syntactic and logical correctness, and for exporting them in standard OWL 2 syntax, it has lacked one aspect which is critical in order to ensure full interoperability with the most popular ontology-based applications, i.e., the capability to import ontologies originally specified in OWL 2. In this demo we will present the most recent enhancement to EDDY, which aims to fill this gap by providing a set of functionalities that allow users to import external OWL 2 ontologies into their GRAPHOL projects through an incremental process. This process is tailored towards taking advantage of EDDY's modular ontology editing environment, obtaining a visually and conceptually rational layout of

P. Groth et al. (Eds.): ESWC 2022 Satellite Events, LNCS 13384, pp. 143–147, 2022.
https://doi.org/10.1007/978-3-031-11609-4_27

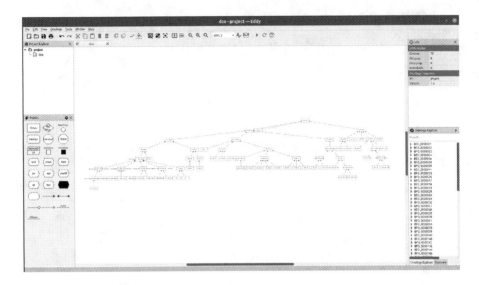

Fig. 1. An example of a class hierarchy rendering in EDDY

the ontology which users can then tweak to their linking, and highlighting the typically most important aspects of an OWL 2 ontology.

EDDY[1] is developed and distributed under GPL-3.0 License by OBDA Systems, a start-up of Sapienza University of Rome.

2 Importing OWL 2 Ontologies in Eddy

When tackling the issue of transforming an OWL 2 ontology into a graphical representation or diagram, regardless of the visual language of choice, the first, and arguably main, questions that need to be answered are which axioms must be preserved in the graphical rendering of the ontology, and how to go about achieving a layout of the elements in the ontology that will allow the end user to make sense of the diagram and to be able to work with it, making modifications and advancing the model in the new graphical form. In the context of EDDY, the answer to the first question is imposed by the expressive capabilities of GRAPHOL, which as we have stated are exactly equivalent to OWL 2. Therefore, the first of our goals was to devise a solution to the import problem which would allow us to maintain each and every possible OWL 2 axiom when transforming from OWL 2 to GRAPHOL in EDDY.

Compatibly with this first design objective, the answer to the second question was in our case to forego the strategy that is most commonly adopted by graphical ontology editing tools [2,8] which provide OWL 2 importing capabilities, which is to draw the whole ontology at once, and instead adopt a more incremental approach to the importing process, which guides the user through a set of steps which automatically compose the backbone of the ontology, and then allow to decide which axioms to draw, and where

---

[1] https://github.com/obdasystems/eddy.

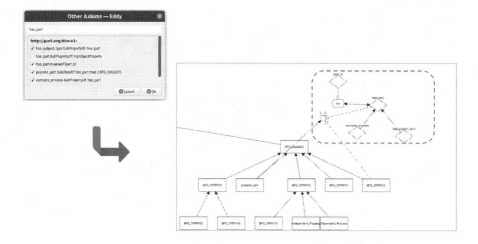

Fig. 2. Automatic drawing of set of OWL 2 axioms in EDDY

in the diagram. In essence, the importing process implemented in EDDY is divided into three separate problems: *(1)* calculating and rendering the class hierarchy of the OWL 2 ontology; *(2)* importing all the metadata of the ontology, i.e., its annotations; *(3)* importing all the remaining ontology axioms. The first two of these tasks are handled automatically by the system, while the latter is implemented through a wizard-like procedure which guides the user towards the finalization of the OWL 2 ontology import.

In any ontology, the most characterizing axioms of the ontology itself are those that contribute to defining the class hierarchy of the ontology, meaning the set of *subclass* relations between the named class entities of these ontologies. It therefore stands to reason that any visual representation of the ontology must provide the class hierarchy in its entirety, and must do so in a fully automatic way, as to not make the import process excessively cumbersome. In EDDY, this is achieved through an algorithm which traverses the *subclass* axioms in the ontology recursively, in order to first reconstruct the tree-like shape of the hierarchy, and then to calculate the optimal layout, both in terms of horizontal and vertical distances between the class nodes in the diagram, and in terms of the semantic "closeness" of the class nodes. In Fig. 1 we show an example of the class hierarchy rendering of the Data Collection Ontology (DCO) ontology[2].

The second step of the importing process, which incorporates all *annotation* axioms of the OWL 2 ontology into its GRAPHOL counterpart, is fairly straightforward, as EDDY already provides the infrastructure to fully host all annotation type axioms, which can feature both standard and user-defined annotation properties.

The third and final step of the procedure allows the user to select one or more of any of the remaining axioms in the ontology, and EDDY will automatically draw them, seamlessly integrating them with the existing diagrams. This step has two main prerequisites: being able to store the axioms that have yet to be imported in such a way that these can be retrieved at any time (guaranteeing the capability of picking up the import

---

[2] https://bioportal.bioontology.org/ontologies/GDCO.

procedure through different work sessions), and being able to process, translate, and draw any OWL 2 axiom in GRAPHOL form. To achieve the first objective, we have first added a data layer into EDDY, physically implemented through an SQLite database, which stores the relevant information and logical representation of the previously mentioned remaining axioms. Then, we have equipped Eddy with a dedicated widget for the exploration, selection, and retrieval of these axioms to be drawn in the diagram from the data layer. Finally, we have designed and implemented an algorithm for the rendering of each possible OWL 2 axiom type, which not only recursively deconstructs the OWL 2 axioms and recompiles them into a GRAPHOL axiom, but also automatically optimizes the drawing of the axioms, i.e., the placement of its nodes and edges, by considering where to place the axiom according to which entities in the axioms have already been drawn, and in which diagram of the GRAPHOL ontology. In Fig. 2, we show an example of the translation of a set of axioms that do not appear in the class hierarchy of the ontology into the preexisting diagram.

One further implementation choice that we made that warrants mentioning is that, unlike in previous attemps with implementing the importing feature in Eddy, when calculating the class hierarchy of the ontology, we have not used an external OWL 2 reasoners such as HermiT [4] or ELK [5] to calculate the inferred relations in the hierarchy, but rather we have strictly adhered to what is asserted in the OWL 2 ontology. This choice was primarily made in order to be able to provide an exact recap to the user, throughout the import process, of which axioms of the original ontology have been drawn in the GRAPHOL ontology, and to keep the diagram as adherent as possible to the original ontology.

3 Application Scenarios and Demo Session Overview

We demonstrate EDDY's new importing features through a suite of ontologies designed to highlight the capability of the system to handle the importing of both large ontologies and ontologies with particularly complex axioms. We will use several ontologies from real-world industrial projects, including the SIR (System of Integrated Registers) ontology, which is being built in a joint project between OBDA Systems and the Italian National Institute of Statistics (ISTAT) and which integrates information from Italian statistical censuses regarding, among others, demographic, territorial, and public administration data, and the ACI (Italian Automobile Club) ontology, which models information regarding italian motorvehicle registration and tax data. Another specification that will be featured in the demo is the Movie Ontology [3], which provides a vocabulary to semantically describe movie related concepts. Finally, we will also use a set of ontologies extracted from Bioportal [9], the world's most extensive repository of biomedical ontologies. During the demo, attendees will interact with EDDY in the above scenarios and will be introduced to its main new features.

References

1. Bao, J., et al.: OWL 2 Web Ontology Language Document Overview (second edition). W3C Recommendation (2012). http://www.w3.org/TR/owl2-overview/
2. Barzdins, J., Barzdins, G., Cerans, K., Liepins, R., Sprogis, A.: UML style graphical notation and editor for OWL 2. In: Forbrig, P., Günther, H. (eds.) BIR 2010. LNBIP, vol. 64, pp. 102–114. Springer, Heidelberg (2010). https://doi.org/10.1007/978-3-642-16101-8_9
3. Bouza, A.: MO - The Movie Ontology (2010). 26 January 2010
4. Glimm, B., Horrocks, I., Motik, B., Stoilos, G., Wang, Z.: HermiT: an OWL 2 reasoner. J. Autom. Reason. **53**(3), 245–269 (2014). https://doi.org/10.1007/s10817-014-9305-1
5. Kazakov, Y., Krötzsch, M., Simancik, F.: The incredible ELK - from polynomial procedures to efficient reasoning with EL ontologies. J. Autom. Reason. **53**(1), 1–61 (2014)
6. Lembo, D., Pantaleone, D., Santarelli, V., Savo, D.F.: Easy OWL drawing with the graphol visual ontology language. In Baral, C., Delgrande, J.P., Wolter, F. (eds.), Principles of Knowledge Representation and Reasoning: Proceedings of the Fifteenth International Conference, KR 2016, Cape Town, South Africa, 25–29 April 2016, pp. 573–576. AAAI Press (2016)
7. Lembo, D., Pantaleone, D., Santarelli, V., Savo, D.F.: Drawing OWL 2 ontologies with Eddy the editor. AI Commun. **31**(1), 97–113 (2018)
8. Lohmann, S., Negru, S., Haag, F., Ertl, T.: Visualizing ontologies with VOWL. Semant. Web **7**(4), 399–419 (2016)
9. Whetzel, P.L., et al.: Bioportal: ontologies and integrated data resources at the click of a mouse. In Bodenreider, O., Martone, M.E., Ruttenberg, A., (eds.) Proceedings of the 2nd International Conference on Biomedical Ontology, Buffalo, NY, USA, 26–30 July 2011, vol. 833 of CEUR Workshop Proceedings. CEUR-WS.org (2011)

Audio Ontologies for Intangible Cultural Heritage

Mary Ann Tan[1,2](✉) ⓘ, Etienne Posthumus[1] ⓘ, and Harald Sack[1,2] ⓘ

[1] FIZ Karlsruhe - Leibniz Institute for Information Infrastructure,
Karlsruhe, Germany
{ann.tan,harald.sack}@fiz-karlsruhe.de, ep@poz.org
[2] Karlsruhe Institute of Technology, Institute AIFB, Karlsruhe, Germany

Abstract. Cultural heritage portals often contain intangible objects digitized as audio files. This paper presents and discusses the adaptation of existing audio ontologies intended for non-cultural heritage applications. The resulting alignment of the German Digital Library-Europeana Data Model (DDB-EDM) with Music Ontology (MO) and Audio Commons Ontology (ACO) is presented.

Keywords: Ontology · Digital library · Digital humanities · Cultural heritage · Audio

1 Introduction

Cultural heritage defines the identity of a community through its history, traditions, practices, and ideals. It fosters continuity between generations and connection among the members of a community. The role it plays in "education, research, creation and recreation"[1] is crucial, such that its preservation is of utmost importance. Digitization of cultural heritage objects (CHOs) ensures its preservation – a far-reaching initiative spearheaded by the Europeana, of which the German Digital Library or *Deutsche Digitale Bibliothek*[2] is a part.

The extensive collections of the DDB include CHOs from different memory institutions or sectors, such as libraries, archives, museums, as well as multimedia libraries, research institutions, and institutions preserving historical sites and monuments. Challenges common to digital libraries also exist in the DDB. Retrieval and exploration are further hampered by the sheer volume[3] and the highly heterogeneous nature of its collection. Some of these challenges are addressed using semantic web technologies, such as development and adaptation of sector-specific ontologies. Initial work focused on the alignment of library objects (Tan et al. 2021a) from the DDB-EDM[4] to FaBiO (Peroni

---

[1] Europeana, https://www.europeana.eu.
[2] Deutsche Digitale Bibliothek, https://www.deutsche-digitale-bibliothek.de.
[3] 41M unique objects as of April 2022.
[4] a DDB-specific extension of the Europeana Data Model (EDM).

P. Groth et al. (Eds.): ESWC 2022 Satellite Events, LNCS 13384, pp. 148–152, 2022.
https://doi.org/10.1007/978-3-031-11609-4_28

and Shotton 2012), an extension of FRBR (IFLA Study Group On The Functional Requirements For Bibliographic Records 1998). In FRBR, the conceptual structure of bibliographical information resources is represented using several entities and their relationships to facilitate efficient access and retrieval. Objects from archives and museums undergo a similar alignment process using suitable ontologies, details of which are beyond the scope of this paper.

DDB's vast collection includes objects that the UNESCO cultural heritage hierarchy (Ronchi 2009, Chap. 5) classified as intangible. Examples of intangible objects include musical works, natural heritage, and oral traditions, to name a few. These are often digitized as audio or video. Semantic web studies in the field of cultural heritage are often skewed towards tangible objects. To help filling this gap, this paper presents and discusses the alignment of DDB-EDM to several audio-specific ontologies intended for non-cultural heritage applications.

2   Audio Ontologies in the DDB

Audio content in the DDB can be found across several sectors: audio books from libraries, interviews of significant German personalities from research institutions, commercial jingles from archives, recordings of animal sounds from natural museums and music from gramophone records often found in multimedia libraries. To be able to represent the semantics of these diverse objects, the selection of target ontologies is based on the following considerations: interoperability, suitability to the domain, and the application profile.

With audio content, adapting a FRBR-aligned ontology facilitates interoperability. A song in FRBR is composed of 4 entities: 1) its intellectual or creative content (*frbr:Work*); 2) how the content was conveyed, whether sound or text, (*frbr:Expression*); 3) how the sound materialized, as e.g., CD or vinyl (*frbr:Manifestation*); and 4) the instance one finds in the library (*frbr:Item*).

Consequently, an audio book is considered an expression of its respective literary works. The same holds true for any musical composition and its text; for instance, a recording of Carl Orff's Carmina Burana is considered an expression of the 13th century manuscript[5] containing a collection of poems it was based on.

Although, FaBiO, as a FRBR-aligned bibliographic ontology, provides subclasses relating to musical works (*fabio:Song, fabio:MusicalComposition*) and their expression (*fabio:AudioDocument*), these subclasses cannot represent the full range of audio content described above. To address this limitation, ontologies aimed at representing the audio domain are considered.

Music Ontology (MO[6]) (Raimond et al. 2007). This ontology aims to model the semantics of music production workflows and their editorial metadata. FRBR plays a central role in the definition of its classes. Parallels can be drawn between the super-classes of MO (*mo:MusicalWork, mo:MusicalExpression, mo:Musical*

---

[5] Carmina Burana manuscript, https://bit.ly/ddb-carmina-burana.

[6] MO Specifications, http://musicontology.com/specification/.

Manifestation, and *mo:MusicalItem*) and the 4 conceptual layers of FRBR. Since the original intention of the authors is to model the different workflows, events are central to this ontology. Entities that are usually found as attributes of a *frbr:Endeavor* sub-class require intermediate events to link them to that endeavor: the attribution of an *mo:MusicalArtist* (Agent) to its *mo:MusicalWork* requires an instance of the *mo:Composition* event, in contrast to the widely-adopted convention of linking agents directly to the *frbr:Work*.

Audio Commons Ontology (ACO[7]) (Ceriani and Fazekas 2018). As mentioned, not all audio files in the DDB possess intellectual or artistic content. Examples of these are natural sounds and field recordings. An ontology that provides classes and properties to allow representations of non-musical audio content exists in ACO. Being an upper-level ontology for audio content, the authors' initial intention is to provide interoperability across repositories on the Web. The FRBR-aligned classes of ACO are generalizations of MO classes. However, a *frbr:Work* sub-class specific to ACO was not defined, since it does not generalize to all types of sounds. Similarly to MO, events also play a central role in ACO.

Event- vs Object-Centric Modeling. Cultural heritage object descriptions often follow either an event-centric, an object-centric or a combination of both modeling approaches. Event-centric modeling puts a premium on completeness by representing significant events relating to a CHO, such as creation, production, revision, enhancement, etc. In contrast, object-centric modeling opts for accessibility by relating the object to pertinent information that describes its context, such as agent, time, and place.

The primary application profile of the DDB is the publication of metadata that directly describes the CHOs. For instance, the description of a gramophone record includes the names of the composer, performer/s and publisher. However, details of the performance of this specific record which is crucial for modeling a music production workflow is not available.

For this reason, an object-centric approach is followed, by foregoing the usage of *event:Event* sub-classes, namely, *mo:Composition*, *mo:Performance*, and *mo:Recording*. Consequently, the generic property *dcterms:contributor* is used in lieu of *mo:performer*, since the latter strictly defines the domain to be of class *mo:Performance*, an event which is not utilized in the alignment.

Alignment. In Fig. 1, a snapshot of the alignment for a gramophone record of Robert Foster's "Old Folks at Home"[8] is shown. Similar to the work described by Tan et al. (2021) (Tan et al. 2021a), *edm:ProvidedCHO* is aligned to a specialization of *frbr:Item*. The original resource, an instance of *edm:WebResource*, is now an *aco:AudioFile*. The item and its reproduction are linked using the object property *fabio:hasReproduction*. Other FaBiO properties used to relate non-adjacent endeavors are also adapted, e.g. *fabio:hasPortrayal*, a relationship that exists between a Work and an Item. The main difference between audio

---

[7] ACO Specifications, http://www.audiocommons.org/ac-ontology/aco.

[8] "Old Folks at Home" in the DDB, https://bit.ly/3IJgJld.

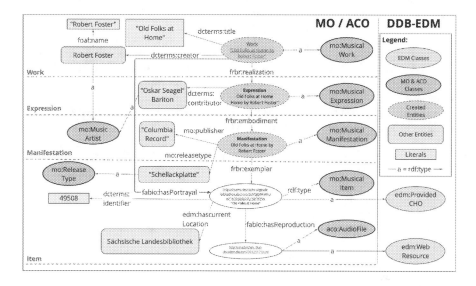

Fig. 1. Alignment of "Old Folks at Home" from DDB-EDM to MO and ACO

content of a musical nature and some non-musical audio content is that only the instance of *mo:AudioManifestation* is created for the latter. For a detailed illustration and comparison, refer to this documentation page[9].

3   Conclusion and Future Work

The diversity of CH objects in a portal such as the DDB requires domain-specific ontologies to represent their semantics. By putting emphasis on interoperability, efficiency of search and retrieval is not restricted by this form of specialization. Although MO and ACO were intended by the original authors for other applications, adopting an object-centric representation is shown to suit intangible CHOs for publication purposes. Hence, this work may serve as a reference for portals that utilize generic EDM classes. Using the proposed alignment, representative audio objects are made available in the DDB-KG (Tan et al., 2021b). Additionally, competency questions, sample SPARQL queries and dataset statistics are provided in the documentation page. The alignment activities will continue with the remaining CHOs: videos, research datasets, historical sites and monuments. Eventually, these changes will improve the organization, access and exploration of German Cultural Heritage.

Acknowledgements. This work was carried out as part of the project "User-Oriented Restructuring of the German Digital Library Portal", funded by the German Federal Commissioner for Culture and the Media (BKM) in the NEUSTART KULTUR funding program.

---

[9] DDB-KG   Documentation   Page,   https://ise-fizkarlsruhe.github.io/ddbkg/docs/ alignment/audio/.

References

Ceriani, M., Fazekas, G.: Audio commons ontology: a data model for an audio content ecosystem. In: Vrandečić, D. (ed.) ISWC 2018. LNCS, vol. 11137, pp. 20–35. Springer, Cham (2018). https://doi.org/10.1007/978-3-030-00668-6_2

Saur, K.G.: IFLA study group on the functional requirements for bibliographic records. Functional requirements for bibliographic records - final report. New Series, vol. 19. UBCIM Publications, München (1998). http://archive.ifla.org/VII/s13/frbr/frbr.pdf

Peroni, S., Shotton, D.: FaBiO and CiTO: ontologies for describing bibliographic resources and citations. J. Web Semant. **17**, 33–43 (2012). https://doi.org/10.2139/ssrn.3198992

Raimond, Y., Abdallah, S., Sandler, M., Giasson, F.: The music ontology. In: Proceedings of the 8th International Conference on Music Information Retrieval, ISMR 2007, Vienna, Austria, 23–27 September 2007, Austrian Computer Society, pp. 417–422 (2017)

Ronchi, A.M.: eCulture: Cultural Content in the Digital Age. Springer, Berlin, Heidelberg (2009). https://doi.org/10.1007/978-3-540-75276-9

Tan, M.A., Tietz, T., Bruns, O., Oppenlaender, J., Dessì, D., Sack, H.: DDB-EDM to FaBiO: the case of the german digital library. In: Proceedings of the 20th International Semantic Web Conference - Posters and Demos - ISWC 2021, CEUR-WS.org, vol. 2980 (2021a)

Tan, M.A., Tietz, T., Bruns, O., Oppenlaender, J., Dessì, D., Sack, H.: DDB-KG: the german bibliographic heritage in a knowledge graph. In: 6th International Workshop on Computational History at JCDL - Histoinformatics, CEUR-WS.org, vol. 2981 (2021b)

Ontology Matching Through Absolute Orientation of Embedding Spaces

Jan Portisch[1,2]([✉]), Guilherme Costa[1][iD], Karolin Stefani[1][iD],
Katharina Kreplin[1][iD], Michael Hladik[1][iD], and Heiko Paulheim[2][iD]

[1] SAP SE, Walldorf, Germany
{jan.portisch,guilherme.costa,karolin.stefani,katharina.kreplin,
michael.hladik}@sap.com
[2] Data and Web Science Group, University of Mannheim, Mannheim, Germany
{jan,heiko}@informatik.uni-mannheim.de

Abstract. Ontology matching is a core task when creating interoperable
and linked open datasets. In this paper, we explore a novel structure-
based mapping approach which is based on knowledge graph embeddings:
The ontologies to be matched are embedded, and an approach known as
absolute orientation is used to align the two embedding spaces. Next to
the approach, the paper presents a first, preliminary evaluation using
synthetic and real-world datasets. We find in experiments with synthetic
data, that the approach works very well on similarly structured graphs;
it handles alignment noise better than size and structural differences in
the ontologies.

Keywords: Ontology matching · Embeddings · Absolute orientation

1 Introduction

Ontology matching describes the complex process of finding an alignment A
between two ontologies O_1 and O_2. An alignment is a set of correspondences
where a correspondence is, in its simplest form, a tuple of $\langle e_1, e_2, R \rangle$ where
$e_1 \in O_1$ is an element from one ontology, $e_2 \in O_2$ is an element from the other
ontology, and R is the relation that holds between the two elements. Typically,
R is equivalence ($\equiv$).

In this paper, we examine the use of embedding two ontologies for finding an
alignment between them. Given two embeddings of the ontologies, we use a set
of anchor points to derive a joint embedding space via a rotation operation.

2 Related Work

Knowledge Graph Embeddings. Given be a (knowledge) graph $G = (V, E)$
where V is the set of vertices and E is the set of directed edges. Further given be
a set of relations R, $E \subseteq V x R x V$. A knowledge graph embedding is a projection

P. Groth et al. (Eds.): ESWC 2022 Satellite Events, LNCS 13384, pp. 153–157, 2022.
https://doi.org/10.1007/978-3-031-11609-4_29

$E \cup R \rightarrow \mathbb{R}^{d1}$. In this paper, we use the RDF2vec approach, which generates multiple random walks per vertex $v \in V$. An RDF2vec sentence resembles a walk through the graph starting at a specified vertex v. Those random walks are fed into a *word2vec* algorithm, which treats the entities and relations as words and the random walks as sentences, and consequently outputs numeric vectors for entities and relations.

Absolute Orientation. Multiple approaches exist for aligning embeddings. In this paper, the extension by Dev et al. [2] of the *absolute orientation* approach is used. The approach showed good performance on multilingual word embeddings. The calculation of the rotation matrix is based on two vector sets $A = \{a_1, a_2, ...a_n\}$ and $B = \{b_1, b_2, ...b_n\}$ of the same size n where $a_i, b_i \in \mathbb{R}^d$. In a first step, the means $\bar{a} = \frac{1}{n}\sum_{i=1}^{n} a_i$ and $\bar{b} = \frac{1}{n}\sum_{i=1}^{n} b_i$ are calculated. Now, $\bar{a}$ and $\bar{b}$ can be used to center A and B: $\hat{A} \leftarrow (A, \bar{a})$ and $\hat{B} \leftarrow (B, \bar{b})$. Given the sum of the outer products $H = \sum_{i=1}^{n} \hat{b}_i \hat{a}_i^T$, the singular value decomposition of H can be calculated: $svd(H) = [U, S, V^T]$. The rotation is $R = UV^T$. Lastly, $\hat{B}$ can be rotated as follows: $\widetilde{B} = \hat{B}R$.

Matching with Embeddings. Embedding-based matching approaches have gained traction recently, mostly using embeddings of the textual information contained in ontologies [7]. OntoConnect [1], for example, uses fastText within a larger neural network to match ontologies; DOME [3] exploits doc2vec; TOM [5] and F-TOM [4] use S-BERT. With the exception of ALOD2vec Matcher [8], knowledge graph embeddings are rarely used. The work presented in this paper is different in that it does not rely on labels or an external knowledge graph. Instead, an embedding is learnt for the ontologies to be matched.

3   Approach

We first train two separate embedding spaces for the two ontologies to be matched (i.e., O_1 and O_2). This is done in two independent RDF2vec training processes. In a second step, we then perform the absolute orientation operation to rotate one embedding space onto the other.

For the matching operation, we assign for each node in $e \in O_1$ the closest node $e \in O_2$ according to Euclidean distance (Fig. 1).

4   Experiments

For the experiments, jRDF2vec[2] [6] was used to obtain RDF2vec embeddings. We chose the following hyper parameter values: *dimension* = 100, *window* = 6,

---

[1] Variations of this formulations are possible, e.g., including different dimensions for the vector spaces of E and R, and/or using complex instead of real numbers.

[2] see https://github.com/dwslab/jRDF2Vec.

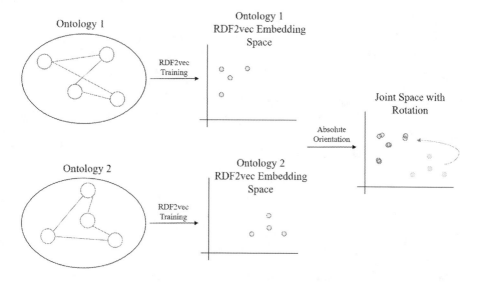

Fig. 1. High-level overview of the absolute orientation approach.

$depth = 6$, $walks = 150$. The code together with the complete set of figures and results is available online[3].

4.1   Synthetic Experiments

In a first step, we perform sandbox experiments on synthetic data. We generate a graph G with 2,500 nodes V. For each node $v \in V$, we draw a random d number using a Poisson distribution $f(k; \lambda) = \frac{\lambda^k e^{-\lambda}}{k!}$ with $\lambda = 4$. We then randomly draw d nodes from $V \setminus v$ and add the edge between v and the drawn node to G. We duplicate G as G' and generate an alignment A where each $v \in V$ is mapped to its copy $v' \in V'$. We define the matching task such that G and G' shall be matched. The rotation is performed with a fraction α from A, referred to as the anchor alignment A'. In all experiments, we vary α between 0.2 and 0.8 in steps of size 0.2.

Training Size. In order to test the stability of the performed rotation, also referred to herein as training, we evaluate varying values for α. Each experiment is repeated 5 times to account for statistical variance. The matching precision is computed for each experiment on the training dataset A' and on the testing dataset $A \setminus A'$. The split between the training and the testing datasets is determined by α. We found that the model is able to map the entire graphs regardless of the size of the training set A' (each run achieved a precision of 100%).

---

[3] see https://github.com/guilhermesfc/ontology-matching-absolute-orientation.

Alignment Noise. In order to test the stability in terms of noise in the anchor alignment A', we distort a share of the training correspondences by randomly matching other than the correct nodes. We vary this level of alignment noise between 0 (no noise introduced) and 0.9 (90% of the alignments are randomly matched) in steps of size 0.1. Figure 2 (left) shows the performance with $\alpha = 0.2$. We observe that the test performance declines with an increasing amount of noise. Interestingly, this relation is not linear. It is visible in Fig. 2 (left) that the approach can handle 40% of noise before dropping significantly in terms of test performance.

Graph Heterogeneity. In order to test the stability in terms of graph heterogeneity, we randomly remove triples from the target graph G' after setting up the alignment between the source graph G and the target graph G'. We vary the fraction of randomly removed triples in G' between 0 (no triples removed) and 0.9 (90% of the triples removed) in steps of size 0.1. In Fig. 2 (right) it can be observed that with a size deviation of 30%, the performance starts to drop rapidly. Comparing the two plots in the figure, it can be seen that the approach handles noise significantly better than size and structure deviations in graphs.

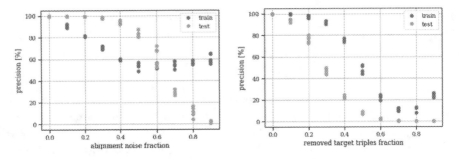

Fig. 2. The effect of distortions. (1) alignment noise (left) and (2) size differences (right). Graphs are given for $\alpha = 0.2$.

4.2   Experiments on Real Data

We also test our approach on the OAEI[4] multifarm dataset. Here, multilingual ontologies from the conference domain have to be matched. Since the absolute orientation approach does not use textual data, we only evaluate the German-English test case. This is sufficient because the other language combinations of the multifarm dataset use structurally identical graphs. With a sampling rate of 20%, our approach achieves micro scores of $P = 0.376$, $R = 0.347$, and

---

[4] The Ontology Alignment Evaluation Initiative (OAEI) provides reference alignments and carries out yearly evaluation campaigns since 2004. For more information, see http://oaei.ontologymatching.org/.

$F_1 = 0.361$. Compared to the systems participating in the 2021 campaign [11], the recall is on par with state of the art systems; an overall lower F_1 is caused by a comparatively low precision score. While not outperforming top-notch OAEI systems in terms of F_1, the performance indicates that the approach is able to perform ontology matching and may particularly benefit from the addition of non-structure-based features.

5   Conclusion

In this paper, we showed early work on aligning graphs through a graph embedding algorithm combined with an absolute orientation rotation approach. In multiple experiments we showed that the approach works for structurally similar ontologies. It handles alignment noise better than varying sizes and structures of graphs. In the future, we plan to conduct experiments with different variants of embedding approaches [9,10], as well as to combine the approach with further text-based features in a hybrid matching system.

References

1. Chakraborty, J., Zahera, H.M., Sherif, M.A., Bansal, S.K.: ONTOCONNECT: domain-agnostic ontology alignment using graph embedding with negative sampling. In: ICMLA 2021, pp. 942–945. IEEE (2021)
2. Dev, S., Hassan, S., Phillips, J.M.: Closed form word embedding alignment. Knowl. Inf. Syst. **63**(3), 565–588 (2021). https://doi.org/10.1007/s10115-020-01531-7
3. Hertling, S., Paulheim, H.: DOME results for OAEI 2019. In: OM 2019. CEUR Workshop Proceedings, vol. 2536, pp. 123–130. CEUR-WS.org (2019)
4. Knorr, L., Portisch, J.: Fine-tom matcher results for OAEI 2021. In: OM 2021. CEUR Workshop Proceedings, vol. 3063, pp. 144–151. CEUR-WS.org (2021)
5. Kossack, D., Borg, N., Knorr, L., Portisch, J.: TOM matcher results for OAEI 2021. In: OM 2021. CEUR Workshop Proceedings, vol. 3063, pp. 193–198. CEUR-WS.org (2021)
6. Portisch, J., Hladik, M., Paulheim, H.: Rdf2vec light - a lightweight approach for knowledge graph embeddings. In: ISWC 2020 Demos and Industry Track, vol. 2721, pp. 79–84 (2020)
7. Portisch, J., Hladik, M., Paulheim, H.: Background knowledge in ontology matching: a survey (2022)
8. Portisch, J., Paulheim, H.: Alod2vec matcher results for OAEI 2021. In: OM 2021. CEUR Workshop Proceedings, vol. 3063, pp. 117–123. CEUR-WS.org (2021)
9. Portisch, J., Paulheim, H.: Putting rdf2vec in order. In: ISWC Posters and Demos, vol. 2980, pp. 1–5 (2021)
10. Portisch, J., Paulheim, H.: Walk this way! entity walks and property walks for rdf2vec. In: ESWC Posters and Demos (2022)
11. Pour, M.A.N., et al.: Results of the ontology alignment evaluation initiative 2021. In: OM 2021. CEUR Workshop Proceedings, vol. 3063, pp. 62–108. CEUR-WS.org (2021). http://ceur-ws.org/Vol-3063/oaei21_paper0.pdf

Semantic Modeling and Reconstruction of Drones' Trajectories

Andreas Soularidis and Konstantinos Kotis[✉] [iD]

i-Lab, Department of Cultural Technology and Communication, University of the Aegean,
83100 Mytilene, Greece
cti21008@ct.aegean.gr, kotis@aegean.gr

Abstract. Research on semantic trajectories' modeling, analytics, and visualization has been conducted for a wide range of application domains. In contrast to raw trajectories, semantically annotated trajectories provide meaningful and contextual information to movement data. Unmanned Aerial Vehicles (UAVs), also known as drones, are becoming more and more widely used in modern battle-fields as well as in search and rescue (SAR) operations. Semantic trajectories can effectively model the movement of swarms of drones towards enabling decision makers/commanders to acquire meaningful and rich contextual information about Points of Interest (PoI) and Regions of Interest (RoI) that will eventually support simulations and predictions of high-level critical events in the real field of operations. The goal of this paper is to present our position related to the semantic trajectories of swarms of drones, towards proposing methods for extending MovingPandas, a widely used open-source trajectory analytics and visualization tool. Such an extension is focused on the semantic modeling of drone trajectories that are automatically reconstructed from geo-tagged data, such as photographs taken during a flight mission of a swarm of UAVs, where its flight plan or real-time movement data have been either lost or corrupted, or there is a need for semantic trajectory cross-validation.

Keywords: Semantic trajectory · UAV · Geo-tagging · MovingPandas

1 Introduction

A swarm of drones is a group of unmanned aerial vehicles that fly in collaboration to complete a specific mission. Depending on the type of swarm, single-layered (each drone is leading) or multi-layered (multiple leaders at different levels), different communication and interoperation strategies are feasible between units (drones), given that interoperability issues at different levels (network, syntactic, semantic, organizational) are already facilitated.

Effective semantic modeling and analysis of trajectories of swarms of drones enable the decision makers/commanders to acquire meaningful and enriched information about the current situation in the field of operations, supporting, eventually, tool-based automated or semi-automated simulations for making predictions of high-level critical events

P. Groth et al. (Eds.): ESWC 2022 Satellite Events, LNCS 13384, pp. 158–162, 2022.
https://doi.org/10.1007/978-3-031-11609-4_30

e.g., rescue or no-rescue due to the severity of weather condition at specific region of interest and time-window.

A *semantic trajectory of swarm of drones* is a synthesis of *semantic trajectories* [1] of multiple units moving (flying) in a specified formation, sharing common origin-destination points, having a common mission, enriched with *semantic annotations* at different levels of detail, having one or more complementary segmentations, where each segmentation consists of a list of annotated episodes. A *drone trajectory* is a sequence of points (*trace*) that specify the position of the *moving entity* in space and time. A *segment* is a part of the trajectory that contains a list of *episodes*. Each episode has a starting and ending timestamp, the segmentation criterion (annotation type) and the episode annotation. For example, an annotation type can be the "weather conditions" and an episode annotation can be "a storm", "heavy rain", "extremely high waves", etc.

Swarms of drones are becoming widely used in modern battlefields as well as in search and rescue (SAR) operations [2, 3]. To create the semantic trajectory of a swarm of drones, raw movement data collected from each unit is necessary. However, unpredicted threats (e.g., unit malfunction, hacking, weather condition) and known vulnerabilities of drones (e.g., operation conditions) can be the cause of incorrect, invalid, or missing movement data. To solve this problem, there is need to introduce methods for reconstructing the semantic trajectories using other data available during a mission, and cross-validate them against the movement data generated ones. In our work we propose to utilize the geo-tagged photos taken by drones' carrying equipment during a mission, since they provide suitable meta-data for semantic trajectory reconstruction.

The aim of our work is a) to design and implement an ontology-based framework for the semantic modeling of trajectories of swarms of drones, reconstructed by geo-tagged photos, b) the development of a method for constructing semantic trajectories from geo-tagged photos. Although related research work exists in both directions, currently there isn't any free and open-source integrated development environment available for supporting both tasks. The goal of our work is to do so by implementing both as extensions of the open-source and widely-used free environment for spatiotemporal trajectory analytics and visualization, namely MovingPandas [4]. Moreover, we plan to evaluate the implemented tasks with real data of drone flights that we are continuously collecting from our drones, as well as from open data. Last but not least, we plan to reuse datAcron ontology [5] in the semantic annotation task of the proposed framework, extending it were necessary, delivering a new UAV-specific ontological model.

The structure of this paper is as follows: Sect. 2 presents the state-of-the-art in related topics, and Sect. 3 briefly introduces the proposed approach.

2 Related Work

Grasier proposes a general-purpose Python library for the analysis and visualization of trajectory data called MovingPandas [4]. In MovingPandas the trajectory is the core object, and modelled as time-ordered series of geometries, stored as GeoDataFrame and integrated with coordinate reference system information. A trajectory object in Moving-Pandas can represent its data either as point-based, or as line-based, while the analysis process and the visualization are executed in two-dimensional space. The proposed library can be used as a stand-alone Python script, as well as within the desktop GIS application QGIS as a plugin called Trajetools.

In the work of Cai et al. [6], the focus is on extracting Semantic Trajectory Patterns from geo-tagged data. They propose a semantic trajectory pattern mining framework, from geo-tagged data taken from social media, to create raw geographic trajectories. These raw trajectories are enriched with contextual semantic annotations, using a RoI as stop to illustrate a place of interest. The algorithm returns basic and multidimensional semantic trajectory patterns.

Santipatakis et al. [5] propose the datAcron ontology for representing semantic trajectories at varying levels of spatiotemporal analysis. Mobility analysis tasks are based on a wealth of disparate and heterogeneous sources of information that need to be integrated. The proposed ontology, as a generic conceptual framework, tackles this challenging problem. The experimental results (Air Traffic Management domain) demonstrate that the proposed ontology supports the representation of trajectories at multiple, interlinked levels of analysis.

3 Proposed Approach

As already stated, the goal of our work is to design and implement both a) a method for the semantic modeling of trajectories of swarms of drones, and b) a method for the reconstruction of semantic trajectories from geo-tagged photos, as extensions of the open-source and widely used free environment for trajectory analytics and visualization, namely the MovingPandas.

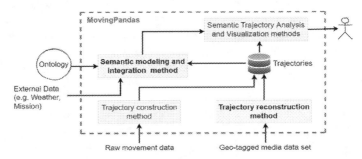

Fig. 1. High-level architectural design of the proposed approach (new methods appear in bold)

Towards this direction we propose a combination of approaches, ontologies, tools and methods for reconstructing and semantically annotating trajectories. Particularly, we propose the extension of MovingPandas with a trajectory reconstruction method using the suitable metadata of geo-tagged images (timestamp: date/time taken, GPS data: latitude, longitude, altitude) taken by drones during flights, along with the semantic modeling of trajectories of swarms of drones reusing the datAcron ontology within a new drone-related ontology (for modeling knowledge related to swarms of drones, their flights and missions, their recordings, etc.) which is currently under development in our laboratory. Figure 1 depicts the high-level architectural design of the proposed methods integrated in MovingPandas. The ontological approach ensures a high-level formalism for the representation of a semantic trajectory, as various heterogenous data such as altitude, sensor (attached to drones or gathered from terrestrial IoT platforms), and weather data (gathered from open Web services), along with mission (who, why, and what) and geographic data (e.g., shape files of documenting/recording areas), etc., are used for the enrichment of raw trajectories. Figure 2 depicts the high-level design of the core semantics of the proposed ontology. At this stage, a first draft version (1.0.0) of the semantic model (namely, Onto4drone) has been developed and it is available in OWL[1]. It is directly based on the datAcron ontology, and indirectly on the DUL, SKOS, SOSA/SSN, SF, GML, and GeoSparql ontologies. The model was developed following the HCOME collaborative engineering methodology, supported by Protégé 5.5 (for personal space model engineering), and WebProtégé (for shared space model engineering). In addition, Google docs and Meet have been used for further collaborative engineering tasks.

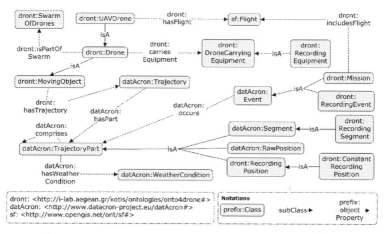

Fig. 2. Basic concepts and relations of the Onto4drone ontology.

The basic concepts and semantic relations of the model which were implemented in the Onto4drone ontology are briefly presented in Fig. 2 in the form of a concept map. This version of Onto4drone includes classes, object properties, and data properties based on the motivated use case of a documentation flight with a mission to record a SAR event related to a sinking ship during a storm. A representative restriction that a RecordingEvent (e.g., a SAR event) occurs in at least one RecordingPosition or in a RecordingSegment. Additionally, a number of individuals have been added in order to evaluate the engineered model in different scenarios.

Beyond the development of the ontological model, current implementation of the proposed approach includes the following:

---

[1] https://github.com/KotisK/onto4drone.

- The extraction of the metadata (timestamp: date/time, latitude, longitude, altitude) from geo-tagged images taken by drone during flight (several inhouse and open datasets from different types of drones have been already tested).
- The reconstruction of drone's raw trajectory using the extracted metadata, and their visualization in MovingPandas.
- The enrichment of drones' trajectories with the injection of additional data (currently missing from MovingPandas' representation capabilities) such as altitude, weather data, geographic data.

4 Conclusion

Managing data of drones' flights/missions are becoming more and more popular in a wide range of applications. To be able to derive meaningful and rich information from drones' movement in the field of operation, it is necessary to semantically enrich them with relevant heterogeneous data/information. In addition, it is necessary to find alternative ways of constructing their semantic trajectories. Towards this direction, we propose the development of a free and open-source semantic trajectory reconstruction module, along with a semantic modeling and integration module for the contextual enrichment of trajectories within MovingPandas.

References

1. Parent, C., et al.: Semantic trajectories modeling and analysis. ACM Comput. Surv. **45**, 1–32 (2013). https://doi.org/10.1145/2501654.2501656
2. Cook, K.L.B.: The silent force multiplier: the history and role of UAVs in warfare. In: IEEE Aerospace Conference Proceedings (2007). https://doi.org/10.1109/AERO.2007.352737
3. Burridge, B.: UAVs and the dawn of post-modern warfare: a perspective on recent operations. RUSI J. **148**, 18–23 (2003). https://doi.org/10.1080/03071840308446924
4. Graser, A.: MovingPandas: efficient structures for movement data in Python. GI_Forum **7**, 54–68 (2019). https://doi.org/10.1553/GISCIENCE2019_01_S54
5. Vouros, G.A., et al.: The datAcron ontology for the specification of semantic trajectories. J. Data Semant. **8**(4), 235–262 (2019). https://doi.org/10.1007/s13740-019-00108-0
6. Cai, G., Lee, K., Lee, I.: Mining semantic trajectory patterns from geo-tagged data. J. Comput. Sci. Technol. **33**(4), 849–862 (2018). https://doi.org/10.1007/s11390-018-1860-1

How to Search and Contextualize Scenes Inside Videos for Enriched Watching Experience: Case Stories of the Second World War Veterans

Eero Hyvönen[1,2]([✉]), Esko Ikkala[1], Mikko Koho[1], Rafael Leal[1],
Heikki Rantala[1], and Minna Tamper[1,2]

[1] Semantic Computing Research Group (SeCo), Aalto University, Espoo, Finland
{eero.hyvonen,esko.ikkala,mikko.koho,rafael.leal,heikki.rantala,
minna.tamper}@aalto.fi
[2] HELDIG – Helsinki Centre for Digital Humanities, University of Helsinki, Helsinki,
Finland
{eero.hyvonen,minna.tamper}@helsinki.fi
https://seco.cs.aalto.fi, https://heldig.fi

Abstract. This demo paper demonstrates the idea of publishing and watching videos on the Semantic Web. An in-use application, WARMEM-OIRSAMPO, is presented that enables scene segments in videos to be searched by their semantic content. While watching a video, additional contextual information is provided dynamically. The system is based on a SPARQL endpoint whose knowledge graph has been extracted automatically from timestamped natural language descriptions of the video contents.

1 Introduction and Related Work

More and more content on the Web is published as videos[1]. Often the videos are long and may contain heterogenous scene segments, such as news in a longer broadcast or scenes of different topics in a film or an interview. Traditional search for whole videos is then not enough but tools for searching and accessing particular scene segments inside the videos are needed.

This paper presents an in-use semantic portal for annotating and searching scenes inside videos. When viewing a video, the annotations can be used for contextualizing the scenes with additional linked data for enriched watching experience. As a case study, a collection of interviews of the Second World War (WW2) veterans is considered. Here timestamped textual descriptions of the videos were available written by the interviewer. Our challenge was to create a knowledge graph of the videos based on their textual descriptions, and on top of it a portal for searching, exploring, and viewing the videos.

---

[1] E.g., https://youtube.com/, https://tiktok.com/, https://vimeo.com/, etc.

P. Groth et al. (Eds.): ESWC 2022 Satellite Events, LNCS 13384, pp. 163–167, 2022.
https://doi.org/10.1007/978-3-031-11609-4_31

Related Work. The research area of video indexing is surveyed in [1]. Indexing can be done by analyzing the frames and/or audio of the recording to find, e.g., the spots where goals are made in a football match. Another option is to use the textual subtitles (dialogues, commentaries) of the video. In some cases, e.g., in historical film archives, manually curated textual descriptions or commentaries of the videos may be available for preserving cultural heritage—they can be used for annotations and indexing, too, as in our case study. Various methods and tools are available for extracting linked data from texts [6]. Providing contextual information and ads while watching videos has been suggested already in the 80's in systems, such as Hypersoap[2]. Works on enriching video watching experience using linked data-based recommendations include, e.g., [7].

2 WarMemoirSampo System: Data Service and Portal

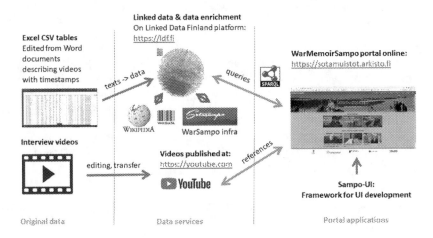

Fig. 1. Publication pipeline from source data to the semantic video viewing portal

Publishing Model. The publication pipeline of the WARMEMOIRSAMPO system is illustrated in Fig. 1. The original data on the left are 1) a set of interview videos and 2) timestamped notes made by the interviewer about the contents of the videos, transformed into spreadsheets with timestamps and corresponding texts. The videos were published on YouTube and its IFrame player[3] is used. The spreadsheets were transformed into a knowledge graph (KG) of 323 000 triples. Its data model contains the core class for an interview whose instances refer to sets of timestamped scene instances. The scenes are annotated with instances of named entities, based on their mentions in the texts describing the scenes, and

---

[2] www.media.mit.edu/hypersoap/.

[3] https://developers.google.com/youtube/iframe_api_reference.

topical keywords linked to an ontology. The entities were linked to resources in the WarSampo KG [4], an extensive data infrastructure for the Finnish WW2, and Wikidata/Wikipedia for further information. The semantic scene annotation and indexing process using natural language processing tools is presented in [5].

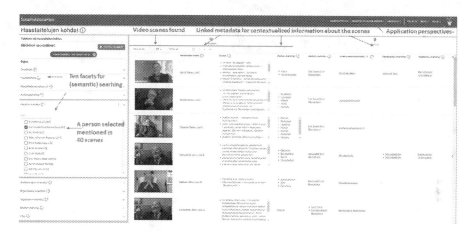

Fig. 2. Faceted search for scenes inside videos.

Semantic Portal. Based on the Sampo model [2] and Sampo-UI framework [3], the landing page of WARMEMOIRSAMPO portal provides three application perspectives to the KG with faceted semantic search: 1) *Interviews perspective* is used for searching whole videos based on their nine key properties: Interviewee, Interview notes, Gender, and mentioned Place, Person, Military unit, Organization, Event, Other entity, and Topic. There is also a facet for traditional text-based search. 2) *Scenes perspective* is used for searching video scenes using the same facets. 3) *Directory perspective* contains all ca. 3000 entities mentioned in the texts with direct links to scenes where the entities were mentioned.

Figure 2 depicts the Scenes perspective, where the user has selected "Carl Gustav Emil Mannerheim" on the facet Person: the 40 scenes mentioning this marshal are shown on the right with metadata links for further information. By clicking on a video, its is opened for dynamic viewing as depicted in Fig. 3. Links to additional information are provided on the fly. Selecting the tab Map on top shows the places mentioned on a map; Fig. 4 shows all 4566 of them. Clicking a marker on the map opens a popup with links to all related scenes. Finally, the tab Word cloud summarizes the topics of the video interview.

Technology. The data model of the underlying knowledge graph contains classes for videos and their scenes annotated by entities extracted from their natural language descriptions, including people, places, military units, organizations, and events. In addition, metadata about the videos, such as the names

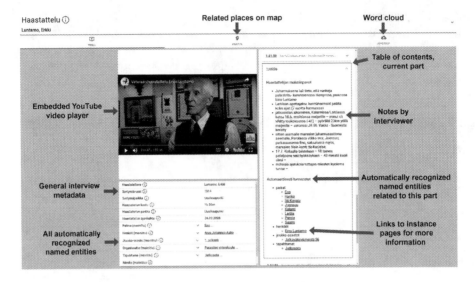

Fig. 3. Video viewing page with a dynamic table of contents for contextual linked data.

of the interviewee and interviewer and the date of interview, were available. The facets ontologies for entities were created bottom-up based on the entities found in the texts and the data was indexed accordingly. In addition, entities were linked to the knowledge graph of WarSampo and Wikidata/Wikipedia for contextual information. The process is explained in more detail in [5]. The state-of-the-art NER/NEL tools used were able to find entities from textual data and categorize them with high enough recall and precision to be useful for building facet ontologies, without involving considerable manual domain ontology engineering. Finally, the knowledge graph was published on the Linked Data Finland platform LDF.fi with a SPARQL endpoint[4] for application development.

3　Summary of Contributions

The novelty of the presented WARMEMOIRSAMPO system lays in the consolidated publication model of Fig. 1 for publishing, enriching, searching, and watching video segments in a linked data context, based on the Sampo model [2], Sampo-UI framework [3], and using natural language knowledge extraction [5].

The underlying data of the in-use portal[5] is available on the Linked Data Finland Platform LDF.fi as an open SPARQL endpoint, and the portal code on GitHub[6], for the community to study, apply, and develop the model further.

---

[4] https://ldf.fi/warmemoirsampo/sparql.

[5] The portal can be used at: https://sotamuistot.arkisto.fi.

[6] https://github.com/SemanticComputing/veterans-web-app.

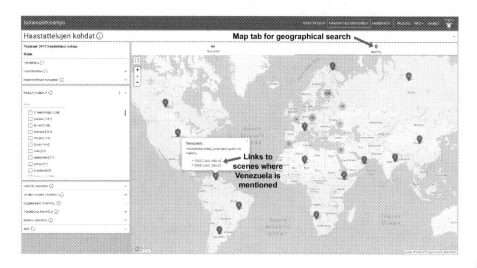

Fig. 4. Map view to access scenes that mention a place.

Acknowledgements. Markus Merenmies, Ilpo Murtovaara, and Kare Salonvaara provided the data and videos. Tammenlehvän Perinneliitto ry funded our work, and CSC – IT Center for Science provided computational resources.

References

1. Hu, W., Xie, N., Li, L., Zeng, X., Maybank, S.: A survey on visual content-based video indexing and retrieval. IEEE Trans. Syst. Man Cybern. **41**(6), 797–819 (2011). https://doi.org/10.1109/TSMCC.2011.2109710
2. Hyvönen, E.: Digital humanities on the semantic web: sampo model and portal series. Semantic Web - Interoperability, Usability, Applicability (2022). http://www.semantic-web-journal.net/content/digital-humanities-semantic-web-sampo-model-and-portal-series-0. Accepted
3. Ikkala, E., Hyvönen, E., Rantala, H., Koho, M.: Sampo-UI: a full stack javascript framework for developing semantic portal user interfaces. Seman. Web - Interoperability Usability Applicability **13**(1), 69–84 (2022). https://doi.org/10.3233/SW-210428
4. Koho, M., Ikkala, E., Leskinen, P., Tamper, M., Tuominen, J., Hyvönen, E.: WarSampo knowledge graph: Finland in the second world war as linked open data. Seman. Web - Interoperability Usability Applicability **12**(2), 265–278 (2021). https://doi.org/10.3233/SW-200392
5. Leal, R., Rantala, H., Koho, M., Ikkala, E., Merenmies, M., Hyvönen, E.: WarMemoirSampo: a semantic portal for war veteran interview videos. In: 6th Digital Humanities in Nordic and Baltic Countries Conference (2022). submitted paper
6. Martinez-Rodriguez, J.L., Hogan, A., Lopez-Arevalo, I.: Information extraction meets the semantic web: a survey. Seman. Web - Interoperability Usability Applicability **11**(2), 255–335 (2020). https://doi.org/10.3233/SW-180333
7. Nixon, L., Bauer, M., Bara, C.: Connected media experiences: web based interactive video using linked data. In: Proceedings of the 22nd International Conference on World Wide Web, pp. 309–312. ACM, New York (2013). https://doi.org/10.1145/2487788.2487931

PhD Symposium

(Semi-) Automatic Construction of Knowledge Graph Metadata

Maryam Mohammadi[✉] [ORCID]

Institute of Data Science, Maastricht University, Maastricht, The Netherlands
m.mohammadi@maastrichtuniversity.nl

Abstract. Recently a huge number of knowledge graphs (KGs) has been generated, but there has not been enough attention to generate high-quality metadata to enable users to reuse the KGs for their own purposes. The main challenge is to generate standardized and high quality descriptive metadata which helps users understand the content of the large KGs. Some existing solutions make use of a combination of schema-level patterns derived from graph summarization with instance-level snippets. I will follow this trend and develop a method based on a combination of content-based patterns with user activity data such as SPARQL query logs to make generated metadata more informative and useful than other developed approaches. The problem of current models is generating complex, long or insufficient metadata which I plan to tackle by proposing a guideline to generate standard metadata during my Ph.D.

Keywords: Metadata · Knowledge graph · FAIR · Graph summarization · SPARQL query logs

1 Motivation

Analyzing and mining Big Data provides a precious opportunity to solve a variety of problems. Increasingly, data is organized as a knowledge graph, in which data are represented as nodes and edges, and this representation facilitates data integration and knowledge discovery. Enormous amounts of Knowledge Graphs (KGs) have been published by researchers in academia and industry. However, there has not been enough attention to generate high-quality metadata to sufficiently describe these datasets which specify what these data are and how they were produced [1, 11]. The lack of standardized metadata also makes comparing possible datasets extremely difficult. Therefore, it is quite challenging for users to find pertinent datasets and reuse them for analyses or other aims without high quality metadata [8].

According to the FAIR principles [7], datasets and their metadata should be represented in a way that makes the dataset more Findable, Accessible, Interoperable, and Reusable. However, creating metadata manually is time-consuming, often incomplete, and prone to error. Towards improving the findability and reusability of the KG datasets, there is an urgent need to provide a rich, structured and understandable description of the dataset in a cost-effective and scalable way [14].

P. Groth et al. (Eds.): ESWC 2022 Satellite Events, LNCS 13384, pp. 171–178, 2022.
https://doi.org/10.1007/978-3-031-11609-4_32

My work aims to increase FAIRness of KGs by generating high quality descriptions of KGs. Increasing FAIRness will enable people and machines to discover relevant resources, and reuse them for new tasks instead of investing their time and money to create their own dataset. It is estimated that the European economy loses more than €10.2 billion euros per year [6] owing to a lack of FAIR data, based on five quantifiable indicators: time spent, cost of storage, license costs, research retraction and double funding. I believe that improving the amount and quality of metadata will improve overall productivity, reduce duplicative costs, and generate new opportunities. For instance, even assuming one has sufficient knowledge about SPARQL query language, it is important to understand the content of the dataset to write the query. Providing enriched metadata that present schemas as well as connections between entities of a KG extremely helps users in query writing tasks [1].

The rest of the paper is organized as follows. I review State-of-the-Art methods in Sect. 2. I introduce problem formulation and research questions in Sect. 3, research hypotheses and research steps are outlined in the Sect. 4 followed by an evaluation plan in Sect. 5. Section 6 presents preliminary results. Lessons learned and conclusions are described in Sect. 7.

2   State-of-the-Art

Several approaches have been proposed to generate high quality descriptive metadata, but many of these rely on human curation, which is expensive, time consuming, and may be limited by the availability of experts. In contrast, semi-automatic and automatic methods offer another way forward. For example, the health care and life sciences community have proposed a generic profile for dataset descriptions and provided SPARQL-based templates for automatic data summarization [3]. Yike et al. [17] have described several graph summarization methods, as well as their different types of input and output. Safavi et al. [18] have proposed GLIMPSE for creating personalized knowledge graph summarization. Ayak et al. [2] have conducted an automatic method for predicting experimental metadata from scientific publications. Martínez-Romero M et al. [4] have developed a method for generating metadata with using ontology-based recommendations. Moreover, there are variant works based on graph summarization models [1, 5], which create schema-level patterns to represent content of a KG. Some works generate instance-level triples by the use of graph snippet generation methods [13]. Wang et al. [9] have proposed a Pattern-Coverage Snippet generation for RDF Datasets based on a combination of schema-level and instance-level data.

As I am using SPARQL query logs in my proposed method, I have done some literature review on SPARQL query logs analysis. Through an analysis on Bio2RDF SPARQL query logs Carlos et al. [14] reported some statistics about SPARQL query keywords and triple patters. In addition, they found that there is a large amount of repeated queries and only 20 query patterns represent 90% of the whole Bio2RDF query logs. Saleem et al. [15] proposed The Linked SPARQL Queries Dataset (LSQ), which describes SPARQL queries issued to endpoints of four datasets with providing statistics of SPARQL features and classes. Claus et al. [16] developed LSQ 2.0: A Linked Dataset of SPARQL Query Logs and extended the work of [15] to 27 different endpoints.

In contrast, in my work, I am focusing on each element of the triple patterns namely subjects, predicates, and objects rather than SPARQL keywords or features. For instance, I list the top 20 frequent subjects, predicates, and objects that indicate the interests of the users based on the query logs.

3 Problem Statement and Contributions

In this section, I introduce problem formulation and research questions that will be focused on during my Ph.D. and the expected contributions I aim to make by answering the research questions.

My PhD research focuses on developing computational approaches for generating high quality machine-readable and human-readable descriptive metadata for knowledge graphs. Generated metadata will help users in two tasks; 1) summarizing the content of a dataset and therefore, increasing the discoverability of a dataset, 2) helping users in SPARQL query writing. My work will explore ways to make generated metadata more informative and useful than other developed approaches. A key direction will be explored lies in the combination of content-based patterns data with external user activity data such as SPARQL query logs. I hypothesize that different metrics will be of value for different KG-related tasks, and intend to learn about these user preferences. The research will study the following research questions:

RQ1- To what extent do the analysis of external knowledge sources (e.g. query logs) inform users of its most relevant content?
RQ2- To what extent sensible natural language summaries could be generated from knowledge graphs?

4 Research Methodology and Approach

Graph summarization can generate metadata about the content of the graph by quantifying how many times certain patterns occur. For a very large graph, it may not be easy for somebody to quickly determine what the graph is about due to a high number of emerging patterns. On the other hand, I hypothesize the users' query logs (against the SPARQL endpoint of a KG) could potentially reveal valuable information about what is interesting to the users of that particular KG. To the best of our knowledge, none of the existing work has used SPARQL query logs in their proposed method. I aim to propose a method to prioritize the patterns driven from graph summarization based on what users ask about the graph, in other words, based on the information from query logs. Additionally queries can contain constants, which are potentially informative to users. According to this idea, three hypotheses are shaped as below:

Hypothesis 1: Frequently occurring SPARQL queries are more useful as metadata than frequently occurring graph summaries (frequently occurring concepts) for large graphs, as qualitatively evaluated by potential users of the graph.

Hypothesis 2: Query filtered graph summaries are more useful as metadata than either ranked lists of SPARQL queries or graph summaries.

Hypothesis 3: Frequently occurring patterns derived from SPARQL queries are more useful as metadata than ranked lists of SPARQL queries or ranked lists of graph summaries.

Research steps for exploring an answer for RQ1 and RQ2 and my progress in each step is as follows:

Step1: Retrieve SPARQL query logs from the endpoint or available resources for a KG (e.g. Bio2RDF Kg or Wikidata KG)
Step2: Remove personal data and prepare the SPARQL query data in a format that is clean for processing
 For cleaning data I delete some basic automatic SPARQL queries that has been sent by machines such as "select* where {?s ?p ?o}". However, I keep more complex SPARQL queries that has been sent by machines or web interfaces, which I believe they are interesting and informative.
Step 3. Isolate query patterns or keywords from SPARQL query logs using a library such as RDF4J, Apache Jena or RDFLib. Generated keywords for an example query is shown in Fig. 1.
Step 4. Apply a graph summarization algorithm [9] or a rule-mining algorithm to the KG and rank the output patterns based on their frequency. (We call these patterns, content-based patterns)
Step 5. Rank query patterns or keywords according to their frequency of use in the SPARQL queries.
Step 6. Merge results of step 3 and 4 to produce metadata for the KG
 One idea is to select high frequent patterns generated from executing step 4 only if they contain highly frequent keywords from step 3.
Step 7. Convert graph summaries (metadata) to sensible natural language summaries (metadata) (RQ2)

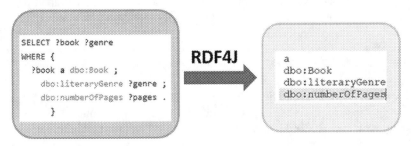

Fig. 1. Generated subject, predicate and object keywords from an example query using RDF4J

Step 8. Evaluate the quality and utility of derived metadata with user study and FAIRness evaluation.

I proposed a workflow to generate descriptive metadata for a KG or a SPARQL endpoint by providing two use cases, Bio2RDF and Wikidata KGs. I chose these KGs because the goal of my work is to create a method which is able to support large scale KGs. I believe that this approach is generalizable; a limitation of method could be the difficulty of obtaining such SPARQL logs. Accessing SPARQL logs data might not always be possible. Depending on the tools used to store the logs, the process for obtaining the logs could be different. About our use cases, for Bio2RDF triplestore, because we had full control over it and we had added a service to store the logs, we were able to retrieve them. Wikidata logs were accessible through a public dataset from international center for computational logic.

5   Evaluation Plan

In this section, I explain three different experiments that I will conduct to evaluate my method. I intend to perform two types of user study mentioned in [1] and [9]. Spahiu et al. [1] have designed a SPARQL query formulation task for two groups of the people, control group and ABSTAT group to evaluate if generated metadata can help users in SPARQL query formulation. Formulating SPARQL queries is a task that requires prior knowledge about the dataset. In this work, five queries (with different complexity) in natural language format together with their incomplete SPARQL formulation were given to 20 participants. The participants were equally splitted into two groups and only one group could use their framework (ABSTAT) in order to get help and complete SPARQL queries. Authors measured the time spent to complete each query and the correctness of the answers and compared the performance of the groups based on completion time and accuracy of the answers. In an experiment by Wang et al. [9], participants of the user study are 20 computer science students that all have the essential knowledge about RDF. Each participant were given ten RDF datasets together with metadata about each RDF dataset. Participants have been asked to rate the quality of two snippets generated by their method and a baseline method, in the range from 1 to 5 expressing how well that snippet exemplified the content of the RDF dataset and have asked to briefly explain the rating. Finally, I will introduce a new evaluation, based on assessing and comparing FAIRness of KG before and after importing generated metadata to the KG with different automatic or semi-automatic FAIR evaluation tools such as FAIR CHECKER [10] and F-UJI [12]. These tools take a resource as the input and check all the FAIR principles for that resource and assign a number indicating percentage of FAIRness of the resource.

6   Preliminary Results

The results of the conducted research steps for each use case are described in this section. Bio2RDF SPARQL queries log has been dumped from ElasticSearch and its personal data has been removed. The code and data is accessible through kg-metadata-generation GitHub page. Organic SPARQL queries of Wikidata that are clean to process and do not contain personal data are downloaded from international center for computational logic. Using RDF4J package in java, all triple patterns of Wikidata queries has been extracted. Then each element of subject, predicate and object is extracted from the triple patterns. In the next step, frequency of the keywords has been calculated. Frequency of the keywords extracted from Organic SPARQL queries of Wikidata is shown in Table 1. and Table 2.

These results suggest that another criterion such as validity of the keyword in addition to the frequency must be considered for step 5 of methodology to avoid meaningless keywords such as "string1". On the other hand, for generating content-based patterns different graph summarization models are explored. Rule base methods due to their scalability for large size of input will be studied.

Table 1. Frequency of the predicate keywords extracted from organic SPARQL queries

Top 10 frequent predicate keywords (the labels)	Frequency
Language	88072
Instance of (P31)	63927
Label	47823
Image (P18)	35315
Coordinate location (P625)	28912
Subclass of (P279)	27832
Description	22334
About	14825
Commons category (P373)	12711
Located in the administrative territorial entity (P131)	11717

Table 2. Frequency of the subject or object keywords extracted from Organic SPARQL queries of Wikidata

Top 10 frequent subject or object keywords (the labels)	Frequency
"en"	35781
"string1"	15326
Human (Q5)	9527
"en,en"	6420
"fr"	5449
"None"	4029
Wiki_Main_Page	3690
"POINT(9"	3017
"de"	2874
'41)"^^ < http://www.opengis.net/ont/geosparql#wktLiteral > '	2813

7 Conclusions and Lessons Learned

Lack of high quality metadata hinders users to better understand existing datasets and reuse them for more analyses and other purposes. The informative, machine- and human-readable metadata (that describes relevant features of the data in the KGs) would increase reusability of the data from existing KGs. Generating metadata for KGs in automatic manner is essential in order to decrease socio-economic impact of not having metadata or high quality metadata. My work aims to propose computational methods to generate descriptive metadata for KGs based on the combination of their internal (e.g. content-based patterns) and external (e.g. user activity) data. Generated results on a sample of small size of the Wikidata dataset are very promising.

Acknowledgements. This research has been funded by the European Union's Horizon 2020 research and innovation program under the Marie Skłodowska-Curie project Knowgraphs (grant agreement ID: 860801). I would like to express my special thanks of gratitude to my advisors and collaborators Prof. Michel Dumontier, Prof Christopher Brewster, Dr. Remzi Celebi, Chang Sun and Vincent Emonet.

References

1. Spahiu, B., Porrini, R., Palmonari, M., Rula, A., Maurino, A.: ABSTAT: ontology-driven linked data summaries with pattern minimalization. In: Sack, H., Rizzo, G., Steinmetz, N., Mladenić, D., Auer, S., Lange, C. (eds.) ESWC 2016. LNCS, vol. 9989, pp. 381–395. Springer, Cham (2016). https://doi.org/10.1007/978-3-319-47602-5_51
2. Nayak, S., Zaveri, A., Serrano, P.H., Dumontier, M.: Experience: automated prediction of experimental metadata from scientific publications. J. Data Inf. Qual. **13**(4), 1–11 (2021). https://doi.org/10.1145/3451219
3. Dumontier, M., et al.: The health care and life sciences community profile for dataset descriptions. PeerJ **4**, e2331 (2016)
4. Martínez-Romero, M, O'Connor, M.J., Shankar, R.D., et al.: Fast and accurate metadata authoring using ontology-based recommendations. In: AMIA Annual Symposium Proceedings 2018, vol. 2017, pp. 1272–1281. Published 16 April 2018
5. Song, Q., Wu, Y., Dong, X.L.: Mining summaries for knowledge graph search. In: 2016 IEEE 16th International Conference on Data Mining (ICDM), pp. 1215–1220 (2016). https://doi.org/10.1109/ICDM.2016.0162
6. European commission, directorate-general for research and innovation, cost-benefit analysis for FAIR research data: cost of not having FAIR research data. Publications Office (2019). https://doi.org/10.2777/02999, https://op.europa.eu/en/publication-detail/-/publication/d375368c-1a0a-11e9-8d04-01aa75ed71a1/language-en
7. Wilkinson, M.D., et al.: The FAIR guiding principles for scientific data management and stewardship. Sci. data **3**(1), 1–9 (2016). https://www.nature.com/articles/sdata201618
8. Pietriga, E., et al.: Browsing linked data catalogs with LODAtlas. In: Vrandečić, D., et al. (eds.) ISWC 2018. LNCS, vol. 11137, pp. 137–153. Springer, Cham (2018). https://doi.org/10.1007/978-3-030-00668-6_9
9. Wang, X., et al.: PCSG: pattern-coverage snippet generation for RDF datasets. In: Hotho, A., et al. (eds.) ISWC 2021. LNCS, vol. 12922, pp. 3–20. Springer, Cham (2021). https://doi.org/10.1007/978-3-030-88361-4_1

10. Rosnet, T., de Lamotte, F., Devignes, M.D., Lefort, V., Gaignard, A.: FAIR-checker–supporting the findability and reusability of digital life science resources

11. Palmonari, M., Rula, A., Porrini, R., Maurino, A., Spahiu, B., Ferme, V.: ABSTAT: linked data summaries with abstraction and statistics. In: Gandon, F., Guéret, C., Villata, S., Breslin, J., Faron-Zucker, C., Zimmermann, A. (eds.) ESWC 2015. LNCS, vol. 9341, pp. 128–132. Springer, Cham (2015). https://doi.org/10.1007/978-3-319-25639-9_25

12. Huber, R., Devaraju, A.: F-UJI: an automated tool for the assessment and improvement of the FAIRness of research data. In: EGU General Assembly Conference Abstracts, pp. EGU21–15922 (2021)

13. Liu, D., Cheng, G., Liu, Q., Yuzhong, Q.: Fast and practical snippet generation for RDF datasets. ACM Trans. Web (TWEB) **13**(4), 1–38 (2019)

14. Buil-Aranda, C., Ugarte, M., Arenas, M., Dumontier, M.: A preliminary investigation into SPARQL query complexity and federation in Bio2RDF. In: Mendelzon, A. (ed.) International Workshop on Foundations of Data Management, p. 196 (2015)

15. Saleem, M., Ali, M.I., Hogan, A., Mehmood, Q., Ngomo, A.-C.: LSQ: the linked SPARQL queries dataset. In: Arenas, M., Corcho, O., Simperl, E., Strohmaier, M., d'Aquin, M., Srinivas, K., Groth, P., Dumontier, M., Heflin, J., Thirunarayan, K., Staab, S. (eds.) ISWC 2015. LNCS, vol. 9367, pp. 261–269. Springer, Cham (2015). https://doi.org/10.1007/978-3-319-25010-6_15

16. Stadlera, C., et al.: LSQ 2.0: a linked dataset of SPARQL query logs

17. Liu, Y., Safavi, T., Dighe, A., Koutra, D.: Graph summarization methods and applications: a survey. ACM Comput. Surv. (CSUR) **51**(3), 1–34 (2018)

18. Safavi, T., Belth, C., Faber, L., Mottin, D., Müller, E., Koutra, D.: Personalized knowledge graph summarization: from the cloud to your pocket. In: 2019 IEEE International Conference on Data Mining (ICDM), pp. 528–537. IEEE (2019)

Towards a Similarity Algorithm for Controlled Vocabularies Within the Digital Humanities

Felix Ernst(✉) ⓘ

Karlsruhe Institute of Technology, Karlsruhe, Germany
felix.ernst@kit.edu

Abstract. With a growing amount and increasing complexity of data and metadata in the Digital Humanities, the use of semantic tools such as controlled vocabularies and taxonomies becomes more and more important to gain new research insights. Their use enables new research possibilities by introducing machine readable semantic links and standardised data and metadata. A validation and recommender system that ensures a quick development of high quality vocabularies is essential in such a scientific workflow. The base of this system is a similarity algorithm. State of the art algorithms and editors for controlled vocabularies do not meet the special requirements of the Digital Humanities domain. Therefore, this work proposes to fill the research gap in the Digital Humanities domain with a similarity algorithm and a recommender and validation system for controlled vocabularies. The methodology and evaluation for achieving this goal as well as preliminary results are presented in this contribution.

Keywords: Semantic web · Similarity metrics · Recommender system · Controlled vocabularies · Vocabulary editor · SKOS

1 Introduction and Motivation

Computer-based methods for answering research questions in the Digital Humanities (DH) pose special challenges: The research data are diverse and oftentimes do not consist of machine readable text but rather of textual fragments, images, 3D models, illustrations and many more, all in multiple (historical) languages and writing systems. Additionally, they are often incomplete, distributed across different data sources or over multiple countries and growing in complexity. Knowledge enrichment of data and metadata by semantic methods plays an important role to overcome these difficulties [6].

This can be best illustrated on a simplified exemplary DH use case of an ongoing research project that is studying different historical language learning books which is part of the Collaborative Research Centre (CRC) 980 'Episteme in Motion'[1]. The group's research interests focus on various aspects of the text-

---

[1] Funded by the German Research Foundation (Deutsche Forschungsgemeinschaft, DFG), see https://www.dfg.de/sfb/.

books, one of which is the book's target audiences. The scholars annotate the digital images of the book pages with machine readable tags to enable further data analysis. A problem arises when tagged historical terms that refer to the same target group differ due to grammar, synonyms or different languages. A controlled vocabulary[2] for all tags solves this problem by semantic links. Synonyms or terms in different languages are incorporated and linked to the single item they refer to. Together with a vocabulary for descriptive metadata about the books such as author, place of printing or writing language, it results in a Knowledge Organisation System (KOS) with well categorised and interlinked tags and metadata. This enables the development of advanced computer-assisted methods for analysing, managing and visualising data. In the DH case, existing vocabularies found in vocabulary registries oftentimes are either too broad or do not match the scholar's needs or required language. Thus, there is a need for developing own vocabularies that are tailored to the data, to the research questions and that are easily shareable. This gives rise to new research possibilities since the reuse of results as well as the collaboration of both disciplinary and interdisciplinary research groups is simplified [5]. Unfortunately, building subject-specific, high-quality vocabularies often is not feasible for domain experts in a reasonable amount of time with currently available vocabulary editors. This is due to the fact that these are either outdated, lack well-written documentation and usability or do not support widely used standards which prevents their use.

One important step to build vocabularies in a fast and efficient way is the use of validation and recommender systems. The latter presents terms and term sets from existing vocabularies and knowledge bases to the researcher that match the current topic or field. Integration of the recommendations allows for a faster vocabulary development. A semantic and content-wise validation system ensures accurate and error-free high quality vocabularies [15]. Both systems rely on similarity algorithms for vocabularies and its terms. The algorithms are not only capable of finding similar terms but also compare semantic relations. Developing a semantic similarity algorithm and a validation and recommender system for the DH faces several challenges. The number of relevant existing domain specific vocabularies or knowledge bases is oftentimes low. Additionally, not only the research data are multilingual, but also the research and the output itself which results in challenges when mapping terms of different (sometimes dead) languages. Furthermore, material and human resources of DH projects often are tight. This leads to the need of specifically designed similarity metrics.

These and the validation and recommender systems have to meet the following **requirements** in order to overcome the aforementioned challenges of the DH: (a) support of heterogeneous, multilingual vocabularies and data; (b) applicability even when preexisting vocabularies are scarce; (c) high usability since DH scholars typically have less background in technical computer science issues such as algorithm improvement or adapting research software; (d) utilisation in projects with limited human resources for acquiring knowledge about ontology

---

[2] In the following, thesauri and taxonomies are subsumed under the term vocabulary.

development; (e) applicability in projects with restricted possibilities of running resource intensive algorithms or software.

The overarching goal is to propose a validation and recommender system for vocabularies which can easily be integrated into a vocabulary editor. It aims to support researchers by lowering the barrier of entry for building high-quality vocabularies. No prior knowledge is needed, thus it facilitates computer-aided research.

2   State of the Art

In order to find relevant vocabularies or terms for a particular research area, there are various **vocabulary registries** that contain humanities specific terms. These include *Linked Open Vocabularies*[3], *DARIAH EU back bone thesaurus*[4], *Linked open terminology resources*[5], *CLARIAH awesome humanities ontologies*[6] or the *Basic Register of Thesauri, Ontologies & Classifications*[7]. Some exemplary tasks taken from sub-projects of CRC 980 include the description of old Greek texts and Egyptian hieroglyphs as well as multilingual terms for ancient plant names. For these tasks, no adequate vocabularies could be found due to the lack or incompleteness of non-English vocabularies. Nevertheless, registries are a valuable source to find vocabularies that can serve as starting point for the development process.

SKOS[8] (Simple Knowledge Organization System) is a data model for representing controlled vocabularies which became a formal W3C recommendation in 2009. It is well suited for building vocabularies because there are several advantages compared to other data models such as a simple integration in the Semantic Web, a flexible and standardised development and its simplicity [10].

Having a suitable data model for controlled vocabularies is not sufficient. A **vocabulary editor** that supports the researcher during the entire process and facilitates building, curating and publishing SKOS vocabularies is essential. In addition to the special DH requirements mentioned in Sect. 1, the application in research projects poses additional ones such as open source software, a customisable web interface, exchangeable backend storage, importing vocabularies as well as a flexible user management. These are taken into account but are not the scope of this contribution and thus not elaborated on further. Although numerous tools were examined (40 in total including Protegé, CESSDA Vocabulary Editor, Neologism 2.0, Vocbench, iQVoc, Bioportal, Vocoreg, Themas, HIVE, NERC Vocabulary Server, OpenSKOS, PoolParty, SissVoc, TemaTres, Unilexicon, VocPrez, Wikibase), none of these fulfilled the requirements or were easily extendible to do so. Furthermore, there is always a trade-off between usability

---

[3] https://lov.linkeddata.es/.

[4] https://www.backbonethesaurus.eu/.

[5] https://www.loterre.fr/.

[6] https://github.com/CLARIAH/awesome-humanities-ontologies/.

[7] https://bartoc.org/.

[8] https://www.w3.org/TR/skos-reference/.

and the number of features. For instance, Protegé and VocBench are feature rich and in general suitable for a large amount of classes and triples. When only using a small subset of the functions to build a SKOS vocabulary, both tools are not able to support and guide a researcher well in the development process who is typically not an ontology expert. This leads to a high barrier in adopting the tools into the daily routine. The Austrian Centre for Digital Humanities (ACDH) at the Austrian Academy of Sciences is developing an editor within the DH context.[9] At the time of evaluation, it was still in the development process and could not be assessed in regards to all key requirements.

Similarity algorithms for vocabularies are able to quantify the similarity of two terms or two term sets with an individual semantic structure. They form the basis for a recommender system and a content-wise validation for vocabularies. The similarity measures can be split into two different main methods: Deep learning and non deep learning methods. In the former, different measures using neural networks are used to compute similarity between texts, phrases or terms which requires a large number of domain specific vocabularies [9]. Those exist in disciplines such as biomedical sciences, but usually not in the humanities or small disciplines. Furthermore, the infrastructure requirements for deep learning methods are demanding, as stated by Nguyen et al. [9], and often cannot be met by a large part of research projects, especially in the humanities and smaller fields or projects. Since preparing a well suited training dataset and performing algorithm training is not feasible for most projects (lack of human, material and fitting data resources), it would only be possible to provide a training model for similarity prediction. However, this would introduce a quality loss when applied to other languages or fields. This contradicts the aim for a sustainable algorithm that can be applied independent of domain and language without the need of constant improvement. For an overview about deep learning methods see [2].

Non deep learning methods can be further broken down into text corpus-based[10] methods and knowledge-based methods. Similarity measures using a text corpus are used to thematically group terms and phrases and generate a vocabulary [2]. These are based on the 'distributional hypothesis' that 'similar words appear in similar contexts' [3]. Following the distributional model, a large corpus is needed such that infrequent words can be represented accordingly. For the previously presented DH use case, such a large amount of data, especially machine readable digitised texts, is not available. Hence, corpus-based methods are not suitable in this case.

Knowledge-based methods (KB methods) use sources with structured knowledge content such as ontologies, thesauri or lexicons for defining the similarity of terms or vocabularies [2,4]. The different KB methods are presented and contextualised in the following. The simplest way to define similarity is to take the taxonomical structure into account and calculate the path length between two terms in a KB tree as proposed by Rada et al. [11]. The lower the distance, the closer the relationship between two terms. Path length based methods rely on

---

[9] https://github.com/acdh-oeaw/vocabseditor/.

[10] A text corpus is a large, structured collection of texts.

well built knowledge bases by domain experts that contain all relevant terms. If a term is missing, the path length and thus the similarity cannot be calculated. The overall goal of the proposed algorithm is to eventually support domain experts in building high quality vocabularies. Such vocabularies would be needed for all path based measures but these do not exist yet. Hence, this approach is not feasible for our case.

A more advanced KB method is based on the information content (IC) of a term. IC can be described as 'the amount of information provided by the term when appearing in a context' [13]. The IC is either derived from the Inverse Document Frequency of the term in a text corpus [2] or from the structure of the knowledge base itself [14]. The former depends on text corpora, the latter on a pre-existing, distinct and well built vocabulary. Since neither is available in the DH use case, IC based methods are not suitable in this case.

Another KB method compares the features and attributes of two terms [4]. The similarity increases the more features and attributes they share, such as description, related terms and others [2,13]. In particular, the overlap of term descriptions can be well suited to define semantic similarity [1]. This approach is suitable for the present use case because multiple vocabularies can be incorporated and used for similarity computation, a pre-existing universal vocabulary is not needed. In case that a term lacks attributes but includes information about exact or close matches in a network KB such as Wikipedia[11], this can be exploited to calculate similarity using the description and semantics of the term in the network knowledge-base [7].

Apart from a plain syntax validation, two types of **vocabulary validation** are introduced in the following. Semantic validation means that there are no logical errors and there is no violation of the data model. Skosify is a Python library which provides such a validation [15] and is well suited for the integration into the proposed validation system. Content-wise validation means that a vocabulary which follows all SKOS rules does not include content that would be judged wrong by a user, e.g. assigning a term accidentally to the wrong branch in the hierarchy. Furthermore, vocabularies such as the Shapes Constraint Language[12], Shape Expressions[13] or Resource Shape[14] are promising candidates for specifying integrity constraints in the validation system. Up-to-date, there exists no tool that provides content-wise validation for SKOS vocabularies which poses a research gap that is addressed in this work.

Concerning **recommender systems** for vocabularies, only Neologism 2.0 [8] offers a basic one. The search of its recommender system is mainly based on term labels which means that semantic features are omitted when giving recommendations. This leads to a limited value because only terms with an identical label in external vocabularies can be found. Synonyms, different languages or a differ-

---

[11] https://en.wikipedia.org/.

[12] https://www.w3.org/TR/shacl/.

[13] https://www.w3.org/community/shex/.

[14] https://www.w3.org/Submission/shapes/.

ent spelling for relevant terms prevent the recommender of finding them. Hence it falls short of the potential of recommenders for vocabulary development.

3   Problem Statement and Contributions

Hypothesis: The developed similarity metrics deliver better results than the state of the art concerning suitability in small research fields, resource consumption and application to a multilingual database.

RQ1: To what extent are knowledge-based similarity algorithms superior to other methods when calculating the similarity of controlled vocabularies in the DH domain?

RQ2: To what extent can a knowledge-based similarity algorithm be modelled to be applicable for small research fields, low resource consumption and a multilingual database as found in the DH context?

RQ3: To what extent can the resulting algorithm be applied to other disciplines, e.g. materials science?

RQ4: To what extent can the recommender and validation system support the development of subject-specific, multilingual DH vocabularies?

The research will contribute as follows:

- Design of a reference vocabulary in the field of DH for evaluation of similarity algorithms,
- development of a similarity algorithm for vocabularies suitable for small research fields, low resource consumption and a multilingual database,
- elaboration of a semantic and content-related validation for vocabularies,
- design of a recommender system for vocabularies,
- evaluation of the recommender and validation system within multidisciplinary projects of the CRC 1475 'Metaphors in Religion' and the CRC 980 'Episteme in Motion'.

4   Research Methodology and Approach

In this section, the methodology and approach is elaborated for each research question.

RQ1: The first step is to collect state of the art similarity metrics that are in general suitable for vocabularies. All gathered methods are then evaluated with respect to the present DH use case and its specific demands. As a result, the best state of the art algorithms are assessed and their performance quantified. This is done using a DH reference vocabulary whose design is also part of the research since there are no such reference datasets available.

RQ2: So far, there exists no knowledge-based similarity algorithm that fits the requirements of the present DH use case. Therefore, the challenge is to develop an algorithm that is capable of providing sufficient results in similarity detection while being used in small research fields with a limited number of knowledge bases and vocabularies, low resource consumption and suitable for a multilingual database. It needs to be assessed to what extent existing algorithms can serve as a starting point for the algorithm development.

RQ3: The objective is to provide a similarity algorithm that is not limited to DH but adaptable to other disciplines, for instance material science. Hence, close cooperation with researchers of other domains is established such that different reference vocabularies can be provided and evaluated. The results are then compared to the DH use case and to other algorithms.

RQ4: The recommender system proposes matching terms or branches of external vocabularies during the development process. The validation system evaluates if there are any semantic or content-wise mistakes by comparing neighbouring terms in both the source and the external vocabulary and by using predefined integrity constraints. If an internal threshold is reached which suggests a content-wise mistake, there will be a corresponding user output. Both systems will be integrated into a vocabulary editor which is currently being developed within the information infrastructure sub-project of CRC 980. Close cooperation is already established to researchers of CRCs 980 and 1475 which allows for receiving early user feedback and eventually answer the research question.

5   Evaluation Plan

5.1   Reference Datasets and Algorithm Evaluation

A crucial element in designing similarity metrics is performance monitoring including a comparison to the state of the art as early as possible. To achieve this, a domain specific vocabulary is built together with DH scholars and serves as base data for evaluation. Since there is no default way to objectively rate the accuracy of computational similarity, the results for each algorithm can be compared to human similarity ratings given by domain experts which represent the baseline [12]. Even though machine learning based methods were shown to be unsuitable for the presented case, their results are also compared to the developed similarity metrics.

Furthermore, the computational similarity of terms in the domain specific vocabulary and other terms in multiple publicly available vocabularies is used as performance indicator. To obtain domain independent results, vocabularies outside the DH are considered as well. If it is not feasible to obtain human similarity judgements as baseline for domain independent vocabularies, high quality lexical-semantic networks such as WordNet[15] or GermaNet[16] are used. In this case, the focus is to find close or exact matches of terms (meaning high computational similarity) and compare it to the ground truth (meaning synonyms) as specified by the utilised lexical-semantic networks.

---

[15] https://wordnet.princeton.edu/.

[16] https://weblicht.sfs.uni-tuebingen.de/rover/.

5.2   Validation and Recommender System Evaluation

The semantic and content-wise validation of vocabularies is evaluated by randomly modifying the vocabulary created by domain experts and introducing false content and wrong semantic links, e.g. closed loops. To ensure neutrality, the modification is done by independent individuals. When performing the validation, the number of detected faults or imperfections in the vocabulary can be quantified and compared to the actual number of introduced errors.

The performance assessment of the recommender system is challenging. Since it is highly subjective if a recommendation is helpful or not, competency questions are defined together with domain experts. This means that fragments of vocabularies X are given as system input ('Which terms and/or vocabularies are similar to X?'), the output ('Term t and vocabulary Y have high computational similarity to X') is then compared to what domain experts are expecting or considering as helpful. The question formulation is done in close contact with researchers of ongoing DH projects within the CRCs 1475 and 980. To avoid tuning the algorithm's performance to the competency questions, these are formulated on an ongoing basis during the whole development process.

6   Preliminary Results

Since this work is at an early stage, only preliminary results regarding similarity algorithms and vocabulary editors are presented. To find state of the art similarity algorithms that are well suited for the DH case, a literature study was conducted. The algorithms were classified into different groups and evaluated. The results are the basis of this work and are summarised in Sect. 2.

Concerning the vocabulary editor, a survey with prospective users of four different humanities projects was conducted to determine the needs of the user base. The state of the art was evaluated against these requirements and is planned to be published as survey paper because to the best knowledge this has not been done so far. As the currently available methods do not fulfil the requirements, a basic vocabulary editor was developed in cooperation with computer science students. This editor addresses the additional, domain independent requirements outlined in Sect. 2: It is written in python, easily extensible, uses SKOS as data model, offers a web interface, provides user management and is capable of collaboratively developing vocabularies.

To include future users as early as possible on in the development process, a hands-on workshop for scholars was held in October 2021 where the participants developed a simple vocabulary and used it to annotate digital images which closely resembles the present DH use case. Additionally, the editor and its prospective use was presented in September 2021 to members of the German engineering community to include future fields of application early on. As a next step, the DH reference vocabulary will be addressed and built such that algorithm performance can be quantified.

7   Conclusions and Lessons Learned

This work contributes to the design, development and evaluation of a validation and recommender system for vocabularies. The underlying similarity metrics are the main object of research and are tuned to be well applicable within the DH community such that they deliver better results than the state of the art. A reference dataset is built and used for evaluation of the similarity algorithm and the validation and recommender system. A user evaluation is carried out to assess both systems as well as the user experience. In the first year of this work, the collection and evaluation of state of the art vocabulary editors and similarity algorithms has been conducted. In parallel, the basis of the enclosing vocabulary editor has been designed and implemented according to the results of a requirement analysis. The first version of the editor has been presented to users within and outside of the DH community. The comments and positive feedback of the participants strengthened the need for a simple to use, domain independent tool for building, curating and publishing vocabularies.

One challenge is to reach enough researchers for the recommender assessment and for giving valuable feedback. Another one is that all evaluation is carried out as neutral as possible to avoid tuning criteria to match a desired outcome. Among the countermeasures taken are increased cooperation with scholars and scientists, a continuous comparison of results with the state of the art and the use of reference datasets outside the DH domain.

Acknowledgments. This research is funded by the German Research Foundation (Deutsche Forschungsgemeinschaft, DFG)—CRC 980 Episteme in Motion. Transfer of Knowledge from the Ancient World to the Early Modern Period. Project-ID 191249397, and supported by the Helmholtz Metadata Collaboration Platform and the German National Research Data Infrastructure (NFDI).

References

1. Banerjee, S., Pedersen, T.: Extended gloss overlaps as a measure of semantic relatedness. In: IJCAI 2003, Acapulco, Mexico, pp. 805–810, May 2003
2. Chandrasekaran, D., Mago, V.: Evolution of semantic similarity - a survey. ACM Comput. Surve. **54**(2), 41:1–41:37 (2021). https://doi.org/10.1145/3440755
3. Gorman, J., Curran, J.R.: Scaling distributional similarity to large corpora. In: Proceedings of the 21st International Conference on Computational Linguistics and the 44th Annual Meeting of the Association for Computational Linguistics, pp. 361–368. ACL-44, Association for Computational Linguistics, USA, July 2006. https://doi.org/10.3115/1220175.1220221
4. Han, M., Zhang, X., Yuan, X., Jiang, J., Yun, W., Gao, C.: A survey on the techniques, applications, and performance of short text semantic similarity. Concurr. Comput. Pract. Exp. **33**(5), e5971 (2021). https://doi.org/10.1002/cpe.5971
5. Haslhofer, B., Isaac, A., Simon, R.: Knowledge graphs in the libraries and digital humanities domain. arXiv:1803.03198 [cs], pp. 1–8 (2018). https://doi.org/10.1007/978-3-319-63962-8_291-1

6. Hyvönen, E.: Using the Semantic Web in digital humanities: shift from data publishing to data-analysis and serendipitous knowledge discovery. Semant. Web **11**(1), 187–193 (2020). https://doi.org/10.3233/SW-190386
7. Jiang, Y., Zhang, X., Tang, Y., Nie, R.: Feature-based approaches to semantic similarity assessment of concepts using Wikipedia. Inf. Process. Manag. **51**, 215–234 (2015). https://doi.org/10.1016/j.ipm.2015.01.001
8. Lipp, J., et al.: Towards easy vocabulary drafts with neologism 2.0. In: Verborgh, R., et al. (eds.) ESWC 2021. LNCS, vol. 12739, pp. 21–26. Springer, Cham (2021). https://doi.org/10.1007/978-3-030-80418-3_4
9. Nguyen, V., Yip, H.Y., Bodenreider, O.: Biomedical vocabulary alignment at scale in the UMLS metathesaurus. In: Proceedings of the Web Conference 2021, pp. 2672–2683. ACM, Ljubljana, April 2021. https://doi.org/10.1145/3442381.3450128
10. Pastor-Sánchez, J., Martinez-Mendez, F.J., Rodríguez, J.: Advantages of thesaurus representation using the simple knowledge organization system (SKOS) compared with proposed alternatives. Inf. Res. **14**(4), 10 (2009). ISSN 1368-1613
11. Rada, R., Mili, H., Bicknell, E., Blettner, M.: Development and application of a metric on semantic nets. IEEE Trans. Syst. Man Cybern. **19**(1), 17–30 (1989). https://doi.org/10.1109/21.24528
12. Resnik, P.: Semantic similarity in a taxonomy: an information-based measure and its application to problems of ambiguity in natural language. J. Artif. Intelli. Res. **11**, 95–130 (1999). https://doi.org/10.1613/jair.514
13. Sánchez, D., Batet, M.: A semantic similarity method based on information content exploiting multiple ontologies. Expert Syst. Appl. **40**, 1393–1399 (2013). https://doi.org/10.1016/j.eswa.2012.08.049
14. Sánchez, D., Batet, M., Isern, D.: Ontology-based information content computation. Knowl.-Based Syst. **24**, 297–303 (2011). https://doi.org/10.1016/j.knosys.2010.10.001
15. Suominen, O., Mader, C.: Assessing and improving the quality of SKOS vocabularies. J. Data Semant. **3**(1), 47–73 (2013). https://doi.org/10.1007/s13740-013-0026-0

Causal Domain Adaptation
for Information Extraction
from Complex Conversations

Xue Li[✉] [iD]

University of Amsterdam, Amsterdam, The Netherlands
x.li3@uva.nl

Abstract. *Complex conversations* can be seen everywhere on the web from email lists to discussion forms. Being able to more effectively extract entities and their relations from these conversations would be an important contribution to conversational content analysis. Despite the success of current information extraction systems, their use in complex conversations is challenging due to, among other reasons, the existence of *long-tail* entities that are unrepresented in standard training corpora (e.g. news). Moreover, in general the distribution of entities in the target domain is frequently different from that of the training domain, which requires the algorithms to be able to perform domain adaptation. In this research, we will focus on identifying domain shifts that might impact information extractions systems and we aim to propose a causal framework for domain adaptation in information extraction.

Keywords: Complex conversations · Information extraction · Domain adaptation · Causality

1 Introduction

Complex conversations are characterized by 1) their long-form nature; 2) extension across sessions; and 3) frequent reference to domain-specific background knowledge and material. Examples of a complex conversation include:

- a mailing list where participants discuss the development of a new standard for 5G;
- a long-running Slack chat on the development of an EU proposal with multiple partners;
- meeting minutes from a series of meetings discussing the development of new governmental policy.

Recent work on conversational AI and dialogue extraction have primarily focused on the development of interactive systems such as chatbots or assistants [11], while complex conversations remain an under-explored topic.

P. Groth et al. (Eds.): ESWC 2022 Satellite Events, LNCS 13384, pp. 189–198, 2022.
https://doi.org/10.1007/978-3-031-11609-4_34

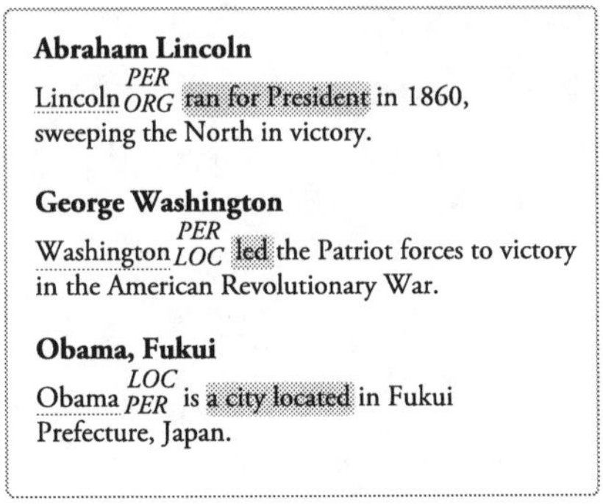

Fig. 1. Examples extracted from Wikipedia (title in bold) illustrate bias in NER. Entities of interest are underlined, green superscript indicates the correct category for the entity and red subscript indicates the prediction from the Stanford NER tagger [17]. The related contextual information to infer the correct types is highlighted in yellow. These failing results show that the model relies heavily on the representation learned from the training dataset. (Color figure online)

One way to analyze conversations is through the construction and use of Knowledge Graphs (KGs) [28]. KGs are graph-structured knowledge bases (KBs) that store factual information in form of relationships between entities [20]. To construct knowledge graphs from complex conversations, we need to extract the entities (nodes) with their types and their relations (edges). In particular, the process includes a set of core Natural Language Processing (NLP) tasks related to entities in Information Extraction (IE): Named Entity Recognition (NER) and Coreference Resolution (CR). More broadly information extraction is a key topic for web research [18] and in particular the semantic web [18].

A challenge with applying information extraction, especially in complex conversations, is the existence of long-tail entities [6,9,12,13,15,26]. This is exemplified in Fig. 1, which shows for an NER task that given biases in the training dataset, current models can fail to to categorize entity mentions correctly even with related context.

Even with the advent of highly successful deep learning based information extraction models using large-scale pre-trained language models (e.g. Bert [8]), challenges in dealing with long-tail data still exist [1,19]. This is because many machine learning models have the default assumption that the training and target data follow the same distribution. However, as mentioned, in real-world applications, this assumption is often not true, especially in-cases with rare, *long-tail* entities. This phenomenon is referred to as *domain shift* [24]. Effectively adapting to changes in the test distribution is referred to as *domain adaptation* [24]. For IE/NLP tasks, there are several types of domain adaption methods including sample-based, feature-based, and inference-based methods [14].

One problem of domain shift is that the data representation is domain-specific when transforming data from one domain to match another. For example, the same entity mention Lincoln is more likely to be an organization in the automotive domain than when it occurs in the American history domain. Therefore, developing approaches that represent data in a domain-invariant space is important avenue for investigation [14]. We would like to learn invariant predictors that perform consistently irrespective of domain.

To that end, causality presents an avenue worth exploring, as it is a principled way to reason about shifts [2, 16, 22, 23]. Only very recently has this been explored in the context of "stress tests" for NLP models [27] as well as distantly supervised NER [31]. However, both these approaches require that the causal graph is known a priori, including the graphical structure of the domain shift. In a general setting we might not know, in advance, the true underlying causal graph, or how the domain affect the features or the label.

Our goal, therefore, is to investigate new methods that are able to learn predictors that transfer across domains and do not require a known causal graph. We will focus on domain adaption specifically for information extraction tasks.

2   State of the Art

2.1   Information Extraction on the Web

Web data normally contains a large amount of data without annotations in various domains. There are a number of approaches for IE on web [18]. These approaches can be categorized broadly into two main classes: (1) semi-supervised and unsupervised systems and (2) supervised systems.

For the semi-supervised setting, many works tackle this problem with distant-supervised data-centric methods that generate distant annotations for unlabelled data. One recent work that focuses on IE from conversational data on the web is ConvSearch [29]. This paper addresses two main challenges in conversational search of online shopping domain: the imperfect entity attributes with multi-turn utterances in conversations and the lack of in-domain annotations for training due to the long-tail entities. ConvSearch combines dialogues and search systems to tackle the first challenge, as well as a jump-start dialog generation method (M2M-UT) for generating utterance and building dialogues to solve the second challenge. M2M-UT builds dialog outlines for online shopping from e-commerce search behavior data, and fills them with the generated utterances. As a result they introduce a new dataset CSD-UT for the online shopping domain. Though training with the newly introduced distantly annotated dataset improved performance, the method is limited to the shopping domain. To use this method in different domains, new datasets need to be generated. Additionally, the method does not take potential biases in the data generating process into consideration.

For supervised systems, recent work [21] introduces Learning To Adapt with Word Embeddings (L2AWE), a model-centric method that exploits the distributional representation of named entities for adapting the entity types predicted by a NER system trained on source generic schema (pre-defined entity types in any NER system) to a given schema. L2AWE takes word embeddings obtained from word2vec or Bert and learns to map between the source schema and target schema. L2AWE is able to achieve fairly good results on the target datasets #Microposts2015, #Microposts2016 and WNUT-17, however there is no comparisons between the distributional changes of the source domain and the target domain.

There is also work on generating knowledge graphs from a different domain. [7] proposed an overall pipeline for generating knowledge graphs from scientific domains by integrating different NLP tasks into the framework. The work aims to utilize state-of-the-arts from different NLP tasks such as entity extraction and relation extraction for knowledge graph generation. However, academic data normally has more structured formats and formal language than conversational data. Using a pipeline with unified dictionaries makes it possible to use different models from NLP tasks to generate knowledge graphs. The work does not aim at improving individual model performance. Instead, we focus on improving robustness of each model for different domains.

2.2 Causal NLP

Until recently, there has been limited attention at the intersection of causal inference and NLP. A recent survey [10] provides a systematic review of the existing literature, classifying it in two general directions: 1) NLP helps causality (i.e. estimating causal effects from text); 2) Causality helps NLP (i.e. improving the robustness and interpretability of NLP through the use of causal reasoning). In our research, we focus on the latter direction, and in particular on IE tasks.

Causality for Improving Robustness in NLP. Veitch et al. [27] describe one of the few methods that exploit the knowledge of the causal relationship between features, labels and domain variables to improve model robustness. In particular, they consider the problem of learning a predictor f that predicts a label Y from features X, assuming there is an additional variable Z that captures the domain information. They consider two settings: (1) the relationship between the features X and the label Y is causal, i.e. $X \rightarrow Y$, or (2) this relationship is anti-causal, i.e. $X \leftarrow Y$. For each of these two settings, they propose different regularization terms.

Veitch et al. [27] consider a general setting in which the label Y and the domain Z might be confounded, which means that there is no general predictor f that can transfer stably across domains since $P(Y|f(X))$ might change for different values of Z. Thus, as a second-best option, they propose to identify sets of features that are not caused by the domain Z. In contrast, our research focuses on the case in which these stable predictors exist. Furthermore, we will also consider the case in which the causal graph is unknown.

Moreover, in this work the tasks addressed are easier to manipulate than typical NER tasks. In particular, the tasks are predicting the usefulness and sentiment of online reviews, in which a synthetic confounder is generated by substituting some tokens that should have no effect on the prediction. Both tasks use binary variables for the domain and label, which simplifies the problem, while in IE tasks we have often several possible classes.

Causality for Distant Supervision in NER. Another example of using causality in NLP is the work of Zhang et al. who apply it to the task of distantly supervised NER [31]. Their method D-DSNER [31] addresses the *intra-dictionary bias* and *inter-dictionary bias* for this task in which dictionaries are mention-type pairs pre-acquired from existing knowledge bases such as Wikipedia.

In the current NER model they investigate, positive and negative instances are generated by matching input texts with the dictionary. The problem they identify is that these distantly supervised models are highly dependent on the quality of the dictionary.

To address this problem, D-DSNER [31], they employ a causal graph to identify bias in the NER model stemming from the dictionary and subsequently propose corresponding adjustments (e.g. to the dictionary) based on the causal theory.

In summary, the current state-of-the-art methods for IE on the web still have limitations generalizing across different domains and identifying the biases in data generating processes. Causality provides a powerful tool for tackling domain shifts in the invariant-feature space, however, using causality to help with domain adaptation in information extraction is under-explored.

3 Problem Statement

Given the above, our main research question is:

To what extent can domain adaptation for information extraction in the context of complex conversations be improved through the use of causality?

Specifically, we can break down this into the following sub-research questions:

- **RQ1** *What is the performance of current state-of-the-art methods of IE for complex conversations in different domains?*
  Here, we aim to characterize the performance of information extraction models when applied to complex conversations in the setting where there are domain shifts. These experimental results can also be seen as baseline results. Preliminary results are shown in Sect. 6.
- **RQ2** *What are the types of domain shifts in IE tasks and how can we systematically identify them?*
  This research question focuses on identifying various distribution shifts between training data (source domain) and test data (target domain) that occur frequently in IE tasks. We are interested in what are the characteristics of the benchmark datasets that state-of-the-art models leverage to make predictions, e.g. spurious correlations. For example, most models fail to use the context, but only rely on the mention representations, which introduces bias and lack of robustness [12]. In our work, we would like to identify distributional shifts systematically. In particular, we will start by focusing on NER.

- **RQ3** *How can we use causality to reason about domain shift, even without a known causal graph?*
This is the most challenging part of the research. The goal is to learn an invariant predictor so that the performance on IE tasks is consistent between domains. The first step to address this will be applying the causal invariant regularizer [27] in an NER task. In particular, we will modify the approach of Zhang et al. to see if the use of this regularizer improves performance. Subsequently, if this is effective, we will investigate performance for domain adaptation given the distribution shifts identified in sub-question 2.

The targeted contributions of this research can be summarized as:

- a characterization of the performance of the state-of-the-art IE models on complex conversations from different domains;
- identification of distribution shifts for IE tasks; and
- novel methods for domain adaptation in IE based on causality.

4   Research Methodology and Approach

With the aim of addressing the research questions in Sect. 3, we will use different methodologies in different phrases. We first carry out experimental research and use empirical analysis to understand the performance of the state-of-the-art models from benchmarks in IE for complex conversations in the target domain as the baseline. We then use exploratory research to understand the specific type of distribution shifts in IE tasks. With this better understanding, we can carry out theoretical research to adapt existing causal inference frameworks for reasoning about such shifts. Last, we will evaluate the proposed framework on complex conversations across different domains and compare the results with the baseline.

IE systems contain many different tasks such as NER, CR, etc. We propose to start our research with NER first, and then extend to other tasks. Our aim is to create a framework that attempts to identify distribution shifts automatically and learn invariant predictors across different domains based on ideas from causality. This framework should be able to adapt across different domains.

Experiments will be carried out with Pytorch[1] as the training framework for machine learning models. Several NLP toolkits will be used such as NLTK[2], spacy[3] and sikit-learn[4]. The Huggingface[5] package will also be used for comparing performance with state-of-the-art Bert-based models.

---

[1] https://pytorch.org/.
[2] https://www.nltk.org/.
[3] https://spacy.io/.
[4] https://scikit-learn.org/stable/.
[5] https://huggingface.co/.

5   Evaluation Plan

As mentioned in Sect. 4, we first carry out our research on NER tasks. The benchmark dataset CoNLL-2003 [25] will be used as our source domain. Two other datasets are proposed as target domains to evaluate our proposed approach, specifically, email conversations (CEREC) [5] and social media (W-NUT) [6].

CoNLL-2003 contains 1393 news articles from the Reuters Corpus with 4 different types.

The email conversation dataset CEREC [5] contains 36,448 email messages with 4 types of entities. Email conversations are one type of complex conversation which is characterized by their long forms, diverse language variations, and a huge variety of surface forms for each entity.

The W-NUT dataset [6], focuses on emerging and rare entities. W-NUT dataset consists of annotated texts from YouTube comments, Twitter posts, and StackExchange contents, which is composed of 5,691 posts and 3,890 entity mentions. Although some of the data might not have the long-form back and forth conversational features, it is still valuable to evaluate the performance on long-tail entities. All contents are user-generated and across different domains.

State-of-the-art NER models (e.g. Bert) will be trained on the CoNLL-2003 dataset combined with small amounts of data from the CEREC and W-NUT datasets. The model will be tested on the rest of the CEREC and W-NUT datasets. This unregularized model is our baseline. A causally-regularized model will be trained and tested on the same split as above and compared.

The evaluation metrics that will be used are *Accuracy, Precision, Recall,* and *F-measure*. Since the distribution of the data over the entity types is unbalanced, we will also calculate the *macro-average* and *micro-average* [30]. The macro-averaged measure gives equal weight to each class, regardless of their frequencies. Micro-averaged weight each class with respect to its number of instances.

6   Results

In our K-CAP 2021 paper [15], we started investigating IE in complex conversations by focusing on the performance of the current state-of-the-art models for cross-document coreference resolution in emails. Coreference resolution is the task of finding all mentions in text that refer to the same real-world entities. We can see that the coreferent relations in ECB+ are more structural and formal. The entities are more likely to exist in Wikipedia or other knowledge bases. On the other hand, the entities in the email conversations are contextual and require additional background knowledge.

In our paper, we investigated the different performances of state-of-the-art models (e.g. [3]) on the hand annotated corpus from the CEREC email dataset [5] with respect to the benchmark ECB+ news dataset [4]. The CD-CR model in [3] contains three components: a span_embedder, a span_scorer and a pairwise_scorer. In the first step, it extracts all possible mentions from the text and encodes them with the span_embedder, then it prunes the mentions given the score generated by span_scorer. Next, the mentions are paired and the pairs of mentions are scored by pairwise_scorer in terms of likelihood of being coreferent. Finally, the coreference chain will be obtained by agglomerative clustering. The results in [15] show that the CD-CR model for the email test set has an F1 score of 27.4, which is a 7 points drop compared to an F1 score of 34.4 for the ECB+ dataset. This drop has shown that the CD-CR model cannot generalize easily to the email setting due to the language variation in the email conversations and the less-frequently-used-entities caused distribution shift from different domains.

Our first next step will be applying the causal invariant regularizer [27] to the D-DSNER approach [31]. If the approach is effective, we will then apply the regularized model to the CEREC and W-NUT datasets as described in our evaluation plan.

7   Conclusions and Future Work

Complex conversations are important source of data on the web. They show a large distribution shift from benchmark datasets due to language variation and long-tail entities. Thus, applying current state-of-the-art IE models is challenging because of they struggle with generalization on data from different domains. Causality is a principled way to help with domain adaptation. Our research will investigate new methods for using such a principled approach in the context of information extraction.

Acknowledgements. I would like to thank my supervisors Prof. Dr. Paul Groth and Dr. Sara Magliacane for their supervision and feedback. This research is funded by the Dutch Research Council (NWO) through grant MVI.19.032

References

1. Bommasani, R., et al.: On the opportunities and risks of foundation models (2021). CoRR abs/2108.07258. https://arxiv.org/abs/2108.07258
2. Bühlmann, P.: Invariance, causality and robustness. Stat. Sci. **35**(3), 404–426 (2020)
3. Cattan, A., Eirew, A., Stanovsky, G., Joshi, M., Dagan, I.: Streamlining cross-document coreference resolution: evaluation and modeling (2020). abs/2009.11032
4. Cybulska, A., Vossen, P.: Using a sledgehammer to crack a nut? lexical diversity and event coreference resolution. In: LREC 2014 (2014)
5. Dakle, P.P., Moldovan, D.: CEREC: a corpus for entity resolution in email conversations. In: Proceedings of the 28th International Conference on Computational Linguistics, pp. 339–349. International Committee on Computational Linguistics, Barcelona, Spain (2020). https://www.aclweb.org/anthology/2020.coling-main.30
6. Derczynski, L., Nichols, E., van Erp, M., Limsopatham, N.: Results of the WNUT2017 shared task on novel and emerging entity recognition. In: Proceedings of the 3rd Workshop on Noisy User-generated Text, pp. 140–147. Association for Computational Linguistics, Copenhagen, Denmark (2017). https://doi.org/10.18653/v1/W17-4418, https://aclanthology.org/W17-4418

7. Dessì, D., Osborne, F., Recupero, D.R., Buscaldi, D., Motta, E.: Generating knowledge graphs by employing natural language processing and machine learning techniques within the scholarly domain (2020). CoRR abs/2011.01103. https://arxiv.org/abs/2011.01103

8. Devlin, J., Chang, M., Lee, K., Toutanova, K.: BERT: pre-training of deep bidirectional transformers for language understanding (2018). CoRR abs/1810.04805. http://arxiv.org/abs/1810.04805

9. van Erp, M., et al.: Evaluating entity linking: an analysis of current benchmark datasets and a roadmap for doing a better job. In: Proceedings of the Tenth International Conference on Language Resources and Evaluation (LREC 2016), pp. 4373–4379. European Language Resources Association (ELRA), Portorož, Slovenia (2016). https://aclanthology.org/L16-1693

10. Feder, A., et al.: Causal inference in natural language processing: estimation, prediction, interpretation and beyond (2021)

11. Gao, J., Galley, M., Li, L.: Neural approaches to conversational AI (2018). CoRR abs/1809.08267. http://arxiv.org/abs/1809.08267

12. Ghaddar, A., Langlais, P., Rashid, A., Rezagholizadeh, M.: Context-aware adversarial training for name regularity bias in named entity recognition. Trans. Assoc. Comput. Linguist. 9, 586–604 (2021). https://doi.org/10.1162/tacl_a_00386

13. Ilievski, F., Vossen, P., Schlobach, S.: Systematic study of long tail phenomena in entity linking. In: Proceedings of the 27th International Conference on Computational Linguistics, pp. 664–674. Association for Computational Linguistics, Santa Fe, New Mexico, USA (2018). https://aclanthology.org/C18-1056

14. Kouw, W.M., Loog, M.: A review of domain adaptation without target labels. IEEE Trans. Pattern Anal. Mach. Intell. 43(3), 766–785 (2021). https://doi.org/10.1109/TPAMI.2019.2945942

15. Li, X., Magliacane, S., Groth, P.: The challenges of cross-document coreference resolution for email. In: Proceedings of the 11th on Knowledge Capture Conference, pp. 273–276. K-CAP 2021, Association for Computing Machinery, New York, NY, USA (2021). https://doi.org/10.1145/3460210.3493573

16. Magliacane, S., van Ommen, T., Claassen, T., Bongers, S., Versteeg, P., Mooij, J.M.: Domain adaptation by using causal inference to predict invariant conditional distributions (2017). CoRR abs/1707.06422. http://arxiv.org/abs/1707.06422

17. Manning, C.D., Surdeanu, M., Bauer, J., Finkel, J.R., Bethard, S., McClosky, D.: The stanford corenlp natural language processing toolkit. In: ACL (System Demonstrations), pp. 55–60. The Association for Computer Linguistics (2014). http://dblp.uni-trier.de/db/conf/acl/acl2014-d.html#ManningSBFBM14

18. Martínez-Rodríguez, J., Hogan, A., López-Arévalo, I.: Information extraction meets the semantic web: a survey. Seman. Web 11(2), 255–335 (2020). https://doi.org/10.3233/SW-180333

19. McCoy, T., Pavlick, E., Linzen, T.: Right for the wrong reasons: diagnosing syntactic heuristics in natural language inference. In: Proceedings of the 57th Annual Meeting of the Association for Computational Linguistics, pp. 3428–3448. Association for Computational Linguistics, Florence, Italy (2019). https://doi.org/10.18653/v1/P19-1334, https://aclanthology.org/P19-1334

20. Nickel, M., Murphy, K., Tresp, V., Gabrilovich, E.: A review of relational machine learning for knowledge graphs. Proc. IEEE, 104(1), 11–33 (2016). https://doi.org/10.1109/jproc.2015.2483592, http://dx.doi.org/10.1109/JPROC.2015.2483592

21. Nozza, D., Manchanda, P., Fersini, E., Palmonari, M., Messina, E.: Learningtoadapt with word embeddings: domain adaptation of named entity recognition sys-

tems. Inf. Proc. Manag. **58**(3), 102537 (2021). https://doi.org/10.1016/j.ipm.2021.
102537, https://www.sciencedirect.com/science/article/pii/S0306457321000455

22. Peters, J., Bühlmann, P., Meinshausen, N.: Causal inference by using invariant prediction: identification and confidence intervals. J. Royal Stat. Soc. Series B (Stat. Methodol.) **78**(5), 947–1012 (2016)

23. Peters, J., Janzing, D., Schölkopf, B.: Elements of Causal Inference: Foundations and Learning Algorithms. The MIT Press (2017)

24. Ramponi, A., Plank, B.: Neural unsupervised domain adaptation in NLP–a survey. In: Proceedings of the 28th International Conference on Computational Linguistics, pp. 6838–6855. International Committee on Computational Linguistics, Barcelona, Spain (2020). https://doi.org/10.18653/v1/2020.coling-main.603, https://aclanthology.org/2020.coling-main.603

25. Tjong Kim Sang, E.F., De Meulder, F.: Introduction to the CoNLL-2003 shared task: Language-independent named entity recognition. In: Proceedings of the Seventh Conference on Natural Language Learning at HLT-NAACL 2003, pp. 142–147 (2003). https://aclanthology.org/W03-0419

26. Tu, J., Lignos, C.: TMR: evaluating NER recall on tough mentions. In: Proceedings of the 16th Conference of the European Chapter of the Association for Computational Linguistics: Student Research Workshop, pp. 155–163. Association for Computational Linguistics (2021). https://doi.org/10.18653/v1/2021.eacl-srw.21, https://aclanthology.org/2021.eacl-srw.21

27. Veitch, V., D'Amour, A., Yadlowsky, S., Eisenstein, J.: Counterfactual invariance to spurious correlations: why and how to pass stress tests (2021)

28. Weikum, G., Dong, L., Razniewski, S., Suchanek, F.M.: Machine knowledge: creation and curation of comprehensive knowledge bases (2020). CoRR abs/2009.11564, https://arxiv.org/abs/2009.11564

29. Xiao, L., et al.: End-to-end conversational search for online shopping with utterance transfer. In: Proceedings of the 2021 Conference on Empirical Methods in Natural Language Processing, pp. 3477–3486. Association for Computational Linguistics, Online and Punta Cana, Dominican Republic (2021). https://doi.org/10.18653/v1/2021.emnlp-main.280, https://aclanthology.org/2021.emnlp-main.280

30. Yang, Y., Liu, X.: A re-examination of text categorization methods. In: Proceedings of the 22nd Annual International ACM SIGIR Conference on Research and Development in Information Retrieval, pp. 42–49. SIGIR 1999, Association for Computing Machinery, New York, NY, USA (1999). https://doi.org/10.1145/312624.312647, https://doi.org/10.1145/312624.312647

31. Zhang, W., Lin, H., Han, X., Sun, L.: De-biasing distantly supervised named entity recognition via causal intervention (2021)

Knowledge Graph Population
with Out-of-KG Entities

Cedric Möller[✉] [ID]

Semantic Systems Group, Universität Hamburg,
Mittelweg 177, 20148 Hamburg, Germany
`cedric.moeller@uni-hamburg.de`

Abstract. Existing knowledge graphs are incomplete. A lot of unstructured documents are hiding valuable information. But extracting and structuring that information is expensive. To help, the knowledge graphs can be populated (semi-) automatically. But knowledge graph population methods often assumes existing entities, yet, this is not the reality. To solve this, missing entities need to be detected and distinguished. To support an incoming stream of documents the out-of-KG entities are incrementally modelled. The first goal of the thesis is hence to create a novel entity linking method able to detect, distinguish and incrementally model out-of-KG entities.

While the identification and modelling of potential out-of-KG entities are a step in the right direction, they still need to be included in the knowledge graph. To simplify the process, another goal is to generate short descriptions of newly identified entities. To accomplish that, a method building upon the representation of out-of-KG entities will be created which combines the properties of both graph-to-text and abstractive summarization methods.

For training and evaluation, two silver-standard datasets, as well as one gold-standard dataset, will be created.

Keywords: Knowledge graph population · NIL Clustering · Emerging entity discovery · Entity description

1 Introduction

Today, we are confronted with an ever-increasing number of textual documents in unstructured form. For example, in 2013, every day, around 500 million tweets were published [22]. Now, the number is certainly higher and is further accompanied by other social media posts, news articles and older but now digitized documents. All these documents often contain valuable information but reading them all is no option. Manually extracting relevant information from thousands of documents regarding one's use case is extremely labor-some. To store structured information, KGs are employed in numerous different domains [19]. Having information available in a KG enables the use of powerful services like Question Answering, Recommender Systems, or Reasoning. For instance, the Google search engine relies on an underlying KG [50]. Yet, getting the information, e.g. from tweets, into the KG is often complicated. Even if an ontology for the KG already exists, domain experts are commonly employed to add new information. Novel knowledge graph population (KGP) methods, also known as knowledge base population, allow that this process can be (semi-) automated [21]. However, existing KGP methods still have several shortcomings which need to be addressed. We will investigate one such shortcoming, which is described next, in the thesis, resulting in two major goals.

Commonly, KGP methods assume that extractable entities and relations are known and part of the underlying KG [2,8,26,53,56,60]. But tweets or historical documents often contain entities, which do not exist in a KG yet (**out-of-KG entities**) [29]. Hence, the **recognition** of out-of-KG entities is necessary. To include the entities in the KG in the future, they also need to be put into relation to existing entities. Furthermore, out-of-KG entity might be mentioned repeatedly across documents. To handle this, representations of out-of-KG entities need to be **incrementally modelled**. The **first goal** is therefore the creation of a novel entity linking method supporting out-of-KG entities. It will be able to detect, distinguish and incrementally model out-of-KG entities (see Fig. 1). This was, to the best of our knowledge, not pursued to its full potential in research until now.

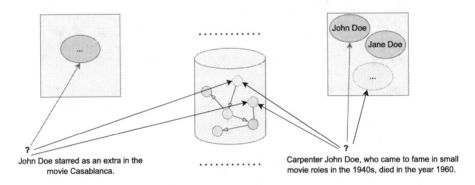

Fig. 1. Out-of-KG entity detection and modelling. An entity mention "John Doe" does not occur in the KG and is identified as an out-of-KG entity, a new intermediary representation is created, which is later used for further linking.

This brings us to our **second goal**. With accomplishment of the first goal the out-of-KG entities are now identified. But before including them in the KG, it might be wise to check whether they are really suitable. To reduce the effort of this process, another goal of this thesis is the **creation of textual entity descriptions** out of the representations of the new entities. This makes it possible for non-KG experts to quickly understand what a newly identified entity is about, and whether or where to insert it. Furthermore, the description can also be included in the KG itself (see Fig. 2). To accomplish that, structured information in the KG and information in the text needs to be combined. More concretely, a novel method will be developed that will build on existing graph-to-text and text summary methods.

When and how exactly the entities are included in the KG, is out of scope of this work. The focus solely lies on the identification of such entities and creating descriptions. How they are used, will be the responsibility of the curator of the KG.

2 State of the Art

2.1 Knowledge Graph Population

Knowledge Base Population was first defined in TAC-2009 [21,28] and is concerned with extracting structured information out of text while being constrained to an existing knowledge base. Notably, in TAC-2009 it is also specified that out-of-KG entities should be identified too. However, such entities are not used further. Here, the term Knowledge Graph Population is used as a synonym for KBP. A related task is Open Information Extraction. Here, the goal is to extract structured information while only relying on the input document and no KG. Its main purpose is to pre-process text to improve downstream tasks such as KGP. However, the methods still struggle with coreference resolution and the canonicalization of relations, which are vital for KGP [36].

Most Knowledge Graph Population methods employ a pipeline-based approach [2,8,47,60] using separate entity linking and relation extraction methods. However, as a pipeline always suffers from error propagation, end-to-end approaches are becoming more popular [23,26,53,56]. Not many of those methods consider the possibility of out-of-KG entities. Notable exceptions are KBPearl [23] and the baseline methods used to evaluate the KnowledgeNet dataset [47]. However, they are restricted to only output non-linked triples (by using the entity mentions of the subject and/or object) if an out-of-KG entity is detected. Thus, there is still space for improvement which this thesis desires to fill.

2.2 Out-of-KG Entity Discovery and Representation

Out-of-KG entities were of interest the first time in 2011 when the NIL-clustering task was included in TAC-2011 [21]. NIL-entities are a different term for out-of-KG entities. Here, the goal is to assign the same out-of-KG entities into the same clusters. Important is that all documents are available from the start. Hence, most methods ran clustering algorithms over all documents while calculating different similarity measures between entity mentions [4,7,11,12,15,16,20,31,54]. Clustering is usually done by employing rule-based, graph-based or agglomerative-hierarchical clustering methods. The most recent method solving this problem is from 2021 and employs hierarchical clustering over a created mention/entity graph [1]. While offline clustering works well it fails if documents are not available all at once. This is the case when one has a continuous stream of news or tweets. But also in the context of historical documents, it is the case that not the full batch of documents is available from the get-go. Digitizing and preprocessing documents is a time-consuming endeavor. However, time is precious and waiting until all documents are available can be a critical disadvantage. That is why it is necessary to be able to process the available documents when they arrive.

Hoffart et al. [18] introduced a similar task. However, the focus lies not on out-of-KG entities in general but only on emerging entities. These are recent entities that occur currently in the media and thus are of importance to the public interest. This is typically solved by including auxiliary sources in temporal proximity [18,59,62]. Most work focusing on this task is not able to identify the same emerging entities in multiple documents [59,62]. They are limited to just identifying them. The notable exception is the aforementioned work by Hoffart et al. They represent each emerging entity by the key phrases surrounding it. This makes it possible to link, if the entity linker relies on key phrases, to emerging entities in new incoming documents [18].

This thesis differs in two main aspects. First, the representation will not rely on key phrases but will be based on more informative **dense-embeddings**, second as the support of not only emerging entities but also other out-of-KG entities is of importance, the **availability of auxiliary sources is not assumed**. The feasibility of representing out-of-KG entities by dense embeddings is supported by the impressive performance of recent inductive or zero-shot entity linker relying on such dense embeddings [5,42,58]. As no auxiliary sources are assumed to be available, all information used needs to lie in the input documents and KG. Another point differentiating the work of this thesis from all the previous methods is that it will focus on knowledge graphs like Wikidata. Previous methods were only suitable for encyclopedias like Wikipedia or Fandom. This makes different methods necessary and possible.

While similar, the work differs from (cross-document) coreference resolution due to the existence of the large number of entities in the KG which also need to be considered.

Note that there is a debate on what is defined as an entity being desirable to link. Often, this depends on the desired use-case and underlying knowledge graph [43,44]. As we are concerned with entities not yet existing in the KG, this certainly also affects this work. However, we assume that entity mentions are already available and that any such entity mention does indeed point to an entity of interest, whether in the KG or not. Furthermore, as described in Sect. 2.3, another goal of the thesis, is the creation of small descriptions of entities. These help to decide whether to include the entity when the entity recognizer is unreliable in identifying entities of interest.

2.3 Entity Description

As the representations of out-of-KG entities will be a combination of structured and unstructured information, the methods to produce a description of the entity will also need to include the combined properties of methods employed on two common tasks: **Text summarization** and **graph-to-text** generation.

In the past, to tackle graph-to-text generation, sequence-to-sequence models were often employed to map a graph to a text [32, 41, 55]. However, as graphs are unordered by nature, the latest methods usually employ graph neural networks (GNN) to encode the graph and then map the graph representation to output text [3, 10, 27, 33, 39, 40, 51, 64]. This summarizes the state of the art to transform structured information into text.

To transform unstructured text into summaries, two different kinds of text summarization problems are considered: abstractive and extractive summarization. The difference is that extractive summarization chooses certain phrases out of the input document as a summary while abstractive summarization creates an entirely new summary.

As abstractive summarization is more relevant to our problem, the related works in text summarization are dedicated it. Abstractive summarization is a sequence-to-sequence problem which is why most methods follow the encoder-decoder framework [9, 13, 34, 35, 37, 46, 49]. Many different model types, such as pointer networks, convolutional networks or attention-based networks, were employed. In recent years, the best-performing models are based on pre-trained transformer models [6, 25, 48, 61]. Important work is here the one by See et al. [49] as it focuses on the problem of summarization methods often responding with wrong facts. As the planned method of the thesis focuses on summarizations supporting graph information (including factual knowledge) and textual information, producing factual correct summarizes is the goal.

3   Problem Statements, Research Questions and Contributions

There are two problems to solve. First, out-of-KG entities need to be detected and incrementally modelled (see Fig. 1). Second, summaries need to be created based on the intermediary representations which are the product of the solution to the first problem (see Fig. 2).

Problem 1. Assign each entity mention $m \in M_d$ occurring in an input document d to an entity in one of the three sets $E_{KG}, E_I, E_{out\text{-}of\text{-}KG}$. E_{KG} contains all entities in the KG, E_I all entities with intermediary entity representations and $E_{out\text{-}of\text{-}KG}$ all other entities. If an entity belonging to the set $E_{out\text{-}of\text{-}KG}$ is encountered, create an intermediary representation of such an entity and insert it into E_I. It holds that $E_{KG} \cap E_I = E_I \cap E_{out\text{-}of\text{-}KG} = E_{KG} \cap E_{out\text{-}of\text{-}KG} = \emptyset$.

Problem 2. Create a textual summary s of an entity e using the context information of the entity, available in a document d and in the KG. The information in the document is of primary importance in the summary while the KG information provides the holistic frame.

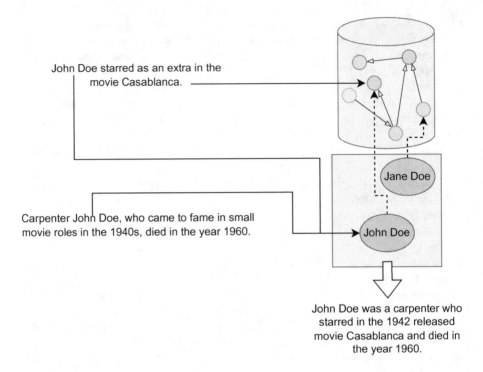

Fig. 2. Out-of-KG entity description creation. Given the intermediary representation of "John Doe", a description is created using the representation and additional information in the KG.

In accordance with the previous two problems the following research questions were identified:

RQ 1: To what extent are out-of-KG entities incrementally identifiable and modellable?

RQ 2: How do existing non-incremental NIL-clustering methods compare to an incremental method?

RQ 3: Does an incremental method utilizing a KG deliver comparable or better performance than emerging entity discovery methods using external documents and encyclopedias?

RQ 4: To what extent are graph-to-text and text summary methods able to be combined to describe out-of-KG entity representations?

In connection with answering the research questions, multiple contributions will be made (more information in Sect. 5):

– Entity linker supporting out-of-KG entities
– Silver-standard entity linking dataset with focus on out-of-KG entities
– Gold-standard entity linking dataset with focus on out-of-KG entities
– Silver-standard entity description generation dataset
– Gold-standard entity description generation dataset

4 Research Methodology and Approach

The first step is to decide on a suitable dataset for measuring the performance of an entity linker supporting the detection and modelling of out-of-KG entities. While some datasets exist, they are often too small to be able to train complex models on them. That is why a new artificially created dataset is necessary. Hence, potential documents need to be searched for and then processed and labeled to be usable.

To be able to deliver an answer to **RQ 1**, the following steps are followed to design an entity linker supporting out-of-KG entities. Afterward, based on extensive literature review, an entity linking architecture will be created fulfilling both the needs for satisfying entity linking performance and the ability to detect and model out-of-KG entities. The model will be trained and evaluated on the artificially created dataset but also evaluated on the few existing datasets compatible with the problem definition. The entity linking method will be based on one mention encoding model and one entity encoding model. The former model is based on a language model with the input being the document in which each mention is marked via special tokens. This results in a dense embedding of each entity mention. The entity encoding is the concatenation of a label embedding, a type embedding and the output of a graph neural network run over the word embeddings of the n-hop neighborhood of each entity. By not relying on pre-computed graph embeddings, it is on the one hand possible for the entity linking method to link to entities not seen during training and on the other hand it allows to represent out-of-KG entities similar to the in-KG entities. Concerning the out-KG-entity, there are currently two options for the detection and two options for the modelling under discussion. For the detection, the first option is to calculate the ranking score for each potential entity and if the score is below some hyper-parameter, the entity mention is deemed to be out-of-KG. The other option is to use a reinforcement-learning-based approach where the action space consists of all possible entity candidates plus the possibility of an out-of-KG entity. The modelling aspect works as follows: An entity mention is detected to belong to an out-of-KG entity. Then, an artificial graph is built for the out-of-KG entity mention. It consists of the mention itself and all other entity mentions in the document. The entity mentions are linked by extracted relations. Furthermore, for each other entity mention in the document not belonging to an out-of-KG entity, the neighborhood is also added to the artificial graph. Hence, it contains the context information of the document and the graph information of the other entities in the document. One problem is the addition of new information into existing representations as the extension of the corresponding graphs is not straightforward. Also, it might be that an existing representation stands for two entities instead of one, so it is necessary to split the graph which is not trivial. To solve that, the second option will use latent representations in the form of elliptical embeddings, more specifically Gaussian embeddings [17,57]. When each entity in the knowledge graph and outside of the knowledge graph is embedded as such, incremental clustering methods can be applied [38,52]. They enable to seamlessly include new information by adding new clusters, updating them with new samples and even splitting them.

Relation extraction is a smaller focus point and as such a state of the art relation extractor [30,45,63] will be used. However, it will be inspected whether the resulting relations can be used to improve the representations of out-of-KG entities. In the case of the symbolic representations in the form of graphs, this is straightforward as the edges between mentions can be refined using the extracted relations. In the case of the latent representations, the inclusion is still under investigation.

After the creation and evaluation of the entity linking method, the representation of out-of-KG entities is specified. Hence, the work on the development of an entity description method can begin. To accomplish that, another comprehensive review of existing abstractive summarization and graph-to-text methods will be carried out. Based on that, a novel method will be designed. As this depends on the literature review, no design decisions are made yet. Here, a dataset does, to the best of my knowledge, not exist. Hence, another dataset will be automatically created from Wikipedia similar to WikiSum [24]. The difference is that here not only documents are assumed as input but also Wikidata as an additional knowledge source. As there exists no comparable work, the evaluation will be done in comparison to created baselines.

Lastly, to evaluate both methods together on a gold-standard dataset, a new one based on historical documents will be annotated. Currently, letters out of the 19th century are considered to be annotated. These will certainly contain out-of-KG entities. However, the letters are not yet available for inspection. If they do not contain enough information on existing entities in, for instance, Wikidata, they are not suitable. The annotation for the EL task will be straightforward. However, for the entity summary task, characteristics defining a "good" summary need to be defined, especially the difference in relevance of the information in the KG and the documents. The plan is to rely on a crowdsourcing platform such as Amazon Mechanical Turk.

See Fig. 3 for an overview of the created modules.

5   Evaluation Plan

Entity linking supporting out-of-KG entity detection and modelling is evaluated as follows. As no fully comparable method exists until now, several baselines varying in complexity will be constructed. For example, a simple baseline would be that any entity mention not corresponding to any label of an existing entity, corresponds to an out-of-KG entity, and all such entity mentions correspond to the same entity. A more complex baseline might use the same EL method as the newly designed method but again rely only on entity mention matching to connect out-of-KG entities. However, no final decisions are yet made. The evaluation will be done by using **precision**, **recall** and **F1**. This evaluation will also contribute to answering **RQ 1**. Next, one comparison to NIL-clustering methods and a second to emerging entity discovery methods is planned as these are related, but not identical, tasks. The former comparison answers **RQ 2**, while the latter will answer **RQ 3**. For NIL-clustering, the commonly used measures, such as **normalized mutual information, adjusted rand index** or **B-Cubed+**, will be used. For emerging entity discovery, precision, recall and F1, are again the preferred measures. The method is compared to the baselines on AIDA-EE [18], an automatically created silver-standard dataset and a manually annotated gold-standard dataset. AIDA-EE is also the dataset used for the comparison to the emerging entity discovery methods. For NIL clustering, the methods will be evaluated on the silver-standard and the gold-standard dataset as well as datasets used in NIL-clustering [14].

Lastly, to answer **RQ 4**, the entity description method is evaluated. Here, the **Rouge** score is used, which measures the quality of textual summaries. Baselines need to be created as no comparable methods exist. The baselines will, for example, either only use text or only use graph information. The evaluation will be done on another automatically created silver-standard dataset and the gold-standard dataset based on the same data as used for the entity linking benchmarks.

See Fig. 3 for all created datasets and the corresponding modules.

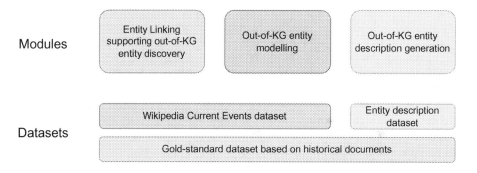

Fig. 3. Overview of created modules and datasets.

6 Preliminary Results

It was already identified that many datasets are not suitable for entity linking with out-of-KG entity detection and the subsequent modelling problem. Often they do not contain out-of-KG entities at all. Other datasets do contain out-of-KG entity mentions but they are only marked as such. It is not specified whether two out-of-KG entity mentions refer to the same entity.

The silver-standard dataset was based on the "Current Events" section of Wikipedia[1]. More specifically, all current events posts between 2017-12-01 and

---

[1] https://en.wikipedia.org/wiki/Portal:Current_events.

2022-01-01 were crawled. Then, each hyperlink in the posts was taken as an initial entity mention. To only focus on named entities, each entity mention was further examined. If it is a class, the entity mention was removed. If some document did not contain any entity mention anymore, it was removed. Then, the Wikidata dump of 2017-12-01 was taken and each entity **not** existing in the dump was marked as being out-of-KG. This resulted in a dataset of documents, being sequential in time and containing out-of-KG entities. Statistics on the dataset can be found in Table 1. It is planned to release the dataset together with the first work using the dataset to be confident of its quality.

Table 1. Statistics of Current-Events dataset

# examples	23.046
# mentions	64.317
# out-of-KG mentions	7.739
# unique entities	16.175
# unique out-of-KG entities	2.356
Average of # mentions per example	2.8

7   Conclusion and Future Work

It was argued that while some works on knowledge graph population with out-of-KG entities exist, the topic is still less widespread. Especially regarding the incremental detection and modeling of out-of-KG entities, the research landscape is still rather sparse. Most of the existing work focuses on emerging entities and not out-of-KG entities in general. Furthermore, nearly all such methods have encyclopedias as their target knowledge base.

Hence, one of the main goals will be the creation of a knowledge graph population method with a focus on the incremental detection and modelling of out-of-KG entities. The target knowledge graph will be Wikidata or other graphs which differentiates this work from others focusing on the discovery of out-of-KG entities.

As discovered out-of-KG entities still need to be added to the KG, another goal is the creation of a description of the new entity. While methods exist which can transform graphs to textual descriptions or create summaries of short texts, the combination of both is usually not done. But as out-of-KG entities in our use case are partially grounded in a KG but also part of the textual information of the input documents, combining both subtasks is a necessity and hence another goal.

Acknowledgements. This work is supervised by Prof. Dr. Ricardo Usbeck.

References

1. Agarwal, D., et al.: Entity linking and discovery via arborescence based supervised clustering. CoRR abs/2109.01242 (2021). arXiv:2109.01242
2. Angeli, G., et al.: Bootstrapped self training for knowledge base population. In: Proceedings of the 2015 Text Analysis Conference, TAC 2015, Gaithersburg, Maryland, USA, 16–17 November 2015. NIST (2015). https://tac.nist.gov/publications/2015/participant.papers/TAC2015.Stanford.proceedings.pdf
3. Beck, D., Haffari, G., Cohn, T.: Graph-to-sequence learning using gated graph neural networks. In: Gurevych, I., Miyao, Y. (eds.) Proceedings of the 56th Annual Meeting of the Association for Computational Linguistics, ACL 2018, Melbourne, Australia, 15–20 July 2018, Volume 1: Long Papers, pp. 273–283. Association for Computational Linguistics (2018). https://aclanthology.org/P18-1026/. https://doi.org/10.18653/v1/P18-1026
4. Blissett, K., Ji, H.: Cross-lingual NIL entity clustering for lowresource languages. In: Proceedings of the Second Workshop on Computational Models of Reference, Anaphora and Coreference, Minneapolis, USA, June 2019, pp. 20–25. Association for Computational Linguistics (2019). https://aclanthology.org/W19-2804. https://doi.org/10.18653/v1/W19-2804
5. Botha, J.A., Shan, Z., Gillick, D.: Entity linking in 100 languages. In: Webber, B., et al. (eds.) Proceedings of the 2020 Conference on Empirical Methods in Natural Language Processing, EMNLP 2020, 16–20 November 2020, pp. 7833–7845. Association for Computational Linguistics (2020). https://doi.org/10.18653/v1/2020.emnlp-main.630
6. Cao, Y., et al.: MultiSumm: towards a unified model for multi-lingual abstractive summarization. In: The Thirty-Fourth AAAI Conference on Artificial Intelligence, AAAI 2020, The Thirty-Second Innovative Applications of Artificial Intelligence Conference, IAAI 2020, The Tenth AAAI Symposium on Educational Advances in Artificial Intelligence, EAAI 2020, New York, NY, USA, 7–12 February 2020, pp. 11–18. AAAI Press (2020). https://aaai.org/ojs/index.php/AAAI/article/view/5328
7. Cassidy, T., et al.: CUNY-UIUC-SRI TAC-KBP2011 entity linking system description. In: Proceedings of the Fourth Text Analysis Conference, TAC 2011, Gaithersburg, Maryland, USA, 14–15 November 2011. NIST (2011). https://tac.nist.gov/publications/2011/participant.papers/CUNY_UIUC_SRI.proceedings.pdf
8. Chaganty, A.T., et al.: Importance sampling for unbiased on-demand evaluation of knowledge base population. In: Palmer, M., Hwa, R., Riedel, S. (eds.) Proceedings of the 2017 Conference on Empirical Methods in Natural Language Processing, EMNLP 2017, Copenhagen, Denmark, 9–11 September 2017, pp. 1038–1048. Association for Computational Linguistics (2017). https://doi.org/10.18653/v1/d17-1109
9. Chopra, S., Auli, M., Rush, A.M.: Abstractive sentence summarization with attentive recurrent neural networks. In: Knight, K., Nenkova, A., Rambow, O. (eds.) NAACL HLT 2016, The 2016 Conference of the North American Chapter of the Association for Computational Linguistics: Human Language Technologies, San Diego California, USA, 12–17 June 2016, pp. 93–98. The Association for Computational Linguistics (2016). https://doi.org/10.18653/v1/n16-1012
10. Damonte, M., Cohen, S.B.: Structural neural encoders for AMR-to-text generation. In: Burstein, J., Doran, C., Solorio, T. (eds.) Proceedings of the 2019 Conference of the North American Chapter of the Association for Computational Linguistics:

Human Language Technologies, NAACL-HLT 2019, Minneapolis, MN, USA, 2–7 June 2019, Volume 1 (Long and Short Papers), pp. 3649–3658. Association for Computational Linguistics (2019). https://doi.org/10.18653/v1/n19-1366

11. Dutta, S., Weikum, G.: C3EL: a joint model for cross- document co-reference resolution and entity linking. In: Màrquez, L., et al. (eds.) Proceedings of the 2015 Conference on Empirical Methods in Natural Language Processing, EMNLP 2015, Lisbon, Portugal, 17–21 September 2015, pp. 846–856. The Association for Computational Linguistics (2015). https://doi.org/10.18653/v1/d15-1101

12. Fahrni, A., et al.: HITS monolingual and cross-lingual entity linking system at TAC 2013. In: Proceedings of the Sixth Text Analysis Conference, TAC 2013, Gaithersburg, Maryland, USA, 18–19 November 2013. NIST (2013). https://tac.nist.gov/publications/2013/participant.papers/HITS.TAC2013.proceedings.pdf

13. Gehrmann, S., Deng, Y., Rush, A.M.: Bottom-up abstractive summarization. In: Riloff, E., et al. (eds.) Proceedings of the 2018 Conference on Empirical Methods in Natural Language Processing, Brussels, Belgium, 31 October–4 November 2018, pp. 4098–4109. Association for Computational Linguistics (2018). https://doi.org/10.18653/v1/d18-1443

14. Getman, J., et al.: Laying the groundwork for knowledge base population: nine years of linguistic resources for TAC KBP. In: Calzolari, N., et al. (eds.) Proceedings of the Eleventh International Conference on Language Resources and Evaluation, LREC 2018, Miyazaki, Japan, 7–12 May 2018. European Language Resources Association (ELRA) (2018). http://www.lrec-conf.org/proceedings/lrec2018/summaries/1047.html

15. Graus, D., et al.: Context-based entity linking - University of Amsterdam at TAC 2012. In: Proceedings of the Fifth Text Analysis Conference, TAC 2012, Gaithersburg, Maryland, USA, 5–6 November 2012. NIST (2012). https://tac.nist.gov/publications/2012/participant.papers/UvA.proceedings.pdf

16. Greenfield, K., et al.: A reverse approach to named entity extraction and linking in microposts. In: Dadzie, A.S., et al. (eds.) Proceedings of the 6th Workshop on 'Making Sense of Microposts' co-located with the 25th International World Wide Web Conference (WWW 2016), Montréal, Canada, 11 April 2016, vol. 1691. CEUR Workshop Proceedings. CEUR-WS.org, pp. 67–69 (2016). http://ceur-ws.org/Vol-1691/paper_11.pdf

17. He, S., et al.: Learning to represent knowledge graphs with Gaussian embedding. In: Bailey, J., et al. (eds.) Proceedings of the 24th ACM International Conference on Information and Knowledge Management, CIKM 2015, Melbourne, VIC, Australia, 19–23 October 2015, pp. 623–632. ACM (2015). https://doi.org/10.1145/2806416.2806502

18. Hoffart, J., Altun, Y., Weikum, G.: Discovering emerging entities with ambiguous names. In: Chung, C.-W., et al. (eds.) 23rd International World Wide Web Conference, WWW 2014, Seoul, Republic of Korea, 7–11 April 2014, pp. 385–396. ACM (2014). https://doi.org/10.1145/2566486.2568003

19. Hogan, A., et al.: Knowledge Graphs. Synthesis Lectures on Data, Semantics, and Knowledge. Morgan & Claypool Publishers (2021). https://doi.org/10.2200/S01125ED1V01Y202109DSK022

20. Huynh, H.M., Nguyen, T.T., Cao, T.H.: Using coreference and surrounding contexts for entity linking. In: 2013 IEEE RIVF International Conference on Computing and Communication Technologies, Research, Innovation, and Vision for the Future, RIVF 2013, Hanoi, Vietnam, 10–13 November 2013, pp. 1–5. IEEE (2013). https://doi.org/10.1109/RIVF.2013.6719856

21. Ji, H., Grishman, R.: Knowledge base population: successful approaches and challenges. In: Lin, D., Matsumoto, Y., Mihalcea, R. (eds.) The 49th Annual Meeting of the Association for Computational Linguistics: Human Language Technologies, Proceedings of the Conference, Portland, Oregon, USA, 19–24 June 2011, pp. 1148–1158. The Association for Computer Linguistics (2011). https://aclanthology.org/P11-1115/

22. Krikorian, R.: New Tweets per Second Record, and How!, April 2013. https://blog.twitter.com/engineering/en_us/a/2013/new-tweets-per-secondrecord-and-how. Accessed 29 Mar 2022

23. Lin, X., et al.: KBPearl: a knowledge base population system supported by joint entity and relation linking. Proc. VLDB Endow. **13**(7), 1035–1049 (2020). http://www.vldb.org/pvldb/vol13/p1035-lin.pdf. https://doi.org/10.14778/3384345.3384352

24. Liu, P.J., et al.: Generating Wikipedia by summarizing long sequences. In: 6th International Conference on Learning Representations, ICLR 2018, Vancouver, BC, Canada, 30 April–3 May 2018, Conference Track Proceedings. OpenReview.net (2018). https://openreview.net/forum?id=Hyg0vbWC-

25. Liu, Y., Lapata, M.: Text summarization with pretrained encoders. In: Inui, K., et al. (eds.) Proceedings of the 2019 Conference on Empirical Methods in Natural Language Processing and the 9th International Joint Conference on Natural Language Processing, EMNLP-IJCNLP 2019, Hong Kong, China, 3–7 November 2019, pp. 3728–3738. Association for Computational Linguistics (2019). https://doi.org/10.18653/v1/D19-1387

26. Liu, Y., et al.: Seq2RDF: an end-to-end application for deriving triples from natural language text. In: van Erp, M., et al. (eds.) Proceedings of the ISWC 2018 Posters & Demonstrations, Industry and Blue Sky Ideas Tracks co-located with 17th International Semantic Web Conference (ISWC 2018), Monterey, USA, 8–12 October 2018, vol. 2180. CEUR Workshop Proceedings. CEUR-WS.org (2018). http://ceurws.org/Vol-2180/paper-37.pdf

27. Marcheggiani, D., Perez-Beltrachini, L.: Deep graph convolutional encoders for structured data to text generation. In: Krahmer, E., Gatt, A., Goudbeek, M. (eds.) Proceedings of the 11th International Conference on Natural Language Generation, Tilburg University, The Netherlands, 5–8 November 2018, pp. 1–9. Association for Computational Linguistics (2018). https://doi.org/10.18653/v1/w18-6501

28. McNamee, P., Dang, H.T.: Overview of the TAC 2009 knowledge base population track. In: Text Analysis Conference (TAC), vol. 17, pp. 111–113 (2009)

29. Menzel, S., et al.: Named Entity Linking mit Wikidata und GND - Das Potenzial handkuratierter und strukturierter Datenquellen für die semantische Anreicherung von Volltexten. In: Franke-Maier, M., et al. (eds.) Qualität in der Inhaltserschließung. De Gruyter, September 2021, pp. 229–258 (2021). ISBN 978-3-11-069159-7. https://doi.org/10.1515/9783110691597-012. https://web.archive.org/web/20220121094046/. https://www.degruyter.com/document/doi/10.1515/9783110691597-012/html

30. Mihindukulasooriya, N., et al.: Leveraging semantic parsing for relation linking over knowledge bases. In: Pan, J.Z., et al. (eds.) ISWC 2020. LNCS, vol. 12506, pp. 402–419. Springer, Cham (2020). https://doi.org/10.1007/978-3-030-62419-4_23

31. Monahan, S., et al.: Cross-lingual cross-document coreference with entity linking. In: Proceedings of the Fourth Text Analysis Conference, TAC 2011, Gaithersburg, Maryland, USA, 14–15 November 2011. NIST (2011). https://tac.nist.gov/publications/2011/participant.papers/lcc.proceedings.pdf

32. Moryossef, A., Goldberg, Y., Dagan, I.: Step-by-step: separating planning from realization in neural data-to-text generation. In: Burstein, J., Doran, C., Solorio, T. (eds.) Proceedings of the 2019 Conference of the North American Minneapolis, MN, USA, 2–7 June 2019, Volume 1 (Long and Short Papers), pp. 2267–2277. Association for Computational Linguistics (2019). https://doi.org/10.18653/v1/n19-1236

33. Moussallem, D., Gnaneshwar, D., Castro Ferreira, T., Ngonga Ngomo, A.-C.: NABU – multilingual graph-based neural RDF verbalizer. In: Pan, J.Z., et al. (eds.) ISWC 2020. LNCS, vol. 12506, pp. 420–437. Springer, Cham (2020). https://doi.org/10.1007/978-3-030-62419-4_24

34. Nallapati, R., et al.: Abstractive text summarization using sequence-to-sequence RNNs and beyond. In: Goldberg, Y., Riezler, S. (eds.) Proceedings of the 20th SIGNLL Conference on Computational Natural Language Learning, CoNLL 2016, Berlin, Germany, 11–12 August 2016, pp. 280–290. ACL (2016). https://doi.org/10.18653/v1/k16-1028

35. Narayan, S., Cohen, S.B., Lapata, M.: Don't give me the details, just the summary! topic-aware convolutional neural networks for extreme summarization. In: Riloff, E., et al. (eds.) Proceedings of the 2018 Conference on Empirical Methods in Natural Language Processing, Brussels, Belgium, 31 October–4 November 2018, pp. 1797–1807. Association for Computational Linguistics (2018). https://doi.org/10.18653/v1/d18-1206

36. Niklaus, C., et al.: A survey on open information extraction. In: Bender, E.M., Derczynski, L., Isabelle, P. (eds.) Proceedings of the 27th International Conference on Computational Linguistics, COLING 2018, Santa Fe, New Mexico, USA, 20–26 August 2018, pp. 3866–3878. Association for Computational Linguistics (2018). https://aclanthology.org/C18-1326/

37. Paulus, R., Xiong, C., Socher, R.: A deep reinforced model for abstractive summarization. In: 6th International Conference on Learning Representations, ICLR 2018, Vancouver, BC, Canada, 30 April–3 May 2018, Conference Track Proceedings. OpenReview.net (2018). https://openreview.net/forum?id=HkAClQgA

38. Pinto, R.C., Engel, P.M.: A fast incremental Gaussian mixture model. CoRR abs/1506.04422 (2015). arXiv:1506.04422

39. Ribeiro, L.F.R., Gardent, C., Gurevych, I.: Enhancing AMR-to-text generation with dual graph representations. In: Inui, K., et al. (eds.) Proceedings of the 2019 Conference on Empirical Methods in Natural Language Processing and the 9th International Joint Conference on Natural Language Processing, EMNLP-IJCNLP 2019, Hong Kong, China, 3–7 November 2019, pp. 3181–3192. Association for Computational Linguistics (2019). https://doi.org/10.18653/v1/D19-1314

40. Ribeiro, L.F.R., Zhang, Y., Gurevych, I.: Structural adapters in pretrained language models for AMR-to-text generation. In: Moens, M.-F., et al. (eds.) Proceedings of the 2021 Conference on Empirical Methods in Natural Language Processing, EMNLP 2021, Virtual Event/Punta Cana, Dominican Republic, 7–11 November 2021, pp. 4269–4282. Association for Computational Linguistics (2021). https://doi.org/10.18653/v1/2021.emnlp-main.351

41. Ribeiro, L.F.R., et al.: Smelting gold and silver for improved multilingual AMR-to-text generation. In: Moens, M.-F., et al. (eds.) Proceedings of the 2021 Conference on Empirical Methods in Natural Language Processing, EMNLP 2021, Virtual Event/Punta Cana, Dominican Republic, 7–11 November 2021, pp. 742–750. Association for Computational Linguistics (2021). https://doi.org/10.18653/v1/2021.emnlp-main.57

42. Ristoski, P., Lin, Z., Zhou, Q.: KG-ZESHEL: knowledge graph-enhanced zero-shot entity linking. In: Gentile, A.L., Gonçalves, R. (eds.) K-CAP 2021: Knowledge Capture Conference, Virtual Event, USA, 2–3 December 2021, pp. 49–56. ACM (2021). https://doi.org/10.1145/3460210.3493549
43. Rosales-Méndez, H., Hogan, A., Poblete, B.: Fine-grained entity linking. J. Web Semant. **65**, 100600 (2020). https://doi.org/10.1016/j.websem.2020.100600
44. Rosales-Méndez, H., Poblete, B., Hogan, A.: What should entity linking link? In: Olteanu, D., Poblete, B. (eds.) Proceedings of the 12th Alberto Mendelzon International Workshop on Foundations of Data Management, Cali, Colombia, 21–25 May 2018, vol. 2100. CEUR Workshop Proceedings. CEUR-WS.org (2018). http://ceurws.org/Vol-2100/paper10.pdf
45. Rossiello, G., et al.: Generative relation linking for question answering over knowledge bases. In: Hotho, A., et al. (eds.) ISWC 2021. LNCS, vol. 12922, pp. 321–337. Springer, Cham (2021). https://doi.org/10.1007/978-3-030-88361-4_19
46. Rush, A.M., Chopra, S., Weston, J.: A neural attention model for abstractive sentence summarization. In: Màrquez, L., et al. (eds.) Proceedings of the 2015 Conference on Empirical Methods in Natural Language Processing, EMNLP 2015, Lisbon, Portugal, 17–21 September 2015, pp. 379–389. The Association for Computational Linguistics (2015). https://doi.org/10.18653/v1/d15-1044
47. de Sá Mesquita, F., et al.: KnowledgeNet: a benchmark dataset for knowledge base population. In: Inui, K., et al. (eds.) Proceedings of the 2019 Conference on Empirical Methods in Natural Language Processing and the 9th International Joint Conference on Natural Language Processing, EMNLP-IJCNLP 2019, Hong Kong, China, 3–7 November 2019, pp. 749–758. Association for Computational Linguistics (2019). https://doi.org/10.18653/v1/D19-1069
48. Saito, I., et al.: Length-controllable abstractive summarization by guiding with summary prototype. CoRR abs/2001.07331 (2020). arXiv:2001.07331
49. See, A., Liu, P.J., Manning, C.D.: Get to the point: summarization with pointer-generator networks. In: Barzilay, R., Kan, M.-Y. (eds.) Proceedings of the 55th Annual Meeting of the Association for Computational Linguistics, ACL 2017, Vancouver, Canada, 30 July–4 August, Volume 1: Long Papers, pp. 1073–1083. Association for Computational Linguistics (2017). https://doi.org/10.18653/v1/P17-1099
50. Singhal, A.: Introducing the Knowledge Graph: Things, Not Strings, May 2012. https://blog.google/products/search/introducing-knowledgegraph-things-not/. Accessed 29 Mar 2022
51. Song, L., et al.: A graph-to-sequence model for AMR-to-text generation. In: Gurevych, I., Miyao, Y. (eds.) Proceedings of the 56th Annual Meeting of the Association for Computational Linguistics, ACL 2018, Melbourne, Australia, 15–20 July 2018, Volume 1: Long Papers, pp. 1616–1626. Association for Computational Linguistics (2018). https://doi.org/10.18653/v1/P18-1150. https://aclanthology.org/P18-1150/
52. Song, M., Wang, H.: Highly efficient incremental estimation of Gaussian mixture models for online data stream clustering. In: Intelligent Computing: Theory and Applications III, vol. 5803, pp. 174–183. SPIE (2005)
53. Sui, D., et al.: Set generation networks for end-to-end knowledge base population. In: Moens, M.-F., et al. (eds.) Proceedings of the 2021 Conference on Empirical Methods in Natural Language Processing, EMNLP 2021, Virtual Event/Punta Cana, Dominican Republic, 7–11 November 2021, pp. 9650–9660. Association for Computational Linguistics (2021). https://doi.org/10.18653/v1/2021.emnlp-main.760

54. Tamang, S., Chen, Z., Ji, H.: CUNY BLENDER TACKBP2012 entity linking system and slot filling validation system. In: Proceedings of the Fifth Text Analysis Conference, TAC 2012, Gaithersburg, Maryland, USA, 5–6 November 2012. NIST (2012). https://tac.nist.gov/publications/2012/participant.papers/Blender_CUNY.proceedings.pdf

55. Trisedya, B.D., et al.: GTR-LSTM: a triple encoder for sentence generation from RDF data. In: Gurevych, I., Miyao, Y. (eds.) Proceedings of the 56th Annual Meeting of the Association for Computational Linguistics, ACL 2018, Melbourne, Australia, 15–20 July 2018, Volume 1: Long Papers, pp. 1627–1637. Association for Computational Linguistics (2018). https://doi.org/10.18653/v1/P18-1151. https://aclanthology.org/P18-1151/

56. Trisedya, B.D., et al.: Neural relation extraction for knowledge base enrichment. In: Korhonen, A., Traum, D.R., Màrquez, L. (eds.) Proceedings of the 57th Conference of the Association for Computational Linguistics, ACL 2019, Florence, Italy, 28 July–2 August 2019, Volume 1: Long Papers, pp. 229–240. Association for Computational Linguistics (2019). https://doi.org/10.18653/v1/p19-1023

57. Vilnis, L., McCallum, A.: Word representations via Gaussian embedding. In: Bengio, Y., LeCun, Y. (eds.) 3rd International Conference on Learning Representations, ICLR 2015, San Diego, CA, USA, 7–9 May 2015, Conference Track Proceedings (2015). http://arxiv.org/abs/1412.6623

58. Wu, L., et al.: Scalable zero-shot entity linking with dense entity retrieval. In: Webber, B., et al. (eds.) Proceedings of the 2020 Conference on Empirical Methods in Natural Language Processing, EMNLP 2020, 16–20 November 2020, pp. 6397–6407. Association for Computational Linguistics (2020). https://doi.org/10.18653/v1/2020.emnlp-main.519

59. Wu, Z., Song, Y., Lee Giles, C.: Exploring multiple feature spaces for novel entity discovery. In: Schuurmans, D., Wellman, M.P. (eds.) Proceedings of the Thirtieth AAAI Conference on Artificial Intelligence, Phoenix, Arizona, USA, 12–17 February 2016, pp. 3073–3079. AAAI Press (2016). http://www.aaai.org/ocs/index.php/AAAI/AAAI16/paper/view/12261

60. Zhang, C., et al.: DeepDive: declarative knowledge base construction. Commun. ACM **60**(5), 93–102 (2017). https://doi.org/10.1145/3060586

61. Zhang, J., et al.: PEGASUS: pre-training with extracted gap-sentences for abstractive summarization. In: Proceedings of the 37th International Conference on Machine Learning, ICML 2020, 13–18 July 2020, Virtual Event, vol. 119, pp. 11328–11339. Proceedings of Machine Learning Research. PMLR (2020). http://proceedings.mlr.press/v119/zhang20ae.html

62. Zhang, L., Wu, T., Xu, L., Wang, M., Qi, G., Sack, H.: Emerging entity discovery using web sources. In: Zhu, X., Qin, B., Zhu, X., Liu, M., Qian, L. (eds.) CCKS 2019. CCIS, vol. 1134, pp. 175–184. Springer, Singapore (2019). https://doi.org/10.1007/978-981-15-1956-7_16

63. Zhang, Y., et al.: Adversarial training improved multi-path multi-scale relation detector for knowledge base question answering. IEEE Access **8**, 63310–63319 (2020). https://doi.org/10.1109/ACCESS.2020.2984393

64. Zhao, C., Walker, M.A., Chaturvedi, S.: Bridging the structural gap between encoding and decoding for data-to-text generation. In: Jurafsky, D., et al. (eds.) Proceedings of the 58th Annual Meeting of the Association for Computational Linguistics, ACL 2020, 5–10 July 2020, pp. 2481–2491. Association for Computational Linguistics (2020). https://doi.org/10.18653/v1/2020.acl-main.224

Dynamic Knowledge Graph Embeddings via Local Embedding Reconstructions

Franz Krause[✉] [iD]

Data and Web Science Group, University of Mannheim, Mannheim, Germany
franz.krause@uni-mannheim.de

Abstract. Knowledge graph embeddings and successive machine learning models represent a topic that has been gaining popularity in recent research. These allow the use of graph-structured data for applications that, by definition, rely on numerical feature vectors as inputs. In this context, the transformation of knowledge graphs into sets of numerical feature vectors is performed by embedding algorithms, which map the elements of the graph into a low-dimensional embedding space. However, these methods mostly assume a static knowledge graph, so subsequent updates inevitably require a re-run of the embedding process. In this work the **Navi Approach** is introduced which aims to maintain advantages of established embedding methods while making them accessible to dynamic domains. Relational Graph Convolutional Networks are adapted for reconstructing node embeddings based solely on local neighborhoods. Moreover, the approach is independent of the original embedding process, as it only considers its resulting embeddings. Preliminary results suggest that the performance of successive machine learning tasks is at least maintained without the need of relearning the embeddings nor the machine learning models. Often, using the reconstructed embeddings instead of the original ones even leads to an increase in performance.

Keywords: Knowledge graph · Semantic web · Dynamic embeddings

1 Introduction and Motivation

Knowledge graphs (KGs) have emerged as an effective tool for managing semi-structured domain knowledge so that it can be made available in a human- and machine-interpretable way. Their inherent information is encoded as triples $(subject, predicate, object)$ and used to improve the performance in areas such as question answering [5] and recommendation [9]. Moreover, KGs play a key role in data-intensive domains like Industry 4.0, where they have so far mostly been used for interconnecting technologies to improve efficiency and productivity of existing processes [2]. In order to make the information encoded within the knowledge graph available for machine learning models, representational learning methods are used to map its entities into a low-dimensional numerical space.

F. Krause—Category: Early Stage PhD.

These representations of the entities, so-called embeddings, can then be processed by successive machine learning models. In the context of Industry 4.0, for example, embeddings are increasingly used as inputs for domain applications. Furthermore, current developments in this field, such as the transition to Industry 5.0, focus on human-machine collaboration, making a well-defined communication and interaction a crucial component for promoting trust [7]. The relevance of knowledge graphs as common specifications of a shared conceptualization will therefore increase even further.

Besides that, accumulation of interconnected devices in this context, as well as in other domains, is causing an increase in updates to KGs in the form of additions or deletions of edges and nodes. A knowledge graph should therefore be considered as dynamic, i.e., its topological structure or attributive information is changing over time. However, current methods lack this kind of flexibility. Usually, static KGs are assumed whose encoded information changes little or not at all. As soon as the graph is updated, the embeddings have to be relearned for the whole KG in order to include the updated information. For large-scale graphs, this relearning can be very time and resource intensive. Furthermore, retraining usually provides structurally similar but not identical embeddings for existing nodes, which is why successive machine learning models have to be adapted as well. Therefore, due to the increasing dynamics and scope of prospective KGs, these methods cannot be considered a suitable solution.

In this PhD, the Navi Approach is introduced to fill this gap towards the application of KG embeddings in dynamic domains. State of the art embedding algorithms for static knowledge graphs are solely used as blueprints for simplified and local reconstructions. It is shown that in this way established embedding methods are adapted such that dynamics are enabled as well.

2   State of the Art

Static Knowledge Graph Embeddings. In order to be able to use contextual information from a knowledge graph, embedding methods are usually considered, which assign numerical feature vectors to the nodes based on the topology of the graph. In this context, Relational Graph Convolutional Networks (R-GCNs) [15] accumulate the feature vectors of neighboring nodes based on the local structure of a KG. However, R-GCNs are inevitably customized to a specific use case and usually not all nodes in the graph are assigned an embedding. In contrast, RDF2Vec [11] generates all-embracing embeddings for different data mining tasks [20]. However, as a transductive method, the embeddings must always be relearned when the graph is updated. ConvE [4], as being another neural network based approach, uses two-dimensional embeddings as input, as well as convolutional layers and fully connected layers to reduce the number of parameters. It has been shown that extensions of TransE [3] are capable of embedding symmetric, asymmetric, inverse and compositional relations, though the basic idea of using a translation-based scoring function is preserved in all of them [16]. In contrast, compositional models apply tensor factorizations to compute the embeddings [8,23] and extensions to the compositional models employ complex numbers to be able to model binary relations [19]. Moreover, embedding methods exist which also take literals into account [13]. However, the embedding methods mentioned so far are trained for an entire static knowledge graph at once. Thus, possible dynamics of a graph in the form of additions and deletions of edges are not considered, which often impairs their use in practice.

Dynamic Knowledge Graph Embeddings. As an adaptation of the static embedding method TransE, puTransE [17] allows parallelization and orchestration across multiple machines and is thus capable of handling the dynamics in KGs. Another of the few approaches to dynamic embeddings is represented by DKGE [22], which is also based on TransE. Here, dynamics are enabled by restricting the retraining of the embeddings to the context of updated nodes, i.e., their neighboring nodes. Thus, the integration of new information is accelerated compared to full relearning. In the area of dynamic graphs in general, methods employ deep recurrent architectures [18], as well as self-attention layers [14] which encode temporally evolving structural information. However, none of the existing approaches is general enough to handle arbitrary embedding methods. In addition, updates in the graph necessarily require a relearning of embeddings, even if only for subgraphs, which in turn affects the overall structure of the embeddings and therefore also successive machine learning applications.

3 Problem Statement and Contributions

Based on the motivation and the state of the art in learning representations for knowledge graphs, there is a gap that we intend to fill in this PhD. We plan to provide a method that reuses existing embeddings, even if they assume static knowledge graphs, to make them usable for dynamic knowledge graphs as well. Thus, we formulate the following hypothesis with the related research questions.

Hypothesis. Static embeddings for a knowledge graph $\mathcal{G}$ can serve as input of a generalized and simplified method that incorporates the neighborhood of a node in order to derive its corresponding embedding independently of itself, thus enabling the generation of dynamic embeddings.

RQ1. Can static embedding methods be adapted to obtain dynamic embeddings for new or updated nodes without relearning the original model?

RQ2. What impact do knowledge graph updates, such as the addition of entities and removal of edges, have on the performance of generated embeddings with respect to entity classification and link prediction?

With this hypothesis and the related research questions, we intend to contribute to the Semantic Web community by developing a generalized method that leverages any numerical embedding by reconstructing it based on local neighborhoods to provide simplified ad-hoc embeddings for dynamic KGs. To the best of our knowledge, such an approach does not exist yet and will have a high impact on the Semantic Web community, as well as in dynamic domains like Industry 4.0.

The first research question RQ1 aims at elaborating methods for the desired dynamic embeddings based on static embedding algorithms. We propose to justify the restriction to local reconstructions within our approach via the so-called message passing paradigm, which states that existing embeddings are derivable from edges to neighboring nodes and their embeddings. It is to be examined whether this paradigm may be assumed for arbitrary embeddings, i.e., whether local topologies are always of relevance for embedding generations.

In RQ2, we further investigate the performance of our reconstruction approach on machine learning tasks with respect to different modifications of the KG. We will also study the performance of dynamic embeddings regarding the amount of modification to a KG. Furthermore, assuming the message passing paradigm, we need to investigate the impact of embedding reconstructions on further nodes, i.e., whether existing embeddings need to be adapted as well.

4   Research Methodology and Approach

The research of this PhD aims to define a generalized approach to the dynamization and simplification of static embeddings $\epsilon : V \mapsto \mathbb{R}^d$ with respect to a KG $\mathcal{G} = (V, E)$ which consists of the sets of nodes V and edges $E \subseteq V \times \mathcal{R} \times V$, where $\mathcal{R}$ denotes the set of valid entity relations. Thus, analogous to existing embeddings, no further information such as temporal edge properties are considered. The presented approach attempts to reconstruct the embedding $\epsilon(s)$ of a node $s \in V$ independently of $\epsilon(s)$ itself. Rather, it derives $\epsilon(s)$ from the neighborhood multiset $N(s)$ with elements from $V \setminus \{s\}$ such that distinct edges with adjacent nodes are taken into account as well. Due to the independence of the reconstruction and $\epsilon(s)$, self-loops are ignored but can be applied consecutively. The reconstructions $\Phi(s) \approx \epsilon(s)$ proposed in this paper are always structured as a composition $\Phi(s) = \phi(s) + \delta_\phi^*(s)$ of a deterministic ground assumption $\phi(s) \in \mathbb{R}^d$ and a trainable refinement term $\delta_\phi^*(s) \in \mathbb{R}^d$. By defining $\delta_\phi(s) := \epsilon(s) - \phi(s)$ as the noise term, the reconstruction error to be minimized is determined as

$$\epsilon(s) - \Phi(s) = \phi(s) + \delta_\phi(s) - \left[\phi(s) + \delta_\phi^*(s)\right] = \delta_\phi(s) - \delta_\phi^*(s).$$

By inserting this error into a suitable loss function $\mathcal{L} : \mathbb{R}^d \to \mathbb{R}_0^+$ and applying a backpropagation method such as Adam [6], the reconstructed embedding $\Phi(s)$ is approximated to the target $\epsilon(s)$. In the following, analogous to [15], for each relation $r \in \mathcal{R}$ an inverse relation r' is assumed, such that each edge $(s, r, o) \in E$ implies an inverse edge (o, r', s) to simulate the varying influence of relations on subject and object nodes. Without loss of generality, the relations $\widehat{\mathcal{R}} = \bigcup_{r \in \mathcal{R}} \{r, r'\}$ are assumed in the following. Furthermore, $N_r(s) = \{v \in V | \exists e \in E : e = (v, r, s)\}$ is defined as the set of all parent nodes of $s \in V$ with respect to $r \in \widehat{\mathcal{R}}$. This implies the neighborhood multiset $N(s) = \bigcup_{r \in \widehat{\mathcal{R}}} N_r(s)$, consisting of all parent and child nodes of s. As of now, reconstruction mappings $\Phi(\cdot)$ based on $N(s)$ are also referred to as **Navi Layers**, like the **Connectivity Navi Layer** $\Phi_C(\cdot)$, defined by

$$\epsilon(s) \approx \Phi_C(s) = \tfrac{1}{|N(s)|} \left(\textstyle\sum_{r\in\widehat{\mathcal{R}}} \sum_{y\in N_r(s)} \left[W_r + Id \right] \cdot \epsilon(y) + b_r \right) \tag{1}$$

with weight matrices $W_r \in \mathbb{R}^{d\times d}$ and bias terms $b_r \in \mathbb{R}^d$ for all relations $r \in \widehat{\mathcal{R}}$. With respect to the parameter initializations $W_r = 0$ and $b_r = 0$, the ground assumption $\phi_C(s) = \tfrac{1}{|N(s)|} \sum_{y\in N(s)} \epsilon(y)$ thus follows that the centroid of the neighbor embeddings should be close to the destined embedding $\epsilon(s)$. Finally, the refinement is achieved by training the weight matrices W_r and biases b_r in

$$\delta_{\phi_C^*}(s) = \tfrac{1}{|N(s)|} \left(\textstyle\sum_{r\in\widehat{\mathcal{R}}} \sum_{y\in N_r(s)} W_r \cdot \epsilon(y) + b_r) \right)$$

for all relations $r \in \widehat{\mathcal{R}}$ such that the loss $\mathcal{L}\big(\epsilon(s) - \Phi_C(s)\big)$ is minimized. In particular, this approach resembles the idea of RDF2Vec embeddings, since the ground assumption does not include any information about the specific relations and considers connectedness as a cause of similarity. In contrast, the **Translational Navi Layer** $\Phi_T(\cdot)$ takes these relations into account by adapting translational approaches like TransE. These embed triples $(s, r, o) \in E$ such that $\epsilon(o) \approx \epsilon(s) + h(r)$ holds, where $h(r) \in \mathbb{R}^d$ is the embedding of relation r. By introducing the set $E_r := \{(\cdot, r, \cdot) \in E\}$ and the deterministic approximations $h_r := \tfrac{1}{|E_r|} \sum_{(s,r,o)\in E_r} [\epsilon(o) - \epsilon(s)] \approx h(r)$, the Navi Layer $\Phi_T(\cdot)$ is defined by

$$\epsilon(s) \approx \Phi_T(s) = \tfrac{1}{|N(s)|} \left(\textstyle\sum_{r\in\widehat{\mathcal{R}}} \sum_{y\in N_r(s)} \left[W_r + Id \right] \cdot \left[\epsilon(y) + h_r \right] + b_r \right), \tag{2}$$

where the ground assumption and the refinement are defined analogously to $\Phi_C(\cdot)$, considering the transformations $\epsilon(y) \mapsto \epsilon(y) + h_r$.

The Navi Layers $\Phi_C(\cdot)$ and $\Phi_T(\cdot)$ can be interpreted as special cases of R-GCN layers according to [15] with the corresponding forward pass from layer l to $l + 1$

$$h_s^{(l+1)} = \sigma \left(\left[W_0^{(l)} \cdot h_s^{(l)} + b_0^{(l)} \right] + \textstyle\sum_{r\in\widehat{\mathcal{R}}} \sum_{y\in N_r(s)} \left[\tfrac{1}{c_{s,r}} W_r^{(l)} \cdot h_y^{(l)} + b_r^{(l)} \right] \right).$$

By specifying $h_s^{(l+1)} := \epsilon(s)$ and $h_y^{(l)} := \epsilon(y)$ or $h_y^{(l)} := \epsilon(y) + h_r$ with respect to the corresponding relation r, one obtains equations similar to (1) and (2). The required independence of $h_s^{(l+1)}$ and $h_s^{(l)}$ is preserved by defining $W_0^{(l)}$ and $b_0^{(l)}$ as deterministic zero elements. Finally, setting the activation function σ as the identity function and the normalization term $c_{s,r} := |N(s)|$ independent of relation r yields the forward passes of the Navi Layers $\Phi_C(\cdot)$ and $\Phi_T(\cdot)$, respectively. In addition, composite reconstructions of multiple Navi Layers are enabled via so-called **Navi Mergers**. These are defined as mappings $\gamma : \mathbb{R}^{d\times n} \to \mathbb{R}^d$, where n is the number of Navis Layers. A possible Navi Merger is the weighted mean

$$\gamma^{(wm)} \left(\Phi_1(s), ..., \Phi_n(s) \right) =: \gamma_n^{(wm)}(s) = \tfrac{1}{n} \textstyle\sum_{i=1}^n W_i \cdot \Phi_i(s) + b_i,$$

with the trainable weight matrices $W_i \in \mathbb{R}^{d\times d}$ and biases $b_i \in \mathbb{R}^d$. In the following we denote a **Navi Approach/Reconstruction** $\gamma(\cdot) := \gamma(\Phi_1(\cdot), ..., \Phi_n(\cdot))$ as a combination of $n \in \mathbb{N}$ Navi Layers $\Phi_1, ..., \Phi_n$ and a Navi Merger γ. The associated training is performed as an end-to-end procedure and the set of reconstructed embeddings for a KG $\mathcal{G} = (V, E)$ is denoted as $\Gamma = \{\gamma(v) : v \in V\}$.

5   Evaluation Plan

The evaluation of the Navi Approach is supposed to clarify whether and to what extent it answers the research questions RQ1 and RQ2 from Sect. 3. To assess the dynamics of Navi Reconstructions Γ, common benchmark methods like link prediction and entity classification are used. The latter is explained in the following as an example for the evaluation procedure depicted in Fig. 1. However, the setting can be used almost analogously for link predictions, which take into account the deletion and addition of edges.

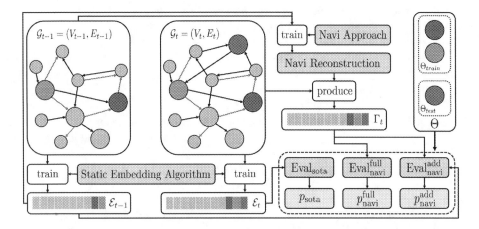

Fig. 1. Architecture of the Navi Reconstruction approach including the evaluation setup for simulating dynamic knowledge graphs.

The knowledge graphs AIFB, MUTAG, BGS and AM from [12] are particularly suitable as evaluation data as they each contain labeled nodes $\Theta \subset V$ including a split into train and test nodes $\Theta_{train}, \Theta_{test} \subset \Theta$. The dynamics of a KG $\mathcal{G}$ are then simulated via the temporal transition from $\mathcal{G}_{t-1}$ with an embedding $\mathcal{E}_{t-1}$ at time $t-1$ towards $\mathcal{G}_t$ at time t by removing the test nodes in $\mathcal{G}_{t-1}$. The reconstructed embeddings of $\mathcal{G}_t$ based on $\mathcal{G}_{t-1}$ and $\mathcal{E}_{t-1}$ are denoted as $\Gamma_t^{(t-1)} = \{\gamma_n^{(t-1)}(v) : v \in V_t\}$. Subsequently, three different performances p are determined as accuracies of successive classifiers.

1. p_{sota}: The state of the art (sota) approach for integrating the new nodes Θ_{test} is to retrain an embedding $\mathcal{E}_t$ for the KG $\mathcal{G}_t$. The classifier is retrained on these embeddings $\{\epsilon_t(v) : v \in \Theta_{train}\}$ and evaluated for $\{\epsilon_t(v) : v \in \Theta_{test}\}$.
2. $p_{\text{navi}}^{\text{add}}$: A Navi Approach $\gamma_n^{(t-1)}$ is trained on $\mathcal{E}_{t-1}$ and $\mathcal{G}_{t-1}$. The classifier is trained on $\{\epsilon_{t-1}(v) : v \in \Theta_{train}\}$ and evaluated for $\{\gamma_n^{(t-1)}(v) : v \in \Theta_{test}\}$.
3. $p_{\text{navi}}^{\text{full}}$: The same Navi Approach $\gamma_n^{(t-1)}$ is assumed as for $p_{\text{navi}}^{\text{add}}$. However, the classifier is trained on the reconstructions $\{\gamma_n^{(t-1)}(v) : v \in \Theta_{train}\}$ as well.

For the evaluation, it is of relevance whether the performance $p_{\text{navi}}^{\text{add}}$ maintains a similar level as p_{sota} despite reusing the classifier and not retraining the static embedding model. This comparison is also needed for link predictions, although other metrics as performances must be considered in this case [19]. On the other hand, p_{navi}^{full} evaluates a novel and dynamic embedding method by reconstructing the full graph and training a new classifier based on these reconstructions.

6   Preliminary Results

The preliminary results are initially limited to the AIFB KG and the entity classification task for a Support Vector Machine with RBF kernel and regularization $C = 1$. As static embedding methods, RDF2Vec [11], TransE [3], TransD [10], CrossE [24], RotatE [16], ConvE [4], RESCAL [8] and DistMult [23] are considered. The RDF2Vec embeddings were generated with pyrdf2vec [21] and the remaining embeddings via pykeen [1] with the default settings. Navi Reconstructions of these embeddings are always achieved via $\gamma(\cdot) := \gamma^{(wm)}(\Phi_C(\cdot), \Phi_T(\cdot))$ with the Navi Merger $\gamma^{(wm)}$ and the Navi Layers Φ_C, Φ_T from Sect. 4. The training runs are performed using Adam, a learning rate of 0.001, dropout 0.5, the epochs $\{0, 100, 500\}$ and the following modified mean squared error (MSE)

$$\mathcal{L}\big(\gamma(x), \epsilon(x)\big) = \tfrac{1}{d} \sum_{j=1}^{d} \left\{ \left| \frac{\exp(\min(\gamma(x)_j, \epsilon(x)_j))}{\exp(\max(\gamma(x)_j, \epsilon(x)_j))} - 1 \right| + \big[\gamma(x)_j - \epsilon(x)_j\big]^2 \right\}.$$

The exponential summand takes into account that, due to the squaring, absolutely small entries are mostly neglected by the standard MSE.

Table 1. Evaluation of the entity classification task. The 3-tuples $(p_{sota}, p_{navi}^{add}, p_{navi}^{full})$ represent the evaluation performances (here classification accuracies in percent). For RESCAL with the epoch number 1000 the performances $(53, 53, 67)$ were obtained.

Epochs	RDF2Vec	TransE	TransD	CrossE	RotatE	ConvE	RESCAL	DistMult
0	83, 89, 92	83, 72, 89	83, 86, 92	69, 44, 86	89, 56, 89	78, 42, 89	53, 31, 58	92, 47, 89
100	83, 86, 92	83, 89, 89	83, 86, 86	69, 53, 86	89, 86, 89	78, 83, 89	53, 33, 58	92, 83, 86
500	83, 89, 92	83, 89, 89	83, 86, 92	69, 81, 86	89, 89, 89	78, 86, 89	53, 47, 67	92, 92, 92

The results from Table 1 suggest that, at least in the present setting, the research questions RQ1 and RQ2 could be solved by the Navi Approach. Sufficiently large epoch numbers apparently lead to $p_{navi}^{add} \geq p_{sota}$, which exceeds the minimum goal of approximately maintaining the state of the art performance p_{sota} without the need of relearning the embedding model after each update to the graph. Further, the performances p_{navi}^{full} suggest some sort of regularization of the data. Without a single training run, the use of Navi Reconstructions mostly yields better performances and simultaneously allows the desired dynamics in the KG. The still ongoing evaluation of the Navi Reconstructions implies that these results and observations also apply to the knowledge graphs MUTAG, BGS and AM.

7   Conclusions and Lessons Learned

In this paper, we presented the Navi Approach as a possible enabler of simplified and dynamic knowledge graph embeddings. It is gratifying and not to be taken for granted that these promising results are already available at such an early stage of this PhD, justifying further research in this direction. Thus, an extension of the evaluation to large-scale graphs like DBpedia, Wikidata and YAGO is planned already. In the process, further forms of dynamics are to be highlighted and tested. Based on this, we will investigate whether and to what extent the Navi Approach already provides an answer to the research questions RQ1 and RQ2. This phase of research will also clarify whether, as conjectured in Sect. 6, a form of regularization actually occurs when existing embeddings are replaced by their reconstructions. Furthermore, there is the possibility to use the Navi Approach as a simplified surrogate model of static embedding methods and thus try to improve the interpretability of KG embeddings in future work as well.

In summary, this PhD's research will contribute to the ability to process dynamic knowledge graphs, making them accessible to humans as well as machines as a basis for their communication. This result would represent a fundamental step towards current research fields like Industry 5.0 and at the same time have a major impact on all areas involving dynamic knowledge graphs.

Acknowledgements. This PhD is part of the TEAMING.AI project which receives funding in the European Commission's Horizon 2020 Research Programme under Grant Agreement Number 957402 (www.teamingai-project.eu). Furthermore, I would like to thank my supervisor Prof. Dr. Heiko Paulheim and my co-supervisor Dr. Tobias Weller for their continuous support.

References

1. Ali, M., Berrendorf, M., et al.: PyKEEN: a python library for training and evaluating knowledge graph embeddings. J. Mach. Learn. Res. **22**(82), 1–6 (2021)
2. Bader, S.R., Grangel-Gonzalez, I., Nanjappa, P., Vidal, M.-E., Maleshkova, M.: A knowledge graph for industry 4.0. In: Harth, A., et al. (eds.) ESWC 2020. LNCS, vol. 12123, pp. 465–480. Springer, Cham (2020). https://doi.org/10.1007/978-3-030-49461-2_27
3. Bordes, A., Usunier, N., et al.: Translating embeddings for modeling multi-relational data. In: Advances in Neural Information Processing Systems, vol. 26. Curran Associates, Inc. (2013)
4. Dettmers, T., Pasquale, M., et al.: Convolutional 2d knowledge graph embeddings. In: Proceedings of the 32th AAAI Conference on Artificial Intelligence (2018)
5. Diefenbach, D., Giménez-García, J., Both, A., Singh, K., Maret, P.: QAnswer KG: designing a portable question answering system over RDF data. In: Harth, A., et al. (eds.) ESWC 2020. LNCS, vol. 12123, pp. 429–445. Springer, Cham (2020). https://doi.org/10.1007/978-3-030-49461-2_25
6. Kingma, D.P., Ba, J.: Adam: a method for stochastic optimization. In: 3rd International Conference on Learning Representations, ICLR 2015, San Diego, CA, USA, 7–9 May 2015, Conference Track Proceedings (2015)
7. Nahavandi, S.: Industry 5.0-a human-centric solution. Sustainability **11**(16), 4371 (2019)
8. Nickel, M., Tresp, V., et al.: A three-way model for collective learning on multi-relational data. In: Proceedings of the 28th International Conference on International Conference on Machine Learning. Omnipress (2011)

9. Palumbo, E., Rizzo, G., Troncy, R., Baralis, E., Osella, M., Ferro, E.: Knowledge graph embeddings with node2vec for item recommendation. In: Gangemi, A., et al. (eds.) ESWC 2018. LNCS, vol. 11155, pp. 117–120. Springer, Cham (2018). https://doi.org/10.1007/978-3-319-98192-5_22

10. Rahman, M.M., Takasu, A.: Knowledge graph embedding via entities' type mapping matrix. In: Cheng, L., Leung, A.C.S., Ozawa, S. (eds.) ICONIP 2018. LNCS, vol. 11303, pp. 114–125. Springer, Cham (2018). https://doi.org/10.1007/978-3-030-04182-3_11

11. Ristoski, P., Paulheim, H.: RDF2Vec: RDF graph embeddings for data mining. In: Groth, P., et al. (eds.) ISWC 2016. LNCS, vol. 9981, pp. 498–514. Springer, Cham (2016). https://doi.org/10.1007/978-3-319-46523-4_30

12. Ristoski, P., de Vries, G.K.D., Paulheim, H.: A collection of benchmark datasets for systematic evaluations of machine learning on the semantic web. In: Groth, P., et al. (eds.) ISWC 2016. LNCS, vol. 9982, pp. 186–194. Springer, Cham (2016). https://doi.org/10.1007/978-3-319-46547-0_20

13. Sack, H., Biswas, R., Gesese, G.A., Alam, M.: A survey on knowledge graph embeddings with literals: which model links better literal-ly? Semant. Web J. **12**(4), 617–647 (2020)

14. Sankar, A., Wu, Y., et al.: Dysat: deep neural representation learning on dynamic graphs via self-attention networks. In: Proceedings of the 13th International Conference on Web Search and Data Mining (2020)

15. Schlichtkrull, M., Kipf, T.N., Bloem, P., van den Berg, R., Titov, I., Welling, M.: Modeling relational data with graph convolutional networks. In: Gangemi, A., et al. (eds.) ESWC 2018. LNCS, vol. 10843, pp. 593–607. Springer, Cham (2018). https://doi.org/10.1007/978-3-319-93417-4_38

16. Sun, Z., Deng, Z., et al.: Rotate: knowledge graph embedding by relational rotation in complex space. In: International Conference on Learning Representations (2019)

17. Tay, Y., Luu, A., et al.: Non-parametric estimation of multiple embeddings for link prediction on dynamic knowledge graphs. In: Proceedings of the AAAI Conference on Artificial Intelligence, vol. 31(1) (2017)

18. Trivedi, R., Farajtabar, M., et al.: Dyrep: learning representations over dynamic graphs. In: International conference on learning representations (2019)

19. Trouillon, T., Welbl, J., et al.: Complex embeddings for simple link prediction. In: Proceedings of the 33rd International Conference on International Conference on Machine Learning (2016)

20. El Vaigh, C.B., Goasdoué, F., Gravier, G., Sébillot, P.: A novel path-based entity relatedness measure for efficient collective entity linking. In: Pan, J.Z., et al. (eds.) ISWC 2020. LNCS, vol. 12506, pp. 164–182. Springer, Cham (2020). https://doi.org/10.1007/978-3-030-62419-4_10

21. Vandewiele, G., Steenwinckel, B., et al.: pyRDF2Vec: python implementation and extension of RDF2Vec (IDLab) (2020)

22. Wu, T., Khan, A., et al.: Efficiently embedding dynamic knowledge graphs. arXiv preprint arXiv:1910.06708 (2019)

23. Yang, B., Yih, W., et al.: Embedding entities and relations for learning and inference in knowledge bases. In: 3rd International Conference on Learning Representations (2015)

24. Zhang, W., Paudel, B., et al.: Interaction embeddings for prediction and explanation in knowledge graphs. In: Proceedings of the Twelfth ACM International Conference on Web Search and Data Mining. WSDM 2019. Association for Computing Machinery (2019)

Leveraging Standards in Model-Centric Geospatial Knowledge Graph Creation

Diego Vinasco-Alvarez[✉] 🆔

Université Lumière Lyon 2, LIRIS UMR-CNRS 5205, Université de Lyon,
Lyon, France
diego.vinasco-alvarez@univ-lyon2.fr
https://liris.cnrs.fr/page-membre/diego-vinasco-alvarez

Abstract. Understanding the complex urban landscapes of cities and
their evolution is becoming an ever more essential area of research for
urbanists, city planners, historians, and industry leaders. Toward this
endeavor, data-driven 3D semantic city models can be implemented to
create tools for understanding, simulating, and modeling these urbanization processes and many other urban phenomena. These implementations often require integrating multidimensional (2D/3D, temporal, and
thematic), heterogeneous, and multisource urban data to provide users
with more complete views of the changing urban landscape. In recent
years, researchers have turned toward Semantic Web technologies such
as knowledge graphs as common platforms for integrating these data
and their underlying data models. However, simple transformation or
conversion of urban data towards these formats is prone to data loss,
and integration of urban data model standards lacking interoperability
poses its own challenges. This work proposes a model-centric urban data
transformation approach towards Semantic Web data formats, based on
international standards for facilitating the integration of these urban
data and promoting their interoperability in the context of multidimensional city modeling.

Keywords: Ontologies · Data integration · Urban data ·
Multidimensional data · Conceptual modeling

1 Introduction and Motivation

Urbanization is a complex and increasingly relevant change process. In 2018 the
United Nations reported that 55% of the world's inhabitants live in urban areas
and predicted that number to increase to 68% by 2050 [23]. Today, the utiliza-
tion of 3D and 4D semantic city models [2,27], urban digital twins, and smart
city applications [20] is a growing area of research for understanding these urban
processes. These approaches often go beyond purely spatial 2D and 3D city models and incorporate more complex multidimensional (nD) structured city data
including temporal data such as 4D (3D+Time) [1] and thematic or categori-
cal data defined by urban data vocabularies and data model standards such as

P. Groth et al. (Eds.): ESWC 2022 Satellite Events, LNCS 13384, pp. 224–233, 2022.
https://doi.org/10.1007/978-3-031-11609-4_37

CityGML[1] and BIM-IFC[2]. In addition, these data are produced from a variety of data sources and data capturing techniques such as LIDAR, photogrammetry, Internet of Things (IoT) sensors, etc. leading to a large heterogeneity in data formats.

To provide users a more complete view of the evolving urban landscape, multidimensional city models often require the combination of these heterogeneous urban data [22]. Consequently, they must overcome the data integration challenges that arise from a lack of interoperability between these structured and semi-structured urban data formats and data models. To this end, approaches relying on Semantic Web technologies as a platform for urban data integration are being proposed [8,9,16] where both these data and their underlying data models can be represented, formalized, combined, and shared as machine processible open-linked-data through the use of Resource Description Framework (RDF) knowledge graphs and Ontology Web Language (OWL) ontologies.

These approaches often take either a bottom-up or a top-down method of integration [10]. Bottom-up approaches such as Ontology-Based Data Access (OBDA) can bridge the interoperability gap between heterogeneous urban data by mapping the schema of existing relational databases to a common ontological model [14,19]. Conversely, top-down (or model-centric) approaches such as Model-Driven-Development (MDD) or Model-Driven-Architecture (MDA) [13] rely on data models and data transformations to provide effective and reproducible methods for creating OWL ontologies from existing urban data models and datasets. These approaches may provide the possibility of reusing existing urban data model standards with existing structured data as opposed to creating new ontologies manually.

This evolving **middle-stage** work proposes a model-centric standards-based data transformation approach for improving nD urban data quality and interoperability during urban data integration as RDF knowledge graphs.

This paper presents the work as follows: Sect. 2 describes the state of the art and related works in nD urban data modeling, transformations to semantic web formats, and heterogeneous urban data integration; Sect. 3 presents the problem statement and each contribution; Sect. 4 presents the research methodology and the implementation of the proposed approach; Sect. 5 details how the approach will be evaluated; Sect. 6 will present the intermediate results achieved thus far; and Sect. 7 will present the lessons learned and conclude.

2   State of the Art

The representation and querying of geospatial and spatio-temporal urban data with Semantic Web technologies have seen much advancement in recent years with proposals such as GeoSPARQL, stRDF, Building Topology Ontology, Ontology for Managing Geometry, and BimSPARQL [3,29]. In the context of

---

[1] https://www.ogc.org/standards/citygml.

[2] https://www.buildingsmart.org/standards/bsi-standards/industry-foundation-classes/.

using transformation towards these technologies to facilitate nD urban data integration for enriching 3D semantic city models, there are several existing works in the literature to take into consideration.

2.1 nD Urban Data Model Transformation and Alignment

When creating ontologies with transformation approaches, it is important to consider the modeling language with which the input data model is formalized in, as the same data model formalized in different languages can produce OWL ontologies with varying structure and vocabulary.

In general, there are two primary kinds of urban data models used as input in these transformations:

- Conceptual data models (such as UML models) [6,11]
- Physical data models (such as XML schema) [24].

Top-down approaches using conceptual data model formats such as UML can exploit the similar modeling concepts and relationships to OWL (e.g. classes, attributes, properties, cardinality, etc.) to propose more straightforward mappings compared to XML Schema-based transformations [4]. To this end, geospatial model transformation standards such as ISO 19150-2[3] have been defined by international organizations such as ISO[4] and the Open Geospatial Consortium[5] for defining transformation mapping rules between geospatial UML models to OWL. In the case of both UML and XML Schema-based approaches - which use more constrained, closed-world formalizations of data models compared to OWL's open-world interpretation - a choice exists in how constrained the generated ontology should be. Which method of transformation should be implemented may vary based on the motivation for integration or use-case [4].

After a data model is expressed in OWL, it can be integrated with other OWL ontologies through alignment and ontology matching techniques [21]. In nD urban data integration, much research has been proposed with commonly implemented data models in Geographic Information Systems (GIS) and Building Information Modeling (BIM) [7,18,24], 3D Cultural Heritage Applications [17], and 4D urban data modeling [22].

2.2 Model-Centric nD Urban Data Transformation

Model-centric transformation approaches such as Extract-Transform-Load (ETL) data pipelines can use data models or schema to define or guide the transformation of heterogeneous urban data towards RDF and OWL [4,12] with some works proposing scalable data-lake integration solutions [15]. Similar to the data model transformations noted in Sect. 2.1, the data format used to represent the underlying data models of the data to be transformed affects the structure of

---

[3] https://www.iso.org/standard/57466.html.

[4] https://www.iso.org/home.html.

[5] https://www.ogc.org/.

the output data. Here, bottom-up approaches are more commonly used as relying on schemas that directly define the structure of the data to be transformed may have the benefit of better preserving the geospatial semantics of these data [4].

3   Problem Statement and Contributions

Limiting semantic data loss and maximizing data interoperability are crucial to improving heterogeneous multisource nD urban data integration for enriching 3D semantic city models, Smart City Applications, and Urban digital Twins. This work hypothesizes that *a standards-based model-centric data transformation approach guided by conceptual, as opposed to physical, data models can improve the quality and interoperability of generated nD urban data models and data during integration as linked-open-data.*

To evaluate this hypothesis, three research questions arise:

Q1: *How can geospatial model transformation standards such as ISO 19150-2 be used to create more concise and useful nD urban data ontologies for nD city modeling while facilitating the integration of existing spatio-temporal ontologies?*

Q2: *What data quality issues arise (e.g. semantic data loss, inconsistencies) when using either conceptual or physical data models to guide data transformation pipelines and how can they be mitigated?*

Q3: *How can these transformations be structured to improve scalability when integrating large datasets covering the district and city-sized urban areas?*

Towards this end, several contributions have been realized [25,26]:

– A state of the art study in creating OWL ontologies from nD urban data UML and XML Schema data models
– A reproducible nD urban data model transformation pipeline based on the ISO standard 19150-2:2015 UML to OWL mappings
– An nD urban data ontology network based on urban data standards
– A proposed approach for integrating heterogeneous multisource nD urban data as linked-open-data with a model-centric data transformations.

4   Research Methodology

To confront the aforementioned problem statement, this work utilizes the following research methodology: Firstly, several state-of-the-art studies must be conducted to better understand the domain of nD urban data integration. Two studies are conducted in the creation of OWL ontologies from nD urban data models to compare the use of conceptual and physical data models. In addition, a study of data integration approaches of nD urban data as RDF knowledge graphs will be done to better understand how to limit data loss during these processes and produce interoperable linked-open-data. These studies will also take into consideration which data models are being commonly implemented in these applications as reusing vocabularies is key to improving interoperability in OWL [4]; Secondly, a data model transformations will be implemented using the information gleaned from the state of the art to create ontologies from widely used urban data model standards. These ontologies will be aligned with existing spatio-temporal ontologies to create an nD urban data ontology network and ensure their interoperability as linked-open-data vocabularies; Thirdly, a data integration methodology (see Fig. 1) is proposed based on model-centric data transformations that exploit the nD urban ontology network to define their trans-formation mappings to RDF; Finally, this approach (and its resulting data and data models) will be tested according to an evaluation plan (detailed in Sect. 5) to validate if it promotes the data quality of nD urban data standards during transformation and to determine its viability for data integration in enriching nD semantic city models, urban digital twins, and smart city applications.

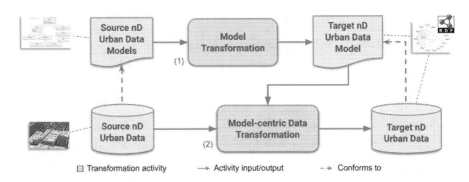

Fig. 1. Proposed integration methodology

5   Evaluation Plan

To test the hypothesis stated in Sect. 3, this work will measure and profile several criteria of the proposed integration approach and resulting knowledge graphs. In regards to **Q1**, two OWL ontologies representing the same data model stan-dard will be automatically generated (one from a UML model and another from an XML Schema) and then compared on criteria such as consistency and con-ciseness in the context of nD urban data applications using requirements and tests developed using the ROMEO [28] ontology evaluation methodology. In response to **Q2** and **Q3**, several knowledge graphs will be created from real-world open urban data repositories using model-centric transformations guided by the generated ontologies and their respective physical schemas. Profiling will be implemented to re-evaluate these graphs when combined with their previ-ously generated ontologies. A method for determining if, and how much data loss has occurred during transformation is also in development. Additionally, the SPARQL query execution time of oft-asked nD questions from historians and urban planners (such as how city objects and urban phenomena evolve over time [5]). A synthesis of these tests will be done to measure the possibility of real-time analysis and scalability of these data in urban digital twins and smart city applications.

6 Intermediate Results

At this point, this work has achieved several initial results. A reproducible urban data transformation tool, UD-Graph, was implemented to generate urban data RDF knowledge graphs. This tool can currently be used to implement two types of transformations for generating OWL ontologies from either:

– Geospatial XML Schema [25] extending the mappings based on [24] to take advantage of geospatial standards in the Semantic Web
– Geospatial OWL ontologies created from UML models using the ISO 19150-2 standard [26].

Thus far, an initial comparison of the resulting ontologies and datasets has been performed using the CityGML 2.0 and 3.0 conceptual models [26] within the context of improving the integration of 3D city model snapshots to model spatio-temporal building evolution. These data models were chosen for their rich vocabularies and widespread use in nD urban data research and industry. In the UML-based approach, the generated ontology is queried using to determine how XML (where nodes and attributes are represented as a tree) should be converted into RDF triples. Since a conceptual model does not directly define the structure of the data instances, some human intervention is required in defining mappings in the case where the structure of the data diverges from the UML model. For example, in the case where an element in XML uses a different name or namespace in its XML schema compared to the UML model. Defining custom mappings has the added benefit of being able to reuse existing OWL vocabularies such as SKOS, GeoSPARQL, OWL-Time, and ISO standard ontologies similarly generated from geospatial UML models[6].

Alongside these contributions, some work has been done in conjunction with the OGC's CityGML 3.0 XML Encoding Sub-working Group[7] to produce standardized 4D urban data (Fig. 2).

---

[6] https://def.isotc211.org/ontologies/.
[7] https://github.com/opengeospatial/CityGML-3.0Encodings/tree/master/
CityGML/Examples/Versioning.

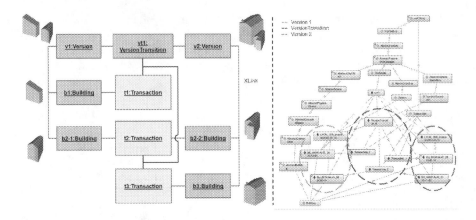

Fig. 2. 3 building historical successions based on the CityGML 3.0 Versioning module; Version graph overview (see footnote 7) (left); Ontograf visualization of generated RDF graph produced by UD-Graph [26] (right)

Reproducibility

This work makes use of open data, especially city models of Lyon in CityGML format[8]. We also use SoftwareHeritage persistent identifiers[9] for sharing code and data presented in Table 1.

Table 1. Reproducibility: URLs of code, proposed data model, and produced data

S.No.	Name	SWHID
1	(Transformation tool) UD-Graph	https://github.com/VCityTeam/UD-Graph
2	Proposed model	https://github.com/VCityTeam/UD-Graph/tree/master/Ontologies/CityGML/3.0
3	Generated datasets	https://github.com/VCityTeam/UD-Graph/tree/master/Transformations/test-data/RDF

7   Conclusions and Lessons Learned

This work explores a method for model-centric data integration with semantic web technologies based on standards to create interoperable data models and improve data interoperability of nD urban linked-open-data. By using semi-automated mapping transformations, as proposed in UD-Graph [25,26], existing nD urban data standard data models and data can be combined with existing spatio-temporal semantic web standards.

---

[8] https://data.grandlyon.com/.

[9] https://archive.softwareheritage.org/swh:1:dir:222696a70325b62af1b728b20714a5a0 e0d415d9.

Currently, using UML models appears to be a favorable approach for creating OWL ontologies [26] due to the similarity in modeling concepts between UML and OWL, but a more formal evaluation of this approach is needed to measure how much semantic data may be lost in the case of urban data standards which present a large divergence between their conceptual and physical data models, and thus more human intervention is required to converge on a complete mapping. Additionally, this approach requires testing with additional data models aside from CityGML, such as IndoorGML[10], or BIM-IFC and profiling the data volume and query execution time of the datasets generated.

Once this work is concluded, the proposed approach can be implemented to integrate heterogeneous urban data sources for enriching nD city models, urban digital twins, and smart city applications.

Acknowledgments. This research is funded by the Université Lumière Lyon 2, as a part of the Virtual City Project (https://projet.liris.cnrs.fr/vcity/) within the LiRiS laboratory (https://liris.cnrs.fr/). I would like to thank my thesis advisors Gilles Gesquière, Sylvie Servigne, and John Samuel for their invaluable guidance and support, in addition to Clément Colin and Eric Boix for their insights.

References

1. Beck, S.F., Abualdenien, J., Hijazi, I.H., Borrmann, A., Kolbe, T.H.: Analyzing contextual linking of heterogeneous information models from the domains BIM and UIM. ISPRS Int. J. Geo-Inf. **10**(12), 807 (2021). https://doi.org/10.3390/ijgi10120807

2. Biljecki, F., Stoter, J., Ledoux, H., Zlatanova, S., Çöltekin, A.: Applications of 3D city models: state of the art review. ISPRS Int. J. Geo-Inf. **4**(4), 2842–2889 (2015). https://doi.org/10.3390/ijgi4042842

3. Bonduel, M., Wagner, A., Pauwels, P., Vergauwen, M., Klein, R.: Including widespread geometry formats in semantic graphs using RDF literals. In: Proceedings of the 2019 European Conference for Computing in Construction, pp. 341–350. European Council on Computing in Construction (2019). https://doi.org/10.35490/ec3.2019.166. iSSN: 2684-1150

4. Brink, L., Janssen, P., Quak, W., Stoter, J.: Linking spatial data: automated conversion of geo-information models and GML data to RDF. Int. J. Spat. Data Infrastruct. Res. **9**, 59–85 (2014). https://doi.org/10.2902/1725-0463.2014.09.art3

5. Chaturvedi, K., Kolbe, T.: A requirement analysis on extending semantic 3D city models for supporting time-dependent properties. ISPRS Ann. Photogramm. Remote Sens. Spat. Inf. Sci. **IV-4/W9**, 19–26 (2019). https://doi.org/10.5194/isprs-annals-IV-4-W9-19-2019

6. Chávez-Feria, S., García-Castro, R., Poveda-Villalón, M.: Converting UML-based ontology conceptualizations to OWL with Chowlk. In: Verborgh, R., et al. (eds.) ESWC 2021. LNCS, vol. 12739, pp. 44–48. Springer, Cham (2021). https://doi.org/10.1007/978-3-030-80418-3_8

---

[10] http://indoorgml.net/.

7. Chiang, Y.H., Huang, C.Y., Fuse, M.: The integration of OGC SensorThings API and OGC CITYGML via semantic web technology. In: Di Martino, S., Fang, Z., Li, K.J. (eds.) Web and Wireless Geographical Information Systems, pp. 55–67. Springer International Publishing, Cham (2020)

8. Claramunt, C.: Ontologies for geospatial information: progress and challenges ahead. J. Spat. Inf. Sci. (2020). https://doi.org/10.5311/JOSIS.2020.20.666

9. Daniil, R., Wohlgenannt, G., Pavlov, D., Emelyanov, Y., Mouromtsev, D.: A new tool for linked data visualization and exploration in 3D/VR space. In: Hitzler, P., et al. (eds.) ESWC 2019. LNCS, vol. 11762, pp. 167–171. Springer, Cham (2019). https://doi.org/10.1007/978-3-030-32327-1_33

10. Daraio, C., Glänzel, W.: Grand challenges in data integration—state of the art and future perspectives: an introduction. Scientometrics **108**(1), 391–400 (2016). https://doi.org/10.1007/s11192-016-1914-5

11. De Paepe, D., Thijs, G., Buyle, R., Verborgh, R., Mannens, E.: Automated UML-based ontology generation in OSLO^2. In: Blomqvist, E., Hose, K., Paulheim, H., Lawrynowicz, A., Ciravegna, F., Hartig, O. (eds.) ESWC 2017. LNCS, vol. 10577, pp. 93–97. Springer, Cham (2017). https://doi.org/10.1007/978-3-319-70407-4_18

12. Hor, A.H., Sohn, G.: Design and evaluation of a BIM-GIS integrated information model using RDF graph database. ISPRS Ann. Photogram. Remote Sens. Spat. Inf. Sci. **VIII-4-W2-2021**, 175–182 (2021). https://doi.org/10.5194/isprs-annals-VIII-4-W2-2021-175-2021. iSSN: 2194-9042

13. Kutzner, T.: Geospatial data modelling and model-driven transformation of geospatial data based on UML profiles. Ph.D. thesis, Technische Universität München (2016)

14. Lefrançois, M., Zimmermann, A., Bakerally, N.: A SPARQL extension for generating RDF from heterogeneous formats. In: Blomqvist, E., Maynard, D., Gangemi, A., Hoekstra, R., Hitzler, P., Hartig, O. (eds.) ESWC 2017. LNCS, vol. 10249, pp. 35–50. Springer, Cham (2017). https://doi.org/10.1007/978-3-319-58068-5_3

15. Mandilaras, G., Koubarakis, M.: Scalable transformation of big geospatial data into linked data. In: Hotho, A., et al. (eds.) ISWC 2021. LNCS, vol. 12922, pp. 480–495. Springer, Cham (2021). https://doi.org/10.1007/978-3-030-88361-4_28

16. Métral, C., Falquet, G.: Extension and contextualization for linked semantic 3D geodata. ISPRS - Int. Arch. Photogramm. Remote Sens. Spat. Inf. Sci. **XLII-4-W10**, 113–118 (2018). https://doi.org/10.5194/isprs-archives-XLII-4-W10-113-2018. iSSN: 1682-1750

17. Nishanbaev, I., Champion, E., McMeekin, D.A.: A survey of geospatial semantic web for cultural heritage. Heritage **2**(2), 1471–1498 (2019). https://doi.org/10.3390/heritage2020093

18. Psyllidis, A.: Ontology-based data integration from heterogeneous urban systems: a knowledge representation framework for smart cities. In: 14th International Conference on Urban Planning and Urban Management, July 2015

19. Rodríguez-Muro, M., Kontchakov, R., Zakharyaschev, M.: Ontology-based data access: *Ontop* of databases. In: Alani, H., et al. (eds.) ISWC 2013. LNCS, vol. 8218, pp. 558–573. Springer, Heidelberg (2013). https://doi.org/10.1007/978-3-642-41335-3_35

20. Santos, H., Dantas, V., Furtado, V., Pinheiro, P., McGuinness, D.L.: From data to city indicators: a knowledge graph for supporting automatic generation of dashboards. In: Blomqvist, E., Maynard, D., Gangemi, A., Hoekstra, R., Hitzler, P., Hartig, O. (eds.) ESWC 2017. LNCS, vol. 10250, pp. 94–108. Springer, Cham (2017). https://doi.org/10.1007/978-3-319-58451-5_7

21. Shvaiko, P., Euzenat, J.: Ontology matching: state of the art and future challenges. IEEE Trans. Knowl. Data Eng. **25**(1), 158–176 (2013). https://doi.org/10.1109/TKDE.2011.253

22. Tran, B.H., Aussenac-Gilles, N., Comparot, C., Trojahn, C.: Semantic integration of raster data for earth observation: an RDF dataset of territorial unit versions with their land cover. ISPRS Int. J. Geo-Inf. **9**(9), 503 (2020). https://doi.org/10.3390/ijgi9090503

23. United Nations, Department of Economic and Social Affairs, P.D.: World urbanization prospects: the 2018 revision. Technical report ST/ESA/SER.A/420, United Nations, New York (2019). oCLC: 1120698127

24. Usmani, A.U., Jadidi, M., Sohn, G.: Towards the automatic ontology generation and alignment of BIM and GIS data formats. ISPRS Ann. Photogramm. Remote Sens. Spat. Inf. Sci. **VIII-4-W2-2021**, 183–188 (2021). https://doi.org/10.5194/isprs-annals-VIII-4-W2-2021-183-2021. iSSN: 2194-9042

25. Vinasco-Alvarez, D., Samuel, J.S., Servigne, S., Gesquière, G.: Towards a semantic web representation from a 3D geospatial urban data model. In: SAGEO 2021, 16ème Conférence Internationale de la Géomatique, de l'Analyse Spatiale et des Sciences de l'Information Géographique, pp. 227–238. Actes de la Conférence SAGEO 2021, La Rochelle, May 2021

26. Vinasco-Alvarez, D., Samuel, J.S., Servigne, S., Gesquière, G.: Towards limiting semantic data loss in 4D urban data semantic graph generation. ISPRS Ann. Photogramm. Remote Sens. Spat. Inf. Sci. **VIII-4/W2-2021**, 37–44 (2021). https://doi.org/10.5194/isprs-annals-VIII-4-W2-2021-37-2021

27. Virtanen, J.P., Jaalama, K., Puustinen, T., Julin, A., Hyyppä, J., Hyyppä, H.: Near real-time semantic view analysis of 3D city models in web browser. ISPRS Int. J. Geo-Inf. **10**(3) (2021). https://doi.org/10.3390/ijgi10030138

28. Yu, J., Thom, J.A., Tam, A.: Requirements-oriented methodology for evaluating ontologies. Inf. Syst. **34**(8), 766–791 (2009)

29. Zhang, C., Beetz, J., de Vries, B.: BimSPARQL: domain-specific functional SPARQL extensions for querying RDF building data. Semant. Web **9**, 1–27 (2018). https://doi.org/10.3233/SW-180297

Building Narrative Structures
from Knowledge Graphs

Inès Blin[1,2(✉)] ⓘD

[1] Sony Computer Science Laboratories, Paris, France
ines.blin@sony.com
[2] Computer Science, Vrije Universiteit Amsterdam, Amsterdam, The Netherlands

Abstract. Humans constantly create narratives to provide explanations for how and why something happens. Designing systems able to build such narratives would therefore contribute to building more human-centric systems, and to support uses like decision-making processes. Here, a narrative is seen as a sequence of events. My thesis investigates how a narrative can be built computationally. Four research questions are identified: representation, construction, link prediction and evaluation. A case study on the French Revolution, based upon Wikidata and Wikipedia is presented. This prototype helps identifying the first challenges such as dynamic representation and evaluation of a narrative.

Keywords: Narratives · Semantic web · Ontologies · Reasoning

1 Introduction

Telling stories and creating narratives is suggested to be part of what makes us human [9,23]. Indeed, such narratives encompass key capabilities like making sense of experiences and providing explanations for a series of events [9]. These capabilities come natural for humans, who can identify participants and make connections between them. Furthermore, narratives are part of the understanding process of an experience [63]. Building systems able to represent and generate narratives would thus contribute to having more human-centric systems. Indeed, such systems would emulate better human processes such as creating narratives.

Studying narratives has gained growing interest in the latest years, and this also applies to the computer science domain. The Computational Models for Narratives Workshop Series (2009–2016, [39]) first attempted to better define narratives, and to better highlight their importance. The aim of the Text2Story Workshop (2018–2021, [11]) series focused on extracting narrative structures

The work reported in this paper was funded by the European MUHAI project from the Horizon 2020 research and innovation programme under grant number 951846 and the Sony Computer Science Laboratories Paris. I. Blin—Early Stage Ph.D. (First Year).

P. Groth et al. (Eds.): ESWC 2022 Satellite Events, LNCS 13384, pp. 234–251, 2022.
https://doi.org/10.1007/978-3-031-11609-4_38

from text input. Recently, [12] explores how to leverage streams of news data to extract events and narrative structures. It provides an overview of the state-of-the-art in event extraction, temporal and causal relations, as well as storyline extraction.

Despite the existing research on narratives, no consensus was reached on how to represent and construct them. To make their construction more manageable, the literature has proposed breaking it down into smaller tasks. One simplification is to distinguish between the *fabula*, i.e. the story as it happened, and the *narration*, i.e. one expression of the fabula [38]. Take the example of a politician X giving a speech. If you are biased in favor of X, you might say that the speech was admirable, whereas if you are biased against X, you might say that the speech was political rhetoric. These two versions would be considered two different narrations of the same initial fabula: X gave a speech.

The dual process theory in cognition [18–20,56] states that a thought is the result of two processes. The first one searches relevant cues among a massive memory, and the second one analyses and reasons about these clues. One possible direction for implementing systems able to reproduce these two processes is to use knowledge graphs. Processes like vector space similarity, knowledge graph retrieval or graph search can be seen as the former first process Likewise, reasoning and building a narrative based on these facts can be mapped to the second process.

My Ph.D. will use the model of a narrative as a sequence of events. Methods and approaches described in [12] also address this event-sequence type of story. The model has one perspective, hence one narration per fabula. Describing a narrative therefore boils down to identifying, describing and linking events. Categories for such representation include people, objects and locations. The aim of my Ph.D. is to leverage knowledge graphs to automatically build structured representations of narratives. System-wise, that consists in building a system that takes a graph as input and outputs a narrative graph.

Motivations for creating narratives in the form of knowledge graphs are numerous. On the representation side, knowledge graphs permit to unify data sources and enable reasoning capabilities. On the application side, they allow for semantic navigational search and reasoning on hierarchical levels. [34] furthermore argues that knowledge graphs can bring artificial intelligence to the right level of semantics and interpretability.

Lastly, narrative graph structures have multiple usages. They can first support navigation across events. In digital humanities for instance, users would first explore the collections by looking at entities and their collections, thus creating a narrative chain of events. [7]. Second, they can help in decision-making or hypotheses generation by extracting explanations, predicting events or completing a graph. Such representations have been used in domains like the biomedical domain, where a graph representation of patients' medical events is used to detect patients with venous thromboembolism [3] or maritime transportation [15].

2   Related Work

Narratives are being more and more researched, yet there is no established benchmarks on structured narratives. This section provides an overview of tasks and techniques that are relevant for narratives, even if the term "narrative" is not necessarily used. It first discusses Natural Language Processing (NLP) tasks with a focus on understanding. It then introduces graph-related tasks to help us build the narrative: graph structure and embeddings, graph search and commonsense knowledge graphs. It finally presents tasks that explicitly mention narratives.

Natural Language Processing Tasks. Machine Reading Comprehension (MRC) includes tasks that aim to assess better human-like understanding. Despite recent successes on benchmarks like SQuAD 1.1 [47], there is still a gap between MRC models and human-like comprehension. [67] surveys the tasks, metrics and datasets related to this MRC research field to address these issues. It classifies the tasks according to four attributes: type of corpus, type of questions, type of answers and source of answers. Since MRC is an NLP task, most of the datasets and outputs are textual, hence not using structured representations. However, some of the datasets explicitly use the word "narrative" or "story", like the ROCStories [41], or have inputs that could be considered narratives, like TellMeWhy [33]. Examples of tasks include next event prediction [41], story completion [26,35,40,68] and missing element prediction [41]. There is also work on combining language models and knowledge graphs for story generation [66]. More recently, [17] argued that MRC tasks assessed more *(text, question) pair* comprehension than *text* comprehension, and proposed text-based Noun Phrase enrichment, to recover all relations between Noun Phrases through prepositions.

Graph-Related Tasks. Other relevant research includes more graph-related tasks. Even if most of the research does not use the term "narrative" explicitly, it can help building components of the system.

One first area of research is graph representation, as either the graph structure itself or as graph embeddings. More recent research on knowledge graphs emphasises the need to have more event-centric structures to facilitate the analysis of sequence of events. A few event-centric knowledge graphs were built from existing generic knowledge graphs [21], whereas others were built from text in a domain like the news [49] or a novel [31]. Such structures also acknowledge the fundamental need to integrate the temporal dimension of events, and temporal and dynamic knowledge are currently being more investigated. Some work focuses on encoding the time component [10,50], whereas others investigate dynamic structures or embeddings [10,14,37,51,59,64]. A few also use a temporal representation to improve tasks like question-answering [29,36], knowledge graph completion [22,30,65], or link prediction [46,69]. Furthermore, datasets specifically targeted towards temporal question answering have also been released [28].

As mentioned in Sect. 1, the first process in the dual theory in cognition is to search relevant cues among a massive memory. To implement this process with a knowledge graph, techniques like entity linking or subgraph extraction can be used. Indeed, such techniques involve extracting relevant elements for a specific query. On one hand, current work in entity linking include entity-oriented search [16,43], relation discovery [27,60,61] and linking text pages to graph nodes [54]. On the other hand, subgraph extraction aims to select parts of a knowledge that are most coherent to reason about a specific query [24,58].

Section 1 also mentions a second process whose aim is to reason about collected relevant cues. There has been recent significant effort to build more specific, commonsense knowledge graphs. Such efforts comprise areas like generic commonsense [8,52], actions [31,42], social interactions [53] or psychology [55].

Finally, some work focuses on how to formally represent narratives and to extract them from inputs like texts or knowledge bases. For text, [4] inspects evolving stories in news articles, [13] proposes a benchmark for extracting temporal and causal relations from text, and [31] proposes a graph-based reasoning challenge to find the criminal in a Sherlock Holmes novel. [5] surveys methods to extract processes from text in business process management and emphasises process elements identified and evaluations performed. [32] lastly uses structured narrative representations and grounds them to knowledge repositories.

3   Problem Statement

The main novelty of my work will be to use knowledge graphs to build narratives in the form of structured graphs. Each one of the research questions below will contribute to building narrative structures from knowledge graphs.

1. **RQ-I: Representation of the Narrative.** Which representation to use for a narrative and for an event? Is there a representation that generalises well over different types of narratives?
2. **RQ-II: Construction of the Narrative.** How to gradually shift from a manual data exploration to a more automated one? How to best select relevant entities for a narrative, and extract the most meaningful subgraph from an input knowledge graph? How to convert this extracted subgraph into a narrative graph whose ontology is more suited for narratives?
3. **RQ-III: Link Prediction for Narrative Building.** Two types of links are meaningful for building a narrative. The first type of links complete the current representation, and the second ones connect past and next events. Therefore, how to predict meaningful links between events? When should two nodes be linked, and provided with which explanation? What types of links should be generated, and when should an entity be added to the graph? The main challenges will be to find adequate benchmarks and to handle the dynamic and temporal aspects of the narrative representation.
4. **RQ-IV: Evaluation of the Narrative.** Which metrics should be used to assess the quality of the constructed narrative?

Advancing in one of these research questions will permit to enhance the final system. This is particularly true for the construction of the narrative (RQ-II) and the hypothesis generation for a narrative (RQ-III), since both are complementary. Indeed, constructing a better narrative enables better hypotheses, and hypothesis generation enriches the final narrative.

4   Research Methodology and Approach

A first start is to use an intuitive representation for a narrative (RQ-I). [12] makes the distinction between two levels of analysis. The first one focuses on the event level (representation of each events separately) whereas the second one focuses on the narrative level (linking events). The Simple Event Model [62] can be the basis for describing the first level: it has four core classes describing the what, who, where and when parts of an event. [12] identifies temporal and causal links as crucial to describe event-event links, which will be the basis for the second level. Consequently, this representation can be seen as a modified version of the Five Ws: who, what, when, where, and why.

RQ-I still remains a complex challenge. Some of those elements might be missing, incomplete or even contradictory depending on the sources. Thinking how to fill those Five Ws: the who part could be objects, animals or humans, the where part a location or a historical entity, the when part a date but also a historical entity, and the why part would be a link between two different events. Each W is hereafter depicted as a narrative dimension. RQ-I should also handle the dynamic and temporal aspect of a narrative. The aim of RQ-I will therefore be to think about how to represent a narrative, and to see if it is possible to find a common representation, or if there is a need for more specificity.

I will illustrate this with the example of a coup d'état. A coup is the seizure and deposition of a government and its powers. It is considered successful if the power is held for at least seven days [44]. For an event e_1 that is a coup, representing it in a graph would be identifying the participant p_1, the timestamp t_1, the location l_1 and the cause e_0, encoded as follows: $hasParticipant(e_1, p_1)$, $hasTimestamp(e_1, t_1)$, $hasLocation(e_1, l_1)$, $hasCause(e_1, e_0)$. Furthermore, if e_1 is successful, there is change of government, hence the representation is different before and after t_1. If e_1 happened in country c_1, encoded information could for instance be $hasGovernment(c_1, gov_{old}, t_1^-)$ and $hasGovernment(c_1, gov_{new}, t_1^+)$.

Two main components were identified for the construction of the narrative (RQ-II): collecting elements, and building the narrative graph. The first component consists in collecting relevant elements for a given narrative, e.g. all events. One technique would be finding good techniques to optimally search this graph. The second component consists in adapting the structure and completing the graph. For instance in the aforementioned coup e_1 with participant p_1, the input knowledge graph can include $commander(e_1, p_1)$, where the wanted output is $hasParticipant(e_1, p_1)$. In that case, the narrative graph construction model should learn to map $commander$ to $hasParticipant$.

As for hypothesis generation on narratives (RQ-III), [37] makes the distinction between offline inference (called interpolation, or graph completion) and online inference (called extrapolation, or next event prediction). Two graph-related techniques were identified: graph completion and event prediction. In a narrative setting, the former would be completing and therefore enriching an existing narrative (i.e. adding nodes and edges), while the latter would be next event prediction. One hypothesis generation could be to generalise a successful coup: $outcome(e_1, \text{success}) \leftarrow ends(e_1, gov_{old}), starts(e_1, gov_{new})$. A successful coup causes the ending of a government and the beginning of a new one.

Different hierarchies of narratives can also be defined, related to RQ-I, RQ-II and RQ-III. At least a distinction between generic and instantiated narratives can be made. An instantiated narrative has only grounded variables, a more generic narrative can also have variables. This is therefore related to graph patterns that aim to identify common sub graphs in a graph [6]. Detecting patterns in narrative graphs can thus contribute to building more generic narratives, and can furthermore be used for next event prediction or graph completion.

5   Evaluation Plan

The evaluation part of the narrative was included as a whole separate question (RQ-IV), since it is a non trivial question. Indeed, it might be complicated to evaluate a narrative benchmark as a complete end-to-end task. Nevertheless, the objective of RQ-IV will be to tackle certain components of building a narrative, and evaluate them separately. RQ-IV will also attempt to define and formalise metrics for narrative understanding.

Techniques to evaluate the narrative representation (RQ-I) include ontology evaluation methods. [45] surveys methods evaluating an ontology according to its quality and correctness and using criteria like accuracy, completeness, conciseness, adaptability, clarity, computational efficiency or consistency.

As described in Sect. 4, the construction of the narrative (RQ-II) can be decomposed into two steps: retrieving relevant content, then building the narrative graph. If there is the ground truth of events for a given topic, metrics like precision, recall and f1 can be used. Once the event-centric graph is built, schema-correctness can also be a way to evaluate the coherence of the graph.

For link prediction to complete a graph representation (RQ-III), one way to evaluate is to complete related challenges or benchmarks. In that case, the evaluation will use the metrics defined by those tasks. For prediction tasks, metrics like Precision, Recall or F1-score are often used. For question-answering tasks, metrics could be Mean Reciprocall Rank or hits@k. Another way of evaluating the narrative will be to define beforehand measures that can assess the understanding of the narrative [57]. In that case, the aim will be to maximise or minimise those dimensions of understanding to assess the narrative output. Such dimensions could include compatibility and relevance.

6   Preliminary Results

This section describes an initial prototype for one historical narrative, the French Revolution. Its aim was to explore Wikidata and Wikipedia to build a narrative on the French Revolution. As a historic event, the events that are part of the

French Revolution are breaking points: there is a before and an after. Therefore, studying this example ensures to have a series of events referenced in knowledge bases. The case study mainly focuses on RQ-I, RQ-II, and RQ-III.

6.1   A Modified Simple Event Model to Represent the Narrative

For the representation of the narrative (RQ-I), a modified version of the Simple Event Model [62] was used. There are four core classes in this model: `sem:Event` (what), `sem:Actor` (who), `sem:Place` (where), and `sem:Time` (when). The constraints classes `sem:Role`, `sem:Temporary` and `sem:View` can respectively add information on the role of an actor, a temporal constraint or on a specific viewpoint. This model does not however permit to link different events, nor gives relations between classes of the same type. Two types of links were thus added. The first types of links are temporal or causal links between events. Allen's relations [2] were used for temporal links. The `wikidata: has effect` predicate was used for causal links. The second types of links are links between core classes of the same type. The predicate `dbo:alongside` was used to denote relations across participants. An example is given in Appendix B.

There are several advantages to use the modified Simple Event Model [62]. First, it is possible to include different perspectives in this model. Indeed, the `sem:View` class allows to add properties that only hold according to a certain authority, hence allowing to compare different viewpoints. Second, regarding uncertainty in the graph, it is possible in the model to add uncertainty on time intervals. Third, the core predicates of this model allow to easily separate different types of subgraphs, like temporal or causal subgraphs for instance. It therefore permits to analyse the narrative under different angles. Lastly, the types classes `sem:EventType`, `sem:RoleType`, `sem:ActorType` and `sem:PlaceType` can help identify more generic narratives to identify narrative schemes rather than instantiated narratives.

Some other aspects are however less straightforward with that model. Indeed, the Simple Event Model described above resembles more the format of a timeline with some causal links rather than a state-based representation. Therefore, the model is less flexible to represent changes over time (either changes of nodes' attributes and new nodes or edges that are added). With this model, temporal constraints would be the way to represent those changes, since they enable properties that hold only during a certain time interval.

6.2   Gathering Data from Wikidata and Wikipedia

Regarding RQ-I, the French Revolution narrative was defined as a set of events. An event here is a node in Wikidata with a path to the French Revolution node[1]. The paths were manually chosen based on a Wikidata exploration and are described in Table 1. These paths enabled to collect 59 events, among which 53 unique collected events and 48 unique ones with a human-readable label.

---

[1] https://www.wikidata.org/wiki/Q6534.

Table 1. Graph paths used to retrieve events during the French Revolution. The path (event, part of, French Revolution) reads as follows: there is a directed edge with the label part of in the graph from the event node to the French Revolution node. *wd* is the prefix for the namespace http://www.wikidata.org/wiki/.

#	Human-readable path	URI Path	Number of events collected
1	(French Revolution, has significant event, event)	(wd:Q6534, wd:Property:P793, ?e)	7
2	(event, part of, French Revolution)	(?e, wd:Property:P361, wd:Q6534)	48
3	(event, is instance of, historical country) & (event, has country, c)	(?e, wd:Property:P31, wd:Q3024240) (?e, wd:Property:P17, wd:Q142)	4

The next step was to see how much information it was possible to gather for each narrative dimension. Specifically, the main points of interest were participants, locations and dates, as well as temporal and causal links between events – equivalent to the event-level and narrative-level links depicted by [12] and mentioned in Sect. 4. Two main sources of data were used:

– The attributes of each node in Wikidata, i.e. outgoing predicates and edges.
– Wikipedia Infoboxes. An Infobox in Wikipedia is a table with textual properties and attributes that contains the most important information about the current page. Most interestingly, the infoboxes contain URL links to other Wikipedia pages, which can be linked again to Wikidata.

Relevant predicates in Wikidata and attributes in Infoboxes were manually selected for narrative building. A predicate was considered relevant if it was adding information on either a participant, the type of event, a timestamp, a location or a cause. Details of predicates are available in Appendix A. Table 2 shows the number and percentage of events that contain at least one information for each narrative dimension. Overall, we see that more information is retrieved regarding places, times and temporal links between events, with Wikidata having a bit more information than Wikipedia. On the other hand, Wikipedia contains more information on participants and causal links between events. Out of the 48 events retrieved in Wikidata, only 26 of them had a corresponding Infobox in Wikipedia, resulting in loss of information and lower numbers. Furthermore, the temporal links between events are artificially boosted by the "part of" predicate in Wikidata and the "partof" attribute in Wikipedia: 42 events are directly linked to the "French Revolution" with predicate "part of", whereas 12 events are linked to the French Revolution Wikipedia page with attribute "partof". These do not add much information, since it was one of the path described in Fig. 1. Such pairs were removed for comparison, and it was found that 8 events had a temporal link for both Wikidata and Wikipedia, 8 events a temporal link for Wikidata only and 1 event a temporal link for Wikipedia only.

Table 2. Number and percentage of events that contain at least one information for each type. WD stands for Wikidata and WP for Wikipedia. WD∩WP indicates events that were retrieved both by WD and WP for a given type, WD\WP events that were retrieved by WD only and WP\WD events that were retrieved by WP only.

Type	WD∩WP		WD\WP		WP\WD		Total		Not retrieved	
	Count	Perc.	Count	Perc.	Count	Perc.	Count.	Perc.	Count	Perc.
Who	5	10	0	0	15	31	20	42	28	58
When	25	52	17	35	0	0	42	87	6	13
Where	17	35	19	40	4	8	40	83	8	17
Causal link	1	2	0	0	12	25	13	27	35	73
Temp. link	21	44	27	56	0	0	48	100	0	0

6.3   Building the Narrative Network

The final step was to construct a narrative graph from the content gathered and described in Sect. 6.2 (RQ-II). Figure 1 presents the steps followed to build the final output graph. As described in Sect. 6.2, events are first searched manually through Wikidata, and relevant paths are chosen. Using those paths, all events for the experiment are then collected, and enriched with infobox information from Wikipedia. The data collected is then converted to triples that enrich the final graph. This section describes more in details how the graph was built.

Fig. 1. Pipeline of the steps followed to build the final graph. Related research questions are also added. Data was used from Wikidata and Wikipedia.

For the construction of the narrative (RQ-II), the objective was to convert the original triples in Wikidata and the key-value pairs in Wikipedia to a format for narratives. The rules for conversion were manually designed, with the following strategy: for each event i) for each url link in the infobox, find the corresponding Wikidata URI and add the triples to the output graph ii) convert the triples (s, p, o), with s the URI of the event and p a relevant predicate, from Wikidata.

The graph for the event 13 Vendémiaire is displayed in Fig. 2. One can understand that 13 Vendémiaire was a coup d'état between Royalists and Republicans, and that Paul Barras and Napoleon were Republicans. Some limitations also appear in that representation. First, the output of this coup is missing: who was at the origin of this coup, was it successful? Second, the node "First French Republic" is overloaded with too many meanings, as it is both a place and an actor. Semantically, it should probably be considered two different entities.

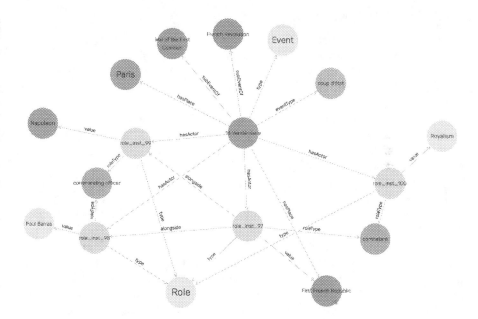

Fig. 2. Visual graph of the 13 Vendémiaire event. The role_inst_{k} nodes are encodings for blank nodes in the graph. One can see that the event is a coup d'état with two combatants: the First French Republic and Royalism. One therefore concludes that the event was a conflict between royalists and republicans.

For hypothesis generation on the graph (RQ-III), the main reasoning step was to manually define the rules defined above, however it does not add new knowledge with regards to the data gathered. Simple reasoning steps could be to enrich the types of nodes added to the graph: for instance, if an event X is a sub-event of another node Y unseen so far in the graph, then Y is also of type event. To prepare for future reasoning, using labels that give us more information about semantics could also help this process.

One improvement to the manual path selection would be to have the machine learning how to collect such events automatically with a knowledge graph. A graph search experiment is currently being worked on, where the aim is to find good heuristics to explore a knowledge graph to retrieve events for a narrative.

7   Conclusions and Lessons Learnt

In this paper, I presented my Ph.D. work that aims to construct narrative networks based on knowledge graphs. It explained the research questions addressed and provided a survey of the state-of-the-art of relevant research. The prototype described in Sect. 6 focused on using information from Wikidata and Wikipedia to build a narrative network. The aim was to see how much information was available to describe elements like participants, locations and causations, as well as to provide a first structured representation.

The prototype furthermore enabled to identify the first challenges for building narrative networks from knowledge graphs. First, there is the fundamental question of the temporality and the dynamicity of the graph representation. Furthermore, how to best represent temporal changes in the narrative network? Second, there is the challenge of evaluating the narrative, and assess whether a set of events is a good one to describe a narrative. How many links should be added to the graph to consider the narrative complete, or correct? Third, there is the scaling question, related to how many narratives one can build re using the same process. For instance, using the same process as for the French Revolution, how easy or hard would that be for another revolution? Lastly, there is the question of relevant input resources to use to build the narrative. Using generic knowledge graphs [25] can be a starting point, but sometimes domain-specific knowledge graphs [1,48] are more suited. In any case, it is important to remember that the final narrative structure will have be biased towards the content of the input resources.

The next steps for my Ph.D. will be to refine over the initial prototype to improve the narrative building process. Future work will especially be about automating more the components for narrative building, like searching relevant entities or completing the graph. Furthermore, the work presented on RQ-I and RQ-II focused more on the representations of events than representations of temporal relations. Future work will therefore also be on such temporal relations.

Acknowledgements. I thank Annette ten Teije (VUA), Ilaria Tiddi (VUA), and Remi van Trijp (CSL) for their comments and feedbacks on this paper. I also thank Frank van Harmelen (VUA) for valuable advice and discussion. I thank David Colliaux (CSL), Michael Anslow (CSL), Martina Galletti (CSL) and Adam Dahlgren (Umeå University) for interesting discussion and feedbacks.

A   Predicates Selected for Each Narrative Dimension

(See Figs. 3, 4, 5 and 6)

Type of predicate	Predicates label
who	participant, organizer, founded by
where	country, location, coordinate location, located in the administrative territorial entity, continent
when	point in time, start time, end time, inception, dissolved, abolished or demolished date, publication date
temporal link between events	part of, followed by, replaces, replaced by, follows, time period
causal link between events	has effect

Fig. 3. Selected predicates for each of the narrative dimension in Wikidata.

Type of predicate	Predicates label
who	Participants, appointer, combatant{k}, commander{k}, commanders, deputy{k}, founder, house, leader{k}, legislature, organisers, p{k}, participants, precursor
where	Location, area, coordinates, location, place
when	Date, abolished, date, date_end, date_event, date_pre, date_start, defunct, disbanded, established, formation, founded_date, life_span, year_
temporal link between events	era, event{k}, event_end, event_pre, event_start, partof , preceded_by, succeeded_by, succession
causal link between events	Result, cause, outcome, result, territory

Fig. 4. Selected predicates for each of the narrative dimension in Wikipedia.

B   Example of One Event Construction

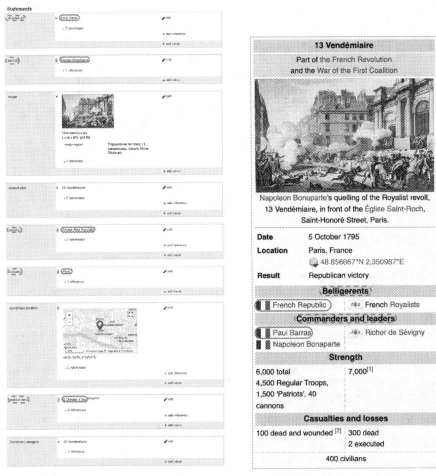

(a) Wikidata page of 13 Vendémiaire

(b) Wikipedia infobox of 13 Vendémiaire

Fig. 5. Wikidata and Wikipedia page content used to build an event representation for 13 Vendmiaire. Dashed lines indicates predicates or keys that were used, and full lines values. For clarity in visualisation, not all predicates related to the narrative dimensions were used, but only a subset of them.

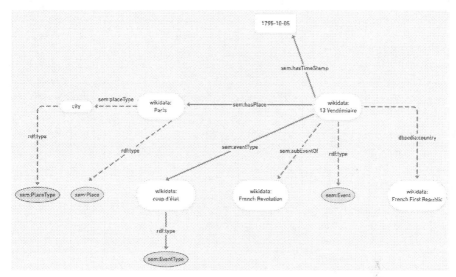

(a) Event representation using Wikidata useful predicates only.

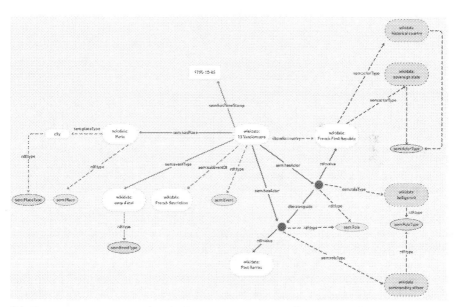

(b) Event representation after both content from Wikidata and Wikipedia has been added.

Fig. 6. Event representation at different steps: using Wikidata outgoing links of the event (a) and Wikipedia infoboxes (b). On (b), green edges on the right indicate edges and nodes that were newly added with the Infobox. Refer to Figure from [62] for the original example. (Color figure online)

References

1. Abu-Salih, B.: Domain-specific knowledge graphs: a survey. J. Netw. Comput. Appl. **185**, 103076 (2021)
2. Allen, J.F.: Maintaining knowledge about temporal intervals. Commun. ACM **26**(11), 832–843 (1983)
3. Bakalara, J., Guyet, T., Dameron, O., Happe, A., Oger, E.: An extension of chronicles temporal model with taxonomies-application to epidemiological studies. In: 14th International Conference on Health Informatics, HEALTHINF 2021, pp. 1–10 (2021)
4. Camacho Barranco, R., Boedihardjo, A.P., Hossain, M.S.: Analyzing evolving stories in news articles. Int. J. Data Sci. Anal. **8**(3), 241–256 (2017). https://doi.org/10.1007/s41060-017-0091-9
5. Bellan, P., Dragoni, M., Ghidini, C.: Process extraction from text: state of the art and challenges for the future. arXiv preprint arXiv:2110.03754 (2021)
6. Bloem, P., de Rooij, S.: Large-scale network motif analysis using compression. Data Min. Knowl. Disc. **34**(5), 1421–1453 (2020). https://doi.org/10.1007/s10618-020-00691-y
7. de Boer, V., Melgar, L., Inel, O., Ortiz, C.M., Aroyo, L., Oomen, J.: Enriching media collections for event-based exploration. In: Garoufallou, E., Virkus, S., Siatri, R., Koutsomiha, D. (eds.) MTSR 2017. CCIS, vol. 755, pp. 189–201. Springer, Cham (2017). https://doi.org/10.1007/978-3-319-70863-8_18
8. Bosselut, A., Rashkin, H., Sap, M., Malaviya, C., Celikyilmaz, A., Choi, Y.: COMET: commonsense transformers for automatic knowledge graph construction. arXiv preprint arXiv:1906.05317 (2019)
9. Boyd, B.: On the Origin of Stories: Evolution, Cognition, and Fiction. Harvard University Press (2010)
10. Cai, L., Janowicz, K., Yan, B., Zhu, R., Mai, G.: Time in a box: advancing knowledge graph completion with temporal scopes. In: Proceedings of the 11th on Knowledge Capture Conference, pp. 121–128 (2021)
11. Campos, R., Jorge, A., Jatowt, A., Bhatia, S.: The 3rd international workshop on narrative extraction from texts: Text2Story 2020. In: Jose, J.M., et al. (eds.) ECIR 2020. LNCS, vol. 12036, pp. 648–653. Springer, Cham (2020). https://doi.org/10.1007/978-3-030-45442-5_86
12. Caselli, T., Hovy, E., Palmer, M., Vossen, P.: Computational Analysis of Storylines: Making Sense of Events. Cambridge University Press (2021)
13. Caselli, T., Vossen, P.: The event storyline corpus: a new benchmark for causal and temporal relation extraction. In: Proceedings of the Events and Stories in the News Workshop, pp. 77–86 (2017)
14. Cochez, M., Ristoski, P., Ponzetto, S.P., Paulheim, H.: Biased graph walks for RDF graph embeddings. In: Proceedings of the 7th International Conference on Web Intelligence, Mining and Semantics, pp. 1–12 (2017)
15. Del Mondo, G., Peng, P., Gensel, J., Claramunt, C., Lu, F.: Leveraging spatio-temporal graphs and knowledge graphs: perspectives in the field of maritime transportation. ISPRS Int. J. Geo Inf. **10**(8), 541 (2021)
16. Devezas, J., Nunes, S.: A review of graph-based models for entity-oriented search. SN Comput. Sci. **2**(6), 1–36 (2021)
17. Elazar, Y., Basmov, V., Goldberg, Y., Tsarfaty, R.: Text-based np enrichment. arXiv preprint arXiv:2109.12085 (2021)

18. Evans, J.S.B.: Heuristic and analytic processes in reasoning. Br. J. Psychol. **75**(4), 451–468 (1984)
19. Evans, J.S.B.: In two minds: dual-process accounts of reasoning. Trends Cogn. Sci. **7**(10), 454–459 (2003)
20. Evans, J.S.B.: Dual-processing accounts of reasoning, judgment, and social cognition. Annu. Rev. Psychol. **59**, 255–278 (2008)
21. Gottschalk, S., Demidova, E.: EventKG-the hub of event knowledge on the web-and biographical timeline generation. Semant. Web **10**(6), 1039–1070 (2019)
22. Gottschalk, S., Demidova, E.: HapPenIng: happen, predict, infer—event series completion in a knowledge graph. In: Ghidini, C., et al. (eds.) ISWC 2019. LNCS, vol. 11778, pp. 200–218. Springer, Cham (2019). https://doi.org/10.1007/978-3-030-30793-6_12
23. Gottschall, J.: The Storytelling Animal: How Stories Make Us Human. Houghton Mifflin Harcourt (2012)
24. Han, Z., Chen, P., Ma, Y., Tresp, V.: Explainable subgraph reasoning for forecasting on temporal knowledge graphs. In: International Conference on Learning Representations (2020)
25. Heist, N., Hertling, S., Ringler, D., Paulheim, H.: Knowledge graphs on the web-an overview (2020)
26. Huang, C.Y., Huang, T.H.: Semantic frame forecast. arXiv preprint arXiv:2104.05604 (2021)
27. Hyvönen, E., Rantala, H., et al.: Knowledge-based relation discovery in cultural heritage knowledge graphs. In: Digital Humanities in Nordic Countries Proceedings of the Digital Humanities in the Nordic Countries 4th Conference. CEUR-WS.org (2019)
28. Jia, Z., Abujabal, A., Saha Roy, R., Strötgen, J., Weikum, G.: TempQuestions: a benchmark for temporal question answering. In: Companion Proceedings of the the Web Conference 2018, pp. 1057–1062 (2018)
29. Jia, Z., Pramanik, S., Saha Roy, R., Weikum, G.: Complex temporal question answering on knowledge graphs. In: Proceedings of the 30th ACM International Conference on Information & Knowledge Management, pp. 792–802 (2021)
30. Jung, J., Jung, J., Kang, U.: Learning to walk across time for interpretable temporal knowledge graph completion. In: Proceedings of the 27th ACM SIGKDD Conference on Knowledge Discovery & Data Mining, pp. 786–795 (2021)
31. Kawamura, T., et al.: Report on the first knowledge graph reasoning challenge 2018. In: Wang, X., Lisi, F.A., Xiao, G., Botoeva, E. (eds.) JIST 2019. LNCS, vol. 12032, pp. 18–34. Springer, Cham (2020). https://doi.org/10.1007/978-3-030-41407-8_2
32. Kroll, H., Nagel, D., Balke, W.-T.: Modeling narrative structures in logical overlays on top of knowledge repositories. In: Dobbie, G., Frank, U., Kappel, G., Liddle, S.W., Mayr, H.C. (eds.) ER 2020. LNCS, vol. 12400, pp. 250–260. Springer, Cham (2020). https://doi.org/10.1007/978-3-030-62522-1_18
33. Lal, Y.K., Chambers, N., Mooney, R., Balasubramanian, N.: TellMeWhy: a dataset for answering why-questions in narratives. arXiv preprint arXiv:2106.06132 (2021)
34. Lecue, F.: On the role of knowledge graphs in explainable AI. Semant. Web **11**(1), 41–51 (2020)
35. Li, Z., Ding, X., Liu, T.: Constructing narrative event evolutionary graph for script event prediction. arXiv preprint arXiv:1805.05081 (2018)
36. Li, Z., et al.: Search from history and reason for future: two-stage reasoning on temporal knowledge graphs. arXiv preprint arXiv:2106.00327 (2021)

37. Liao, S., Liang, S., Meng, Z., Zhang, Q.: Learning dynamic embeddings for temporal knowledge graphs. In: Proceedings of the 14th ACM International Conference on Web Search and Data Mining, pp. 535–543 (2021)

38. Meghini, C., Bartalesi, V., Metilli, D.: Representing narratives in digital libraries: the narrative ontology. Semant. Web (Preprint) 1–24 (2021)

39. Miller, B., Lieto, A., Ronfard, R., Ware, S., Finlayson, M.: Proceedings of the 7th workshop on computational models of narrative. In: 7th Workshop on Computational Models of Narrative (CMN 2016), vol. 53 (2016)

40. Mori, Y., Yamane, H., Mukuta, Y., Harada, T.: Finding and generating a missing part for story completion. In: Proceedings of the the 4th Joint SIGHUM Workshop on Computational Linguistics for Cultural Heritage, Social Sciences, Humanities and Literature, pp. 156–166 (2020)

41. Mostafazadeh, N., et al.: A corpus and evaluation framework for deeper understanding of commonsense stories. arXiv preprint arXiv:1604.01696 (2016)

42. Narayanan, S.: Reasoning about actions in narrative understanding. In: IJCAI, vol. 99, pp. 350–357. Citeseer (1999)

43. Oza, P., Dietz, L.: Which entities are relevant for the story? In: Text2Story@ ECIR, pp. 41–48 (2021)

44. Powell, J.M., Thyne, C.L.: Global instances of coups from 1950 to 2010: a new dataset. J. Peace Res. **48**(2), 249–259 (2011)

45. Raad, J., Cruz, C.: A survey on ontology evaluation methods. In: Proceedings of the International Conference on Knowledge Engineering and Ontology Development, Part of the 7th International Joint Conference on Knowledge Discovery, Knowledge Engineering and Knowledge Management (2015)

46. Radstok, W., Chekol, M., Velegrakis, Y.: Leveraging static models for link prediction in temporal knowledge graphs. In: 2021 IEEE 33rd International Conference on Tools with Artificial Intelligence (ICTAI), pp. 1034–1041. IEEE (2021)

47. Rajpurkar, P., Zhang, J., Lopyrev, K., Liang, P.: Squad: 100,000+ questions for machine comprehension of text. arXiv preprint arXiv:1606.05250 (2016)

48. Reese, J.T., et al.: KG-Covid-19: a framework to produce customized knowledge graphs for Covid-19 response. Patterns **2**(1), 100155 (2021)

49. Rospocher, M., et al.: Building event-centric knowledge graphs from news. J. Web Semant. **37**, 132–151 (2016)

50. Rossi, E., Chamberlain, B., Frasca, F., Eynard, D., Monti, F., Bronstein, M.: Temporal graph networks for deep learning on dynamic graphs. arXiv preprint arXiv:2006.10637 (2020)

51. Rudolph, M., Blei, D.: Dynamic embeddings for language evolution. In: Proceedings of the 2018 World Wide Web Conference, pp. 1003–1011 (2018)

52. Sap, M., et al.: Atomic: an atlas of machine commonsense for if-then reasoning. In: Proceedings of the AAAI Conference on Artificial Intelligence, vol. 33, pp. 3027–3035 (2019)

53. Sap, M., Rashkin, H., Chen, D., LeBras, R., Choi, Y.: SocialIQA: commonsense reasoning about social interactions. arXiv preprint arXiv:1904.09728 (2019)

54. Schäfer, B.: Exploiting DBpedia for graph-based entity linking to Wikipedia. Ph.D. thesis (2014)

55. Shu, T., et al.: Agent: a benchmark for core psychological reasoning. arXiv preprint arXiv:2102.12321 (2021)

56. Sloman, S.A.: The empirical case for two systems of reasoning. Psychol. Bull. **119**(1), 3 (1996)

57. Steels, L.: Conceptual Foundations of Human-Centric AI (2022)

58. Teru, K., Denis, E., Hamilton, W.: Inductive relation prediction by subgraph reasoning. In: International Conference on Machine Learning, pp. 9448–9457. PMLR (2020)
59. Tiddi, I., Daga, E., Bastianelli, E., d'Aquin, M.: Update of time-invalid information in knowledge bases through mobile agents (2016)
60. Tiddi, I., d'Aquin, M., Motta, E.: Walking linked data: a graph traversal approach to explain clusters (2014)
61. Traverso-Ribón, I., Palma, G., Flores, A., Vidal, M.-E.: Considering semantics on the discovery of relations in knowledge graphs. In: Blomqvist, E., Ciancarini, P., Poggi, F., Vitali, F. (eds.) EKAW 2016. LNCS (LNAI), vol. 10024, pp. 666–680. Springer, Cham (2016). https://doi.org/10.1007/978-3-319-49004-5_43
62. Van Hage, W.R., Malaisé, V., Segers, R., Hollink, L., Schreiber, G.: Design and use of the simple event model (SEM). J. Web Semant. **9**(2), 128–136 (2011)
63. Vilarroya, Ó.: Somos lo que nos contamos. Cómo los relatos construyen el mundo en que vivimos. Editorial Ariel, Barcelona (2019)
64. Wewer, C., Lemmerich, F., Cochez, M.: Updating embeddings for dynamic knowledge graphs. arXiv preprint arXiv:2109.10896 (2021)
65. Xu, C., Chen, Y.Y., Nayyeri, M., Lehmann, J.: Temporal knowledge graph completion using a linear temporal regularizer and multivector embeddings. In: Proceedings of the 2021 Conference of the North American Chapter of the Association for Computational Linguistics: Human Language Technologies, pp. 2569–2578 (2021)
66. Yang, X., Tiddi, I.: Creative storytelling with language models and knowledge graphs. In: CIKM (Workshops) (2020)
67. Zeng, C., Li, S., Li, Q., Hu, J., Hu, J.: A survey on machine reading comprehension-tasks, evaluation metrics and benchmark datasets. Appl. Sci. **10**(21), 7640 (2020)
68. Zhang, M., Ye, K., Hwa, R., Kovashka, A.: Story completion with explicit modeling of commonsense knowledge. In: Proceedings of the IEEE/CVF Conference on Computer Vision and Pattern Recognition Workshops, pp. 376–377 (2020)
69. Zhang, M., Chen, Y.: Link prediction based on graph neural networks. In: Advances in Neural Information Processing Systems, vol. 31, pp. 5165–5175 (2018)

Using Referential Language Games for Task-oriented Ontology Alignment

Nikolaos Kondylidis[(✉)] [ID]

Vrije Universiteit Amsterdam, Amsterdam, The Netherlands
nikos.kondylidis@vu.nl

Abstract. Ontology Alignment (OA) is generally performed by requesting two parties to provide their complete knowledge to a third party that
suggests potential schema alignments. This might however not always
be possible or helpful, as for example, when two organisations want to
query each other's knowledge, and none of them is willing to share their
schema due to information privacy considerations. This Ph.D. explores
how to allow multi-agent communication in cases where agents operate using different ontologies that cannot be fully exposed or shared.
Our preliminary experiments focus on the case where agents' knowledge
is describing a common set of entities and has the form of Knowledge
Graphs (KGs). The suggested methodology is based on the grounded
naming game, where agents are forced to develop their own language in
order to refer to corresponding schema concepts of different ontologies.
This way, agents that use different ontologies can still communicate successfully for a task at hand, without revealing any private information.
We have performed some proof of concept experiments applying our suggested method on artificial cases and we are on the process of extending
our methodology so that it can be applied in real-world KGs.

Keywords: Multi-agent communication · Task-oriented Ontology
Alignment · Instance-based Ontology Matching

1 Introduction and Motivation

A populated ontology is attributing characteristics to a set of instances using its
ontology schema. Different schema designs and characteristics can be used for
describing the same instances, depending on the purpose of the ontology. Even if
these ontologies have common characteristics, these might not be communicated
directly as it is expected to be defined under different symbols or namespaces.

 This work was supported by "MUHAI - Meaning and Understanding in
Human-centric Artificial Intelligence" project, funded by the European
Union's Horizon 2020 research and innovation program under grant agreement No
951846.

N. Kondylidis—Early Stage Ph.D.

P. Groth et al. (Eds.): ESWC 2022 Satellite Events, LNCS 13384, pp. 252–263, 2022.
https://doi.org/10.1007/978-3-031-11609-4_39

Ontology Alignment (OA) techniques attempt to bridge this gap by providing symbol alignments across ontologies, denoting that the meaning of these symbols is equivalent. Provided these alignments, the ontologies are able to represent their knowledge in terms of both ontologies, allowing them to query one another.

These approaches usually require the ontologies to fully expose their schema [2]. However, this might not always be feasible or fruitful. Our method is inspired from natural agent communication i.e. among animals, infants or humans, where the agents do not have access to each other's schema. Instead, these agents can only refer to each other's concepts by interacting with their environment and signaling each other. Language Games (LGs) are used by computational linguists to study and model how natural language emerges in order to cover communication needs among agents [13]. To that end, we are studying how LGs can be applied for Task-oriented Ontology Alignment (TOA), so that the agents can communicate using a newly invented language, without having to fully share their ontologies. Our method can be an alternative approach to TOA that does not require schema sharing, which, can even simplify the problem. This is the case when a layman and an expert interact, as for example, the interaction between a doctor and its patient, or a lawyer and its client. In such cases, although it might be feasible for them to exchange and align their ontologies in order to interact, this might be time-consuming, while also unnecessary depending on the task at hand. Of course, it is challenging to ensure that the new language is interpreted correctly by both parties, which is the focus of this thesis.

We suggest a LG approach, where the agents create a new vocabulary, the interpretation of which is aligned through interaction [14]. We propose such an approach because it has shown to allow successful communication between agents, without requiring them to expose any information explicitly. The interaction is designed in a way that requires the agents to interpret the same words with semantically similar properties across the schemata of different agents. Within LGs, agents are participating in a set of episodes in which they are required to act based on a sophisticated guess; a decision based on assumptions. The assumptions have the form of assertions, while the decision has an observable outcome which is either correct or wrong, i.e. the success of the episode. Depending on the episode's outcome, the agents either accept or reject their own assumptions, updating their knowledge and learn. We have completed early experiments applied on artificial cases reporting encouraging results that motivate us to extend our approach in order to apply it in real-world KGs.

2   State of the Art

In this section, we will introduce studies that are related to our work, ranging from the domain of LGs, where our suggested approach draws inspiration, to OA, where the approach can lead to useful outcomes.

2.1   Language Games

LGs are a common methodology for studying language emergence in populations of agents in a decentralised or self-organised way [13]. Language emerges through communicative interactions, allowing the agents to successfully and efficiently communicate while performing a specific task that the game defines [8]. Although the studies are applied on a set of agents, all interactions happen within communicative interaction rounds that involve two agents acting as Speaker and Listener. The Speaker needs to communicate a piece of information to the Listener by uttering a word, so that the latter can make an informed decision. The word has the same form for the two agents, but they do not necessarily attribute the same meaning to it. Only the Speaker is allowed to create a new word when necessary, while all agents start with an empty vocabulary. The agents behave according to their word interpretations while attempting to cooperate. The communication is deemed successful according to the outcome of the task. In the case of success, the agents increase the probability of reusing the same interpretation in the future, or decrease it otherwise. Eventually, the agents converge to having shared interpretations allowing them to communicate successfully in any episode.

Referential Language Games. Most LG studies are designed around the referential task, where the Speaker needs to inform the Listener regarding the identity of a target object among a set of objects. In the simple, non-grounded, version of the game [14], the agents have their own names for every object in the world and must align words with the names that each agent gives to the same object. The agents make assumptions in the form of weights relating object names with words, which are updated after each interaction following a Reinforcement Learning (RL) setup driven by the outcome of the episodes. In the grounded version of the naming game, the agents are embodied and perceive objects in the form of features that have sub-symbolic values i.e. RGB colour, height, width, etc. Agents use words not to directly refer to an object, but implicitly do so by referring to its characteristics. This way, when the interactions end, the agents use the same word to refer to set of characteristics with similar enough values. Agents relate different characteristic values to the same word, depending on their observational position, the different lighting conditions, etc. This proves that this form of communication allows of bridging such a gap, leading to our motivation of attempting to align concepts that are similar enough across ontologies, not requiring them to have the exact same meaning.

2.2 Ontology Alignment

Traditional OA methods follow a centralised approach [2], where systems are asked to provide their complete knowledge in order to find plausible alignments. This can be a problem in scenarios where agents need to keep their knowledge private, or cannot share it for any other reason. Additionally, such techniques assume that it is known beforehand i) which systems will interact and ii) what types of tasks they will be asked to collaboratively perform. These are usually too strong assumptions, since different methods are resulting in different alignments and not all alignments are equally suitable for all tasks [9,12]. Accordingly, two main streams of work have decided to propose techniques that allow the agents to develop alignments in a decentralised way through iterative agent interaction.

Negotiating Symbol Correspondences while Satisfying Private Constraints. This stream of studies suggests that agents interact in a set of episodes, during which they partly reveal their own knowledge and collaboratively converge to a common set of symbol correspondences [6,7,10,11,15]. These works formally define an argument, which consists of a suggested symbol correspondence together with supporting facts, as well as methods to generate and resolve them, even including rebuttals. The supporting facts either include previously accepted symbol correspondences or exposed facts from the agent's ontology. Each agent independently calculates a level of agreement with each suggested symbol correspondence, according to its ontology and the previously suggested correspondences, based on which, it decides whether to accept the suggestion or not. The method terminates when the agents cannot come up with new arguments and the commonly accepted symbol correspondences are provided as a solution. All these works show that even with partial revealings of the agents' ontologies, their method can achieve up to 95% of aligning accuracy [10], compared to centralised OA-based methods, where the complete information of both agents is accessible, making the task less challenging.

Symbol Correspondence Rectification via Agent Interaction. In a different stream of studies [1,3–5], a population of agents engage in interaction rounds, called episodes, in order to repair or create a public set of symbol correspondences across their personal schemata. These studies are similar to our work because a population of agents engage in pairwise interactions describing an object and learn which symbols each uses for every property. Compared to our work, these studies expose their schemas and cannot create complex alignments. The experiments are performed in artificial ontologies that share partial information and do not contain any contradicting facts. Last but not least, these studies not only measure the evolution of the rate of successful communication as a communication criterion, but further evaluate the consistency, redundancy and other semantic measures, while also compare the produced alignments with a set of reference alignments in the form of recall and precision.

2.3   Differences with this Thesis

Compared to the presented OA studies, our LG-inspired TOA approach does not require the agents to expose any knowledge from their ontologies regarding their schema. Additionally, current studies are restricted to only produce simple alignments, not allowing their application on ontologies that are designed in different granularity, as is the interaction between an expert and a layman. For example, if one ontology defines a class Human for what the other ontology defines either as Woman or Man, simple alignments would face difficulties aligning these concepts. LG studies focus on studying language evolution among agents that sense the environment in an equally expressive way, e.g. centimeters and inches. Our aim is not to study language evolution, but to apply it as a method to perform a particular problem, namely Task-oriented Ontology Alignment (TOA). In such an application the ontologies are not expected to have the same expressiveness and communication success is not guaranteed. Finally, the agents in our case interpret words in terms of ontology concepts, the dependency of which must be taken into account. A summary of the comparisons is presented in Table 1.

Table 1. Comparing the suggested LG-inspired TOA approach to related work.

Method	Task	Assumptions	Exposed knowledge
Negotiation [6]	Simple OA	Heuristic similarity values across ontologies	Minimised number of object properties
Rectification [1]	Simple OA	Sub-sampled ontologies from common ontology	Object properties
Referential LGs [13]	Study language emergence	Common knowledge	None
LG-inspired TOA	Complex TOA	Different ontologies	Indirectly (by inference)

3   Problem Statement and Contributions

As presented earlier, we suggest that there is an overlapping interest between OA and LGs which has not been studied yet, leading us to our research question: *"Can Language Games be used for Task-oriented Ontology Alignment?"*. We break our research question to four smaller ones:

1. To what extend can a LG approach perform TOA, without requiring the agents to reveal any of their schema?
2. What is the efficiency penalty or benefit imposed by restricting agents from exposing their knowledge?
3. Can such an approach be applied to multiple ontologies at the same time?
4. Can the agents extend their ontology or knowledge appropriately to always ensure successful communication?

Our contribution is a novel TOA method inspired by LGs, which will:

1. be able to deal with cases were communication success is not guaranteed;
2. extend current LG approaches to take into account the ontology's concept relationships as interpretation restrictions.

3. provide ontology alignments that are specifically tailored for a particular downstream task
4. broaden the application of OA methods to include cases where knowledge sharing is not possible, that can also be applied to ontologies of different granularity while even between more than two ontologies.

4   Research Methodology and Approach

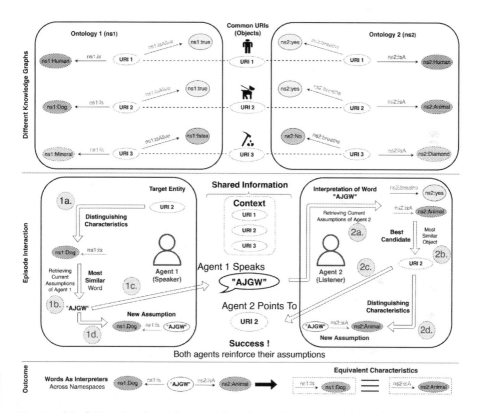

Fig. 1. (Top) Populated ontologies of Speaker and Listener. (Middle) Episode interaction; from top left to bottom right. (Bottom:) The alignment that this successful episode reinforces. The purple circles denote the methodology steps, while the colours indicate known characteristic alignments across ontologies. (Color figure online)

Our method aims to indirectly align terms across ontologies, provided that these ontologies include information regarding a common set of instances identified as Uniform Resource Identifiers (URI), i.e. the **Common URIs**, as depicted at the center top of Fig. 1. We assume this information to be in a Knowledge Graph (KG) form and more specifically in a Object - Property - Value triple format.

We define a **characteristic** to be a property - value pair of a triple, so that the KG of an agent consists of objects and their characteristics. In Fig. 1, characteristics are depicted as coloured property - value pairs, while same colours indicate ground truth equivalent characteristics across the two ontologies. Following the referential game setup and using the example from the middle Fig. 1, Agent 1 acts as Speaker and needs to inform the Listener, impersonated by Agent 2, that the target object is URI 2 among the context objects i.e. URI 1, URI 2 and URI 3. Furthermore, we define the "**distinguishing characteristics**" of one object in the context as the subset of its characteristics that are not shared by any other object in the context, according to an agent's knowledge. Thus, they depend both on the context and the agent. On the middle left side of Fig. 1 we can see the distinguishing characteristics of URI 2 i.e. {(ns1:is,ns1:Dog)}, according to Agent 1, with respect to the episode's context URIs. Within each episode the Speaker communicates one word and the Listener is allowed to communicate one URI in order to "point to" a candidate target item. The process is illustrated in the middle of Fig. 1 starting from the Speaker knowing the target entity i.e. URI 2, and follows the arrow flow. Words are interpreted by relating them with characteristics and interpretations are different per agent. Both the objects and words are related in a boolean manner to a set of characteristics that are defined on the agent's schema. Accordingly, we define the **similarity** between words, objects or any set of characteristics, to be equal to the number of the characteristics that both are related to. We define every word-to-characteristic relation as a single **assumption**; see examples in Fig. 1. When the agents converge to always communicating successfully, they can use the words to refer to each other's equivalent characteristics. At the bottom of Fig. 1, we can see an example of the word "AJGW" being used as an interpreter across namespaces to suggest that its interpretations by the two agents, i.e. {(ns1:is,ns1:Dog)} and {(ns2:isA,ns2:Animal)}, are equivalent.

Episodes: Every agent can operate both as a Speaker or a Listener. An illustration of the episode interaction where Agent 1 and Agent 2 are acting as Speaker and Listener respectively, is given in the middle of Fig. 1. The center depicts the information that is provided to both agents, while the sides are visualising the independent processes of the two agents that solely depend on their private information. As stated before, within each episode the Speaker needs to inform the Listener regarding the identity of the target object from a set of context objects. Every aspect of the episode is randomly sampled, i.e. the agents, their roles, the context and the target.

Speaker Behaviour: The Speaker initially calculates the distinguishing characteristics of the target object: which is {(ns1:is,ns1:Dog)} in the presented example (step 1a.). The same agent then uses its current assumptions to retrieve all words that are related to these characteristics resulting to a set of candidate words to communicate (step 1b.). All words that are more similar to any non-target object in the context are removed from this set, since communicating them would lead to misleading communication. In case the remaining set of words is empty, the speaker generates a new word, otherwise we select the most similar word from that set. Then, the Speaker communicates the selected word (step 1c.), and generates a set of assumptions relating the selected word with the distinguishing characteristics of the target object (step 1d.); i.e. one assumption per characteristic e.g. "AJGW" → (ns1:is,ns1:Dog).

Listener Behaviour: The Listener interprets the communicated word by retrieving from memory all assumptions that relate characteristics to this word. In Fig. 1, you can see the example of interpreting the word "AJGW" as the set of characteristics {(ns2:breaths,ns2:Dog), (ns2:isA,ns2:Animal) }; (step 2a). Note that each agent interprets a word in its own namespace. Similarity scores with context objects are calculated (step 2b.) while ties or lack of similarity scores, due to new words, are resolved randomly. The Listener points to the best matching context object (step 2c.) and generates a set of assumptions relating the communicated word with the distinguishing characteristics of the selected object (step 2d.); e.g. "AJGW" → (ns2:isA,ns2:Animal).

Outcome: The Speaker informs the Listener whether the object selection is correct. In case of successful communication, the two agents save the generated assumptions in their memories. Otherwise, they make sure that these assumptions are not in their memory. This way, the agents can use the interaction and the outcome of an episode in order to learn and update their interpretations. Eventually, the agents end up communicating successfully for enough subsequent episodes, at which point we can safely assume that the agents interpret the words using similar enough terms. For example, the interpretation assumptions that were generated during the depicted example episode interaction in Fig. 1, allow the agents to refer to each other's equivalent characteristics {(ns1:is,ns1:Dog)} ≡ {(ns2:isA,ns2:Animal)} by uttering the word "AJGW", as shown in the bottom of the figure. It should be mentioned that the agents to forget a word when it has not been used for the last 100 episodes, as it happens in the naming game.

5   Evaluation Plan

Proof of Concept. We run some proof of concept experiments towards answering our first research question as defined in Sect. 3. These investigate the successful application of our approach on small artificial ontologies. This stage has been performed and the results are presented in the next section.

RQ1. Next, we aim to apply our methodology to real ontologies, using existing TOA's benchmarks, and study how we need to improve our methodology appropriately. A candidate benchmark will either be found in the Ontology Alignment Evaluation Initiative, or will be constructed. We are aware that some episodes are more informative than others and we aim to allow the agents to design them, according to their state and goals. We estimate this phase to last around 6 months, helping us to answer our first research question.

RQ2. Towards answering out second research question, we will compare our method with other approaches that partly expose ontologies' knowledge and measure the amount of exposed information and the computational cost of each. This process should be performed within a period of 6 months.

RQ3. In order to apply our methodology to a population of ontologies, it is expected that the agents will need to have some theory of mind capabilities. This way, the agents will be able to learn what concepts they can communicate with every other agent separately. The experiments would be performed using benchmarks with more than 2 ontologies, and would help us answer our third research question i.e. the agent population setup. Estimated duration of this phase is around 9 months.

RQ4. The last phase will focus on assisting agents to decide when and how to extend their ontologies so that they learn each other's concepts, attempting to overcome ontology mismatch communication limitations. Experiments will be performed on the same benchmarks as before, but the agents should be able to communicate more concepts than before, if not all. This last phase should be performed within 1 year.

6   Preliminary Results

In this section, we will describe our proof of concept experiments. In each experiment, we provide all agents the same graph defined under different namespaces, except for the objects which have the same URIs across all ontologies. Thus, we know the ground truth alignments of the characteristics across graphs, allowing us to evaluate the output of our method beyond the success of the task. We run different experiments that vary according the number of object in the context (2 or 3) and the agent population size (2 or 3) depicted as "C. Size" and "Agents" respectively in the legends of Fig. 2. Additionally, we use two small artificial KGs consisting of 10 and 20 triples describing 3 and 6 objects, denoted as "tiny" and "small".

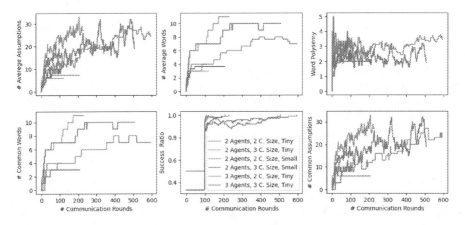

Fig. 2. The measured progression of the executed experiments, as captured by the 6 suggested evaluation metrics over the number of executed episodes. (Color figure online)

Evaluation Metrics. We plan to monitor the progress of the experiments, over the number of episodes, in order to validate whether the agents converge to similar word interpretations and successful communication. Figure 2 presents the evolution of the suggested metrics over the number of completed episodes. We mainly want to measure the success regarding the task at hand. In the presented experiments the task is for the Listener to find the target object. The evaluation metric "Success Ratio" captures this, by calculating the average success value of the last 100 rounds. In case of less executed rounds, the metric is set to be equal to the chance of randomly selecting the target object: 1/context size. Given that the agents are provided the same graphs, we can additionally measure the number current assumptions per agent and the number of common assumptions across agents, axes "#Average Assumptions" and "#Common Assumptions" respectively. We also present the traditional LG evaluation metrics to observe the successful application of the method. These are the average number of words ("#Average Words"), the number of common words across entities ("#Common Words") and the average number of characteristics related to one word ("Word Polysemy").

Table 2. An example of a converged experiment of how the communication symbols can be used as interpreters to align characteristics across namespaces (ns1 and ns2). Colours indicate ground truth characteristic correspondences across namespaces.

ns1 Characteristics		Word	ns2 Characteristics	
Property	Value		Property	Value
ns1:is	ns1:Human	"DFHD"	ns2:isA	ns2:Human
ns1:is	ns1:Dog	"SEWG"	ns2:isA	ns2:Animal
ns1:is	ns1:Dog	"AJGW"	ns2:isA	ns2:Animal
ns1:is	ns1:Mineral	"LWNC"	ns2:isA	ns2:Diamond
ns1:isAlive	ns1:false		ns2:breaths	ns2:No

The behaviour of the experiments according to our evaluation metrics are presented in Fig. 2. First, it is important to note that all experiments converge to successful communication. This allows us to assume that our proof of concepts experiments were successful and motivates us to continue working on our approach. Furthermore, it seems that larger context sizes usually lead to faster convergence. This is intuitive since the larger number of objects within a context, the less number of distinguishing characteristics each object is expected to have, leading to less assumptions per communicated word. This leads to less average assumptions per agent which is also observed in the "#Average Assumptions" plot (orange, brown and red lines in Fig. 2). It is important to point out that the methodology includes some stochasticity, and a more proper evaluation of the experiments would require aggregation over multiple executions of the same experiment. Regarding the alignments that the agents have generated, Table 2 shows how each agent interprets a word. The agents interpret the same words with the corresponding characteristics, even forming complex alignments (e.g. word "LWNC" on Table 2). On the other hand, the current methodology may generate synonyms i.e. two words with the same interpretation, which is an unwanted property (e.g. words "SEWG" and "AJGW" in Table 2).

7   Conclusions and Lessons Learned

To conclude, the success of the proof of concepts experiments suggests the continuation of our study, while also provide us with evidence of shortcomings that should be resolved. Specifically, the current method should be adjusted in order to avoid generating synonyms and the number of required episodes might be disproportional to the complexity of the problem, pointing towards further investigation for improvement. Therefore, the boolean relations between words and characteristics should be replaced to have a probabilistic form, defining a convex continuous space on which words are interpreted, as this allows easier optimisation. Furthermore, following the studies on OA, we should allow agents to store in their memory previous interactions, as a form of episodic memory, also aiming for faster convergence.

Acknowledgments. This work was performed in collaboration with dr. Ilaria Tiddi, prof. Annette ten Teije and prof. Frank van Harmelen. I want to sincerely thank them for their supervision and support.

References

1. van den Berg, L., Atencia, M., Euzenat, J.: A logical model for the ontology alignment repair game. Auton. Agents Multi-Agent Syst. **35**(2), 1–34 (2021). https://doi.org/10.1007/s10458-021-09508-8
2. Euzenat, J., Shvaiko, P.: Ontology Matching. Springer, Heidelberg (2013). https://doi.org/10.1007/978-3-642-38721-0
3. Euzenat, J.: First experiments in cultural alignment repair (extended version). In: Presutti, V., Blomqvist, E., Troncy, R., Sack, H., Papadakis, I., Tordai, A. (eds.) ESWC 2014. LNCS, vol. 8798, pp. 115–130. Springer, Cham (2014). https://doi.org/10.1007/978-3-319-11955-7_10
4. Euzenat, J.: Crafting ontology alignments from scratch through agent communication. In: An, B., Bazzan, A., Leite, J., Villata, S., van der Torre, L. (eds.) PRIMA 2017. LNCS (LNAI), vol. 10621, pp. 245–262. Springer, Cham (2017). https://doi.org/10.1007/978-3-319-69131-2_15
5. Euzenat, J.: Interaction-based ontology alignment repair with expansion and relaxation. In: Proceedings of the Twenty-Sixth International Joint Conference on Artificial Intelligence, pp. 185–191. International Joint Conferences on Artificial Intelligence Organization (2017)
6. Laera, L., Blacoe, I., Tamma, V., Payne, T., Euzenat, J., Bench-Capon, T.: Argumentation over ontology correspondences in MAS. In: Proceedings of the 6th international joint conference on Autonomous agents and multiagent systems - AAMAS 2007, p. 1. ACM Press, Honolulu, Hawaii (2007)

7. Laera, L., Tamma, V., Euzenat, J., Bench-Capon, T., Payne, T.: Arguing over ontology alignments. In: Proceedings 1st ISWC 2006 international workshop on ontology matching (OM), pp. 49–60 (2006)
8. Nevens, J., Eecke, P.V., Beuls, K.: A practical guide to studying emergent communication through grounded language games. CoRR abs/2004.09218 (2020)
9. Payne, T.R., Tamma, V.: Negotiating over ontological correspondences with asymmetric and incomplete knowledge. In: Proceedings of the 2014 International Conference on Autonomous Agents and Multi-agent Systems, pp. 517–524 (2014)
10. Payne, T.R., Tamma, V.: Using preferences in negotiations over ontological correspondences. In: Chen, Q., Torroni, P., Villata, S., Hsu, J., Omicini, A. (eds.) PRIMA 2015. LNCS (LNAI), vol. 9387, pp. 319–334. Springer, Cham (2015). https://doi.org/10.1007/978-3-319-25524-8_20
11. Santos, G., Tamma, V., Payne, T.R., Grasso, F.: Dialogue based meaning negotiation. In: The 15th Workshop on Computational Models of Natural Argument (CMNA 2015) (2015)
12. Shvaiko, P., Euzenat, J.: Ontology matching: State of the art and future challenges. Knowl. Data Eng. IEEE Trans. 25, 158–176 (2013)
13. Steels, L.: The emergence of grammar in communicating autonomous robotic agents, pp. 764–769 (01 2000)
14. Steels, L., Loetzsch, M.: The grounded naming game, pp. 41–59 (2012)
15. Trojahn, C., Euzenat, J., Tamma, V., Payne, T.R.: Argumentation for Reconciling Agent Ontologies. In: Kacprzyk, J., Elçi, A., Koné, M.T., Orgun, M.A. (eds.) Semant. Agent Syst., vol. 344, pp. 89–111. Springer, Berlin Heidelberg (2011). https://doi.org/10.1007/978-3-642-18308-9_5

Balancing RDF Generation
from Heterogeneous Data Sources

Dylan Van Assche$^{(\boxtimes)}$ iD

IDLab, Department of Electronics and Information Systems, Ghent University -
-imec, Technologiepark -Zwijnaarde 122, 9052 Ghent, Belgium
`dylan.vanassche@ugent.be`

Abstract. Knowledge graphs in RDF are often generated from heterogeneous data sources to power services. However, knowledge graph generation is an unbalanced effort for producers compared to consumers of
a knowledge graph. In this paper, I present my research about (i) investigating current RDF knowledge graph production and consumption
approaches, and (ii) how to involve the consumer into a hybrid RDF
generation approach to reduce the necessary resources for generating
RDF for producers & consumers. I discuss the shortcomings of existing approaches for RDF generation from heterogeneous data sources
(i.e., materialization and virtualization) and how I will address these:
a Systematic Literature Review; an analysis and a set of guidelines for
producers to select the right approach for an use case; and a combined
hybrid approach to balance the producer's and consumer's effort in RDF
generation. I already performed a Systematic Literature Review to get
an overview of the existing approaches for RDF production from heterogeneous data sources. These results will be used to establish a set
of producer guidelines, a benchmark to compare the current materialization and virtualization approaches, and evaluate the proposed hybrid
approach. Thanks to my research, knowledge graph production and consumption will be more balanced and accessible to smaller companies and
individuals. This way, they can focus on providing better services on top
of a knowledge graph instead of being limited by the lack of computing resources to harvest enormous amounts of data from the Web and
integrate it into a knowledge graph.

1 Introduction

Over the past two decades, several RDF generation approaches emerged such as
materialization & virtualization. On the one hand, materialization approaches
in the form of Extract-Transform-Load (ETL) [1] extract data from heterogeneous data sources, transform and integrate them completely or partially into a
knowledge graph, and materialize it to a certain target, such as a triple store, a
file, etc. On the other hand, virtualization in the form of Ontology Based Data

---

D. Van Assche—Supervised by Anastasia Dimou https://doi.org/0000-0003-2138-7972
& Ben De Meester https://doi.org/0000-0003-0248-0987.

P. Groth et al. (Eds.): ESWC 2022 Satellite Events, LNCS 13384, pp. 264–274, 2022.
https://doi.org/10.1007/978-3-031-11609-4_40

Access (OBDA) [2] provides query access to a virtual knowledge graph on top of the heterogeneous data. OBDA allows consumers to ask SPARQL queries and get an tailored answer for their query. Only the data necessary to answer the query is used and transformed by the producer.

Currently, producers are solely responsible for generating knowledge graphs. There is no way for a producer to determine which RDF generation approach is the most suitable depending on e.g., the properties of the data or how the RDF is used by consumers. Moreover, integrating enormous amounts of data into RDF is unfeasible since the producer's and consumer's effort is unbalanced.

No guidelines exist for producers to select the right approach depending on how their generated RDF is consumed. Therefore, producers cannot optimize their RDF generation, even though approaches exist which optimize parts of it.

RDF producers and consumers aim to minimize their own effort for producing and consuming a knowledge graph, but these efforts are unbalanced in favour of consumers. Producers are responsible for generating RDF from heterogeneous data sources and answering queries from consumers. Consumers ask queries and consume the answers as RDF, provided by the producer. Consequently, producers not only provide the data but also need to provide the most resources compared to consumers. Alternative approaches involving the consumer in the generation process are not investigated yet. This could better balance the efforts: consumers can contribute to the generation together with producers. This way, the producer's effort is reduced and balanced with its consumers.

In this PhD thesis I aim to (i) investigate which key factors influence RDF generation by analyzing existing approaches, (ii) provide a set of guidelines for producers to select the right RDF generation approach for a given use case, and (iii) introduce a new approach which involves consumers during the generation process. This way, producers' and consumers' efforts can be balanced better. Thanks to my research, smaller companies and individuals will be able to produce and consume knowledge graphs in RDF without having to invest in a large infrastructure to harvest and integrate all data into RDF. Smaller companies and individuals can focus on building products such as virtual assistants or smart route planners instead of entering first a data harvesting competition.

2   State of the Art

I provide an overview of current knowledge graph generation approaches, their strengths and weaknesses, and discuss existing benchmarks for their generation.

Knowledge graph generation. Several approaches exist to generate knowledge graphs based on materialization or virtualization, each with their own merits.

ETL approaches transform all data from heterogeneous data sources into a materialized knowledge graph. Several approaches exist based on the R2RML mapping language [3], e.g. KR2RML [4] or Morph-xR2RML [5], or its extensions, e.g., RMLMapper [6]. Some RML-based ETL approaches optimize the mapping rules execution, e.g., SDM-RDFizer [7] by avoiding duplicates, Morph-KGC[1] through mapping rules partitioning, or Morph-CSV [8] by normalizing and cleaning tabular data. Streaming-based ETL approaches, e.g., RML-Streamer [9] process large heterogeneous data sources in a streaming way. Besides R2RML based, SPARQL query language [10] based approaches exists as well, e.g., SPARQL-Generate [11], SPARQL-Anything [12], or XSPARQL [13]. They repurposed SPARQL to generate RDF from heterogeneous data sources; so does ShExML [14] which repurposes the constraint language ShEx [15].

OBDA approaches, e.g., Morph [16], UltraWrap [17], or Virtuoso[2] answer consumers' SPARQL queries over a virtual knowledge graph from a homogeneous data source, e.g., relational database. The response is generated at query time from a single data source. Recently, OBDA approaches such as Ontop [18], Squerall [19], Ontario [20], or PolyWeb [21] emerged for heterogeneous data.

Both ETL and OBDA approaches answer consumers' queries, but differ in their execution. OBDA provides a query interface for consumers, whereas ETL relies on external RDF triple stores for query executing. If a knowledge graph generated by ETL must be changed, the whole knowledge graph is regenerated. Depending on the data sources, this may take significant resources and execution time. If the data sources change faster than the knowledge graph is regenerated, these changes may not even appear in the generated RDF depending on the frequency of the regeneration process. However, this is not the case for OBDA, as the RDF is generated for each query from the data sources. This way, the generated RDF always has the data changes incorporated. Execution time for both approaches may heavily increase depending on e.g., the query and the size of the data sources. Scalability depends on the RDF generation approach, query execution, query type, size of the data sources, and how frequently they change.

Benchmarks. Over the past decade, several benchmarks were proposed to evaluate and compare knowledge graph generation approaches. Benchmarks such as GTFS-Madrid-Bench [22], Berlin SPARQL Benchmark (BSBM) [23], Lehigh University Benchmark (LUBM) [24], SP^{2}Bench [25], LSLOD [26], DBpedia SPARQL Benchmark [27], Linked Open Data Integration Benchmark (LODIB) [28], or Norwegian Petroleum Directorate Benchmark (NPD) [29] focus on evaluating virtualization approaches but no materialization approaches, as they provide a set of SPARQL queries to be executed by the virtualization query engine.

3   Problem Statement and Contributions

Both ETL materialization and OBDA virtualization for RDF generation from heterogeneous data sources are computationally intensive operations depending on factors e.g. available computing resources, data freshness, etc. These factors and approaches combining both are not investigated yet.

---

[1] https://github.com/oeg-upm/morph-kgc.
[2] https://virtuoso.openlinksw.com/.

Research Question: *How can RDF be generated in balanced way for producers and consumers with respect to execution time, computing resources, and consumers' queries?*

Hypothesis. When producers and consumers collaborate during the knowledge graph generation, a knowledge graph will be generated faster, with less computing resources e.g. CPU, RAM, storage, and network bandwidth, and tailored towards answering queries from consumers.

I split my Research Question (RQ) into three subquestions: RQ1 investigates the factors influencing RDF generation from heterogeneous data sources, the State of the Art, and open issues. These factors are used as a basis for RQ2 to investigate how these factors influence existing RDF generation approaches with a benchmark. The benchmark results can be used as a base to define a set of producer guidelines to better select the right approach. In RQ3, I use the results of RQ2 to introduce a new RDF generation approach.

Research Question 1 (RQ1): *What are the open issues, key factors regarding computing resources or consumers' usage, and available approaches in deciding if (part of) RDF is produced through materialization or virtualization.*

Hypothesis 1 (H1): Several approaches exist for materialization and virtualization based on existing specifications e.g. R2RML [3], or SPARQL query language [10]. Available computing resources, data size, query type, execution time, and update frequency influence when and how an RDF graph should be produced. Several open issues remain regarding transforming heterogeneous data.

Contribution 1: Systematic Literature Review to determine these factors based on the last 20 years of research in this domain.

Materialization vs virtualization. Selecting between virtualization or materialization is highly subjective because there are currently no studies evaluating which approach is the most suitable depending on how consumers access and use the generated RDF graph. Producers are responsible for the complete RDF generation while consumers only use the generated RDF or wait for an answer from the producer for their query. Since no guidelines exist, producers cannot optimize their RDF generation depending on their own resources and RDF use.

Generating materialized and virtualized RDF is constrained with respect to execution time [30], computing resources [18,30], bandwidth [31], performance [32], and query execution [31] because producers do not know which generation approach is the most suitable given its own resources and the RDF use. Since the producer needs to provide most resources for generating RDF from heterogeneous data sources and answering consumers' queries, guidelines for selecting the right approach are needed to minimize its effort. For instance, depending on the size of the data, producers may benefit from materialization because at the crossing point, the query and virtualized access of OBDA may cause more overhead than materializing (part of) a knowledge graph. However, this may influence how frequently a knowledge graph is updated which may affect consumers depending on how they use e.g. route changes with a route planning use case needs frequent updates while a weather prediction for next week may not. These guidelines try to provide for each key factor the trade-off when selecting a certain approach.

Research Question 2 (RQ2): *How influence the identified key factors the producer's effort when selecting either materialization or virtualization?*

Hypothesis 2 (H2): At least one crossing point exists between materialization and virtualization for each key factor. This crossing point determines a set of guidelines for producers to select the most suitable generation approach.

Contribution 2: Set of guidelines to select materialization or virtualization for generating RDF by broadening the GTFS-Madrid-Bench benchmark's scope.

Producer vs Consumer. The producer's effort is unbalanced compared to the consumer's effort since the producer needs to generate RDF but also answer the consumer's query. Moreover, production and consumption are still considered independent tasks. Each party executing one of these tasks, aims to reduce its own effort. This causes an imbalance of the producers' and consumers' efforts. Approaches where consumers and producers both participate in the materialization and/or virtualization process are not investigated yet.

Research Question 3 (RQ3): *How can consumers reduce the producer's effort regarding execution time and computing resources when generating RDF?*

Hypothesis 3 (H3): The execution time and computing resources are significantly reduced for producers when consumers are involved since consumers also generate parts of the RDF instead of only the producer.

Contribution 3: Involving the consumer in the existing materialization and virtualization approaches for generating RDF from heterogeneous data sources to balance the effort better between producers and consumers.

4   Research Methodology and Approach

I execute this research in three parts, each related to a RQ, to investigate the current State of the Art in depth and find a balance between the different key factors. The Systematic Literature Review (Part 1) determined the key factors influencing knowledge graph generation such as computing resources, execution time, etc. These key factors are used in a benchmark to evaluate materialization and virtualization approaches. Based on these results and how their generated RDF is used, I introduce a set of producer guidelines (Part 2) to select the right approach for their own resources. These guidelines can be used on the results of RDF generation benchmarks such as GTFS-Madrid-Bench [22]. I use these guidelines and benchmark results to introduce a new approach (Part 3) which involves the consumer to balance the efforts between producers and consumers.

Contribution 1: Systematic Literature Review. I systematically reviewed the literature of the last 20 years of research in this domain to establish a good overview of which approaches exist, their strengths and weaknesses, etc. This article is at the time of writing under major revision at the Journal of Web Semantics[3]. Relying on these results, I determined a set of key factors, e.g., data size, type of queries, or data freshness that influence an RDF graph's generation.

---

[3] https://www.websemanticsjournal.org/.

Contribution 2: Selection guidelines for materialization and virtualization. I will benchmark materialization and virtualization approaches based on the identified key factors. The results of this benchmark will be used to create a set of guidelines to select the right approach depending on available computing resources and how consumers use a generated knowledge graph. I expect that the results will show at least one crossing point between materialization and virtualization in our benchmark which allows me to define a guideline for each evaluated key factor. These guidelines can be used by producers to select the right approach based on results of RDF generation benchmarks such as GTFS-Madrid-Bench [22]. Materialization is commonly used for generating RDF from one or multiple large heterogeneous data sources. Once the RDF is materialized, it can be used to answer queries from multiple consumers without regenerating it. However, if the original data changes, the materialization process is completely repeated. Virtualization is widely used for answering consumer's queries through virtualized access to the RDF. For each query, the RDF is regenerated, but only from the parts of the heterogeneous data sources necessary to answer the query. If these data sources change, the changes are immediately used to answer a query.

Contribution 3: Producer and consumer involvement. I will balance the producers' and consumers' efforts by involving the consumer in the generation process into a new hybrid approach to divide the efforts among both producers and consumers. Example: producers may provide data to consumers to generate a part of the RDF themselves to answer their own query. The hybrid approach leverages materialization for parts which are heavily used among multiple consumers e.g. *"all departing trains in all stations in Belgium"*, while it leverages virtualization for other parts which are specifically for a single consumer e.g. *"next departing train near my location"*. Consumers can combine these parts together to answer their query. This way, queries can be answered without putting the burden on the producer only. For example, answering the query *"When does the next train depart in the nearest station?"* can use virtualized RDF to retrieve the nearest station and materialized RDF to retrieve the departing trains for the station. While the nearest station is specific for a given consumer, the list of departing trains for a station is re-usable for multiple consumers.

5   Evaluation Plan

This research will be evaluated through a Systematic Literature Review (SLR), a benchmark to measure the various key factors of the existing approaches, and the validation of my hybrid approach. The benchmark results are used to evaluate the proposed guidelines. Moreover, this hybrid approach will be used in several use cases such as public transport route planning and virtual assistants.

Contribution 1: Systematic Literature Review. I executed a SLR to identify key factors, approaches and open issues of RDF generation (Section 4, Part 1).
H1 validation: I accept my hypothesis for RQ1, several approaches e.g. RML [6], SPARQL-Generate [11], or ShExML [14] exist for generating RDF

from heterogeneous data. I identified several key factors e.g. data size, mapping rule execution, joins, and open issues e.g. applying conditions on data during the generation.

Contribution 2: Benchmark. I will establish a benchmark based on GTFS-Madrid-Bench [22] to evaluate existing materialization and virtualization approaches against the key factors determined in the SLR to select the right approach for generating RDF. I chose to build upon the GTFS-Madrid-Bench because it already measures similar metrics, but only for virtualization approaches. I will extend this benchmark and add more metrics to cover materialization approaches. I will use the following scaling parameters: original data size, number of mapping rules, query types, and update frequency of the original data. The following metrics are inherited from the GTFS-Madrid-Bench:

- **Total execution time (s):** Time to return the fully query answer.
- **Number of answers:** Number of answers returned.
- **RAM consumption (GB):** Amount of memory used to answer a query.
- **Initial delay (s):** Time to return the first part of the answer.
- **Loading time (s):** Time for loading the ontology, mappings, and query.
- **Number of requests:** Executed number of requests.
- **Source selection time (s):** Time for selecting all sources for an answer.
- **Results aggregation time (s):** Time for aggregating subqueries' results.
- **Query generation time (s):** Time for generating the query/queries.
- **Query rewriting time (s):** Time for rewriting query into subqueries.
- **Query execution time (s):** Time for executing the query on the sources.
- **Query translation time (s):** Time for translating a query into a different query for a source.

I will add additional metrics to cover materialization approaches as well:

- **Selectivity:** Parts of a dataset used for answering a query.
- **Bandwidth (GB):** Bandwidth necessary to answer a query.
- **CPU usage (%):** CPU usage to answer a query.
- **Storage (GB):** Storage used to store the data to answer a query.
- **Data freshness (s):** Integration time for original data changes in the RDF.

Based on the benchmark results, I will provide producer guidelines to determine if materialization or virtualization is suitable given their own resources and how the generated RDF is consumed. I will apply and validate these guidelines on two use cases: public transport route planning and virtual assistants.
H2 validation: I am currently in the process of extending and setting up this benchmark. I can accept my hypothesis if I have at least one crossing point between materialization and virtualization for each key factor.

Contribution 3: Producer & consumer involvement. I will adapt the benchmark introduced previously for my proposed hybrid approach with additional metrics, e.g., *cacheability* or *type of hardware (embedded systems, desktops, servers)*, and also metrics on the consumer side since the consumer is now involved.

This way, I can compare my hybrid approach with existing materialization and virtualization approaches. These results will validate if the hybrid approach is more suitable for some use cases, e.g., public transport route planning or virtual assistants, compared to only materialization or virtualization.

6   Intermediate Results

This research has already a few intermediate results such as an under-review Systematic Literature Review (SLR) paper at the Journal of Web Semantics[4] and the paper "Leveraging Web of Things W3C recommendations for knowledge graphs generation" [33] at the ICWE 2021 conference[5] (published in May 2021).

In the SLR paper, I collected papers from 42 sources (workshops, journals, conferences, and digital libraries) over the past 20 years, resulting in 52 analyzed papers. This SLR confirmed that two approaches exist for generating RDF: materialization and virtualization. I discussed how these approaches differ in terms of schema transformations, data transformations, implementations and open issues. Moreover, it showed that the producer's and consumer's effort is unbalanced. This SLR answers RQ1, and confirms its hypothesis.

"Leveraging Web of Things W3C recommendations for knowledge graphs generation" [33], paper introduces RML's Logical Target to specify where (parts of) the RDF must be exported, e.g., a triple store, a file, etc. RML's Logical Target is a step towards a hybrid approach since it allows to export parts of the RDF to different targets e.g. an materialization target or an virtualization target. This way, I can export parts which are frequently re-used among multiple consumers through materialization, while other parts with a virtualization approach. For example: a public transport schedule is exported to an materialization target because it is re-used among multiple consumers while the route planning is handled by an virtualization target since routes are consumer-specific.

In the next months, I plan to develop the aforementioned benchmark that evaluates existing materialization and virtualization approaches, providing producer guidelines to select an approach given its resources and how the generated RDF is consumed. Afterwards, I will compare my proposed hybrid approach with existing approaches and investigate when a hybrid approach is more suitable than materialization or virtualization. This will be evaluated through public transport route planning and virtual assistant use cases.

7   Conclusion and Lessons Learned

This research already led to a better understanding of materialization and virtualization approaches for RDF generation and how they are designed to transform large amounts of data or answer specific questions.

---

[4] https://www.websemanticsjournal.org/.
[5] https://icwe2021.webengineering.org/.

Preliminary results of the Systematic Literature Review already highlighted open issues, key factors, and existing approaches of RDF generation. Currently, there is no way to determine which approach should be used depending on computing resources and how the RDF is consumed. Moreover, some use cases, e.g., public transport route planning or virtual assistants, need to answer multiple types of queries. A hybrid approach combining materialization and virtualization may prove to be better than existing approaches.

References

1. Bansal, S., Kagemann, S.: Integrating big data: a semantic extract-transform-load framework. Computer **48**(3), 42–50 (2015)
2. Poggi, A., Lembo, D., Calvanese, D., De Giacomo, G., Lenzerini, M., Rosati, R.: Linking data to ontologies. In: Spaccapietra, S. (ed.) Journal on Data Semantics X. LNCS, vol. 4900, pp. 133–173. Springer, Heidelberg (2008). https://doi.org/10.1007/978-3-540-77688-8_5
3. Das, S., Sundara, S., Cyganiak, R.: R2RML: RDB to RDF mapping language. Working group recommendation, World Wide Web Consortium (W3C) (2012)
4. Slepicka, J., Yin, C., Szekely, P.A., Knoblock, C.A.: Kr2rml: an alternative interpretation of r2rml for heterogenous sources. In: Proceedings of the 6th International Workshop on Consuming Linked Data (COLD 2015) (2015)
5. Michel, F., Djimenou, L., Faron-Zucker, C., Montagnat, J.: Translation of heterogeneous databases into RDF, and application to the construction of a SKOS taxonomical reference. In: Monfort, V., Krempels, K.-H., Majchrzak, T.A., Turk, Ž (eds.) WEBIST 2015. LNBIP, vol. 246, pp. 275–296. Springer, Cham (2016). https://doi.org/10.1007/978-3-319-30996-5_14
6. Dimou, A., Vander Sande, M., Colpaert, P., Verborgh, R., Mannens, E., Van de Walle, R.: RML: a Generic language for integrated RDF mappings of heterogeneous data. In: Proceedings of the 7th Workshop on Linked Data on the Web (2014)
7. Iglesias, E., Jozashoori, S., Chaves-Fraga, D., Collarana, D., Vidal, M.-E.: SDM-RDFizer: an RML interpreter for the efficient creation of RDF knowledge graphs. In: Proceedings of the 29th ACM International Conference on Information & Knowledge Management (2020)
8. Chaves-Fraga, D., Ruckhaus, E., Priyatna, F., Vidal, M.-E., Corcho, O.: Enhancing virtual ontology based access over tabular data with Morph-CSV. Semant. Web **12**(6), 869–902 (2021)
9. Haesendonck, G., Maroy, W., Heyvaert, P., Verborgh, R., Dimou, A.: Parallel RDF generation from heterogeneous big data. In: Proceedings of the International Workshop on Semantic Big Data - SBD 2019 (2019)
10. Harris, S., Seaborne, A.: SPARQL 1.1 Query Language. Recommendation, World Wide Web Consortium (W3C) (2013)
11. Lefrançois, M., Zimmermann, A., Bakerally, N.: A SPARQL extension for generating RDF from heterogeneous formats. In: Blomqvist, E., Maynard, D., Gangemi, A., Hoekstra, R., Hitzler, P., Hartig, O. (eds.) ESWC 2017. LNCS, vol. 10249, pp. 35–50. Springer, Cham (2017). https://doi.org/10.1007/978-3-319-58068-5_3
12. Daga, E., Asprino, L., Mulholland, P., Gangemi, A.: Facade-X: an opinionated approach to SPARQL anything. In: Further with Knowledge Graphs - Proceedings of the 17th International Conference on Semantic Systems, 6–9 September 2021, Amsterdam, The Netherlands, pp. 58–73 (2021)

13. Bischof, S., Decker, S., Krennwallner, T., Lopes, N., Polleres, A.: Mapping between RDF and XML with XSPARQL. J. Data Semant. **3**, 147–185 (2012)
14. García-González, H., Boneva, I., Staworko, S., Labra-Gayo, J.E., Lovelle, J.M.C.: ShExML: improving the usability of heterogeneous data mapping languages for first-time users. PeerJ Comput. Sci. **318**, e318 (2020)
15. Prud'hommeaux, E.: Shape Expressions 1.0 Primer. Member submission, World Wide Web Consortium (W3C) (2014)
16. Priyatna, F., Corcho, O., Sequeda, J.: Formalisation and experiences of R2RML-based SPARQL to SQL query translation using morph. In: Proceedings of the 23rd International Conference on World Wide web, pp. 479–490 (2014)
17. Sequeda, J.F., Miranker, D.P.: Ultrawrap: SPARQL execution on relational data. J. Web Semant. **22**, 19–39 (2013)
18. Calvanese, D., et al.: Ontop: answering SPARQL queries over relational databases. Semant. Web J. **3**, 471–487 (2017)
19. Mami, M.N., Graux, D., Scerri, S., Jabeen, H., Auer, S., Lehmann, J.: Squerall: virtual ontology-based access to heterogeneous and large data sources. In: Ghidini, C., et al. (eds.) ISWC 2019. LNCS, vol. 11779, pp. 229–245. Springer, Cham (2019). https://doi.org/10.1007/978-3-030-30796-7_15
20. Endris, K.M., Rohde, P.D., Vidal, M.-E., Auer, S.: Ontario: federated query processing against a semantic data lake. In: Database and Expert Systems Applications: 30th International Conference, DEXA, Part I, pp. 379–395 (2019)
21. Khan, Y., Zimmermann, A., Jha, A., Gadepally, V., D'Aquin, M., Sahay, R.: One size does not fit all: querying web polystores. IEEE Access **7**, 9598–9617 (2019)
22. Chaves-Fraga, D., Priyatna, F., Cimmino, A., Toledo, J., Ruckhaus, E., Corcho, O.: GTFS-Madrid-bench: a benchmark for virtual knowledge graph access in the transport domain. J. Web Semant. **65**, 100596 (2020)
23. Bizer, C., Schultz, A.: The Berlin SPARQL benchmark. Int. J. Semant. Web Inf. Syst. (IJSWIS) **2**, 1–24 (2009)
24. Guo, Y., Pan, Z., Heflin, J.: LUBM: a benchmark for OWL knowledge base systems. J. Web Semant. **3**(2), 158–182 (2005). Selcted Papers from the International Semantic Web Conference, 2004
25. Schmidt, M., Hornung, T., Lausen, G., Pinkel, C.: Sp̂2bench: a SPARQL performance benchmark. In: 2009 IEEE 25th International Conference on Data Engineering, pp. 222–233 (2009)
26. Hasnain, A., et al.: Biofed: federated query processing over life sciences linked open data. J. Biomed. Semant. **8**(1), 1–19 (2017)
27. Morsey, M., Lehmann, J., Auer, S., Ngonga Ngomo, A.-C.: DBpedia SPARQL benchmark–performance assessment with real queries on real data. In: Aroyo, L., et al. (eds.) ISWC 2011. LNCS, vol. 7031, pp. 454–469. Springer, Heidelberg (2011). https://doi.org/10.1007/978-3-642-25073-6_29
28. Rivero, C.R., Schultz, A., Bizer, C., Ruiz Cortés, D.: Benchmarking the performance of linked data translation systems. In: LDOW 2012: WWW2012 Workshop on Linked Data on the Web (2012)
29. Lanti, D., Rezk, M., Xiao, G., Calvanese, D.: The NPD benchmark: reality check for OBDA systems. In: EDBT, pp. 617–628 (2015)
30. Chaves-Fraga, D., Endris, K.M., Iglesias, E., Corcho, O., Vidal, M.-E.: What are the parameters that affect the construction of a knowledge graph? In: Panetto, H., Debruyne, C., Hepp, M., Lewis, D., Ardagna, C.A., Meersman, R. (eds.) OTM 2019. LNCS, vol. 11877, pp. 695–713. Springer, Cham (2019). https://doi.org/10.1007/978-3-030-33246-4_43

31. Verborgh, R., et al.: Triple pattern fragments: a low-cost knowledge graph interface for the web. J. Web Semant. **37**, 184–206 (2016)
32. Machado, G.V., Cunha, Í., Pereira, A.C.M., Oliveira, L.B.: DOD-ETL: distributed on-demand ETL for near real-time business intelligence. J. Internet Serv. Appl. **10**(1), 1–15 (2019). https://doi.org/10.1186/s13174-019-0121-z
33. Van Assche, D., et al.: Leveraging web of things W3C recommendations for knowledge graphs generation. In: Brambilla, M., Chbeir, R., Frasincar, F., Manolescu, I. (eds.) ICWE 2021. LNCS, vol. 12706, pp. 337–352. Springer, Cham (2021). https://doi.org/10.1007/978-3-030-74296-6_26

Geological Information Capture
with Sketches and Ontologies

Yuanwei Qu[✉]

SIRIUS Centre, University of Oslo, Oslo, Norway
quy@ifi.uio.no

Abstract. Recent groundbreaking research [3] has shown the viability and usefulness of *qualitative information processing* in the digitisation of geosciences, as well as the possible role of semantic knowledge representation as an underlying framework. While there is significant work on e.g. geological ontologies and the integration of geological data, means of data entry that are suitable for geologists remain a bottleneck. Form and table data entry methods are good matches for an ontology-based data entry system; however, they cannot fulfill geologists' needs: to use sketches to express their idea and knowledge. This PhD project will lead to a novel user interface that will allow geologists to use sketches as an information entry method to input and store qualitative geological information in RDF format, which will enable machine-readable qualitative geological data query and reasoning in the future, and bring geology digitization one step forward. In this research work, assuring that qualitative geological information is captured completely and correctly is one of the main challenges.

Keywords: Semantic web · Ontology · Geology digitization

1 Introduction

Geology is the subject of studying the Earth that feeds humankind, both theoretically and practically. The resources, energy, and environment needed for human society rely on a deep understanding of the Earth. Thus, the development of geology is essential to the whole society.

In recent years, the use of information technology in geology has increased, many tools and systems have been developed to assist geologists in overcoming obstacles [7]. Machine learning has assisted geologists in interpreting and predicting results from quantitatively-oriented geological data [15,19]. But there is also a growing body of work on non-numerical information.In semantic technologies, semantics experts and geoscientists have been working together to address the problem of geological data silos [10,21]. Domain ontologies have been provided to avoid ambiguity and to support collecting heterogeneous data [1,6,22].

Recent work like that on the GeologicalAssistant [3] and SiriusGeoAnnotator [9] has shown that qualitative reasoning on geological information and image

© The Author(s), under exclusive license to Springer Nature Switzerland AG 2022
P. Groth et al. (Eds.): ESWC 2022 Satellite Events, LNCS 13384, pp. 275–284, 2022.
https://doi.org/10.1007/978-3-031-11609-4_41

data annotation are also possible, important, and interesting to the industry. Compared with machine learning, the decision support made by qualitative reasoning is an analogue of human inference, which is explainable and reversible. Moreover, it is applicable when extensive numerical data is not available. However, digitizing qualitative geological information is still problematic. In contrast to the maturity of numerical data collection and storage, infrastructure methods for capturing and storing digital qualitative geological information still need investigation. Massive qualitative geological information within sketches, illustrations, and geological photos is still waiting to be digitized.

Multiple easy-to-use front-end applications and user interfaces have been proposed to support RDF data entry and maintenance. It is often pointed out that such ontology-based interfaces for data entry can adapt arbitrary input ontologies, and their user interfaces are novice-friendly [2,5,12]. But apparently, these systems cannot fully meet geology users' needs. Being generic, the interfaces use elements like forms, or reflect the knowledge graph structure, etc. While these interfaces *could* be used for arbitrary domains, they are not necessarily appropriate for the intended users. Geologists prefer to use drawings to express their ideas and knowledge. Geologic sketch tools like [11,13] are designed from on ad hoc needs and aiming for visualisation. The gap between the geological qualitative information entry and geology digitization is still recognizable.

What geologists need is an easy-to-use tool that can allow them to draw sketches as an information entry method and store the information in a format that is machine-readable, suitable for inference and ready to support the rising trend of geology digitization. For this work, we are focusing on building an intelligent system for capturing the geological qualitative information by drawing sketches, and the system will generate knowledge graphs to store captured geological information. An example of this idea has been illustrated in Fig. 1, a schematic geological scenario drawn by a user and a corresponding knowledge graph generated by the system. By providing this system, this work aims to allow geologists to input and update geological information easily, pave the path for digital geoscience query, qualitative reasoning, and support supervised machine learning for both academia and industry.

2   State of the Art

In this section, related work consists of three major parts: 1) how semantics experts tried to offer user interfaces to improve data input efficiency and enhance the user experience for the arbitrary domain. 2) how geology and semantics researchers worked together to harmonize geological data in the context of semantic technologies. 3) how geologists and computer scientists build artifacts to assist researchers in conducting their studies.

2.1   User Interface for RDF Data Entry

UTILIS is a method presented by Hermann et al. [8] that aims to utilize existing objects, their properties, and known information of new objects and assist users

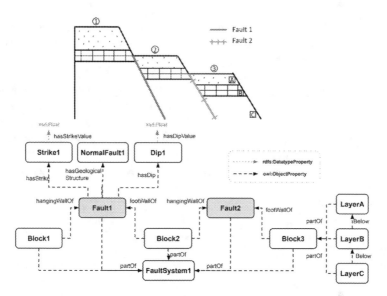

Fig. 1. Above: a sketch containing two geological faults (Faultn), three blocks (Blockn), and each block has layer A, B, and C. Fault 1 is in red and Fault 2 in blue. Below: part of the knowledge graph of the geological scenario above (Color figure online)

when they are adding or updating semantic web data. This system matches similar data objects and uses their properties as suggested descriptions to provide to users when adding new data. Aiming to make casual users create their own RDF data, Butt et al. [2] propose ActiveRaUL, which can automatically generate web form-based user interface from input ontology with no domain-specific limitation. With a similar purpose, Frischmuth et al. [5] present OntoWiki, a user interface for RDF knowledge graphs integrated with data management and visualization method.

Based on the method of UTILIS, FORMULIS was developed by Maillot et al. [12], a form-based user interface for knowledge graph editing. FORMULIS can not only give suggestions while the user is adding or updating RDF data, but also offer users an easy-to-use interface without the need for IT experts have to set it up first, and extended possibility depends on users' needs. With a similar idea of reducing reliance on IT experts in the context of data retrieval, Soylu et al. [17] render an overview and discuss the achievability of ontology-based data access, visual representation and interaction for users in an ontology-based system, and potential user roles within such system. However, all these methods and systems still cannot fully meet geology users' needs.

2.2 Geological Data Integration

Integrating geological data is a well-known challenge in this subject, and diverse approaches have been applied to address this issue. Therein, semantic technologies have been achieved several successes. By applying a shared conceptualization model to describe geological map objects and their properties in the model to bring semantic unification, Laxton [10] has successfully deployed a system to integrate geological map data across several nations.

Holding the vision of breaking the data silos of geological data, the Deep-Time Digital Earth Program was proposed by the International Union of Geological Science and several associations, surveys, and institutions. Scientists are trying to use such platform to link and integrate data in existing databases, and serve for more future knowledge graphs in geoscientific usage [21]. Aiming to integrate subsurface geological data within a digital modelling flow and let experts in diverse disciplines involved, Verney et al. [14] presented their works using designed ontologies as knowledge representations to characterize and correlate subsurface geological structures, and record parameters of characterized targets in the system. Having the goal of integrating multi-source early geological data, Wang et al. [20] proposed a semi-automatic method based on ontology and natural language processing to reconstruct low-cost vector geological profiles.

2.3   Software Assistance for Geological Research

Nowadays, geoscientists, especially geologists, still prefer to use pens to draw sketches on paper to illustrate their ideas or concepts. Following this preference, both Lidal et al. [11] and Natali et al. [13] have presented their approaches for sketching, drawing, and visualizing geological models in a time-efficient way that allows geologists to interact with their sketch model and to communicate and share their conceptualization model with others.

Images are usually considered as a type of critical data for geoscience, because images can contain a large amount of information that is useful for researchers. Aiming to support geoscientists to annotate geological information within the image and make those content accessible, SiriusGeoAnnotator has been deployed [9]. This artifact offers users an interface to annotate geological information. With the help of embedded ontology, the user's annotations will transfer to RDF format data, which can increase image query efficiency.

Din et al. [3] proposed GeologyAssistant, a logic-based formal system for geological reasoning to assist exploration work in the energy industry and reduce the laborious work of geoscientists. The system is designed to infer and generate multiple sound possibilities for an uncertain subsurface interpretation by taking qualitative geological information as input data and combing the formalized geological knowledge in first-order logic. This work proves that qualitative geological reasoning is also executable and essential. But where to find such formalized geological qualitative information?

3   Problem Statement

As mentioned in the previous section, the gap between the geological qualitative information entry and geology digitization is still recognizable. And this work aims to propose an intelligent system for geological qualitative information entry and storage in the RDF format.

Our core hypothesis of this work is that geo-user with no semantic knowledge and experience can use sketches and drawing as satisfactory and efficient information entry options to easily and precisely input and update qualitative geological information in the RDF format, without being highly dependent on data experts to set up and maintain data evolution. Other hypotheses: this intelligent system can be modified to adapt knowledge from different geology sub-domains; the stored geological qualitative information can be used in data query, qualitative reasoning, and supervised machine learning.

3.1   Research Questions

The previous section discussed the need for geologists to entry of geological information, and this research's primary objective has been settled. To achieve this goal, the following research questions have been derived:

RQ1. How can we achieve loose coupling between the generic ontology-driven components and the specialised sketching component?

It should be possible to use the system with different geological ontologies, e.g., covering different areas of geology, using different upper ontologies, etc. A menu-based interface can be made to automatically adapt to any given ontology, but a sketching interface is more intimately tied to the intended domain. Representations of entities as lines, areas, colours cannot be read from the ontology, any more than useful modes of interaction with these graphical elements. The challenge is therefore how to bridge the relatively rigid sketch-based part with the generic ontology-driven components.

RQ2. How can the system's information entry method be sufficient and accessible for users to express their knowledge?

Sufficiency is about allowing users to express all information required for the task at hand. The system should permit users to express their domain knowledge without being hindered by a lack of expressiveness. Accessibility is about ensuring that the information entry methods can easily be adapted to domain users and meet their needs.

RQ3. How can this geological information entry method be precise and avoid users' missing input?

Compared to forms or tables, using a drawing tool as a geological information entry method increases makes it more difficult to ensure that the system store the correct information. What the users draw and what the system stores are may not be the same, the system should be able to confirm its stored information with users. For the users, they shouldn't be expected to understand RDF, their work is to describe scenarios. Checking the RDF quality is not users' but semantic experts' work.

4   Research Methodology

This research work is still in its initial stage. As the research progresses, the current methodologies might be changed to fit evolving and emerging questions and challenges.

The initial idea of designing such a system is inspired by the work of the Geological Assistant [3]. This work has shown the viability and usefulness of qualitative information processing in the digitisation of geology, but where is the formalised geological qualitative information? The geology community needs an easy-to-use method to prepare data for qualitative information processing. The SiriusGeoAnnotator [9] took the first step to annotate image information, based on this, we want to make the system one step forward to allow users to sketch, instead of only annotating. CogSketch [4] is a sketch tool with a knowledge base for cognitive science research purposes, which also inspires us on what could a sketch tool with an ontology look like.

The system consists of an ontology-driven part based on similar concepts to previous ontology-based systems and a graphical part to allow drawing. But designing such a system to balance two parts is a question. Besides, validating the system's usefulness is also a challenge. Due to different domains of geology are having diverse needs, the scope of this work also needs to limit to a suitable sub-domain of geoscience to prove the concept of this work.

To develop the system, first step is to determine the essential elements that need to be implemented for an ontology-based geological sketching tool. This can be done by talking with domain experts and doing a literature review. Once the fundamental elements have been settled, the work on the project can continue.

Research question 1 concerns constructing two parts of the system, bridging the gap between the sketch tool and the geology domain ontology. Compared with current ontology-based systems that use tables or forms as data entry methods, using drawing as geological information entry method requires a more complex and sophisticated ontology-based system. To address this question, we are considering Reasonable Ontology Templates (OTTR) [16] as a technical foundation. OTTR templates are a high-level language that focuses on modeling patterns for building and maintaining ontologies. By providing designed ontology templates, OTTR allows system designers to describe the mapping from high level description like ≪there is a fault through this formation≫, into RDF triples and in a maintainable way. And modifying domain ontology and bridging rigid and nonrigid parts of the system will also be possible by applying OTTR.

The causes and relations of RQ2 and RQ3 are illustrated in Fig. 2. In this figure, the user's intention is about what the user *wants* or tries to do; the user's idea of the system is about the user's understanding of what they have expressed or not expressed in the system; the actual stored data stands for the information that is actually stored by the system. The yellow arrow in Fig. 2 represents the scenario when users want to input some information but soon realize that the system lacks the expressiveness and cannot fulfill their needs. (RQ2). In order to answer RQ2 and to avoid poor usability, a competency question-driven domain-

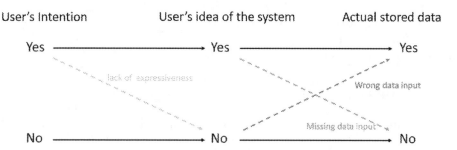

Fig. 2. This figure illustrates the connection between the user's intention, user's idea of what is represented in the system and the actual stored information, and what consequences will wrong connections lead to. (Color figure online)

specific ontology should be provided. Many ontologies relevant to geology have been presented in the literature. Though, most of these ontologies were designed for various purposes and disciplines. Thus, we need specific criteria to evaluate, modify and reuse these available domain ontologies to fit our purpose. Based on this need, a user case survey needs to be designed and conducted to collect the most critical and frequent questions that target domain users ask. After evaluations and modifications that are based on collected competence questions, a question-driven ontology will be presented, which contains sufficient knowledge to answer those questions. Potential users' drawing preferences will also be collected to meet their needs for the graphic drawing part of the system. Thus, the system's expressivity will be made to fit users' intentions and expectations as closely as possible.

As for RQ3, mistakes in the captured information can occur in two ways:

- The user thinks that their sketches should lead to some information being stored, but the actual data does not reflect this information (blue arrow in Fig. 2). For example, in Fig. 1 Fault 1 is on the left of Fault 2. In the missing data input scenario, a user draws this figure to express the fact that geological fault 1 is to the West of fault 2, but the system stores only that there are two faults, not their relative location.
- The user enters a sketch, and the system misinterprets or over-interprets the meaning and stores information that was not intended (red arrow in Fig. 2). For example, in Fig. 1 the user draws the Fault 1 to the left of Fault 2 without intending to express anything about the relative location, but the system stores data to represent that Fault 1 lies to the west of Fault 2.

In order to address this question, the user needs a clear understanding of what the system can do, and they need to be supported by proper information entry methods. In addition to having a tailored domain-specific ontology and providing the instruction book and some demonstrations, the system should also provide users with clear instructions to help users double-check the actual stored information. The work of detailed quality assurance should leave to semantic experts. For the user side, the system can provide a certain degree of query or reasoner to help users test their stored data. Besides, a detailed evaluation study will be performed to distinguish under what circumstances users' information entry will lead to wrong or missing data input, which is in Sect. 5.

5 Evaluation Plan

To validate the usefulness of the proposed system and make sure the proposed research questions are addressed, use cases examinations and qualitative empirical methods such as design workshops, interviews, and observations will be implemented in the evaluation plan. Since this research work is interdisciplinary, geologists and semantics experts will be involved.

Before inviting users, concrete use cases will be used to examine the expressiveness and correctness of the system and its ontology. These real word geological cases will be selected from industrial and academic structural geology analysis publications and reports. The application domain will first concentrate on carbon capture and storage, petroleum exploration, and production. We will first test the correctness and completeness of our ontology. If the ontology can describe scenarios, then the system will be deployed to draw sketches to describe use cases and check the quality of the stored knowledge graphs.

Qualitative empirical evaluation has two main parts. One part is to design and organize workshops with geologists. Before the workshops, several use cases with geological sketches that contain critical geological information will select as entry material. Geologists will be asked to use this system to input geological information in the sketches with a short system introduction. After the information entry, a prepared qualitative survey will give to users for collecting as much feedback as possible concerning the overall solution, and the satisfaction measurements will based on the system usability scale. Then, a group of semantics experts will assess the correctness of stored information. Any mismatch between the captured information and the users' expectations and intentions will lead to a discussion among semantic and domain experts, and they shall solve the problem together.

Another part will be to invite geologists who have attended the workshops to apply this system in day-to-day work, especially in their fieldwork. Raw geological information entry will bring more challenges to the system, allowing us to assess the usability.

The current work focuses on structural geological faults. It is easy to have envisioned that this system could extend to other structural geological subjects or even relevant geologic domains, and be implemented in energy, mining, or construction industries. More implementation possibilities will lead to more future evaluation plans.

On a broader level, based on Verne's analysis [18] of how digitization and automation influences users' experiences, we will take the following aspects into account during the evaluation:

- are domain competency questions covered and answered by using the system?
- is there any essential aspect is not covered by using this system?

- is there any new task, either positive or negative, that is brought by using this system?
- does any new challenge appear outside this system?

6   Conclusions and Further Work

The current semantics-based table/form data entry user interfaces and traditional geological information entry methods cannot fulfill the needs of geology digitization. This work will result in a system that takes digital geoscience a step forward. It allows geologists to input qualitative information in RDF format in a convenient way. The sketching entry method ensures that geologists follow the conceptualizations in their minds to precisely enter geological information, which is convenient for them and keeps the completeness of their ideas. Thus, qualitative geological information will no longer be limited to sketches and figures, it is captured by the system and stored in RDF format. The stored RDF qualitative information will increase the geological information query efficiency. It can also be used for other purposes, such as qualitative information reasoning and supervised machine learning in various industrial domains.

The availability of geological information in RDF format will enable new digitization in the geology domain and support machine-readable geological information query and reasoning. Besides, this work handles the issue of bridging the gap between the ontology part of the system and the graphic drawing part of the system, which can transfer to other ontology-based information systems as well as other interdisciplinary work between geology and semantic technologies.

Acknowledgements. This work is supported by the Norwegian Research Council via PeTWIN (294600) and SIRIUS (237898).

References

1. Abel, M., Lorenzatti, A., Fiorini, S.R., Carbonera, J.: Ontological analysis of the lithology data in PPDM well core model. In: 19th International Conference on Petroleum Data Integration and Data Management (2015)
2. Butt, A., Haller, A., Liu, S., Xie, L.: ActiveRaUL: automatically generated web interfaces for creating RDF data. Semant. Web **2013** (2013)
3. Din, C.C., Karlsen, L.H., Pene, I., Stahl, O., Yu, I.C., Østerlie, T.: Geological multi-scenario reasoning. NIK: Norsk Informatikkonferanse (2019)
4. Forbus, K., Usher, J., Lovett, A., Lockwood, K., Wetzel, J.: CogSketch: sketch understanding for cognitive science research and for education. Top. Cogn. Sci. **3**(4), 648–666 (2011)
5. Frischmuth, P., Martin, M., Tramp, S., Riechert, T., Auer, S.: Ontowiki-an authoring, publication and visualization interface for the data web. Semant. Web **6**(3), 215–240 (2015)
6. Garcia, L.F., Abel, M., Perrin, M., dos Santos Alvarenga, R.: The GeoCore ontology: a core ontology for general use in geology. Comput. Geosci. **135**, 104387 (2020)

7. Gil, Y., Pierce, S.A., Babaie, H., Banerjee, A., Borne, K., Bust, G., Cheatham, M., Ebert-Uphoff, I., Gomes, C., Hill, M., et al.: Intelligent systems for geosciences: an essential research agenda. Commun. ACM **62**(1), 76–84 (2018)
8. Hermann, A., Ferré, S., Ducassé, M.: An interactive guidance process supporting consistent updates of RDFS graphs. In: ten Teije, A., et al. (eds.) EKAW 2012. LNCS (LNAI), vol. 7603, pp. 185–199. Springer, Heidelberg (2012). https://doi.org/10.1007/978-3-642-33876-2_18
9. Jiménez-Ruiz, E., et al.: SiriusGeoAnnotator: ontology-driven knowledge graph population for geological image annotatio. https://sws.ifi.uio.no/project/sirius-geo-annotator/. Accessed 06 Dec 2021
10. Laxton, J.: Geological map fusion: OneGeology-Europe and INSPIRE. Geolog. Soc. London Special Publ. **408**(1), 147–160 (2017)
11. Lidal, E.M., Hauser, H., Viola, I.: Geological storytelling: graphically exploring and communicating geological sketches. In: Proceedings of the International Symposium on Sketch-Based Interfaces and Modeling, pp. 11–20 (2012)
12. Maillot, P., Ferré, S., Cellier, P., Ducassé, M., Partouche, F.: FORMULIS: dynamic form-based interface for guided knowledge graph authoring. In: Ciancarini, P., et al. (eds.) EKAW 2016. LNCS (LNAI), vol. 10180, pp. 140–144. Springer, Cham (2017). https://doi.org/10.1007/978-3-319-58694-6_18
13. Natali, M., Klausen, T.G., Patel, D.: Sketch-based modelling and visualization of geological deposition. Comput. Geosci. **67**, 40–48 (2014)
14. Perrin, M., Thonnat, M., Rainaud, J.F., Verney, P.: A knowledge-based approach of seismic interpretation: horizon and dip-fault detection by means of cognitive vision. In: 2008 SEG Annual Meeting. OnePetro (2008)
15. Rodriguez-Galiano, V., Sanchez-Castillo, M., Chica-Olmo, M., Chica-Rivas, M.: Machine learning predictive models for mineral prospectivity: an evaluation of neural networks, random forest, regression trees and support vector machines. Ore Geol. Rev. **71**, 804–818 (2015)
16. Skjæveland, M.G., Lupp, D.P., Karlsen, L.H., Forssell, H.: Practical ontology pattern instantiation, discovery, and maintenance with reasonable ontology templates. In: Vrandečić, D., et al. (eds.) ISWC 2018. LNCS, vol. 11136, pp. 477–494. Springer, Cham (2018). https://doi.org/10.1007/978-3-030-00671-6_28
17. Soylu, A., Giese, M., Jimenez-Ruiz, E., Kharlamov, E., Zheleznyakov, D., Horrocks, I.: Ontology-based end-user visual query formulation: why, what, who, how, and which? Univ. Access Inf. Soc. **16**(2), 435–467 (2016). https://doi.org/10.1007/s10209-016-0465-0
18. Verne, G.B.: Adapting to a robot: Adapting gardening and the garden to fit a robot lawn mower. In: Companion of the 2020 ACM/IEEE International Conference on Human-Robot Interaction, pp. 34–42 (2020)
19. Waldeland, A.U., Jensen, A.C., Gelius, L.J., Solberg, A.H.S.: Convolutional neural networks for automated seismic interpretation. Lead. Edge **37**(7), 529–537 (2018)
20. Wang, B., et al.: A semi-automatic approach for generating geological profiles by integrating multi-source data. Ore Geol. Rev. **134**, 104190 (2021)
21. Wang, C., et al.: The deep-time digital earth program: data-driven discovery in geosciences. Natl. Sci. Rev. **8**(9), nwab027 (2021)
22. Zhong, J., Aydina, A., McGuinness, D.L.: Ontology of fractures. J. Struct. Geol. **31**(3), 251–259 (2009)

Industry

The Data Value Quest: A Holistic Semantic Approach at Bosch

Baifan Zhou[1(✉)], Zhuoxun Zheng[2,3], Dongzhuoran Zhou[1,2], Gong Cheng[4],
Ernesto Jiménez-Ruiz[1,6], Trung-Kien Tran[2], Daria Stepanova[2],
Mohamed H. Gad-Elrab[2], Nikolay Nikolov[1,7], Ahmet Soylu[1,3,5],
and Evgeny Kharlamov[1,2]

[1] SIRIUS Centre, University of Oslo, Oslo, Norway
baifanz@ifi.uio.no
[2] Bosch Center for Artificial Intelligence, Renningen, Germany
[3] Department of Computer Science, Oslo Metropolitan University, Oslo, Norway
[4] State Key Laboratory for Novel Software Technology, Nanjing University,
Nanjing, China
[5] Department of CS, Norwegian University of Science and Technology,
Trondheim, Norway
[6] City, University of London, London, UK
[7] SINTEF, Trondheim, Norway

Introduction. Modern industry witnesses a fast growth in volume and complexity of heterogeneous manufacturing (big) data [1,2] thanks to the technological advances of Industry 4.0 [1,3], including development in perception, communication, processing, and actuation. Data has become the new oil for industries[1]. However, despite the effort and time invested in the data business, there still exists a big room for improvement in exploiting the value of data. In particular, data is still often scattered and stored in silos affecting its usage [4]; a lot of data generated by sensors is not used in applications; companies possess precious data but do not have a trustworthy scheme to share its value; etc. There are certainly many ways to address these issues. In this paper we discuss the dimension of meaning in data and how we address it at Bosch (Fig. 1) in a holistic semantification fashion that bestows data with meanings which has always been important for humans to perceive, comprehend, reason, and produce. We believe the emphasis, the clarification, and the promotion of the eminent and profound roles of semantic technologies in the industry should lead to considerable opportunities for advances in technology, growth of profitability, and paradigm change in the industrial practice.

Holistic Semantification at Bosch

- **Data collection.** Semantification begins with data collection [5]. During which, vast amounts of heterogeneous data with mutli-faceted variety in locations, formats, physical equipment, customisation, etc. are annotated with precise and uniform meta-data, which sets the first corner stone for many activities that are based on the collected data.

---

[1] https://blog.s4rb.com/data-is-the-oil-of-the-21st-century.

P. Groth et al. (Eds.): ESWC 2022 Satellite Events, LNCS 13384, pp. 287–290, 2022.
https://doi.org/10.1007/978-3-031-11609-4_42

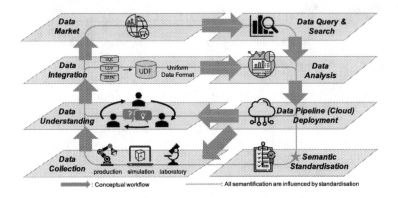

Fig. 1. An overview of our holistic semantification approach

- **Data understanding.** In big manufacturing companies like Bosch, data science projects are typically multi-disciplinary teamwork where experts with asymmetric knowledge backgrounds (e.g., engineers, equipment experts, measurement experts, data managers, data scientists, managers) need to talk to each other, to gain a mutual understanding of the process, data, solution, infrastructure, strategic interests, etc. [6]. These experts with distinct backgrounds speak different technical or management languages, which tends to lead to error-prone and time-consuming communication. Thanks to their conciseness and unambiguity, semantic models play an essential role here, serving as the "lingua franca" between the experts speaking different languages [7,8].
- **Data integration.** We rely on ontologies and knowledge graphs (KG) to annotate heterogeneous welding manufacturing data from Bosch and its partners with unified vocabularies. Then, enhanced by the ontology reshaping method developed in Bosch [9,10], we transform them into uniform data formats/databases that allow uniform access, interoperability, and unified interpretation.
- **Data market.** Bosch participates in a digital open marketplace ecosystem [11], which provides a sustainable approach to connect the data providers and the data consumers to help to connect Bosch and its partners. The ontologies and KGs make the data easier to reach from and by Bosch's production units, suppliers, and customers.
- **Data query & search.** Data like XML files, KGs [12,13] provide an efficient foundation for querying information of interest via clearly defined formats. SPARQL queries or keywords are used to query data [14–17] for inspection, information summary, and diagnostics. Data search outputs datasets, databases, or snippets of datasets [18–21] and relies on the metadata-based query, KG summarisation, natural language-based search [22], or even the content-based search, which Bosch is researching on.
- **AI and Data analysis.** Here Bosch relies on semantics in diversified ways like scaling usability of data analysis (typically machine learning (ML)-based) pipelines [23] with user interface, which improves the adoption of ML [24],

(semi-)automate the generation of ML pipelines with ontologies, templates, and reasoning [25] incorporating domain knowledge via annotation and KG embeddings, etc.

- **Data pipeline deployment (scalability).** Bosch develops semantic abstraction of cloud resources for computing, storage, and networking that facilitate the deployment of distributed ML pipelines, thus scaling the data analysis onto the big data level [26,27]. Adaptive rule-based reasoners help to automate the configuration of resource allocation.
- **Semantic standardisation.** Now Bosch participates in the endeavour [28] working towards addressing the long call of the standardisation of semantic artefacts [29], infrastructure, and best practice via e.g. aligning to ISO standards, existing vocabularies, achieving common agreement.

Conclusion. This work gives a panorama view of semantic technologies in the data business at Bosch that is in development. We aim at advancing the exploitation of the values of data in the manufacturing industry. We envision semantic technologies continuing to be one of the keys to unlocking the potential of the values of data.

Acknowledgements. The work was partially supported by the H2020 projects Dome 4.0 (Grant Agreement No. 953163), OntoCommons (Grant Agreement No. 958371), and DataCloud (Grant Agreement No. 101016835) and the SIRIUS Centre, Norwegian Research Council project number 237898.

References

1. Chand, S., Davis, J.: What is smart manufacturing, Time Magazine Wrapper
2. Horrocks, I., Giese, M., Kharlamov, E., Waaler, A.: Using semantic technology to tame the data variety challenge. IEEE Internet Comput. **20**(6), 62–66 (2016)
3. Kagermann, H.: Change through digitization—value creation in the age of industry 4.0. In: Albach, H., Meffert, H., Pinkwart, A., Reichwald, R. (eds.) Management of Permanent Change, pp. 23–45. Springer, Wiesbaden (2015). https://doi.org/10.1007/978-3-658-05014-6_2
4. Gimpel, G.: Bringing dark data into the light: illuminating existing IoT data lost within your organization. Bus. Horiz. **63**(4), 519–530 (2020)
5. Zhou, B.: Machine learning methods for product quality monitoring in electric resistance welding, Ph.D. thesis, Karlsruhe Institute of Technology, Germany (2021)
6. Svetashova, Y., et al.: Ontology-enhanced machine learning: a Bosch use case of welding quality monitoring. In: Pan, J.Z., et al. (eds.) ISWC 2020. LNCS, vol. 12507, pp. 531–550. Springer, Cham (2020). https://doi.org/10.1007/978-3-030-62466-8_33
7. Zhou, B., et al.: SemML: facilitating development of ML models for condition monitoring with semantics. J. Web Semant. **71**, 100664 (2021)
8. Svetashova, Y., Zhou, B., Schmid, S., Pychynski, T., Kharlamov, E.: SemML: reusable ML for condition monitoring in discrete manufacturing. ISWC (Demos/Ind.) **2721**, 213–218 (2020)
9. Zhou, B., Zhou, D., Chen, J., Svetashova, Y., Cheng, G., Kharlamov, E.: Scaling usability of ML analytics with knowledge graphs: exemplified with a Bosch welding case. In: IJCKG, pp. 54–63 (2021)

10. Zhou, D., Zhou, B., Chen, J., Cheng, G., Kostylev, E., Kharlamov, E.:Towards ontology reshaping for KG generation with user-in-the-loop: applied to Bosch welding. In: IJCKG, pp. 145–150 (2021)
11. DOME4.0, Digital open marketplace ecosystem 4.0. https://dome40.eu/. Accessed 14 Mar 2022 (2022)
12. Z. Zheng, et al.: Query-based industrial analytics over knowledge graphs with ontology reshaping. In: ESWC (Posters & Demos). Springer (2022)
13. Zhou, D., et al.: Enhancing knowledge graph generation with ontology reshaping - Bosch case. In: ESWC (Demos/Industry). Springer (2022)
14. Andresel, M., Stepanova, D., Tran, T. K., Domokos, C., Minervini, P.: Neuro-symbolic ontology-mediated query answering
15. Shi, Y., Cheng, G., Kharlamov, E.: Keyword search over knowledge graphs via static and dynamic hub labelings. In: WWW, pp. 235–245 (2020)
16. Shi, Y., Cheng, G., Tran, T. K., Tang, J., Kharlamov, E.: Keyword-based knowledge graph exploration based on quadratic group Steiner trees. In: IJCAI 2021, pp. 1555–1562 (2021)
17. Shi, Y., Cheng, G., Tran, T.K., Kharlamov, E., Shen, Y.: Efficient computation of semantically cohesive subgraphs for keyword-based knowledge graph exploration. In: WWW, pp. 1410–1421 (2021)
18. Wang, X., et al.: A framework for evaluating snippet generation for dataset search. In: ISWC, pp. 680–697 (2019)
19. ang, X., Cheng, G., Pan, J. Z., Kharlamov, E., Qu, Y.: BANDAR: benchmarking snippet generation algorithms for (RDF) dataset search, IEEE Trans. Knowl. Data Eng
20. Wang, X., Cheng, G., Kharlamov, E.: Towards multi-facet snippets for dataset search. In: PROFILES/SEMEX@ISWC 2019, pp. 1–6 (2019)
21. Wang, X., et al.: PCSG: pattern-coverage snippet generation for RDF datasets. In: Hotho, A., et al. (eds.) ISWC 2021. LNCS, vol. 12922, pp. 3–20. Springer, Cham (2021). https://doi.org/10.1007/978-3-030-88361-4_1
22. Tran, T. K., Le-Tuan, A., Nguyen-Duc, M., Yuan, J., Le-Phuoc, D.: Fantastic data and how to query them. arXiv preprint arXiv:2201.05026
23. Zhou, B., Pychynski, T., Reischl, M., Kharlamov, E., Mikut, R.: Machine learning with domain knowledge for predictive quality monitoring in resistance spot welding. J. Intell. Manufact. **33**(4), 1139–1163 (2022). https://doi.org/10.1007/s10845-021-01892-y
24. Zhou, B., Svetashova, Y., Byeon, S., Pychynski, T., Mikut, R., Kharlamov, E.: Predicting quality of automated welding with machine learning and semantics: a Bosch case study. In: CIKM, ACM, pp. 2933–2940 (2020)
25. Zhou, B., Svetashova, Y., Pychynski, T., Baimuratov, I., Soylu, A., Kharlamov, E.: SemFE: facilitating ML pipeline development with semantics. In: CIKM, ACM, pp. 3489–3492 (2020)
26. DataCloud, Enabling the big data pipeline lifecycle on the computing continuum (2022). https://datacloudproject.eu/. Accessed 14 Mar 2022
27. Roman, D., et al.: Big data pipelines on the computing continuum: ecosystem and use cases overview. In: ISCC, IEEE, pp. 1–4 (2021)
28. OntoCommons, Ontology-driven data documentation for industry commons (2022). https://ontocommons.eu/. Accessed 14 Mar 2022
29. Yahya, M., et al.: Towards generalized welding ontology in line with ISO and knowledge graph construction. In: ESWC (Posters & Demos). Springer (2022)

Extracting Subontologies from SNOMED CT

Warren Del-Pinto[1]([✉]), Renate A. Schmidt[1], and Yongsheng Gao[2]

[1] Department of Computer Science, University of Manchester, Manchester, UK
{warren.del-pinto,renate.schmidt}@manchester.ac.uk
[2] SNOMED International, London, UK
yga@snomed.org

1 Introduction

Computing smaller extracts of a larger ontology has been recognised as important for enabling tasks such as ontology creation, review, updating, debugging, navigation, sharing and integration [2,5,6]. In addition, reasoning tasks such as querying and classification take less time to execute over a smaller extract than over the original ontology. As the most comprehensive clinical healthcare terminology in the world, SNOMED CT is by necessity a large ontology, containing over 350,000 concepts and a large amount of content is contained in various extensions. As a result, the benefits provided by computing smaller extracts are even more pronounced in this setting. Additionally, the ability to extract and extend content focused on specialist domains can facilitate the navigation and utilisation of specific content within a large terminology that are directly relevant to specialist domains for clinicians and healthcare systems.

Often, reference sets (refsets) [3] are computed or curated by experts to list a subset of concepts that are relevant to a given clinical specialty, such as the General Dentistry Diagnostic refset. However, such lists are not sufficient in applications that rely upon the semantics of the source ontology, where an extract in the form of a standalone ontology is needed.

Modularisation approaches [2,5] produce such extracts by computing subsets of the stated axioms in the source ontology, such that all entailments with respect to the included concepts are preserved. The computed modules are useful in that they capture the semantics within a domain of interest and can be used in place of the original, larger ontology. However, in practice modules are often large and contain a significant amount of unnecessary information that is not required to capture the modelling of the specified concepts in the domain of interest.

2 Subontology Extraction

We have developed new software to compute concise extracts of SNOMED CT that are semantically complete with respect to a set of input concepts, called

Thanks to members of our Steering and Working Groups: Rory Davidson, Jim Case, Monica Harry, Kai Kewley and Ghadah Alghamdi. The work was funded by UK EPSRC IAA, the University of Manchester and SNOMED International.

P. Groth et al. (Eds.): ESWC 2022 Satellite Events, LNCS 13384, pp. 291–294, 2022.
https://doi.org/10.1007/978-3-031-11609-4_43

focus concepts. The two main criteria for these extracts, called *subontologies*, are: (i) Focus concepts must be defined equivalently in the subontology and the source ontology. (ii) The transitive closure (with respect to subsumption) between concepts occurring in the extract must be equal in the subontology and the source ontology, up to the signature of concepts in the subontology. The subontology extraction approach automatically identifies additional *supporting concepts* that are required to satisfy condition (i) and includes these in the extracted subontology.

Subontology extraction differs from modularisation approaches in the separation between focus and supporting concepts; while modularisation approaches extract a subset of the original axioms in an ontology, subontology extraction produces equivalent definitions for focus concepts in a compact abstract form, the authoring form (long canonical form in [7]), while supporting concepts are only fully defined if necessary. The hierarchy between concepts in the subontology is then completed by using the classification over the source ontology (SNOMED CT) to identify missing inclusions and add these automatically.

The subontology extraction approach developed in this work supports the language features required by the latest versions of SNOMED CT, including language extensions such as GCI axioms, reflexive roles, transitive roles, role chain axioms and data types, effectively, the description logic ELH^{++} [1].

3   Implementation, Evaluation and Applications

The prototype was implemented in Java, making use of the OWL API and the DL reasoner ELK [4] for classification. A prototype of the tool is available at https://github.com/IHTSDO/snomed-subontology-extraction.

A set of experiments were performed to evaluate the performance of the algorithm in practice. Since the aim is to produce concise extracts, the size of the extracted subontologies was compared to STAR modularisation, which is available as part of the OWL API. The two approaches were compared using real clinical refsets as input, where the refset is used to specify the set of focus concepts for extraction. The results in Table 1 indicate that the extracted subontologies are significantly smaller than STAR modules across all cases. The runtime for subontology extraction ranged from 8–266 s for the smallest to largest refsets respectively.

Figure 1 provides an in-practice comparison between the navigation of a subontology, the ERA-EDTA subontology, and the full release of SNOMED CT. As seen from the subhierarchies displayed, the extracted subontology includes only those hierarchies that contain concepts that are relevant to the domain of interest specified by the ERA-EDTA refset. Hierarchies such as "Pharmaceutical/biologic product (product)" are excluded from the subontology, as no concept in this hierarchy was found to be necessary to preserve the semantics of the focus concepts in the refset. Additionally, for each of the included subhierarchies, the descendent count is smaller in the subontology compared to the original SNOMED CT ontology.

Table 1. A comparison between the sizes of the extracted subontologies and locality-based (STAR) modules for a collection of refsets.

Refset name	Refset size (concepts)	Subontology size		STAR module size	
		Axioms	Concepts	Axioms	Concepts
ERA-EDTA	184	485	475	3076	3086
Dentistry	226	455	642	1449	1478
Nursing	1337	2616	2616	5579	5708
Orphanet	5681	9209	9189	27595	27625
IPS	8182	12793	12745	53736	53708
GPS	26159	33970	33907	86167	86374
Refsets key					
Dentistry	General Dentistry				
ERA-EDTA	European Renal Association/Dialysis and Transplant Association				
GPS	International Global Patient Set				
IPS	International Patient Set				
Nursing	Nursing Activities and Nursing Health Issues (combined)				
Orphanet	Rare diseases, orphan drugs				

In addition to the experiments, a range of subontologies have been computed for standard lists of clinical concepts, including several of the refsets in Table 1. These subontologies, viewable in the browser at https://iaa.snomed. tools, have received qualitative feedback from users (domain experts). The users each answered questions about a subontology that was relevant to their domain of interest, covering their experience of navigating the subontology, the scope of the content contained within them and the potential usefulness in their own work. The feedback indicated that presenting domain specific content via a subontology in the browser was useful, as it made it easier to navigate the relevant content without having to navigate the entirety of SNOMED CT. Additionally, the feedback generated discussion relating to the refsets provided as input. For example, the nursing refset did not contain several concepts that were expected by domain experts, such as those relating to different types of specimens (samples). This was based on navigation of the subontologies, which relies on semantic information retained by subontology extraction such as the definitions of and hierarchy between included concepts. This points to a promising use of subontologies in maintaining domain specific content and assisting with refset curation.

The subontology extraction prototype has already been used in a range of applications within SNOMED International, including the development of a new concept model for anatomy, which is represented as a subontology, and identifying improvements to the modelling of substances by enabling clinical modellers to examine and navigate content via more concise extracts that are compatible with the existing SNOMED CT browser. Subontology extraction is also a core component in the new release of the International Patient Set subontology, which

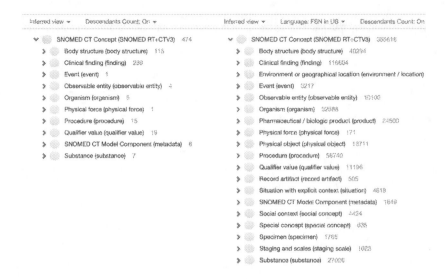

Fig. 1. A screenshot of the top-level subhierarchies of SNOMED CT for the ERA-EDTA subontology at https://iaa.snomed.tools (left) and the full SNOMED CT International Edition (right), viewed using the SNOMED CT browser. The counts beside each concept show the number of inferred subconcepts in the ontology.

aims to enable more effective use of clinical data analytics and decision support over essential healthcare information. Community content regarding traditional medicine, which is not part of the International Edition of SNOMED CT, will also be presented as a subontology to provide a means for users to utilise concepts related to traditional medicines where this is needed in different countries.

References

1. Baader, F., Brandt, S., Lutz, C.: Pushing the EL envelope. In: Proceedings of the Nineteenth International Joint Conference on Artificial Intelligence, vol. 5, pp. 364–369. AAAI Press (2005)
2. Grau, B.C., Horrocks, I., Kazakov, Y., Sattler, U., Theory and practice: Modular reuse of ontologies. J. Artif. Intell. Res. **31**, 273–318 (2008)
3. SNOMED International. Practical guide to reference sets. SNOMED CT Document Library (2017). https://confluence.ihtsdotools.org/display/DOCRFSPG. Accessed 08 Mar 2022
4. Kazakov, Y., Krötzsch, M., Simancik, F.: The incredible ELK: from polynomial procedures to efficient reasoning with EL ontologies. J. Autom. Reason. **53**, 1–61 (2014)
5. Konev, B., Lutz, C., Walther, D., Wolter, F.: Model-theoretic inseparability and modularity of description logic ontologies. Artif. Intell. **203**, 66–103 (2013)
6. Rector, A.L.: Modularisation of domain ontologies implemented in description logics and related formalisms including OWL. In: Proceedings of the 2nd International Conference on Knowledge Capture, pp. 121–128. ACM (2003)
7. Spackman, K.A.: Normal forms for description logic expressions of clinical concepts in SNOMED RT. In: Proceedings of the AMIA Symposium, p. 627. American Medical Informatics Association (2001)

"Semantify" Business and Content to Meet Demands for Expert Solutions in Professional Markets

Christian Dirschl[1], Jamie Schram[2(✉)], Jessica Kent[2], and Quentin Reul[2]

[1] Wolters Kluwer Deutschland GmbH, Alphen aan den Rijn, The Netherlands
Christian.Dirschl@wolterskluwer.com
[2] Wolters Kluwer R&D U.S. LP, Riverwoods, USA
{Jamie.Schram,Jessica.Kent,Quentin.Reul}@wolterskluwer.com

Abstract. Wolters Kluwer aims to provide professionals with timely, more informed, actionable expert insights which can be easily integrated into their workflow and daily routines. It is no longer sufficient to have content as the main focus of Wolters Kluwer solutions with semantics and metadata as secondary concerns. It has become readily apparent that content curation and business processes need to become more knowledge-centric, i.e., to "semantify" the content and the business. To semantify content, we describe how we have developed an enterprise upper ontology based on industry standards and have developed a process to make domain-specific extensions to that ontology. With regards to our business processes, we outline how we are driving a transformational change in editorial staff and developers alike to semantify content curation and development efforts. Providing knowledge-driven expert solutions requires both of these fundamental transformations; it is not sufficient to semantify content without also changing the way the business works, and vice versa.

Keywords: Knowledge workers · Expert solutions · Shared semantics · Business transformation

1 Introduction

Wolters Kluwer has been on a digital transformation journey for the last 15 years and is now focusing on developing expert solutions for our customers [1]. In 2021, over half of Wolters Kluwer revenue was from expert solutions, and it is expected that this will continue to grow [2]. To accommodate this evolution, we aim to provide professionals with timely, actionable expert insights which can be easily integrated into their workflow. However, it is no longer sufficient to have content as the main focus of our solutions with semantics and metadata as secondary concerns. There needs to be a shift to not just "semantify" the content, but also to semantify the business itself.

© The Author(s), under exclusive license to Springer Nature Switzerland AG 2022
P. Groth et al. (Eds.): ESWC 2022 Satellite Events, LNCS 13384, pp. 295–298, 2022.
https://doi.org/10.1007/978-3-031-11609-4_44

2 Semantifying Content

In order to meet changing customer expectations and to stay relevant in professional markets, changing how content is thought about and delivered is paramount. Professionals have little interest in reading mountains of documents returned in search results. They want answers to questions, and *actionable insights* delivered on top of traditional content. For example, a tax practitioner wants to know the 2022 tax rate for a client who owns a small business; a health practitioner formulating a clinical research question needs to find relevant research; an attorney needs to find relevant precedential jurisprudence that matches the unique claims and factual matters for a case [3].

At Wolters Kluwer, each of these use cases (among others) requires us to think of our content not just as simple documents with text or even as documents enriched with descriptive metadata. Rather, we aim to "semantify" our content. That is, to augment our traditional content with semantic knowledge, which can then be used to drive advanced features and actionable insights that customers increasingly demand. To extract this semantic knowledge, we leverage a combination of manual enrichments through editorial staff and specialized AI-based solutions.

To semantify our content in a standard, unified manner with shared, unambiguous meaning, we have built an enterprise upper ontology [3] based on W3C standards. In our upper ontology, we define properties and classes that are germane across all our content domains. And rather than reinventing the wheel, we make use of publicly available ontological standards and vocabularies whenever possible, such as SKOS, FOAF, Dublin Core and FRBR [4].

However, our enterprise upper ontology still cannot deliver the deep, highly domain specialized semantics required for different professional domains by itself. To resolve this gap, we have developed a process for creating and managing domain-specific extensions to our upper ontology. Our process involves direct consultancy between business analysts and the semantic knowledge engineers who manage the upper ontology, where we discuss professionals' requirements and determine a best fit for the situation at hand, e.g., to determine if a domain-specific extension is appropriate, or if perhaps the upper ontology should be extended based on a cross-domain requirement. By following this process, we ensure that our business units all take advantage of the shared semantics and common meaning defined in the upper ontology, yet are free to define additional semantics that are meant to fulfill the needs that are intrinsic to unique domain-specific use cases facing our customers.

As a concrete example of the adoption of this process we are currently developing a divisional content standard ontology extension for our legal and regulatory businesses, that enables us to further semantify the content from different business units in that domain on top of the semantic layer of the enterprise upper ontology for one modular legal expert solution platform.

Of course, this process does present challenges, specifically with regards to the needed business transformation explained in the next section. It has been a challenge to encourage content workers and software developers alike to focus on semantics and shared meaning, and thus to formally register that meaning in an ontology extension rather than simply inventing their own bespoke names for new properties in a simple spreadsheet to meet new requirements.

3 Semantifying the Business

Traditional content applications are mainly based on generic features such as content to be searched, filtered, ranked, and displayed. There is a clear disconnect between content creation and maintenance on the one hand and the application technology on the other. Information is ingested as content blobs where very few dedicated content features like search query parsing for legal entities are widely used.

Expert solutions, however, are more designed for specific recurring expert tasks of legal professionals like, for example, drafting contracts or legal analytics. Therefore, more domain information is processed, and this information needs to be more contextualised - and ideally - the content itself is directly driving functionality on the application side [5, 6].

More awareness and insights in the content is required if a product manager wants to define expert solutions' capabilities. This content knowledge is also helpful further downstream by platform architects and software developers who are implementing these capabilities. And in the end, content knowledge is even transforming the content creation process, with additional business requirements addressing content structure, enrichment, and frequency of delivery. This means that all stakeholders in the content process need to further develop and gain more knowledge about the content and data they are selling to customers as well as the customers' job to be done. In particular, those who have direct access to content creation and maintenance need to evolve from a purely content worker skillset to a knowledge worker skillset, including more knowledge about customer needs and how this impacts content. This is also true for software developers, who need to learn more about the result they produce – no longer an isolated piece of code, but a value-add functionality, directly driven by content capabilities, forcing them to evolve from software developers to expert solution developers. Additionally, business analysts who need to detail requirements to developers using common shared semantics as defined in the previous section.

One concrete example for knowledge worker skills is comprehension of how law sections are perceived with respect to granularity by the users so that we can build metadata on top of that perception, instead of simply copying and pasting from the source what the legislator is directly offering as a whole. In addition, expert solution developers are required to develop dynamic mechanisms for processing variable content entities that directly drive functionality, like dynamic browse trees or analytics capabilities on large and diverse volumes of data.

The overall business changes - based on more sophisticated and advanced customer needs - in turn drive and accelerate the organizational transformation that is focusing on informing and enabling all stakeholders about the impact of content driven customer needs for their own day to day work environment.

4 Conclusion

Semantifying content and the business culture by focusing on knowledge requires a transition from separate and disjoint roles to integrated understanding and contributions from knowledge workers. Integrating content creation and maintenance with application technology, as well as promoting shared understanding of the domain and content knowledge enables expert solutions that are highly informed by customer jobs to be done and a seamless part of the workflow followed to complete those jobs. This change requires a modified methodology for presenting semantics for different stakeholders in a coherent and yet stakeholder specific fashion that still needs to be discovered by the research community.

References

1. Digital transformation. https://www.wolterskluwer.com/en/about-us/digital-transformation. Accessed 8 Apr 2022
2. Kluwer, W.: Full-Year report (2021). https://assets.contenthub.wolterskluwer.com/api/public/content/c53de1c772024d3d96138476b0881680?v=373e7262. Accessed 8 Apr 2022
3. Schram, J., Dirschl, C., Kent, J., Reul, Q., Henderson, V., Sabnani, H.: Providing actionable insights for jurisprudence researchers. In: Qurator (2021)
4. Functional requirements for bibliographic records: final report. https://repository.ifla.org/handle/123456789/811. Accessed 8 Apr 2022
5. Reul, Q., Dirschl, C., Casellas, N., Flannery, W.: Adopting linked data principles for accelerating business transformation processes in Wolters Kluwer. In: ISWC (2015)
6. Dirschl, C., Kent, J., Schram, J., Reul, Q.: Enabling digital business transformation through an enterprise knowledge graph. In: Harth, A., et al. (eds.) The Semantic Web: ESWC 2020 Satellite Events. ESWC 2020. Lecture Notes in Computer Science, vol. 12124. Springer, Cham (2020). https://doi.org/10.1007/978-3-030-49461-2

Enhancing Knowledge Graph Generation with Ontology Reshaping – Bosch Case

Dongzhuoran Zhou[1,2(✉)], Baifan Zhou[2], Zhuoxun Zheng[1,3], Egor V. Kostylev[2],
Gong Cheng[4], Ernesto Jiménez-Ruiz[2,5], Ahmet Soylu[3],
and Evgeny Kharlamov[1,2]

[1] Bosch Center for Artificial Intelligence, Renningen, Germany
`dongzhuoran.zhou@outlook.com`
[2] SIRIUS Centre, University of Oslo, Oslo, Norway
[3] Department of Computer Science, Oslo Metropolitan University, Oslo, Norway
[4] State Key Laboratory for Novel Software Technology, Nanjing University,
Nanjing, China
[5] City, University of London, London, UK

Motivation. In the context of Industry 4.0 [1] and Internet of Things (IoT) [2], modern manufacturing and production [3,4] lines are equipped with software systems and sensors that constantly collect and send a high volume of data. Knowledge Graphs (KGs) allow to represent these data in a semantically structured way and provide a convenient foundation for standardised AI and analytics solutions [5–13]. Thus, KGs opened new horizons [14] and were adapted for a wide range of industrial applications in Bosch [15–17], Siemens [18,19], Equinor [6] and other companies. An important industrial scenario for Bosch where we rely on KGs is *monitoring* of manufacturing processes, including e.g. analysing the quality of the manufactured products with heterogeneous data from various formats. In particular we rely on KGs for *welding quality monitoring* [5,9,15,20,21], where welding is performed with automated machines that connect pieces of metal together by pressing them and passing high current electricity through them [20]. The process is remarkably data intensive and requires efficient data infrastructure like KG databases [21–23].

Challenge. There is a number of approaches to enable (semi-) automatic construction of KGs over industrial data that is typically of high complexity and variety. These approaches typically rely on mappings from the raw data to a given KG schema, namely a domain ontology, and that can be used to construct (in the ETL fashion) the entities and properties of the KGs according to the ontology. However, the existing approaches to generate KGs are not always efficient enough and the resulting KGs are not sufficiently application and user-friendly. This challenge arises from a trade-off between the following two principles:

- It is in general considered a good practice to create domain ontologies in a *knowledge-oriented* way, namely to reflect the general domain knowledge rather than data particularities of arbitrary datasets [24,25].
- On the other hand, to properly reflect the raw data, a *data-oriented* KG schema is required. Raw data often come with diverse specificities, which

P. Groth et al. (Eds.): ESWC 2022 Satellite Events, LNCS 13384, pp. 299–302, 2022.
https://doi.org/10.1007/978-3-031-11609-4_45

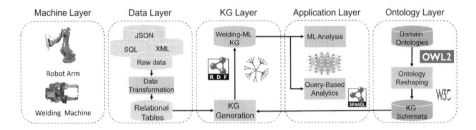

Fig. 1. An overview of our approach of ontology reshaping enhanced KG generation.

may differ significantly from the domain ontologies, e.g., not necessarily all classes in the latter can be mapped to attributes in the former. If a knowledge-oriented domain ontology is directly used as the KG schema, this can cause a series of issues, e.g., blank nodes created due to classes unmapped to the raw data.

Ontology Reshaping Enhanced KG Generation. To address this challenge, we propose our approach of ontology reshaping enhanced KG generation (Fig. 1). The core idea of our approach is to "reshape" a domain ontology to its (often) more compact data-oriented versions, and then to use the latter ones as the KG schemata to construct KGs from relational tables. Our system consists of five layers and several semantic modules.

Our approach consists of Machine Layer, Data Layer, KG Layer, Application Layer and Ontology Layer. In the Machine Layer, manufacturing data are constantly collected from running production lines of automated welding. In the Data Layer, the raw data of various formats e.g., json, SQL, XML are transformed into relational tables by the *Data Transformation* module. In the KG Layer, our Welding-ML KG is generated by populating KG schemata with the relational tables. We call our KG Welding-ML KGs because they contain information of the welding production and ML analysis [26]. The Welding-ML KG are used by a series of applications, e.g., ML Analysis, in the Application Layer. The KG schemata are data-oriented ontologies transformed by the Ontology Reshaping module from knowledge-oriented domain ontologies, in the Ontology Layer.

In particular, our Ontology Reshaping module [27] converts a given domain ontology to (often) compacter ontologies that serves as the KG schema [28]. The intuition behind it is to project the domain ontology to a labelled multi-graph, then select subsets of nodes and edges from it, and then connect the sub-graphs via some optimality criteria based on user heuristics, efficiency, simplicity, etc.

Evaluation at Bosch. We implement and evaluate our approach at Bosch for welding quality monitoring and data analysis [29,30]. The evaluation was done in the offline mode on several car manufacturing lines. These lines generated a great number of heterogeneous data such as historic data with sensor measurements, welding machine configurations, manufacturing specifications, and the quality estimates of finished welding operations. In this work, we select a section of the data for discussion. The selected section contains 4.315 million records. These data account for 1000 welding operations, estimated to be related to 100 cars. Thanks to ontology reshaping, our approach significantly increases time efficiency, space efficiency, and results in KGs with much better simplicity, compared to a baseline approach [27] without ontology reshaping: The KG generation becomes 7 to 8 times faster; the number of entities reduced to merely 1/2 to 1/6 of the baseline, and storage space reduced to 2/3; and the number of blank nodes are reduced to zero and queries over the KGs become shorter and simpler.

Outlook. Our approach is currently deployed in our Bosch evaluation environment, and we are considering to push it further into a more advanced and strict evaluation phase of production that runs in real-time. To show the benefits, we also plan to demonstrate our KG solution with more users and more use cases. In the Application Layer, we plan to develop Query-Based Industrial Analytics. In the future, we plan to develop formal theory of ontology reshaping, to enhance the KG generation modules to improve the compatibility of the KG schema to the domain ontologies; to extend the KG solution for more applications, e.g. question answering, visualisation, statistic analysis.

Acknowledgements. The work was partially supported by the H2020 projects Dome 4.0 (Grant Agreement No. 953163), OntoCommons (Grant Agreement No. 958371), and DataCloud (Grant Agreement No. 101016835) and the SIRIUS Centre, Norwegian Research Council project number 237898.

References

1. Kagermann, H.: Change through digitization—value creation in the age of Industry 4.0. In: Albach, H., Meffert, H., Pinkwart, A., Reichwald, R. (eds.) Management of Permanent Change, pp. 23–45. Springer, Wiesbaden (2015). https://doi.org/10.1007/978-3-658-05014-6_2

2. ITU, Recommendation ITU - T Y.2060: overview of the internet of things, Technical report, International Telecommunication Union

3. Chand, S., Davis, J.: What is smart manufacturing. Time Mag. Wrapper **7**, 28–33 (2010)

4. Wuest, T., Weimer, D., Irgens, C., Thoben, K.-D.: Machine learning in manufacturing: advantages, challenges, and applications. Prod. Manuf. Res. **4**, 23–45 (2016)

5. Zhou, B., Pychynski, T., Reischl, M., Kharlamov, E., Mikut, R.: Machine learning with domain knowledge for predictive quality monitoring in resistance spot welding. J. Intell. Manuf. **33**(4), 1139–1163 (2022)

6. Kharlamov, E., et al.: Ontology based data access in Statoil. J. Web Semant. **44**, 3–36 (2017)

7. Zhou, B.: Machine learning methods for product quality monitoring in electric resistance welding, Ph.D. thesis, Karlsruhe Institute of Technology, Germany (2021)

8. Zou, X.: A survey on application of knowledge graph. In: Journal of Physics: Conference Series, vol. 1487, p. 012016. IOP Publishing (2020)

9. Zhou, B., Svetashova, Y., Pychynski, T., Baimuratov, I., Soylu, A., Kharlamov, E.: SemFE: facilitating ML pipeline development with semantics. In: CIKM, pp. 3489–3492. ACM (2020)

10. Zhou, B., Pychynski, T., Reischl, M., Mikut, R.: Comparison of machine learning approaches for time-series-based quality monitoring of resistance spot welding (RSW). Arch. Data Sci. Ser. A (Online First) **5**(1), 13 (2018)

11. Soylu, A., et al.: TheyBuyForYou platform and knowledge graph: expanding horizons in public procurement with open linked data. Semant. Web **13**(2), 265–291 (2022)
12. Zhou, B., Chioua, M., Schlake, J.-C.: Practical methods for detecting and removing transient changes in univariate oscillatory time series. IFAC-PapersOnLine **50**(1), 7987–7992 (2017)
13. Zhou, B., Chioua, M., Bauer, M., Schlake, J.-C., Thornhill, N.F.: Improving root cause analysis by detecting and removing transient changes in oscillatory time series with application to a 1,3-butadiene process. Ind. Eng. Chem. Res. **58**, 11234–11250 (2019)
14. Horrocks, I., Giese, M., Kharlamov, E., Waaler, A.: Using semantic technology to tame the data variety challenge. IEEE Internet Comput. **20**(6), 62–66 (2016)
15. Zhou, B., Svetashova, Y., Byeon, S., Pychynski, T., Mikut, R., Kharlamov, E.: Predicting quality of automated welding with machine learning and semantics: a Bosch case study. In: CIKM (2020)
16. Zhou, B., et al.: Method for resistance welding, US Patent App. 17/199,904 (2021)
17. Kalaycı, E.G., et al.: Semantic integration of Bosch manufacturing data using virtual knowledge graphs. In: Pan, J.Z., et al. (eds.) ISWC 2020. LNCS, vol. 12507, pp. 464–481. Springer, Cham (2020). https://doi.org/10.1007/978-3-030-62466-8_29
18. Kharlamov, E., et al.: Semantic access to streaming and static data at Siemens. J. Web Semant. **44**, 54–74 (2017)
19. Hubauer, T., Lamparter, S., Haase, P., Herzig, D.M.: Use cases of the industrial knowledge graph at siemens. In: ISWC (P&D/Industry/BlueSky) (2018)
20. Zhou, B., et al.: SemML: facilitating development of ML models for condition monitoring with semantics. J. Web Semant. **71**, 100664 (2021)
21. Svetashova, Y., et al.: Ontology-enhanced machine learning: a Bosch use case of welding quality monitoring. In: Pan, J.Z., et al. (eds.) ISWC 2020. LNCS, vol. 12507, pp. 531–550. Springer, Cham (2020). https://doi.org/10.1007/978-3-030-62466-8_33
22. Svetashova, Y., Zhou, B., Schmid, S., Pychynski, T., Kharlamov, E.: SemML: reusable ML for condition monitoring in discrete manufacturing. In: ISWC (Demos/Industry), vol. 2721, pp. 213–218 (2020)
23. Zhou, B., Svetashova, Y., Pychynski, T., Kharlamov, E.: Semantic ML for manufacturing monitoring at Bosch. In: ISWC (Demos/Ind), vol. 2721, p. 398 (2020)
24. Smith, B.: Ontology. In: The Furniture of the World, pp. 47–68. Brill (2012)
25. Guarino, N., Oberle, D., Staab, S.: What is an ontology? In: Staab, S., Studer, R. (eds.) Handbook on Ontologies. IHIS, pp. 1–17. Springer, Heidelberg (2009). https://doi.org/10.1007/978-3-540-92673-3_0
26. Zhou, B., Zhou, D., Chen, J., Svetashova, Y., Cheng, G., Kharlamov, E.: Scaling usability of ML analytics with knowledge graphs: exemplified with a Bosch welding case. In: IJCKG (2021)
27. Zhou, D., Zhou, B., Chen, J., Cheng, G., Kostylev, E.V., Kharlamov, E.: Towards ontology reshaping for KG generation with user-in-the-loop: applied to Bosch welding. In: IJCKG (2021)
28. Zheng, Z., et al.: Query-based industrial analytics over knowledge graphs with ontology reshaping. In: ESWC (Posters & Demos) (2022)
29. Zhou, B., et al.: The data value quest: a holistic semantic approach at Bosch. In: ESWC (Demos/Industry) (2022)
30. Yahya, M., et al.: Towards generalized welding ontology in line with ISO and knowledge graph construction. In: ESWC (Posters & Demos) (2022)

Semantic Data Integration for Monitoring Operators' Ergonomics in an Automotive Manufacturing Setting

Efstratios Kontopoulos[1(✉)] , Gerasimos Arvanitis[2] , Alessandro Zanella[3] ,
Panagiotis Mitzias[1] , Evangelia I. Zacharaki[2] , Pavlos Kosmides[1] ,
Nikos Piperigkos[4] , Konstantinos Moustakas[2] , and Aris S. Lalos[4]

[1] Catalink Limited, Nicosia, Cyprus
{e.kontopoulos,pmitzias,pkosmidis}@catalink.eu
[2] Electrical and Computer Engineering Department, University of Patras, Patras, Greece
{arvanitis,moustakas}@ece.upatras.gr, ezachar@upatras.gr
[3] Centro Ricerche FIAT SCpA, Orbassano, Italy
alessandro.zanella@crf.it
[4] Industrial Systems Institute, Athena Research Center, Athens, Greece
{piperigkos,lalos}@isi.gr

Abstract. This paper presents a novel semantic data integration framework for monitoring and safeguarding the ergonomics of human operators during a collaborative assembly task in an automotive manufacturing environment.

Keywords: Semantic data integration · Ontologies · Knowledge graphs · Automotive manufacturing

1 Motivation and Setup

This paper presents our work within the H2020 ICT-01–2019 CPSoSaware project [1] in the context of a use case based on a collaborative application in an automotive assembly line. In the scenario, a human operator performs manual assembly operations on a windshield handled and moved by a robot before assembly on the chassis. Our overarching aim is to protect the operators from injuries and muscle strain and to reduce their body's strain by performing biophysics assessment for ergonomic optimization. Towards this end, we deploy a semantic data integration framework for monitoring the human operators' safety and well-being as they are performing the requested operations.

The proposed implementation focuses on adjusting the position of the windshield according to the operator's ergonomics and providing personalized suggestions and warnings to the operator based on their postures and the way that they use their body to perform an operation, in order to avoid long-term musculoskeletal problems and other health and/or safety risks. The foreseen benefits of our solution are: (a) improvement of the workers' wellbeing at work; (b) mitigation of risks and accidents; (c) flexibility of workplace management.

© The Author(s), under exclusive license to Springer Nature Switzerland AG 2022
P. Groth et al. (Eds.): ESWC 2022 Satellite Events, LNCS 13384, pp. 303–306, 2022.
https://doi.org/10.1007/978-3-031-11609-4_46

2 Deployment

A set of IoT sensors submit their measurements to respective analysis components: (a) footage from static cameras analysed by computer vision components for estimating the operator's anthropometrics parameters (i.e., posture); (b) wearables (inertial measurement units – IMUs, i.e., accelerometers and gyroscopes) for motion analysis and body tracking. The analysis outputs (and not the raw sensor measurements) are then fed to an ontology-based semantic Knowledge Graph (KG) through CASPAR [2], a flexible semantic data integration framework, already being deployed in various domains [3, 4]. Our overall aim is to perform a proactive ergonomics optimization of the equipment. Figure 1 gives a diagrammatic overview of the workflow; message exchange and data streams are based on the popular RabbitMQ message broker [5]. Note that only the higher-level analysis outputs are stored and not the raw data itself, preventing issues of performance and storage costs.

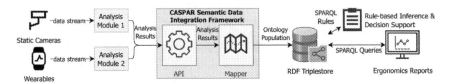

Fig. 1. Workflow overview.

The proposed deployment is currently being tested in a virtual environment (i.e., simulator designed in Unity [6]) and in a real industrial environment. The simulation involves three static RGB cameras located in three different areas of the working environment monitoring the "human's" (i.e., a digital human model) actions, while he collaborates with a robot to perform together a specific task. Figure 2 illustrates a set of snapshots from the three different views in the simulated environment. A pose estimation algorithm extracts in real time the posture landmarks and a confidence rate for each estimation. The outputs are fed into the ontology via semantic data integration, while a set of rules determine the camera with the best view. For instance, Fig. 3 displays the average confidence rate per camera during a testing session, which can help determine the most reliable camera depending on the conditions each time.

Fig. 2. Simulated environment snapshot.

The same pipeline process is adopted in the real-life industrial environment, with camera-based estimations from computer vision algorithms now coupled with body joints' estimation based on the IMU sensors in online monitoring.

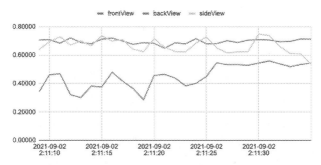

Fig. 3. Evolution of pose estimation confidence rate during a demonstration scenario.

3 Benefits of Applying Semantic Technologies

The application of semantic technologies in this scenario results in: (a) richer representation of the domain knowledge and of the respective provenance of the incoming information; (b) better explainability of the derived outputs; (c) deeper insights, e.g., discovery of underlying patterns "hidden" in the data. Moreover, being naturally inclined to addressing semantic data integration and interoperability issues, semantic technologies offer a significant degree of extensibility, allowing the addition of more input sources as deemed necessary by potential future scenarios.

4 Discussion and Next Steps

In industrial environments, the use of ergonomics aims to optimize the body physical parameters during repetitive tasks, searching for wrong postures and positions in order to help the operator avoid long term health problems. Towards this aim, our solution aspires to deliver a novel tool for optimizing the design of the workplace.

Note that in the current scenario we are not considering the sensors and actuators of the robot as an additional data source. The reason behind this decision is due to the fact that we wanted to avoid continuous adjustments of the robot, because the type of control that should be performed would most probably not be robust, reliable, and fast enough to allow a safe control in the presence of the human operator. At this stage we will use the system information and the anthropometric/ergonomics assessment to evaluate the most suitable height of the gripper, towards making the position as comfortable as possible reducing the ergonomics workload of the operator, and to adjust the gripper height from the ground. The system should adjust the height only when the operator is "far enough", otherwise the actuation could result in a danger.

Our upcoming efforts will be aimed at standardising and improving the cross-domain interoperability of our developed knowledge-based tools for scene analysis, posture recognition, and ergonomic assessment in a manufacturing environment.

Acknowledgment. This work has received funding from the European Union's Horizon 2020 research and innovation programme under Grant Agreement No 871738 - CPSoSaware: Crosslayer cognitive optimization tools & methods for the lifecycle support of dependable CPSoS.

References

1. CPSoSaware project. https://cpsosaware.eu/. Accessed Mar 2022
2. CASPAR framework. https://caspar.catalink.eu/. Accessed Mar 2022
3. Kontopoulos, E., et al.: An extensible semantic data fusion framework for autonomous vehicles. In: The Fifteenth International Conference on Advances in Semantic Processing (SEMAPRO 2021), pp. 5–11. Barcelona, Spain, 3–7 October (2021)
4. Maga-Nteve, C., et al.: A semantic technologies toolkit for bridging early diagnosis and treatment in brain diseases: report from the ongoing EU-funded research project ALAMEDA. In: Garoufallou, Emmanouel, Ovalle-Perandones, María-Antonia., Vlachidis, Andreas (eds.) Metadata and Semantic Research: 15th International Conference, MTSR 2021, Virtual Event, November 29–December 3, 2021, Revised Selected Papers, pp. 349–354. Springer International Publishing, Cham (2022). https://doi.org/10.1007/978-3-030-98876-0_30
5. RabbitMQ. https://www.rabbitmq.com/. Accessed Mar 2022
6. Unity. https://unity.com/. Accessed Mar 2022

Semantic Description of Equipment and Its Controls in Building Automation Systems

Ganesh Ramanathan[✉] and Maria Husmann

Siemens AG, Zug, Switzerland
ganesh.ramanathan@siemens.com

1 Introduction

Building automation (BA) systems orchestrate and monitor the functioning of a wide variety of utilities in a building so that living spaces are kept comfortable, safe, and secure. The complexity of such a system which involves multiple disciplines (heating, air-conditioning, lighting, fire safety, security etc.), coming from multiple vendors, is compounded by the fact that each building differs in the way the equipment operate and coordinate.

So far, efforts involving semantic modeling of BA systems, like Haystack [3], IFC [2], or Brick [1], have been focusing on the description of the building topology, installed equipment, and to a lesser extent, the control strategy, the modeling of the *physical process* and the role of the control program. In addition, the *semantics of interaction* with the devices used in BA, which is essential to establish technical interoperability, has so far not been coupled to the BA semantic models. As a result, planners, project engineers, technical operators, and service technicians have to design and understand the working of the system by piecing together information from different sources.

From our experience at the Smart Infrastructure division of Siemens AG, we describe briefly in the following sections some key use-cases, the challenges faced by us while applying semantic data in BA, and finally describe our approach and its evaluation in real-life buildings.

2 Use Cases for a Holistic Semantic Description

Engineering: Availability of semantic data describing the structural aspects of the building, the equipment installed, the process goals, and the specified control strategy (often called the *sequence of operation*) will help in tracking and validating the installation, and also assists the BA engineer to understand the context during programming of the automation controller.

Fault Detection and Diagnostics: Automated Fault detection and diagnostic (AFDD) methods for BA systems largely rely on rules which are based on the (semantic) knowledge of the process, the control strategy, and the way to interact with the associated sensors and actuators (to retrieve information or trigger test conditions).

P. Groth et al. (Eds.): ESWC 2022 Satellite Events, LNCS 13384, pp. 307–310, 2022.
https://doi.org/10.1007/978-3-031-11609-4_47

Process Optimization: Apart from understanding the functioning of an equipment on its own, the coordination and dependencies at system level is also important to ensure efficient operation, and this often requires exchange of knowledge between sub-systems.

3   Challenges

We have pointed out the need to describe the equipment, processes, and controls in a comprehensive manner so that they weave seamlessly into our engineering process. When we started with the analysis to create such knowledge base in building automation domain, we encountered the following constraints:

– The engineering of BA systems is divided both horizontally in layers of field, automation, and management, and vertically amongst the disciplines. Engineering in each of these aspects is carried out by diverse set of vendors, tools, and information models.
– Though control programs are machine-readable artifacts, they do not express their role in achieving the process goals. Such programs need to be augmented with semantic description of their role in the system.
– Openly available ontologies only partially cover the concepts required to describe a real-life building. Also, combining multiple such ontologies requires hand-crafted bridging and this is cumbersome to maintain as the ontologies evolve.
– Our knowledge consumers, both human and artificial agents, require different levels of abstractions for their operation. Consumers such as those at enterprise-level operate with abstract discipline-independent terms, whereas planning agents need to understand the functional features, while control agents require the implementation details of the features and need to interact with the devices.
– Existing BA (and IoT) ontologies are restricted to describing the presence of a field device (like sensor or actuator) and do not address the need to describe how to interact with such devices (which is essential for applications such as AFDD).

4   Approach

Considering the challenges listed above, we decided to create proprietary ontologies. We realized that this would incur a trade-off between achieving higher semantic richness within our products and a lack of wider interoperability in multi-vendor scenario. So, as a middle-path, we adopted the following approach:

– We structured our proprietary ontologies in three layers (see Fig. 1), such that the upper two layers of domain- and discipline-specific terms were designed in a manner that they either included or bridged to some of the openly available ontologies.

- The discipline- and product-specific ontologies resulted in natural vertical specializations since in the multi-disciplinary domain of BA, expertise is often divided on these lines (for e.g. HVAC, fire-safety, security, etc.)
- The usability of abstract terms was rather low for artificial agents (like AFDD) which needed to understand specific control and equipment configuration. Thus, the product- or system-specific ontologies provided these specialized concepts while relating to concepts in the upper two layers. The product-specific ontologies were meant to provide more flexible evolution.
- Integration of our ontologies in our engineering tools enabled bottom-up specification and extraction of knowledge from workflows where the control and construction aspects are inherently coupled. For example engineering tool meant for room HVAC control could refer to concepts such as *room* and *room segment* from the location ontology whereas the tool meant for lighting controls could define a collection of such *room segments* as a *lighting zone*. As a result, a consumer relying on abstract discipline-specific terms could still understand that the *room segments* had lighting function associated to it.
- The discipline-specific ontology included description of processes like heating, ventilation, lighting, etc. and allowed linking the description of control strategies to the process goals. For example, a cascade control loop could be linked to its role in heat generation process.
- *Things* like sensors, actuators, and controllers need to be integrated as first-class citizens in the semantic description so that agents can discover and interact with them. We achieved this by using the Web of Things semantic *Thing Descriptions (TD)* [4] in way that terms in all three layers could be linked to TDs.

5   Evaluation

The feature of the upper-most domain-wide ontology helped foster re-usability while the discipline-specific verticals enabled experts to formulate their concepts more precisely.

We used our ontology suite to help our engineering tools generate knowledge graphs for five real-life buildings and evaluated its effect on our use-cases. The

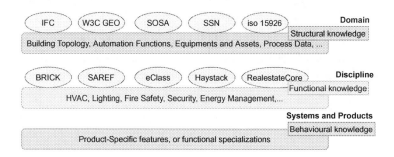

Fig. 1. Layered ontology for BA.

ability to describe control functions and their context of operation enabled our AFDD agents to reason about faults [6]. The description of building structure and related automation functions has facilitated research on its use to automate and manage engineering processes [5]. To demonstrate that our layered ontology can support construction of queries based on different levels of abstraction, we customized the SPARNATURAL[1] UI such that the user could query using broader terms based on open ontologies like BRICK, and then dive into discipline- or product-specific details. Finally, the ability to link entities in our knowledge graph to things representing the field devices (via TDs) enabled both human and artificial agents to interact with the BA system without requiring off-band understanding of protocols and information models.

6   Summary

We have shown that a bottom-up description in building automation should include the physical processes, its automation, and the construction aspects to facilitate software agents like engineering tools and AFDD to reason about the functioning of the system. This requires a flexible and extensible knowledge base which is product-agnostic and yet open to linking against industry-wide ontologies. When such knowledge bases are made available to the engineering tools, it enables the domain expert to create a comprehensive bottom-up description of the system.

References

1. Brick: A uniform metadata schema for buildings. https://brickschema.org/. Accessed 17 Mar 2021
2. Industry foundation classes. https://technical.buildingsmart.org/standards/ifc/ifc-formats/ifcowl/. Accessed 17 Mar 2021
3. Project haystack. https://project-haystack.org/. Accessed 17 Mar 2021
4. Web of things thing description. https://www.w3.org/TR/wot-thing-description/. Accessed 17 Mar 2021
5. Mitzutani, I., Ramanathan, G., Mayer, S.: Semantic data integration with devops to support engineering process of intelligent building automation systems. In: Proceedings of the 8th ACM International Conference on Systems for Energy-Efficient Buildings, Cities, and Transportation, pp. 294–297 (2021)
6. Ramanathan, G., Husmann, M., Niedermeier, C., Vicari, N., Garcia, K., Mayer, S.: Assisting automated fault detection and diagnostics in building automation through semantic description of functions and process data. In: Proceedings of the 8th ACM International Conference on Systems for Energy-Efficient Buildings, Cities, and Transportation, pp. 228–229 (2021)

---

[1] https://sparnatural.eu/.

Author Index

Printed in the United States
by Baker & Taylor Publisher Services